MW01169558

CCM Study Guide

UPDATED All-in-One CCM Review + 750 Practice Questions with Detailed Answer Explanations for the Certified Case Manager Exam (5 Full-Length Tests)

PlanwiseInk Publishing

© 2025-2026

Printed in USA

Disclaimer:

© Copyright 2025 by PlanwiseInk Publishing All rights reserved.

All rights reserved. It is illegal to distribute, reproduce or transmit any part of this book by any means or forms. Every effort has been made by the author and editor to ensure correct information in this book. This book is prepared with extreme care to give the best to its readers. However, the author and editor hereby disclaim any liability to any part for any loss, or damage caused by errors or omission. Recording, photocopying or any other mechanical or electronic transmission of the book without prior permission of the publisher is not permitted, except in the case of critical reviews and certain other non-commercial uses permitted by copyright law.

Printed in the United States of America.

CCM ® is a registered trademark. They hold no affiliation with this product. We are not affiliated with or endorsed by any official testing organization.

<u>CONTENTS</u>

Master the CCM Exam: Key Tips for Success

1. Study Efficiently, Not Extensively
Rather than attempting to memorize every detail, focus on understanding the fundamental concepts and core subjects that are most likely to appear on the test. This approach allows for better retention and quicker recall when answering questions, helping you navigate the exam more confidently.

2. Build a Flexible Study Routine
A study plan doesn't have to be rigid. Creating a flexible yet well-organized schedule allows you to balance your study time effectively, ensuring you dedicate adequate attention to each topic. Consistency and adaptability are key to mastering the material over time.

3. Review the Exam Framework
The exam framework is a guide to what you'll encounter on test day. Take time to study it closely so you can focus on the areas that will be tested. By identifying your weak points, you can direct your study efforts where they'll have the most impact.

4. Simulate the Exam with Practice Tests
Take advantage of practice exams to familiarize yourself with the test format and time constraints. These simulated exams not only reveal areas where you might need further study but also help reduce test anxiety by providing a sense of what to expect.

5. Surround Yourself with a Supportive Community
Engage with peers, online study groups, or mentors who are also preparing for the exam. Sharing experiences, discussing difficult topics, and offering moral support can significantly enhance your preparation and motivate you to stay on track.

6. Stay Motivated and Confident
The right mindset can make a huge difference. Stay focused on your goal, maintain a positive attitude, and believe in your ability to succeed. Confidence and persistence will help you push through any challenges and achieve your certification.

Why This Guide is Essential for Your CCM Exam Prep:

Up-to-Date Material This guide offers the most current practice questions and relevant content, ensuring you are studying with the most up-to-date materials that reflect the exam's current standards.

Expert Advice from Successful Test-Takers Written by professionals who have passed the CCM exam themselves, this guide is packed with expert strategies and advice that will help you tackle the exam with confidence.

Clear Explanations for Better Understanding Each practice question includes detailed explanations, making it easier to understand the reasoning behind the answers. This approach not only strengthens your comprehension but also prepares you for the more difficult questions you might face.

Experience the Real Exam Format The practice exams in this guide are designed to mirror the actual test. Taking these will help you become familiar with the exam's format and reduce any anxiety you may feel on the day of the test.

Sharpen Your Analytical Thinking Engage with questions that challenge you to apply your knowledge and think critically. Developing these skills will help you navigate complex questions more effectively and with greater ease.

Learn in a Clear, Concise Manner This study guide simplifies complex concepts into easy-to-understand explanations. It focuses on delivering the essential information without overwhelming you, making your preparation efficient and stress-free.

With the right study strategies and mindset, you can pass the CCM exam and achieve your certification. Let this guide be your companion as you work toward this important goal!

1   Care Delivery & Reimbursement Strategies:

Care delivery and reimbursement methods are integral components of healthcare management, focusing on how medical services are provided and compensated. Care delivery encompasses the organization, coordination, and provision of healthcare services to patients, ensuring that they receive the right care at the right time. It involves various models such as patient-centered care, coordinated care, and integrated care systems that aim to enhance quality and efficiency.

Reimbursement methods refer to the financial mechanisms through which healthcare providers are paid for their services. These methods include fee-for-service, capitation, bundled payments, and value-based reimbursement. Fee-for-service is a traditional model where providers are paid per service rendered, potentially leading to higher costs due to increased service volume. Capitation involves a fixed payment per patient, regardless of the number of services provided, encouraging cost-effective care management.

Bundled payments offer a single payment for all services related to a specific treatment or condition over a defined period, promoting efficiency and collaboration among providers. Value-based reimbursement ties compensation to the quality of care delivered, rewarding providers for achieving specific health outcomes and cost savings.

Understanding these methods is crucial for case managers as they navigate the complexities of healthcare systems. Effective case management requires knowledge of these models to advocate for patients' needs while ensuring sustainable resource utilization. This understanding allows case managers to effectively coordinate care plans that align with both clinical goals and financial constraints, ultimately enhancing patient outcomes and system efficiency.

1.1 Accountable Care Organizations (ACOs):

Accountable Care Organizations (ACOs) are collaborative networks of healthcare providers, including hospitals, doctors, and other healthcare professionals, who voluntarily come together to provide coordinated, high-quality care to their Medicare patients. The primary aim of ACOs is to ensure that patients receive the right care at the right time while avoiding unnecessary duplication of services and preventing medical errors. By focusing on patient-centered care, ACOs strive to improve health outcomes and reduce healthcare costs.

ACOs operate under a value-based care model, where they are held accountable for the quality, cost, and overall care of the Medicare beneficiaries assigned to them. If an ACO successfully meets quality benchmarks and reduces spending compared to a predetermined financial target, it can share in the savings it achieves for the Medicare program. This incentivizes providers to focus on preventive care and chronic disease management.

To achieve these goals, ACOs utilize data-driven strategies to track patients' health outcomes and identify areas for improvement. They emphasize evidence-based medicine and leverage health information technology to facilitate communication among providers across different settings. This ensures that care is seamless, coordinated, and tailored to individual patient needs.

For case managers, understanding the structure and function of ACOs is crucial, as they play a significant role in coordinating care among various providers within the organization. Their expertise in managing patient transitions and ensuring adherence to care plans is vital for an ACO's success in achieving its objectives.

1.2 Adherence To Care Regimen:

Adherence to a care regimen refers to the extent to which a patient correctly follows medical advice and prescribed treatment plans. This encompasses taking medications as prescribed, following dietary recommendations, attending scheduled appointments, and implementing lifestyle changes. For case managers, ensuring adherence is crucial, as it directly impacts patient outcomes, healthcare costs, and the overall effectiveness of care delivery.

Effective adherence requires a collaborative approach between healthcare providers and patients. Case managers play a pivotal role by assessing barriers to adherence, such as socioeconomic factors, health literacy, and psychological issues. They work to identify these barriers early on and implement strategies to overcome them. This may involve simplifying medication regimens, providing education about the importance of adherence, and employing motivational interviewing techniques to enhance patient engagement.

Additionally, case managers coordinate with multidisciplinary teams to tailor individualized care plans that align with the patient's lifestyle and preferences. Utilizing technology, such as reminders through mobile apps or telehealth consultations, can also support adherence by offering continuous engagement and monitoring.

Monitoring adherence is an ongoing process that requires regular assessment and adjustment of care plans. Case managers must document adherence levels and communicate effectively with all stakeholders involved in the patient's care. By fostering a supportive environment and encouraging active patient participation, case managers can significantly improve adherence rates, leading to better health outcomes and more efficient use of healthcare resources.

1.3 Age-Specific Care: Differences and Applications

Age-specific care involves tailoring healthcare delivery to meet the unique physical, emotional, and developmental needs of individuals at different life stages. This approach is essential for ensuring optimal patient outcomes and enhancing the quality of care. For case managers, understanding these differences is crucial for coordinating and planning effective care strategies.

In pediatric care, emphasis is placed on growth and development milestones, immunization schedules, and family-centered care. Communication is often directed through parents or guardians, with a focus on creating a supportive environment that fosters development. Adolescents require attention to their evolving autonomy, mental health, and risk behaviors, necessitating a balance between parental involvement and privacy.

Adult care varies significantly based on life circumstances, such as pregnancy or chronic disease management. This stage often involves promoting preventive health measures and managing acute conditions. For older adults, care focuses on managing multiple comorbidities, medication reconciliation, fall prevention, and end-of-life planning. Cognitive changes and social support systems become increasingly important.

The application of age-specific care requires case managers to assess individual needs comprehensively and coordinate with multidisciplinary teams to implement personalized care plans. This may involve collaborating with pediatricians, gerontologists, or other specialists to address specific age-related concerns. By recognizing the distinct needs of each age group, case managers can facilitate appropriate interventions that promote health and well-being across the lifespan. This holistic approach not only improves patient satisfaction but also optimizes resource utilization within healthcare systems.

1.4 Life Span Considerations:

Life span considerations in case management involve understanding and addressing the unique healthcare needs and challenges that arise at different stages of an individual's life. This concept is crucial for case managers, as it influences care planning, intervention strategies, and resource allocation to ensure optimal outcomes across the continuum of care.

From infancy to old age, individuals experience varying physiological, psychological, and social changes that affect their health status and care requirements. For instance, infants and children require growth and developmental assessments, immunizations, and parental guidance on nutrition and safety. Adolescents may need support related to mental health, substance use prevention, and sexual health education.

In adulthood, the focus shifts to preventive care, management of chronic conditions, and reproductive health. Case managers must consider occupational hazards, lifestyle factors, and family responsibilities that impact health. As individuals transition into older adulthood, common concerns include managing multiple chronic illnesses, cognitive decline, mobility issues, and end-of-life planning.

Cultural competence is also integral to life span considerations. Case managers should be aware of cultural beliefs and practices that influence health behaviors and decisions at each life stage. Additionally, social determinants of health, such as socioeconomic status, education level, and access to healthcare services, play a significant role in shaping individual needs throughout the lifespan.

By incorporating life span considerations into their practice, case managers can provide personalized care that respects the diverse needs of clients at every stage of life, promoting continuity of care and enhancing quality of life.

1.5 Alternative Care Facilities:

Alternative Care Facilities (ACFs) are healthcare settings that provide a spectrum of care services outside the traditional hospital environment. These facilities cater to individuals who require medical, rehabilitative, or supportive care but do not need the acute care services offered by hospitals. ACFs include nursing homes, assisted living facilities, rehabilitation centers, hospice care, and home health care services.

These facilities aim to deliver patient-centered care tailored to individual needs, focusing on enhancing the quality of life and promoting independence. They often serve populations such as the elderly, those with chronic illnesses, and individuals recovering from surgery or acute medical events. The primary goal is to provide a more cost-effective solution while maintaining high standards of care.

Case managers working with ACFs must understand various aspects, including regulatory requirements, accreditation standards, and the specific services each facility offers. They play a crucial role in coordinating care plans that align with patients' needs and preferences, ensuring seamless transitions between different levels of care.

Moreover, case managers must be adept at evaluating the appropriateness of an ACF for each patient, considering factors such as the patient's medical condition, functional status, and social support systems. By effectively navigating these facilities and leveraging available resources, case managers can significantly enhance patient outcomes and satisfaction while optimizing healthcare resources. Understanding ACFs is essential for case managers to facilitate comprehensive and continuous care across the healthcare continuum.

1.5.1 Assisted Living:

Assisted living is a residential option for individuals who require some level of assistance with daily activities but do not need the intensive medical care provided by nursing homes. These facilities offer a blend of independence and support, catering primarily to older adults who value autonomy yet need help with tasks such as bathing, dressing, medication management, and meal preparation.

In assisted living communities, residents typically reside in private or shared apartments and have access to communal areas for dining and social activities. The environment is designed to be home-like and supportive, promoting dignity and quality of life. Staff members are available 24/7 to provide necessary care and ensure safety, often including emergency call systems in each unit.

A key aspect of assisted living is the personalized care plans tailored to meet the unique needs of each resident. This approach allows for flexibility as needs change over time, ensuring that residents receive appropriate levels of support while maintaining as much independence as possible.

Case managers play a crucial role in evaluating whether assisted living is suitable for a client. They assess the individual's physical, emotional, and social needs, considering factors such as mobility, cognitive function, and personal preferences. Additionally, case managers may assist families in navigating financial considerations and selecting an appropriate facility that aligns with the client's lifestyle and care requirements.

Understanding assisted living is essential for case managers to effectively guide clients through the continuum of care options available within alternative care facilities.

1.5.2 Group Homes:
Group homes are community-based residential facilities designed to provide a structured and supportive living environment for individuals who require assistance with daily living activities but do not need the intensive medical care provided in hospitals or nursing homes. These facilities cater to various populations, including individuals with developmental disabilities, mental health conditions, substance use disorders, or those transitioning from institutional settings back into the community.

The primary goal of group homes is to promote independence while ensuring safety and well-being. They offer a homelike atmosphere where residents can receive personalized care tailored to their specific needs. Services typically include assistance with personal care, medication management, meal preparation, transportation, and access to recreational activities. Additionally, group homes often provide life skills training to help residents develop the competencies necessary for independent living.

Staffing in group homes usually consists of trained professionals such as social workers, nurses, and direct care staff who work collaboratively to deliver holistic care. The staffing ratio is often determined by the needs of the residents and regulatory requirements.

For case managers preparing for the CCM exam, understanding the role of group homes is crucial in developing comprehensive care plans. Case managers must evaluate the appropriateness of a group home placement based on an individual's functional abilities, support needs, and personal preferences. Additionally, they play a vital role in coordinating services and monitoring progress to ensure that residents achieve optimal outcomes within these alternative care settings.

1.5.3 Residential Treatment Facilities:
Residential Treatment Facilities (RTFs) are structured environments that provide intensive therapeutic services and 24-hour care to individuals with complex mental health, behavioral, or substance use disorders. These facilities offer a comprehensive approach that integrates medical, psychiatric, and psychosocial interventions tailored to the unique needs of each resident. RTFs serve as an alternative to hospitalization, aiming to stabilize individuals in crisis while promoting long-term recovery and reintegration into the community.

The multidisciplinary team in RTFs typically includes psychiatrists, psychologists, social workers, nurses, and other specialized therapists who collaborate to develop individualized treatment plans. These plans often encompass a combination of individual therapy, group therapy, family counseling, medication management, and life skills training. The therapeutic milieu in RTFs is designed to foster a supportive community where residents can practice interpersonal skills and receive peer support.

Case Managers play a crucial role in RTFs by coordinating care, facilitating communication among the treatment team, and ensuring continuity of care upon discharge. They assess residents' needs, advocate for necessary resources, and assist in developing discharge plans that may include outpatient therapy, support groups, or transitional housing.

RTFs vary in terms of specialization; some focus on specific populations, such as adolescents or individuals with dual diagnoses. The length of stay can range from several weeks to several months, depending on the individual's progress and specific treatment goals. Understanding the function and operation of RTFs is essential for Case Managers preparing for the CCM exam, as it highlights their role in managing complex cases within alternative care settings.

1.6 Case Management: Models, Processes, Tools
Case management models are structured frameworks that guide case managers in delivering coordinated care to clients. These models include the Brokerage Model, which focuses on connecting clients with necessary resources; the Clinical Model, which emphasizes direct clinical involvement and intervention; and the Strengths-Based Model, which leverages clients' inherent strengths to achieve desired outcomes. Each model offers a unique approach to addressing client needs and optimizing care delivery.

The case management process is a systematic series of steps that ensures comprehensive client care. It typically involves assessment, planning, implementation, coordination, monitoring, and evaluation. During the assessment, case managers gather detailed information about the client's health status and needs. Planning involves developing a tailored care plan with specific goals and interventions. Implementation is the execution of the care plan, while coordination ensures seamless service delivery across different providers. Monitoring involves tracking progress toward goals, and evaluation assesses the effectiveness of the interventions.

Tools used in case management include software systems for documentation and communication, assessment instruments for evaluating client needs, and outcome measurement tools for tracking progress. These tools enhance efficiency and accuracy in managing cases by providing standardized methods for data collection and analysis.

Understanding these models, processes, and tools is crucial for effective case management practice. They enable case managers to provide holistic care that meets individual client needs while ensuring that resource utilization is efficient and outcomes are optimized. Mastery of these elements is essential for success in the CCM exam and professional practice.

1.7 Coding Methodologies:

Coding methodologies refer to the systematic approaches used to classify and categorize medical diagnoses, procedures, and services into standardized codes. These codes are essential for billing, reimbursement, and maintaining comprehensive health records. In the context of case management, understanding coding methodologies is crucial, as they impact care coordination, resource allocation, and the financial aspects of healthcare delivery.

The primary coding systems utilized include the International Classification of Diseases (ICD), Current Procedural Terminology (CPT), and the Healthcare Common Procedure Coding System (HCPCS). ICD codes are used to represent diagnoses and health conditions, while CPT codes describe medical, surgical, and diagnostic services. HCPCS is primarily used for billing Medicare and Medicaid patients and includes additional services not covered by CPT.

Case managers must be adept at interpreting these codes to ensure accurate documentation of patient conditions and treatments. This knowledge aids in verifying insurance coverage, facilitating communication among healthcare providers, and optimizing patient care plans. Additionally, proficiency in coding methodologies enables case managers to identify discrepancies or errors in medical records that could affect patient outcomes or lead to financial penalties for healthcare facilities.

An in-depth understanding of coding methodologies also involves staying updated with annual revisions and changes to coding guidelines. This ensures compliance with regulatory standards and enhances the quality of case management practices. Mastery of coding methodologies is a vital skill set for case managers aiming to achieve certification and excel in their roles within the healthcare system.

1.7.1 Diagnosis-Related Group (DRG):

The Diagnosis-Related Group (DRG) system is used to classify hospital cases into one of originally 467 groups, with the intent of facilitating reimbursement under the Medicare program. Each DRG is designed to reflect the amount of resources required to treat patients in a particular category. Essentially, DRGs are used to determine how much Medicare pays the hospital, as they are based on the patient's diagnosis, procedures performed, age, sex, and discharge status.

The DRG system categorizes patients with similar clinical conditions and resource usage. This classification system is crucial for case managers, as it aids in understanding hospital billing and reimbursement processes. The DRG system ensures that hospitals are incentivized to manage resources efficiently while maintaining quality care. This is because hospitals receive a fixed payment for a patient's stay based on the assigned DRG, regardless of the actual costs incurred.

For case managers, understanding DRGs is vital for managing healthcare costs and ensuring appropriate resource allocation. It assists in discharge planning and in coordinating care transitions effectively. By understanding which DRG a patient falls under, case managers can anticipate potential needs and complications that might arise during a patient's stay and plan accordingly.

In summary, DRGs serve as a cornerstone in hospital reimbursement systems, impacting financial management and operational efficiency. Case managers must be adept at navigating these classifications to optimize patient outcomes and resource utilization within healthcare facilities.

1.7.2 DSM: Overview and Significance

The Diagnostic and Statistical Manual of Mental Disorders (DSM) is a critical tool used by healthcare professionals, including case managers, to diagnose and classify mental disorders. Published by the American Psychiatric Association (APA), the DSM provides standardized criteria and language for diagnosing mental health conditions, ensuring consistency and reliability across various healthcare settings.

The DSM serves as a comprehensive guide that outlines specific symptoms and diagnostic criteria for each mental disorder, facilitating accurate assessment and treatment planning. It is regularly updated to reflect advancements in psychiatric research and clinical practice, with the current edition being DSM-5-TR, which includes updated diagnostic criteria and new disorders based on recent findings.

For case managers, understanding the DSM is essential for coordinating care effectively. It aids in identifying appropriate interventions, planning treatment strategies, and communicating with other healthcare providers. Familiarity with the DSM also enables case managers to advocate for clients' needs, ensuring they receive appropriate services and support.

Moreover, the DSM plays a significant role in insurance reimbursement processes. Accurate diagnosis according to DSM criteria is often required for insurance claims related to mental health services. Therefore, proficiency in utilizing the DSM not only enhances clinical practice but also supports the financial aspects of care management.

In summary, the DSM is an indispensable resource that supports case managers in delivering comprehensive, evidence-based care to individuals with mental health disorders.

1.7.3 Understanding ICD: A Global Health Framework

The International Classification of Diseases (ICD) is a globally recognized system for coding various health conditions and diseases. Developed by the World Health Organization (WHO), the ICD serves as a critical tool for healthcare providers, including case managers, to ensure uniformity and consistency in the documentation and reporting of diseases. The ICD codes are used to classify diagnoses and reasons for visits in all healthcare settings, enabling effective communication across different healthcare systems and facilitating international comparisons in health data.

The ICD system is periodically updated to reflect advances in medical knowledge and changes in disease patterns. As of October 2023, the most current version is ICD-11. This version incorporates significant improvements over its predecessors, including enhanced detail and specificity, which aid in more precise diagnosis and treatment planning. For case managers, understanding ICD codes is essential for accurate documentation, billing, and ensuring compliance with healthcare regulations.

ICD codes play a pivotal role in case management by aiding in the identification of patient needs, planning appropriate interventions, and evaluating outcomes. They also assist in resource allocation and policy development by providing reliable data on disease prevalence and healthcare utilization. Mastery of ICD coding methodologies is crucial for case managers aiming to excel in their roles, as it directly impacts the quality of care coordination and the efficiency of healthcare delivery systems.

1.7.4 Current Procedural Terminology (CPT):
Current Procedural Terminology (CPT) is a comprehensive coding system established by the American Medical Association (AMA) to standardize the reporting of medical, surgical, and diagnostic procedures and services. It is widely used in the United States for billing purposes by healthcare providers, insurers, and government entities. CPT codes ensure uniformity and accuracy in documenting medical services rendered, facilitating efficient communication among healthcare professionals and payers.

CPT codes are five-digit numeric or alphanumeric codes assigned to every task and service a medical practitioner may provide to a patient, including medical, surgical, and diagnostic services. These codes are divided into three categories: Category I for procedures and contemporary medical practices, Category II for performance measurement, and Category III for emerging technologies and experimental procedures.

For case managers, understanding CPT codes is crucial, as they play a pivotal role in managing patient care plans, coordinating with healthcare providers, and ensuring that services are appropriately documented and billed. The accurate use of CPT codes helps avoid claim denials and ensures that patients receive the benefits to which they are entitled under their health plans.

Additionally, CPT codes are regularly updated to reflect advancements in medical technology and practice. Case managers must stay informed about these updates to maintain compliance with current standards. Mastery of CPT coding methodologies is essential for effective case management, as it directly impacts the financial aspects of patient care delivery and reimbursement processes.

1.8 Continuum of Care and Services:
The Continuum of Care refers to a comprehensive, integrated system of care that guides and tracks patients over time through a wide array of health services, spanning all levels and intensities of care. This concept is pivotal for case managers, as it encompasses the entire spectrum of care, from preventive and primary care to acute, chronic, and end-of-life care. The continuum is designed to ensure that patients receive the right care at the right time in the most appropriate setting.

In the context of health and human/social services, the continuum emphasizes coordination among various healthcare providers and social service agencies to address not only medical needs but also social determinants of health. This includes services such as housing assistance, nutritional support, and mental health services. Effective management within this continuum requires case managers to identify gaps in care, facilitate communication among caregivers, and advocate for patient-centered approaches that respect individual preferences and cultural values.

Case managers play a crucial role in navigating this continuum by assessing patient needs, developing personalized care plans, coordinating resources, and monitoring outcomes. Their work ensures continuity and quality of care while optimizing resource utilization. Understanding the Continuum of Care is essential for case managers preparing for the CCM exam, as it underpins many core competencies required for effective practice in diverse healthcare settings.

1.9 Cost Containment Principles:
Cost containment principles in case management refer to strategies and practices aimed at controlling and reducing healthcare expenses while maintaining or improving the quality of care. These principles are crucial for ensuring that healthcare resources are used efficiently, ultimately benefiting both the patient and the healthcare system.

A primary aspect of cost containment is the effective utilization of resources. This involves ensuring that patients receive necessary care without undergoing unnecessary tests or treatments, which can inflate costs. Case managers play a pivotal role in coordinating care to avoid duplication of services and to ensure that interventions are evidence-based and appropriate for the patient's condition.

Another key principle is the management of high-cost cases. By identifying patients who require extensive resources, case managers can implement targeted interventions to manage their care more effectively. This may include coordinating with multiple healthcare providers, facilitating access to community resources, and implementing disease management programs.

Negotiating with providers and payers is also essential for cost containment. Case managers often work to secure favorable rates for services or medications, thus reducing expenses for both patients and insurers. Additionally, promoting preventive care and patient education can lead to long-term cost savings by reducing the incidence of chronic diseases and hospital readmissions.

Overall, cost containment principles require a balance between financial considerations and quality care delivery, necessitating a comprehensive understanding of healthcare systems, reimbursement models, and patient needs.

1.10 Assessing Client Acuity Levels:

Acuity or severity levels in case management refer to the extent of a client's healthcare needs and the complexity of their condition. Identifying these levels is crucial for prioritizing care, allocating resources, and planning interventions effectively. Several factors are utilized to determine a client's acuity or severity levels.

Firstly, clinical indicators such as vital signs, laboratory results, and diagnostic imaging provide objective data on the client's current health status. These indicators help assess the urgency and intensity of the medical intervention required.

Secondly, the client's functional status is evaluated. This includes their ability to perform daily activities and maintain independence. A decline in functional status often signals increased acuity.

Thirdly, psychosocial factors are considered. These encompass mental health conditions, social support systems, and socioeconomic status. Clients with inadequate support or significant psychological distress may exhibit higher acuity levels.

Moreover, comorbidities play a significant role in determining severity. The presence of multiple chronic conditions can complicate treatment plans and elevate acuity levels.

Additionally, healthcare utilization history is analyzed. Frequent hospitalizations or emergency room visits may indicate high acuity due to inadequate outpatient management or uncontrolled symptoms.

Finally, the potential for rapid deterioration is assessed. Clients at risk of sudden health decline require immediate attention and intervention.

Understanding these factors enables case managers to stratify clients accurately based on their needs, ensuring timely and appropriate care delivery while optimizing resource utilization.

1.11 Financial Resources:

Financial resources in the context of case management refer to the monetary assets and funding mechanisms available to support patient care and services. These resources are critical for ensuring that clients receive necessary medical treatments, social services, and other forms of assistance without financial barriers. Case managers play a pivotal role in identifying, accessing, and coordinating these resources to optimize patient outcomes.

A comprehensive understanding of financial resources involves recognizing various funding sources such as private insurance, Medicare, Medicaid, workers' compensation, and other government programs. Additionally, non-profit organizations, community funds, and charitable foundations may offer financial assistance for specific needs or populations.

Case managers must be adept at navigating the complexities of insurance benefits and eligibility criteria to maximize coverage for their clients. This includes understanding policy details, co-payments, deductibles, and out-of-pocket limits. They also need to be familiar with billing procedures and reimbursement processes to ensure that services are delivered efficiently and cost-effectively.

Moreover, financial resources encompass budgeting skills to manage funds effectively within healthcare settings. Case managers must often work within constraints to prioritize interventions that deliver the greatest benefit relative to cost. They also advocate for clients by negotiating payment plans or seeking alternative funding when standard resources fall short.

Ultimately, proficient management of financial resources requires ongoing education and collaboration with financial advisors, social workers, and healthcare providers to develop sustainable care plans that align with clients' financial capacities and health needs.

1.11.1 Waiver Programs:

Waiver Programs are specialized financial resources that allow states to provide Medicaid-funded services to individuals who might not otherwise qualify for standard Medicaid benefits. These programs are designed to offer flexibility in the provision of care, enabling states to waive certain Medicaid requirements to better meet the needs of specific populations. Typically, Waiver Programs target groups such as the elderly, individuals with disabilities, and those requiring long-term care, allowing them to receive care in community settings rather than institutional environments.

The primary objective of Waiver Programs is to enhance the quality of life for beneficiaries by offering services that promote independence and integration into the community. These programs can cover a wide range of services, including personal care assistance, home modifications, respite care, and adult day health services. By providing these services, Waiver Programs help reduce the need for more costly institutional care, ultimately leading to cost savings for both the state and federal governments.

Case managers play a crucial role in navigating Waiver Programs by assessing client eligibility, coordinating necessary services, and ensuring compliance with program requirements. Understanding the nuances of different Waiver Programs is essential for case managers to effectively advocate for their clients and secure appropriate resources. Familiarity with both federal guidelines and state-specific implementations of these waivers is vital for maximizing client outcomes and optimizing resource allocation within the healthcare system.

1.11.2 Special Needs Trusts:

A Special Needs Trust (SNT) is a legal arrangement designed to manage and protect assets for individuals with disabilities, ensuring their eligibility for government benefits such as Medicaid and Supplemental Security Income (SSI). The primary purpose of an SNT is to supplement, not supplant, the beneficiary's public benefits by covering additional expenses that enhance their quality of life without affecting their eligibility for essential support programs.

There are three main types of Special Needs Trusts: first-party, third-party, and pooled trusts. A first-party SNT is funded with the disabled individual's own assets, typically established when they receive a significant sum of money, such as an inheritance or personal injury settlement. This trust must include a Medicaid payback provision upon the beneficiary's death. A third-party SNT is funded by someone other than the disabled individual, such as a parent or grandparent, and does not require a Medicaid payback clause. Pooled trusts are managed by nonprofit organizations and pool resources from multiple beneficiaries for investment purposes while maintaining separate accounts for each.

Case managers should understand that SNTs are crucial tools for preserving the financial security and well-being of individuals with disabilities. They allow beneficiaries to receive funds for non-essential needs like education, transportation, and recreational activities while retaining access to government assistance. Properly managing these trusts requires collaboration with legal professionals to ensure compliance with complex regulations and safeguard the beneficiary's interests.

1.11.3   Viatical Settlements:
A viatical settlement is a financial arrangement in which a life insurance policyholder sells their policy to a third party for a lump sum payment. This transaction typically involves individuals who are terminally ill or have a shortened life expectancy, allowing them to access funds for medical expenses or other needs while they are still alive. The buyer of the policy, often an investment company, assumes responsibility for paying future premiums and becomes the beneficiary of the policy upon the insured's death.

In practice, viatical settlements provide a financial lifeline to individuals facing significant healthcare costs or end-of-life expenses. The lump sum received is generally less than the policy's face value but more than its cash surrender value, offering immediate liquidity. This can be crucial for patients requiring costly treatments or wishing to improve their quality of life during their remaining time.

Case managers should understand the implications of viatical settlements, including potential impacts on eligibility for public assistance programs like Medicaid. It is essential to evaluate whether this option aligns with the client's financial goals and healthcare needs. Additionally, ethical considerations must be taken into account, ensuring that clients are fully informed about the terms and consequences of such transactions.

Overall, viatical settlements can be a valuable resource for those needing immediate funds, but they require careful consideration and guidance from knowledgeable professionals to ensure that clients make informed decisions that best serve their interests.

1.12 Case Management Goals and Objectives:
The goals and objectives of case management practice are foundational elements that guide the actions and decisions of case managers in their professional roles. The primary goal of case management is to improve the client's health, wellness, and autonomy through advocacy, communication, education, identification of service resources, and facilitation of service delivery. This involves a collaborative process that assesses, plans, implements, coordinates, monitors, and evaluates the options and services required to meet the client's health needs.

Objectives within case management practice are specific, measurable actions that support the overarching goals. These objectives include ensuring timely access to appropriate care and services, promoting client safety and quality of life, enhancing client self-management abilities, reducing unnecessary hospitalizations or emergency room visits, and optimizing resource utilization. Case managers work to empower clients by providing them with the information and support needed to make informed decisions about their care.

Additionally, case management objectives emphasize interdisciplinary collaboration among healthcare providers to ensure comprehensive and coordinated care delivery. By focusing on these goals and objectives, case managers aim to achieve positive outcomes for clients while maintaining ethical standards and adhering to best practices within the field. Ultimately, successful case management leads to improved client satisfaction, better health outcomes, and more efficient use of healthcare resources.

1.13 Healthcare Delivery Systems:
Healthcare delivery systems refer to the organized and systematic approaches through which healthcare services are provided to populations. These systems encompass various components, including healthcare providers, institutions, financing mechanisms, and regulatory frameworks, all working collaboratively to deliver care. The primary goal of healthcare delivery systems is to ensure that individuals receive timely, efficient, and effective care that meets their needs.

In the context of case management, understanding healthcare delivery systems is crucial, as it involves navigating complex networks of care. These systems can be categorized into different models, such as managed care, integrated delivery systems, and patient-centered medical homes. Managed care emphasizes cost control and quality improvement through coordinated care and pre-established provider networks. Integrated delivery systems aim to provide a continuum of care by linking various healthcare services and providers under a unified system. Patient-centered medical homes focus on primary care that is comprehensive, coordinated, and accessible.

Case managers must be adept at working within these systems to facilitate optimal patient outcomes. This involves understanding the intricacies of insurance coverage, reimbursement processes, and regulatory compliance. Additionally, case managers play a pivotal role in coordinating care across different settings—such as hospitals, outpatient clinics, and home health services—ensuring seamless transitions for patients.

Overall, healthcare delivery systems form the backbone of how healthcare is accessed and delivered, making it essential for case managers to have a thorough understanding of these structures to effectively advocate for and manage patient care.

1.14 Understanding Hospice and Palliative Care:

Hospice, palliative, and end-of-life care are specialized areas of healthcare focused on providing comprehensive support to patients with life-limiting illnesses. Hospice care is a model designed to offer comfort and dignity to patients in the final stages of terminal illness. It emphasizes pain management, symptom control, and emotional support rather than curative treatment. Hospice care typically involves a multidisciplinary team approach that includes physicians, nurses, social workers, chaplains, and volunteers working collaboratively to address the physical, emotional, and spiritual needs of patients and their families.

Palliative care, while similar to hospice care in its focus on alleviating suffering and improving quality of life, can be provided at any stage of a serious illness and alongside curative treatments. It aims to relieve symptoms such as pain, nausea, fatigue, and anxiety while providing psychosocial support. Palliative care teams work closely with patients and their families to establish goals of care and develop personalized treatment plans.

End-of-life care refers to the support and medical care provided during the time surrounding death. This includes managing physical symptoms, providing psychological support, addressing spiritual concerns, and assisting with decision-making regarding advance directives and treatment preferences.

Case managers play a crucial role in coordinating hospice, palliative, and end-of-life care by ensuring seamless communication among healthcare providers, facilitating access to necessary resources, and advocating for patient-centered care that aligns with the individual's values and wishes.

1.15 Insurance Principles:

Insurance principles are foundational guidelines that govern the operation and management of insurance policies, ensuring fairness, legality, and efficiency in the provision of coverage. These principles are crucial for case managers to understand as they navigate the complexities of patient care and resource allocation.

The first principle is Utmost Good Faith, which requires all parties involved to act honestly and disclose all relevant information. This ensures that insurers can accurately assess risk and provide appropriate coverage. Next is the Principle of Indemnity, which stipulates that insurance should compensate the insured for their loss, restoring them to their financial position prior to the incident, without allowing profit from the insurance claim.

Another key principle is Insurable Interest, which mandates that the insured must have a legitimate interest in the preservation of the subject matter of insurance. This prevents moral hazard and speculative behavior. The Principle of Contribution applies when multiple policies cover a single risk, ensuring equitable distribution of liability among insurers.

The Principle of Subrogation allows insurers to pursue third parties responsible for an insured loss, protecting against unjust enrichment and reducing overall costs. Finally, the Principle of Loss Minimization obligates policyholders to take reasonable steps to mitigate their losses.

Understanding these principles enables case managers to effectively collaborate with insurance providers, advocate for patients' needs, and ensure optimal utilization of healthcare resources within legal and ethical frameworks.

1.15.1   Health:

Health is a multifaceted concept that encompasses physical, mental, and social well-being. It is not merely the absence of disease or infirmity but a holistic state in which an individual can realize their potential, cope with normal stresses, work productively, and contribute to their community. In the context of case management, understanding health involves recognizing the interplay between various factors that influence an individual's overall well-being.

Physical health refers to the efficient functioning of the body and its systems, enabling individuals to perform daily activities without undue fatigue. Mental health encompasses emotional, psychological, and social aspects that influence how people think, feel, and behave. Social health involves having supportive networks and fulfilling relationships that contribute to a person's sense of belonging and purpose.

Case managers play a pivotal role in promoting health by coordinating care that addresses these diverse dimensions. They assess clients' needs, develop personalized care plans, and facilitate access to resources that support comprehensive health management. This includes advocating for preventive measures, ensuring continuity of care, and addressing barriers such as socioeconomic factors and access to healthcare services.

By adopting a holistic approach to health, case managers can enhance clients' quality of life and empower them to achieve optimal health outcomes. Understanding the intricate balance of physical, mental, and social components enables case managers to deliver effective interventions tailored to each individual's unique circumstances. This comprehensive perspective is crucial for fostering sustainable health improvements and advancing the goals of case management practice.

1.15.2   Disability:

Disability, within the context of insurance principles, refers to a physical or mental impairment that substantially limits one or more major life activities. It is a critical concept in case management, particularly when dealing with disability insurance, which provides income protection to individuals who become unable to work due to their disability. Understanding disability is essential for case managers as they navigate the complexities of insurance claims and client advocacy.

Disabilities can be temporary or permanent and may arise from various causes, such as illness, injury, or congenital conditions. The definition and classification of disability can vary depending on the insurance policy, legal jurisdiction, and specific context in which it is being considered. In the realm of insurance, disability is often categorized into short-term and long-term types, each with distinct eligibility criteria and benefit structures.

Case managers must be adept at assessing the impact of disabilities on an individual's ability to perform occupational tasks and daily activities. This involves collaborating with healthcare providers to obtain accurate medical documentation, understanding policy terms, and effectively communicating with clients about their rights and benefits.

Moreover, case managers play a pivotal role in facilitating access to rehabilitation services and vocational training aimed at improving functional capacity and promoting return-to-work outcomes. By comprehensively understanding disability and its implications within insurance frameworks, case managers ensure that clients receive appropriate support and resources to manage their conditions effectively while safeguarding their financial stability.

1.15.3   Workers Compensation:

Workers' compensation is a form of insurance that provides wage replacement and medical benefits to employees injured during the course of their employment. It serves as a critical safety net for workers, ensuring they receive the necessary care and financial support while recovering from work-related injuries or illnesses. This system is designed to protect both employees and employers by establishing a no-fault framework, meaning employees are entitled to benefits regardless of who was at fault for the injury.

For case managers, understanding workers' compensation involves recognizing the nuances of state-specific regulations, as these can vary significantly across jurisdictions. Each state has its own governing body and set of rules that dictate eligibility, benefit levels, and the claims process. Case managers must be adept at navigating these regulations to effectively advocate for their clients.

The role of a case manager in workers' compensation includes coordinating care, facilitating communication between healthcare providers, employers, and insurance companies, and ensuring compliance with treatment plans. They play a pivotal role in helping injured workers return to work safely and efficiently by developing comprehensive rehabilitation plans tailored to individual needs.

Furthermore, case managers must be vigilant in identifying potential barriers to recovery, such as psychosocial issues or non-compliance with treatment protocols, and addressing them proactively. By doing so, they help minimize the duration of disability and optimize outcomes for both the employee and employer. A thorough understanding of workers' compensation enables case managers to provide informed guidance and support throughout the recovery process.

1.15.4   Long Term Care:

Long Term Care (LTC) refers to a range of services and supports necessary for individuals who have lost some degree of independence due to chronic illness, disability, or aging. These services can be provided in various settings, such as nursing homes, assisted living facilities, or within the individual's home. The primary goal of LTC is to assist individuals with activities of daily living (ADLs), which include bathing, dressing, eating, toileting, and transferring.

LTC is not limited to medical care; it encompasses personal and social services that help maintain the quality of life for those who require extended care. Case managers play a crucial role in coordinating these services to ensure that the patients' needs are met efficiently and effectively. They assess the individual's requirements, develop care plans, and collaborate with healthcare providers, caregivers, and family members to implement and monitor these plans.

Financing LTC can be challenging, as it is often not covered by standard health insurance policies. Medicare provides limited coverage for specific conditions and durations, while Medicaid offers more comprehensive support for eligible low-income individuals. Additionally, private long-term care insurance policies are available but can be costly.

Understanding the complexities of LTC is essential for case managers preparing for the CCM exam. They must be adept at navigating insurance options, advocating for patient needs, and ensuring continuity of care across different settings to optimize patient outcomes and resource utilization.

1.16 Interdisciplinary/interprofessional Care Team:

An interdisciplinary/interprofessional care team is a collaborative group of healthcare professionals from diverse fields who work together to deliver comprehensive patient care. This team approach is crucial for managing complex patient needs, ensuring that care is holistic, coordinated, and efficient. Each member of the team brings their unique expertise and perspective, contributing to a more complete understanding of the patient's condition and facilitating optimal health outcomes.

The core of an interdisciplinary/interprofessional care team typically includes physicians, nurses, social workers, pharmacists, physical therapists, dietitians, and case managers. Each professional plays a distinct role: physicians diagnose and treat medical conditions; nurses provide ongoing patient care and education; social workers address psychosocial issues; pharmacists manage medication therapy; physical therapists aid in rehabilitation; dietitians focus on nutritional needs; and case managers coordinate care plans and resources.

Effective communication is essential within this team to prevent errors, reduce redundancies, and ensure that all aspects of a patient's care are addressed. Regular meetings and updates are vital for maintaining alignment on treatment goals and progress. The collaborative nature of the team fosters shared decision-making, where input from all disciplines is valued and utilized in developing patient-centered care plans.

For case managers preparing for the CCM exam, understanding the dynamics of an interdisciplinary/interprofessional care team is critical. They must be adept at facilitating communication among team members, advocating for the patient's needs, and ensuring that care delivery is seamless across different healthcare settings.

1.17 Levels of Care & Settings:

Levels of care refer to the intensity and complexity of medical services provided to patients, while care settings denote the environments in which these services are delivered. Understanding these concepts is crucial for case managers as they coordinate patient care across various healthcare environments.

The levels of care typically include primary, secondary, tertiary, and quaternary care. Primary care serves as the first point of contact and involves general health maintenance and preventive services. Secondary care refers to specialized medical services provided by specialists after a referral from a primary care provider. Tertiary care involves highly specialized medical treatment, often in a hospital setting, such as advanced surgical procedures or cancer treatment. Quaternary care represents an extension of tertiary care, providing even more specialized and experimental treatments.

Care settings vary widely and include hospitals, outpatient clinics, long-term care facilities, home health agencies, rehabilitation centers, and hospice care. Each setting is designed to meet specific patient needs based on their required level of medical attention.

Case managers must adeptly navigate these levels and settings to ensure seamless transitions for patients across the continuum of care. They assess patient needs, develop comprehensive care plans, and coordinate with healthcare providers to optimize outcomes. Proficiency in understanding levels of care and settings enables case managers to advocate effectively for patients, ensuring they receive appropriate services at the right time and place. This knowledge is fundamental for passing the CCM exam and excelling in the role of a case manager.

1.18 Managed Care Concepts:

Managed care is a healthcare delivery system aimed at managing costs, utilization, and quality. It encompasses a variety of techniques intended to reduce the cost of providing health benefits and improve the quality of care. The primary objective is to provide patients with access to necessary medical services while controlling the expenses associated with treatment.

Key components of managed care include a network of contracted healthcare providers, negotiated rates for services, and utilization management strategies. These networks are often organized through Health Maintenance Organizations (HMOs), Preferred Provider Organizations (PPOs), or Point of Service (POS) plans, each offering varying levels of flexibility and cost-sharing for patients.

Utilization management involves pre-authorization for certain procedures, concurrent review during hospital stays, and case management for complex conditions. This ensures that patients receive appropriate care without unnecessary duplication of services or excessive costs.

Managed care also emphasizes preventive care and wellness programs to reduce the incidence of chronic diseases and improve overall health outcomes. By focusing on prevention, managed care aims to decrease long-term healthcare costs and enhance patients' quality of life.

Quality assurance is another critical aspect, involving continuous monitoring and evaluation of healthcare services to ensure they meet established standards. This includes performance measurement, patient satisfaction surveys, and adherence to clinical guidelines.

Overall, managed care concepts are designed to balance cost control with high-quality patient care, making it essential for case managers to understand these principles to effectively coordinate and optimize patient outcomes within the healthcare system.

1.19 Client Management in Acute and Chronic Illnesses:

The management of clients with acute and chronic illnesses involves a systematic approach to healthcare delivery that focuses on optimizing patient outcomes through coordinated care. Acute illnesses are sudden in onset and typically require immediate attention, whereas chronic illnesses are long-term conditions that necessitate ongoing management. Case managers play a pivotal role in the interdisciplinary team by assessing, planning, implementing, coordinating, monitoring, and evaluating the options and services required to meet an individual's health needs.

In managing acute illnesses, case managers must quickly identify the severity of the condition and facilitate prompt interventions. This involves collaborating with healthcare providers to ensure timely diagnostics and treatment while also educating patients about their condition and care plan. Effective communication is crucial to prevent complications and promote recovery.

For chronic illness management, case managers focus on long-term care strategies that emphasize patient education, adherence to treatment plans, lifestyle modifications, and regular monitoring of health status. They work closely with patients to develop personalized care plans that address medical, psychosocial, and functional needs. This includes coordinating with various healthcare professionals to provide comprehensive care that minimizes hospitalizations and improves quality of life.

Case managers also advocate for patients by navigating healthcare systems to access necessary resources and support services. They ensure continuity of care through transitions between different levels of care settings. Overall, effective management of acute and chronic illnesses requires a proactive approach that empowers patients while fostering collaboration among healthcare providers.

1.20 Client Disability Management:

The management of clients with disabilities involves a comprehensive approach to ensure optimal health outcomes, enhance quality of life, and promote independence. Case managers play a pivotal role in coordinating services that address the unique needs of individuals with disabilities. This process begins with a thorough assessment to identify the client's physical, emotional, social, and environmental needs. The assessment guides the development of a personalized care plan that outlines specific goals and interventions.

Effective management requires collaboration with a multidisciplinary team, including healthcare providers, rehabilitation specialists, social workers, and community resources. Case managers advocate for clients by facilitating access to necessary medical care, therapy services, adaptive equipment, and support networks. They also assist in navigating complex healthcare systems and securing financial resources, such as insurance benefits and government assistance programs.

Education is a critical component of managing clients with disabilities. Case managers provide information to clients and their families about the nature of the disability, available services, and strategies for self-management. Empowering clients through education fosters self-advocacy and encourages active participation in their care.

Regular monitoring and evaluation are essential to ensure that the care plan remains relevant and effective. Adjustments may be needed based on changes in the client's condition or circumstances. By maintaining open communication with clients and their families, case managers can address concerns promptly and adapt interventions as necessary.

Ultimately, the goal is to support clients in achieving their highest level of functioning and integration into society while respecting their autonomy and preferences.

1.21 Medication Safety Assessment and Management:

Medication Safety Assessment, Reconciliation, and Management are critical processes in ensuring patient safety and optimizing therapeutic outcomes. They involve a systematic approach to evaluating and managing a patient's medication regimen to prevent errors, adverse drug events, and interactions. The process begins with a thorough Medication Safety Assessment, where case managers evaluate the appropriateness of each medication, considering the patient's current condition, history, and potential for drug-drug or drug-disease interactions.

Medication Reconciliation is an integral part of this process. It involves verifying the accuracy and completeness of a patient's medication list at every transition of care. This includes comparing the patient's current medications with new prescriptions to resolve discrepancies and ensure continuity in treatment. The goal is to maintain an accurate and updated medication profile, thereby reducing the risk of errors such as omissions, duplications, or dosing mistakes.

Medication Management refers to the ongoing oversight of a patient's medication regimen. Case managers collaborate with healthcare providers to optimize drug therapy, monitor patient adherence, and adjust treatment plans as necessary. This may involve educating patients about their medications, addressing barriers to adherence, and coordinating with pharmacists for comprehensive pharmaceutical care.

In summary, Medication Safety Assessment, Reconciliation, and Management are essential components of case management that enhance patient safety by ensuring accurate medication use and preventing potential adverse effects. Through diligent assessment, reconciliation, and management practices, case managers play a pivotal role in promoting effective and safe pharmacotherapy.

1.22 Military and Veteran Benefits Overview:

Military and Veteran Benefit Programs are specialized services and supports designed to assist current and former military personnel, as well as their families, in accessing necessary healthcare, financial assistance, education, and housing benefits. These programs are crucial in facilitating the transition from active duty to civilian life, ensuring that veterans receive the care and support they deserve.

The Department of Veterans Affairs (VA) is the primary federal agency responsible for administering these benefits. Key programs include healthcare services through the Veterans Health Administration, which provides medical care at VA hospitals and clinics. The VA also offers disability compensation for veterans with service-connected disabilities, as well as pension benefits for low-income veterans.

Educational benefits are available under the GI Bill, which covers tuition and fees for veterans seeking higher education or vocational training. Additionally, the VA provides home loan guaranty programs to help veterans purchase homes without requiring a down payment.

Other significant benefits include employment services through the Veterans Employment and Training Service (VETS), which aids in job placement and career development. The VA also offers life insurance options tailored to veterans' needs.

Case managers play a vital role in navigating these complex benefit systems, ensuring that eligible veterans receive timely and appropriate assistance. By understanding the intricacies of Military and Veteran Benefit Programs, case managers can effectively advocate for their clients, maximizing access to these essential resources.

1.22.1   TRICARE And Veterans Administration:

TRICARE is a health care program of the United States Department of Defense Military Health System, providing civilian health benefits for military personnel, military retirees, and their dependents. It offers several plans, including TRICARE Prime, TRICARE Select, and TRICARE for Life, each catering to different needs and eligibility criteria. TRICARE Prime is similar to an HMO, requiring enrollment and offering lower out-of-pocket costs. TRICARE Select resembles a PPO, providing more flexibility in choosing providers but with higher costs. TRICARE for Life serves as Medicare wraparound coverage for those eligible for both Medicare and TRICARE.

The Veterans Administration (VA), on the other hand, is a federal agency responsible for providing comprehensive health care services to eligible military veterans at VA medical centers and outpatient clinics located throughout the country. The VA offers a wide array of services, including primary care, specialized care, mental health services, and rehabilitation. It also administers benefits such as disability compensation, vocational rehabilitation, education assistance, and home loans.

Case managers working with military and veteran populations must understand the intricacies of these programs to effectively navigate benefits and coordinate care. This includes recognizing eligibility requirements, understanding covered services, and knowing how to access additional resources. A thorough grasp of both TRICARE and VA systems ensures that case managers can advocate effectively for their clients, facilitating seamless transitions between military service and civilian life while maximizing available benefits.

1.23 Models Of Care Delivery:

Models of care delivery refer to the structured methods and systems through which healthcare services are organized and delivered to patients. These models are designed to ensure that care is patient-centered, efficient, and effective while meeting the diverse needs of the population served. They encompass various approaches to coordinating care across different settings and providers, aiming to enhance the quality of care, improve health outcomes, and optimize resource utilization.

One common model is the Patient-Centered Medical Home (PCMH), which emphasizes comprehensive primary care facilitated by a personal physician who coordinates all aspects of a patient's healthcare. This model fosters a partnership between patients and their healthcare providers, focusing on holistic and continuous care.

Another model is Accountable Care Organizations (ACOs), which are groups of doctors, hospitals, and other healthcare providers who voluntarily come together to provide coordinated, high-quality care to their Medicare patients. The goal is to ensure that patients receive the right care at the right time while avoiding unnecessary duplication of services and preventing medical errors.

Integrated Care Models focus on combining physical and behavioral health services, recognizing the interdependence of these aspects of health. This approach seeks to provide seamless care across various domains and specialties.

Each model has its unique features but shares common goals of improving patient outcomes, enhancing patient satisfaction, reducing healthcare costs, and promoting the efficient use of resources. Understanding these models is crucial for case managers as they navigate and coordinate complex healthcare systems to deliver optimal patient care.

1.23.1 Patient-centered Medical Home (PCMH):

The Patient-Centered Medical Home (PCMH) is a model of care delivery that emphasizes comprehensive, continuous, and coordinated care centered around the patient's needs. It is designed to enhance the quality of care by fostering a partnership between patients and their primary care providers. In this model, the primary care provider acts as the central hub for managing all aspects of a patient's health, ensuring that care is tailored to individual preferences, needs, and values.

PCMHs focus on delivering care that is accessible, family-centered, compassionate, and culturally effective. The model promotes a team-based approach where healthcare professionals collaborate to provide holistic and integrated care. This includes preventive services, management of chronic conditions, and coordination with specialists when necessary.

Key components of the PCMH include enhanced access to care through extended hours and improved communication channels, such as electronic health records and patient portals. Emphasis is placed on quality improvement processes and evidence-based medicine to drive better health outcomes.

For case managers preparing for the CCM exam, understanding the PCMH model is crucial, as it involves coordinating resources effectively across various healthcare settings. Case managers play an integral role in facilitating communication among providers, ensuring continuity of care, and advocating for patient needs within this framework. Mastery of the PCMH principles allows case managers to contribute significantly to reducing healthcare costs while improving patient satisfaction and health outcomes.

1.23.2 Health Home:

A Health Home is a care delivery model designed to provide comprehensive and coordinated care to individuals with chronic conditions. Established under the Affordable Care Act, Health Homes aim to integrate primary, acute, behavioral health, and long-term services and supports for Medicaid beneficiaries. The primary objective is to enhance the quality of care, improve health outcomes, and reduce healthcare costs through the efficient management of services.

In a Health Home model, a designated provider or team of healthcare professionals coordinates all aspects of an individual's healthcare needs. This includes developing a personalized care plan that addresses the medical, behavioral, and social needs of the patient. The care team typically consists of primary care physicians, nurse practitioners, case managers, social workers, and other relevant specialists who collaborate to ensure seamless service delivery.

Health Homes emphasize patient-centered care by fostering strong relationships between patients and their care teams. They utilize health information technology to facilitate communication among providers and effectively track patient progress. Additionally, they focus on preventive care and chronic disease management to minimize hospital admissions and emergency room visits.

Case managers play a crucial role in Health Homes by coordinating services, facilitating communication among providers, and advocating for the patient's needs. They ensure that patients receive timely interventions and follow-up care while addressing any barriers to accessing services. By promoting holistic and integrated care approaches, Health Homes strive to enhance patient satisfaction and achieve better health outcomes for individuals with complex healthcare needs.

1.23.3   Chronic Care:

Chronic care refers to an integrated, patient-centered approach to managing chronic diseases and conditions over an extended period. It involves a coordinated effort among healthcare providers, patients, and caregivers to address the ongoing needs of individuals with long-term health issues such as diabetes, hypertension, heart disease, and asthma. The primary goal of chronic care is to enhance the quality of life for patients by preventing disease progression, minimizing complications, and promoting self-management.

Effective chronic care requires a comprehensive plan that includes regular monitoring, medication management, lifestyle modifications, and patient education. Case managers play a pivotal role in this process by facilitating communication between patients and healthcare providers, ensuring adherence to treatment plans, and advocating for necessary resources and services. They also assist in navigating the healthcare system to access appropriate levels of care, including primary care, specialty services, and community support.

A successful chronic care model emphasizes proactive rather than reactive care. This involves anticipating potential health issues and implementing preventive measures to avoid hospitalizations and emergency room visits. Chronic care management often employs evidence-based guidelines and utilizes technology such as electronic health records (EHRs) to track patient progress and outcomes.

Ultimately, chronic care aims to empower patients by providing them with the knowledge and tools needed to manage their health effectively. By fostering a collaborative environment, case managers ensure that chronic care is tailored to meet each patient's unique needs, thereby improving overall health outcomes and reducing healthcare costs.

1.24 Population Health:

Population health refers to the health outcomes of a group of individuals, including the distribution of such outcomes within that group. It is an approach aimed at improving the health of an entire human population. In the context of case management, understanding population health is crucial, as it involves assessing and addressing the broad range of factors that impact health outcomes, including social determinants, healthcare access, and individual behaviors.

Case managers play a pivotal role in population health by coordinating care that addresses both medical and non-medical needs. This involves collaborating with healthcare providers, social services, and community resources to develop comprehensive care plans tailored to diverse populations. The goal is to enhance the quality of care while reducing healthcare costs by preventing disease and effectively managing chronic conditions.

By focusing on population health, case managers can identify at-risk groups and implement targeted interventions that promote preventive care and healthy lifestyles. This proactive approach not only improves individual patient outcomes but also contributes to the overall well-being of the community. Population health strategies often include data analysis to track health trends and outcomes, enabling case managers to make informed decisions and advocate for necessary resources.

In preparation for the CCM exam, case managers should be familiar with concepts such as risk stratification, care coordination models, and outcome measurement tools that are integral to effective population health management. Understanding these concepts will enable them to contribute effectively to improving population health outcomes in their professional practice.

1.25 Negotiation Techniques:

Negotiation techniques are strategic approaches used by case managers to reach mutually beneficial agreements between parties involved in patient care. These techniques are vital for resolving conflicts, securing resources, and ensuring optimal patient outcomes. Effective negotiation involves clear communication, understanding the needs and interests of all parties, and finding common ground.

One crucial technique is active listening, which involves paying close attention to what others are saying, asking clarifying questions, and reflecting back what has been heard to ensure understanding. This practice helps build trust and rapport, which are essential for successful negotiations.

Another technique is preparation, which involves gathering all relevant information before entering a negotiation. This includes understanding the patient's needs, the resources available, and the constraints each party faces. Being well-prepared allows the case manager to present informed arguments and anticipate potential objections.

The use of empathy is also critical in negotiations. By recognizing and acknowledging the emotions and perspectives of others, case managers can foster a collaborative atmosphere where all parties feel valued and understood.

Additionally, problem-solving skills are essential. Case managers should aim to identify creative solutions that satisfy the interests of all parties involved. This may involve exploring alternative options or compromises that were not initially considered.

Finally, maintaining professionalism throughout the negotiation process is paramount. This includes being respectful, patient, and focused on achieving positive outcomes for the patient while balancing the needs of all stakeholders involved.

1.26 Assessing Physical Functioning and Behavioral Health:

The Physical Functioning and Behavioral Health Assessment is a critical component of the case management process, focusing on evaluating a client's physical capabilities and mental health status. This assessment is essential for developing a comprehensive care plan tailored to the individual's needs.

The physical functioning assessment involves evaluating the client's ability to perform activities of daily living (ADLs) and instrumental activities of daily living (IADLs). This includes assessing mobility, strength, endurance, and coordination. It also considers the impact of any physical impairments or disabilities on the client's quality of life. Tools such as Functional Independence Measures (FIM) or specific physical performance tests may be used to gather objective data.

The behavioral health assessment, on the other hand, focuses on understanding the client's psychological and emotional state. This includes evaluating mood disorders, anxiety levels, cognitive function, and any history of substance abuse. It involves structured interviews, standardized questionnaires such as the Beck Depression Inventory or the Generalized Anxiety Disorder scale, and observational techniques to gather information.

The integration of both assessments allows case managers to identify barriers to recovery or rehabilitation and to design interventions that address both physical and mental health needs. This holistic approach ensures that all aspects of a client's well-being are considered, promoting optimal outcomes. Understanding these assessments equips case managers with the necessary insights to advocate effectively for their clients' needs within healthcare systems and community resources.

1.27 Private Benefit Programs:

Private Benefit Programs are insurance and financial assistance plans offered by non-governmental entities, such as private companies, non-profit organizations, or employer-sponsored programs. These programs are designed to provide coverage for healthcare services, disability benefits, retirement savings, and other forms of financial support to individuals who qualify based on specific criteria set by the provider.

In the context of case management, understanding Private Benefit Programs is crucial, as they often supplement public health benefits and can significantly impact a client's care plan. These programs may include employer-sponsored health insurance plans, private disability insurance, long-term care insurance, and supplemental health policies, such as dental or vision coverage. Each program has its own eligibility requirements, coverage limits, premium costs, and claims processes.

Case managers must be adept at navigating these programs to optimize their clients' access to necessary services while minimizing out-of-pocket expenses. This involves assessing the client's existing benefits, identifying gaps in coverage, and exploring available private options that align with the client's health needs and financial situation.

Moreover, case managers should be familiar with the legal and regulatory frameworks governing these programs, such as the Employee Retirement Income Security Act (ERISA), which sets standards for most voluntarily established retirement and health plans in the private industry. Proficiency in coordinating between multiple benefit programs ensures comprehensive care delivery and enhances client satisfaction by providing tailored solutions that address both the medical and financial aspects of their well-being.

1.27.1 Pharmacy Benefits Management:

Pharmacy Benefits Management (PBM) refers to the administrative and operational processes involved in managing prescription drug benefits on behalf of health insurers, Medicare Part D drug plans, large employers, and other payers. PBMs play a crucial role in the healthcare ecosystem by negotiating with drug manufacturers to secure favorable pricing and rebates, designing and managing formularies, processing prescription drug claims, and implementing cost-control measures such as generic substitution and mail-order pharmacy services.

A primary function of PBMs is to develop a formulary, which is a list of covered medications typically categorized into tiers based on cost-sharing levels. By determining which drugs are covered and at what level, PBMs can influence prescribing behaviors and promote the use of cost-effective therapies. Additionally, PBMs negotiate discounts and rebates with pharmaceutical companies, which can significantly reduce the overall cost of medications for plan sponsors.

PBMs also provide clinical services such as medication therapy management (MTM), which aims to optimize therapeutic outcomes for patients. MTM services involve reviewing a patient's complete medication regimen to identify potential drug interactions, duplications, or adherence issues.

For case managers preparing for the CCM exam, understanding the role of PBMs is essential because they directly impact patient access to medications and overall healthcare costs. Case managers must be adept at navigating PBM policies to advocate effectively for their clients' medication needs while ensuring cost-effective care delivery.

1.27.2 Indemnity:

Indemnity, in the context of private benefit programs, refers to a type of health insurance plan where the insurer reimburses the insured for medical expenses regardless of where the services are provided. This traditional form of insurance allows policyholders to choose their healthcare providers and facilities without requiring referrals or network restrictions. Indemnity plans typically cover a percentage of the cost for covered services after the insured meets a predetermined deductible.

Under indemnity plans, the insured pays upfront for medical services and submits claims to the insurance company for reimbursement. The reimbursement is usually based on a percentage of usual, customary, and reasonable (UCR) charges for specific services. This means that if a healthcare provider charges more than what is considered standard in a particular geographic area, the insured may be responsible for paying the difference.

Case managers should understand that while indemnity plans offer flexibility and freedom of choice, they often come with higher out-of-pocket costs compared to managed care plans like HMOs or PPOs. Additionally, indemnity plans may require more administrative work due to the need for claim submissions and potential disputes over UCR charges.

In preparing for the CCM exam, case managers should recognize that indemnity insurance plays a critical role in patient advocacy, as it empowers patients with autonomy over their healthcare decisions. However, it also necessitates careful financial planning and an understanding of coverage limitations to effectively manage patient care within budgetary constraints.

1.27.3   Employer-sponsored Health Coverage:

Employer-sponsored health coverage, also known as group health insurance, is a health insurance policy offered by an employer to its employees as part of a benefits package. This type of coverage is a significant component of private benefit programs and plays a crucial role in the healthcare system by providing access to medical care for millions of workers and their families.

In employer-sponsored health plans, the employer typically selects the insurance provider and plan options, negotiating terms that can offer favorable rates due to the collective bargaining power of the group. Employees often share the cost of premiums with their employer, making these plans more affordable compared to individual health insurance policies. The coverage generally includes a range of services such as preventive care, hospitalization, prescription drugs, and sometimes dental and vision care.

From a case management perspective, understanding the nuances of employer-sponsored health coverage is vital. Case managers must be knowledgeable about plan specifics, including covered services, network restrictions, co-payments, deductibles, and out-of-pocket maximums. They play a key role in helping clients navigate these plans to maximize benefits while minimizing costs. Additionally, case managers should be aware of regulatory requirements, such as the Affordable Care Act (ACA) mandates that affect employer-sponsored plans, including essential health benefits and coverage for pre-existing conditions.

Overall, employer-sponsored health coverage is a pivotal element in ensuring that employees have access to necessary healthcare services while managing the financial risks associated with medical expenses.

1.27.4   Individually Purchased Insurance:

Individually purchased insurance refers to health insurance policies that are bought directly by an individual from an insurance provider, rather than being provided through an employer or a government program. This type of insurance is often sought by individuals who are self-employed, unemployed, or whose employers do not offer health insurance benefits.

The primary characteristic of individually purchased insurance is its customization and flexibility. Policyholders have the ability to select plans that best meet their healthcare needs and financial circumstances. Options typically include a variety of coverage levels, such as high-deductible plans, Health Maintenance Organization (HMO) plans, Preferred Provider Organization (PPO) plans, and more comprehensive options. Premiums, deductibles, co-pays, and out-of-pocket maximums vary significantly among these plans.

One of the advantages of individually purchased insurance is the ability to maintain coverage regardless of changes in employment status. However, cost can be a significant factor; premiums for individual plans can be higher compared to group plans due to the lack of shared risk among a larger pool of insured individuals.

Case managers should understand the intricacies of individually purchased insurance to effectively assist clients in navigating plan selections and managing costs. They should be knowledgeable about policy terms, network restrictions, and the implications of Affordable Care Act (ACA) provisions that affect individual market policies. Ensuring clients are aware of subsidies or tax credits available through health insurance marketplaces can also play a crucial role in making individually purchased insurance more affordable for eligible individuals.

1.27.5   Home Care Benefits:

Home care benefits are a crucial component of private benefit programs designed to provide medical and non-medical support to individuals in their own homes. These benefits aim to enhance the quality of life for patients who require assistance due to illness, disability, or aging while also promoting independence and preventing unnecessary hospitalizations or institutional care.

Home care services typically include skilled nursing care, physical therapy, occupational therapy, speech therapy, and assistance with activities of daily living (ADLs) such as bathing, dressing, and meal preparation. Additionally, home care benefits may cover medical equipment and supplies necessary for patient care at home.

For case managers preparing for the CCM exam, it is essential to understand that eligibility for home care benefits often depends on the individual's medical condition, the physician's recommendations, and the specific terms outlined in their insurance policy. Case managers play a pivotal role in coordinating these services by assessing patient needs, developing care plans, and ensuring seamless communication between healthcare providers and insurance companies.

Moreover, case managers must be adept at navigating the complexities of different insurance plans to maximize the patient's coverage while minimizing out-of-pocket expenses. This requires a thorough understanding of policy limitations, prior authorization processes, and potential co-payments associated with home care services.

In summary, home care benefits are integral to patient-centered care strategies that prioritize comfort and autonomy while mitigating healthcare costs through effective management and coordination of in-home services.

1.27.6 COBRA:

The Consolidated Omnibus Budget Reconciliation Act (COBRA) is a federal law that mandates employers with 20 or more employees to offer the continuation of group health benefits to employees and their families upon the occurrence of certain qualifying events that would otherwise result in the loss of coverage. These events include voluntary or involuntary job loss, reduction in hours worked, transition between jobs, death, divorce, and other life events.

Under COBRA, eligible individuals can retain their existing health insurance coverage for a limited period, typically 18 months, although this can extend up to 36 months in specific circumstances. This extension provides a critical safety net for individuals who might otherwise face a gap in healthcare coverage during transitional periods.

The cost of COBRA coverage is generally higher than what employees paid while actively employed because they must pay the full premium, including the portion previously covered by the employer, plus a 2% administrative fee. However, it remains less expensive than purchasing individual health insurance due to the group rate advantage.

Case managers must understand COBRA's provisions to effectively guide clients through transitions that affect their healthcare coverage. This includes educating clients about eligibility criteria, enrollment deadlines, and potential costs associated with COBRA. Additionally, case managers should be knowledgeable about alternative options, such as state continuation programs or marketplace insurance plans, that might offer more affordable solutions. Mastery of COBRA regulations ensures that case managers can provide comprehensive support during critical life changes.

1.28 Public Benefit Programs:

Public benefit programs are government-funded initiatives designed to provide financial assistance and support services to individuals and families in need, ensuring access to essential resources such as healthcare, nutrition, housing, and income support. These programs aim to enhance the well-being of vulnerable populations, reduce poverty, and promote self-sufficiency.

Key public benefit programs include Medicaid, which offers healthcare coverage to low-income individuals and families; Medicare, which provides health insurance to those aged 65 and over or with certain disabilities; and the Supplemental Nutrition Assistance Program (SNAP), which assists low-income families in purchasing food. Additionally, Temporary Assistance for Needy Families (TANF) provides temporary financial aid to families with dependent children, promoting work and self-sufficiency through various support services.

Housing assistance programs, such as Section 8 vouchers, help low-income families afford safe and decent housing. Social Security Disability Insurance (SSDI) and Supplemental Security Income (SSI) offer financial support to individuals with disabilities who are unable to work.

For case managers, understanding these programs is crucial for effectively coordinating care and resources for clients. They must be knowledgeable about eligibility criteria, application processes, and the specific benefits each program provides. Case managers play a pivotal role in advocating for clients' access to these programs, ensuring that they receive the necessary support to improve their quality of life. By navigating these complex systems, case managers help bridge the gap between clients' needs and available resources.

1.28.1 SSI:

Supplemental Security Income (SSI) is a federal program in the United States designed to provide financial assistance to individuals who are aged, blind, or disabled and have limited income and resources. Administered by the Social Security Administration (SSA), SSI aims to meet basic needs for food, clothing, and shelter. Unlike Social Security benefits, SSI is not based on prior work history but rather on financial need.

Eligibility for SSI requires meeting specific criteria: individuals must be 65 or older, blind, or have a disability that severely limits their ability to perform substantial gainful activity. Additionally, applicants must have limited income and resources; generally, resources must not exceed $2,000 for an individual or $3,000 for a couple. Certain assets, such as a primary residence and one vehicle, may be excluded from these calculations.

SSI payments are determined by federal benefit rates (FBR), which are adjusted annually based on cost-of-living increases. Some states supplement the federal payment with additional funds. Recipients may also qualify for Medicaid and other social services.

Case managers play a crucial role in assisting clients with SSI applications by ensuring they understand eligibility requirements and gather the necessary documentation. They also help clients navigate appeals if initial applications are denied. Understanding SSI is essential for case managers, as it enables them to effectively advocate for their clients' financial stability and access to essential services.

1.28.2 SSDI:

Social Security Disability Insurance (SSDI) is a federal program administered by the Social Security Administration (SSA) designed to provide financial assistance to individuals who are unable to work due to a qualifying disability. To be eligible for SSDI, applicants must have accumulated sufficient work credits through prior employment, which involves paying into the Social Security system via payroll taxes. The number of work credits required varies based on the applicant's age at the onset of the disability.

SSDI benefits are intended for individuals with severe, long-term disabilities expected to last at least one year or result in death. The SSA uses a stringent definition of disability, requiring that the condition significantly limits the individual's ability to perform basic work activities. The determination process involves a thorough evaluation of medical records, work history, and other relevant documentation.

Once approved, SSDI beneficiaries receive monthly cash payments intended to help cover living expenses. Additionally, after two years of receiving SSDI benefits, individuals become eligible for Medicare coverage, providing access to essential healthcare services.

Case managers play a critical role in assisting clients with navigating the SSDI application process. This includes gathering necessary documentation, ensuring the timely submission of applications, and advocating on behalf of clients during appeals if initial claims are denied. Understanding the intricacies of SSDI is crucial for case managers, as it enables them to effectively support clients in securing the benefits they need to maintain financial stability and access vital healthcare resources.

1.28.3   Medicare:
Medicare is a federal health insurance program primarily designed for individuals aged 65 and older, although it also covers certain younger individuals with disabilities and those with End-Stage Renal Disease. It consists of four parts: Part A (Hospital Insurance), Part B (Medical Insurance), Part C (Medicare Advantage), and Part D (Prescription Drug Coverage).

Part A covers inpatient hospital stays, care in a skilled nursing facility, hospice care, and some home health care. Most beneficiaries do not pay a premium for Part A if they or their spouse paid Medicare taxes while working. Part B covers outpatient care, preventive services, ambulance services, and durable medical equipment. Beneficiaries typically pay a monthly premium for Part B.

Part C, or Medicare Advantage, is an alternative to Original Medicare provided by private companies approved by Medicare. These plans often include additional benefits such as vision, dental, and wellness programs. They may also incorporate prescription drug coverage.

Part D provides prescription drug coverage through private plans that contract with Medicare. Beneficiaries can choose from various plans offering different levels of coverage and premiums.

Case managers must understand the intricacies of each part to effectively guide clients in choosing appropriate coverage options based on their healthcare needs and financial situations. Additionally, understanding eligibility requirements, enrollment periods, and potential penalties for late enrollment is crucial for accurately advising clients. Familiarity with Medicare's coordination with other types of insurance ensures comprehensive case management and optimal client outcomes.

1.28.4   Medicaid:
Medicaid is a public health insurance program in the United States designed to provide medical assistance to low-income individuals and families. It is jointly funded by the federal and state governments but managed at the state level, allowing for some variability in how it is administered across different states. Medicaid covers a broad range of services, including hospital and nursing home care, physician services, laboratory and X-ray services, and home health care, among others.

Eligibility for Medicaid is primarily determined by income level, family size, disability status, and other factors. The Affordable Care Act (ACA) expanded Medicaid eligibility in many states to include more low-income adults without dependent children. This expansion aimed to reduce the number of uninsured individuals and improve access to healthcare services for vulnerable populations.

For case managers, understanding Medicaid is crucial, as they often assist clients in navigating the complexities of enrollment and ensuring continued eligibility. They must be knowledgeable about each state's specific Medicaid rules and benefits to provide accurate guidance. Additionally, case managers play a vital role in coordinating care for Medicaid recipients, ensuring they receive necessary services while managing costs effectively.

Medicaid also plays a significant role in long-term care funding, covering services that Medicare does not typically include. Case managers must be adept at helping clients access these benefits while planning for future healthcare needs. Overall, proficiency in Medicaid policies and procedures is essential for effective case management practice.

1.29 Employer Health & Wellness Programs:
Employer-based health and wellness programs are structured initiatives implemented by organizations to promote and maintain the health and well-being of their employees. These programs are designed to improve overall employee health, reduce healthcare costs, enhance productivity, and foster a supportive work environment. They often include a variety of services and activities, such as health screenings, fitness classes, smoking cessation programs, stress management workshops, and nutritional counseling.

These programs are tailored to address the specific needs of the workforce and may incorporate incentives to encourage participation. For example, employers might offer discounts on health insurance premiums for employees who engage in wellness activities or meet certain health criteria. The rationale behind these programs is that healthier employees contribute to reduced absenteeism, lower healthcare expenses, and increased job satisfaction.

A critical aspect of these programs is their ability to integrate with broader case management strategies. Case managers play a pivotal role in facilitating access to these resources, ensuring that employees receive the necessary support to manage chronic conditions or prevent potential health issues. By coordinating care and advocating for employees' needs, case managers help optimize the effectiveness of wellness programs.

For case managers preparing for the CCM exam, understanding employer-based health and wellness programs involves recognizing their components, benefits, challenges, and the role of case management in enhancing program outcomes. This knowledge is crucial for developing strategies that align with organizational goals while prioritizing employee health and well-being.

1.30 Reimbursement And Payment Methodologies:

Reimbursement and payment methodologies refer to the systems and processes through which healthcare providers receive payment for their services. These methodologies are crucial for case managers to understand, as they directly impact the financial aspects of patient care and resource allocation. There are several key models used in healthcare reimbursement.

Fee-for-Service (FFS) is a traditional model where providers are paid for each service rendered. While straightforward, it can incentivize higher volumes of care rather than quality.

Capitation involves paying a set amount per patient, regardless of the number of services provided. This encourages cost-effective care but can lead to underutilization if not monitored properly.

Value-Based Purchasing (VBP) ties reimbursement to the quality of care provided, rewarding providers for efficiency and positive patient outcomes. This model aims to improve overall healthcare quality while controlling costs.

Diagnosis-Related Groups (DRGs) are used primarily in inpatient settings, where hospitals receive a fixed payment based on the patient's diagnosis. This encourages efficient resource use but requires accurate coding and documentation.

Bundled Payments involve a single payment for all services related to a treatment or condition over a defined period. This approach fosters collaboration among providers but requires careful coordination.

Understanding these methodologies helps case managers navigate the complexities of healthcare finance, ensuring that patients receive appropriate care while maintaining fiscal responsibility. Mastery of these concepts is essential for effective case management and successful certification as a Certified Case Manager (CCM).

1.30.1   Bundled Payment:

A bundled payment, also known as episode-based payment, is a reimbursement model in healthcare where a single, comprehensive payment is made to cover all services related to a specific treatment or condition over a defined period. This model contrasts with the traditional fee-for-service approach, where providers are paid separately for each individual service. The bundled payment system aims to encourage coordinated care among providers and reduce unnecessary medical expenses by creating financial incentives for efficiency and quality.

Under this model, healthcare providers, including hospitals, physicians, and other relevant professionals, receive a predetermined payment that covers all the care required for a patient's particular episode of care. This can include pre-operative consultations, the surgical procedure itself, post-operative follow-ups, rehabilitation, and any potential complications or readmissions within the specified time frame.

The bundled payment approach emphasizes value over volume, promoting collaboration among multidisciplinary teams to enhance patient outcomes while controlling costs. Providers share in the financial risk and benefit; if the cost of care exceeds the bundled payment amount, they bear the loss. Conversely, if they manage to provide care below the budgeted amount while maintaining quality standards, they can retain the savings.

For case managers preparing for the CCM exam, understanding bundled payments is crucial, as it impacts care coordination strategies. Effective management under this model requires careful planning, communication across care teams, and diligent monitoring of patient progress to ensure both cost-effectiveness and high-quality patient outcomes.

1.30.2   Case Rate:

A case rate, also known as bundled payment or episode-based payment, is a reimbursement methodology in which a single payment is made to cover all services related to a specific treatment or condition over a defined period. This approach contrasts with traditional fee-for-service models, where providers are reimbursed for each individual service rendered. The case rate aims to promote cost efficiency and improve care coordination by encouraging providers to work collaboratively within the established financial parameters.

In this model, healthcare providers—including hospitals, physicians, and other ancillary services—agree upon a predetermined amount for treating a particular condition. This amount is intended to cover all necessary services, from the initial consultation through follow-up care. By doing so, it incentivizes providers to eliminate unnecessary procedures and tests while maintaining quality care standards.

For case managers, understanding the intricacies of case rate reimbursement is crucial, as it directly impacts care planning and resource allocation. They must ensure that patient care remains within the financial constraints of the case rate while also advocating for necessary services that contribute to optimal patient outcomes. Furthermore, case managers play a vital role in coordinating between various healthcare providers to ensure that all aspects of patient care are addressed efficiently within the bundled payment framework.

Overall, the case rate model encourages a more holistic approach to patient care by fostering collaboration among healthcare providers and focusing on outcomes rather than individual service costs.

1.30.3   Prospective Payment Systems:

Prospective Payment Systems (PPS) are reimbursement methodologies used primarily in the healthcare sector to determine payment amounts in advance for specific services. Under PPS, healthcare providers, such as hospitals and clinics, receive a predetermined fixed amount for each episode of care or service provided to patients. This amount is established based on the classification of the patient's diagnosis or the type of care required, rather than the actual cost incurred during treatment.

The primary goal of PPS is to control healthcare costs while ensuring that providers deliver efficient and effective care. By establishing a fixed payment rate, PPS incentivizes providers to manage resources wisely and avoid unnecessary services that could inflate costs. This system contrasts with retrospective payment methods, where providers are reimbursed based on actual expenses after services are rendered.

In PPS, various factors influence the payment rates, including the complexity of the patient's condition, regional cost variations, and historical data on similar cases. For example, Medicare uses Diagnosis-Related Groups (DRGs) within its Inpatient Prospective Payment System (IPPS) to categorize hospital admissions and determine payments.

Case managers play a crucial role in navigating PPS by coordinating care plans that align with reimbursement structures while ensuring quality patient outcomes. They must understand how PPS impacts financial planning and resource allocation within healthcare settings to optimize both patient care and organizational efficiency. Mastery of PPS concepts is vital for case managers to effectively advocate for patients and collaborate with healthcare teams.

1.30.4   Value-based Care:
Value-based care is a healthcare delivery model that incentivizes providers to deliver high-quality care and improve patient outcomes, rather than focusing solely on the volume of services provided. This approach shifts the emphasis from fee-for-service models, where providers are paid based on the quantity of care delivered, to a system where payment is tied to the quality and efficiency of care.

In value-based care, healthcare providers, including physicians, hospitals, and other entities, are rewarded for helping patients achieve better health outcomes in a cost-effective manner. This model encourages preventive care, chronic disease management, and coordination among different healthcare services to reduce unnecessary interventions and hospitalizations.

For case managers, understanding value-based care is crucial, as it involves coordinating comprehensive care plans that align with these principles. Case managers play a key role in ensuring that patients receive appropriate follow-up care, adhere to treatment plans, and access necessary resources to manage their health conditions effectively. They must be adept at navigating different reimbursement structures and working collaboratively with healthcare teams to optimize patient outcomes.

Value-based care models include Accountable Care Organizations (ACOs), Patient-Centered Medical Homes (PCMHs), and bundled payment arrangements. These models aim to reduce healthcare costs while improving the quality of care by fostering accountability and collaboration among providers. By focusing on patient-centered approaches and evidence-based practices, value-based care seeks to enhance the overall healthcare experience for patients while promoting sustainability within the healthcare system.

1.30.5   Financial Risk Models:
Financial risk models are structured frameworks used to assess and manage the uncertainty associated with financial losses in healthcare settings. These models are integral to reimbursement and payment methodologies, as they help predict potential financial outcomes and determine the allocation of resources. In the context of case management, understanding these models is crucial for optimizing patient care while maintaining fiscal responsibility.

There are several types of financial risk models, including capitation, bundled payments, and shared savings. Capitation involves a fixed amount paid per patient to cover all necessary services within a specified period, incentivizing providers to deliver cost-effective care. Bundled payments, on the other hand, involve a single comprehensive payment for all services related to a treatment episode or condition, encouraging coordination among providers to avoid unnecessary costs. Shared savings models reward healthcare providers for reducing healthcare costs while meeting quality benchmarks, allowing them to share in the savings achieved with payers.

Case managers must be adept at navigating these financial risk models to ensure that patients receive appropriate care without incurring excessive costs. They play a pivotal role in coordinating care plans that align with the objectives of these models, promoting efficient resource use and improving patient outcomes. By understanding financial risk models, case managers can effectively advocate for patients and contribute to sustainable healthcare delivery systems. This knowledge is essential for the CCM exam, as it reflects the case manager's ability to balance clinical needs with economic considerations in diverse healthcare environments.

1.31 Case Managers: Roles and Functions Across Settings
Case managers play a crucial role in coordinating and facilitating comprehensive care across diverse practice settings. Their primary function is to ensure that patients receive appropriate, timely, and cost-effective care tailored to their individual needs. In acute care settings, case managers assess patient needs, develop discharge plans, and coordinate post-hospitalization services to prevent readmissions. They work closely with interdisciplinary teams to align treatment plans with patient goals.

In long-term care facilities, case managers focus on maintaining the quality of life for residents by managing chronic conditions and coordinating ongoing care services. They advocate for residents' needs while ensuring compliance with regulatory standards. In rehabilitation settings, case managers facilitate recovery by organizing therapies and support services that promote independence and functional improvement.

Within community-based settings, such as home health or hospice care, case managers assess home environments, coordinate in-home services, and provide education to patients and families about disease management and end-of-life care options. They act as liaisons between patients, families, healthcare providers, and community resources.

In managed care organizations, case managers evaluate the medical necessity of treatments, optimize resource utilization, and implement cost-containment strategies while ensuring quality care delivery. They analyze data to identify trends and improve care processes.

Overall, case managers serve as advocates for patients across all settings, ensuring continuity of care through effective communication, coordination of services, and collaboration with healthcare teams. Their roles are dynamic and adaptable to meet the evolving needs of healthcare systems and patient populations.

1.32 Healthcare Provider Roles in Diverse Settings:

In the diverse landscape of healthcare, various providers play critical roles within different care and practice settings, each contributing uniquely to patient outcomes. Understanding these roles is essential for case managers to effectively coordinate care. Physicians, as primary decision-makers, diagnose conditions and prescribe treatments across settings such as hospitals, clinics, and private practices. Nurses provide direct patient care, administer medications, and educate patients and families in settings including hospitals, home health, and long-term care facilities.

Pharmacists ensure the safe use of medications by reviewing prescriptions and counseling patients, primarily in community pharmacies and hospital settings. Physical therapists focus on improving patient mobility and physical function through rehabilitation programs in outpatient clinics and inpatient rehabilitation centers. Occupational therapists assist patients in regaining daily living skills in various environments, including hospitals and community-based settings.

Social workers address psychosocial needs by providing counseling and connecting patients with community resources across all healthcare settings. Dietitians develop nutrition plans tailored to individual health needs in hospitals, outpatient clinics, and public health departments. Respiratory therapists manage patients with breathing disorders, predominantly in acute care hospitals and home care environments.

Each provider's role is interconnected within the healthcare system, requiring effective communication and collaboration to ensure comprehensive, patient-centered care. Case managers must be adept at navigating these interactions, advocating for patients' needs while coordinating services across multidisciplinary teams to optimize health outcomes.

1.33 Transitions Of Care/Transitional Care:

Transitions of care, also known as transitional care, refer to the coordination and continuity of healthcare during a movement from one healthcare setting to another or to home. This process is critical in ensuring that patients receive seamless, efficient, and effective care as they move between different levels or types of care. Transitional care involves a comprehensive approach that addresses the medical, psychological, and social needs of patients during these transitions.

Effective transitional care requires collaboration among healthcare providers, patients, and their families to develop a personalized care plan that ensures continuity. This includes accurate and timely communication of the patient's health information, medication reconciliation, and patient education to empower them in managing their health. The aim of transitional care is to prevent adverse events, reduce hospital readmissions, and improve health outcomes by providing support during vulnerable periods.

Case managers play a pivotal role in transitional care by assessing the patient's needs, coordinating with multidisciplinary teams, advocating for the patient's preferences, and facilitating access to community resources. They ensure that follow-up appointments are scheduled and that patients understand their discharge instructions. Additionally, case managers monitor the patient's progress and intervene when necessary to address any barriers to effective care transitions.

In summary, transitions of care are essential for maintaining the quality and safety of healthcare delivery. By focusing on comprehensive planning and communication, transitional care helps bridge gaps in care continuity and supports patients in achieving optimal health outcomes during transitions between healthcare settings.

1.34 Utilization Management Guidelines:

Utilization Management (UM) is a critical component of healthcare that ensures the appropriate use of medical services, enhances patient outcomes, and controls costs. It involves evaluating the necessity, appropriateness, and efficiency of healthcare services, procedures, and facilities under the provisions of an applicable health benefits plan. The principles of UM are centered around evidence-based guidelines, which provide a framework for decision-making processes that prioritize the quality of patient care while considering cost-effectiveness.

The primary guidelines of UM include prior authorization, concurrent review, and retrospective review. Prior authorization requires obtaining approval before delivering specific services to ensure they meet established criteria. Concurrent review involves ongoing assessment during a patient's hospital stay or treatment to ensure the continued necessity and appropriateness of care. Retrospective review evaluates the appropriateness of care after services have been provided, primarily for educational purposes or to identify patterns for future improvement.

Case managers play a pivotal role in UM by coordinating with healthcare providers, insurance companies, and patients to facilitate efficient care delivery. They utilize clinical guidelines and protocols to assess treatment plans and advocate for necessary services while minimizing unnecessary interventions. Effective UM requires collaboration among all stakeholders to align healthcare delivery with best practices and regulatory standards.

In summary, the principles and guidelines of Utilization Management aim to optimize healthcare delivery by ensuring that patients receive necessary care without incurring unnecessary costs or delays, thereby improving overall healthcare system efficiency and patient satisfaction.

1.35 Collaborative/comprehensive/integrated/holistic Case Management Services:

Collaborative, comprehensive, integrated, and holistic case management services refer to a multifaceted approach that emphasizes coordination, inclusivity, and client-centered care in case management. This approach involves the integration of various healthcare services and professionals to ensure that all aspects of a client's needs are addressed in a seamless and efficient manner. Collaboration is key, involving active communication and partnership among healthcare providers, clients, families, and community resources to develop a cohesive care plan.

Comprehensive case management encompasses the full spectrum of client needs, from medical to psychosocial, ensuring that no aspect of care is overlooked. It requires a thorough assessment of the client's situation, including physical health, mental health, social support systems, and environmental factors. Integrated services mean that these diverse elements are not treated in isolation but are woven together into a unified plan that addresses the client's overall well-being.

Holistic case management recognizes the importance of treating the whole person rather than just focusing on specific symptoms or conditions. It considers emotional, spiritual, and cultural dimensions as integral parts of the healing process. This approach ensures that care is personalized and respects the client's values and preferences.

Ultimately, this method aims to enhance client outcomes by promoting continuity of care, reducing fragmentation of services, and empowering clients through active participation in their care plans. Case managers play a crucial role in facilitating these processes by coordinating resources, advocating for clients' needs, and ensuring effective communication across all parties involved.

1.36 Caseload Considerations:

Caseload considerations refer to the strategic assessment and management of the number and complexity of cases that a case manager handles at any given time. Effective caseload management is crucial for ensuring quality care, promoting positive outcomes, and maintaining professional well-being. Caseload considerations involve evaluating various factors, including the acuity level of clients, the intensity of services required, and the available resources.

A comprehensive understanding of caseload considerations includes recognizing that each client presents unique needs that may require varying levels of attention and time commitment. High-acuity cases might demand more frequent interventions and coordination with multiple healthcare providers, whereas lower-acuity cases may require less intensive management. Balancing these demands is critical to preventing burnout and ensuring sustainable practice.

Case managers must also consider organizational policies, legal regulations, and ethical standards when determining appropriate caseload sizes. This involves adhering to guidelines set by professional bodies and institutions to ensure compliance and uphold care standards. Additionally, effective time management skills are essential for prioritizing tasks efficiently and allocating resources appropriately.

Regularly reviewing caseloads allows case managers to identify trends, adjust strategies as needed, and advocate for necessary support or resources. By maintaining manageable caseloads, case managers can provide personalized attention to each client, enhance care coordination, and ultimately improve health outcomes. Understanding caseload considerations is vital for case managers preparing for the Certified Case Manager (CCM) exam, as it directly impacts their ability to deliver competent and ethical care.

1.37 Alternative Care Sites:

Alternative Care Sites (ACS) are non-traditional healthcare settings established to provide medical care outside of standard hospital environments, particularly during emergencies or when existing healthcare facilities are overwhelmed. These sites are strategically set up to manage patient overflow, ensuring continuity of care and alleviating pressure on primary healthcare institutions. ACS can be located in a variety of settings, such as schools, community centers, sports arenas, or temporary structures like tents, and are equipped to handle various levels of medical care depending on the resources available.

The primary objective of ACS is to expand capacity for patient care during critical times, such as pandemics, natural disasters, or mass casualty events. They are designed to offer a range of services, from basic triage and stabilization to more comprehensive medical interventions. Case managers play a crucial role in the efficient operation of ACS by coordinating patient care, ensuring appropriate resource allocation, and facilitating communication between healthcare providers and patients.

In establishing an ACS, considerations include site selection based on accessibility and infrastructure, staffing with appropriately trained personnel, and equipping the site with necessary medical supplies and equipment. Additionally, legal and regulatory compliance must be addressed to ensure safety and quality of care.

Case managers must be adept at navigating these alternative settings, understanding the unique challenges they present, and implementing effective care strategies that align with the overarching goals of public health and emergency response initiatives.

1.37.1   Non-traditional Sites Of Care:

Non-traditional sites of care refer to healthcare settings outside the conventional hospital or clinic environments, designed to meet patient needs in more accessible, cost-effective, and often less formal settings. These sites include home healthcare, telehealth services, retail clinics, urgent care centers, and community health programs. As healthcare evolves toward patient-centered models, these sites play a crucial role in delivering timely and efficient care.

Home healthcare allows patients to receive medical services in their own homes, promoting comfort and convenience while reducing hospital readmissions. It is particularly beneficial for chronic disease management and post-operative recovery. Telehealth leverages technology to provide remote consultations, increasing access to care for patients in rural or underserved areas. This mode is not only convenient but also reduces the burden on traditional healthcare facilities.

Retail clinics, often located within pharmacies or supermarkets, offer quick access to basic medical services without the need for appointments. They are ideal for minor illnesses or preventive care, such as vaccinations. Urgent care centers serve as an intermediary between primary care and emergency rooms, providing immediate attention for non-life-threatening conditions outside regular office hours.

Community health programs focus on preventive measures and education within local populations, addressing social determinants of health. These programs often collaborate with local organizations to improve overall community well-being.

For case managers, understanding non-traditional sites of care is essential for coordinating comprehensive care plans that optimize resource use and enhance patient outcomes while maintaining cost-effectiveness and accessibility.

1.37.2   Telehealth:

Telehealth refers to the use of digital information and communication technologies, such as computers and mobile devices, to access healthcare services remotely and manage healthcare. This approach enables patients to consult with healthcare providers without the need for in-person visits, making it a vital component of the continuum of care, especially for individuals in remote or underserved areas.

Telehealth encompasses a wide range of services, including virtual consultations, remote monitoring, patient education, and electronic health records management. For case managers, telehealth is a crucial tool that facilitates efficient coordination of care by enabling real-time communication between patients and multidisciplinary teams. It allows for timely interventions, reducing the need for emergency room visits and hospital readmissions.

The implementation of telehealth services requires adherence to regulatory standards such as HIPAA (Health Insurance Portability and Accountability Act) to ensure patient confidentiality and data security. Case managers must be adept at navigating these technologies and understanding their limitations and potential challenges, such as digital literacy barriers among patients and connectivity issues.

Moreover, telehealth can enhance patient engagement by providing more accessible follow-ups and continuous support. It empowers patients to take an active role in their health management through tools like mobile health apps that track vital signs or medication adherence.

In summary, telehealth is a transformative element in modern healthcare delivery that enhances accessibility, efficiency, and patient-centered care. For case managers preparing for the CCM exam, mastering telehealth concepts is essential for optimizing patient outcomes in diverse care settings.

1.37.3   Virtual Care:

Virtual care refers to the provision of healthcare services through digital platforms, enabling patients to consult with healthcare providers remotely. This approach leverages technology such as video conferencing, mobile apps, and telephonic communication to facilitate interactions between patients and healthcare professionals without the need for in-person visits. Virtual care encompasses a broad range of services, including telemedicine consultations, remote monitoring of chronic conditions, digital prescriptions, and mental health support.

For case managers, virtual care is an essential component of delivering comprehensive and continuous patient management. It allows for real-time monitoring and timely interventions, which are crucial for effectively managing complex cases. By integrating virtual care into their practice, case managers can enhance patient engagement, improve access to care, and reduce healthcare costs by minimizing unnecessary hospital visits.

Furthermore, virtual care supports the coordination of multidisciplinary teams by enabling seamless communication among healthcare providers. This ensures that all stakeholders are informed about the patient's condition and treatment plan, promoting a holistic approach to care management.

In addition to improving patient outcomes, virtual care offers significant benefits in terms of convenience and flexibility for both patients and providers. Patients can receive care from the comfort of their homes, reducing travel time and associated stress. Providers can manage their schedules more efficiently while expanding their reach to underserved populations.

Overall, virtual care is a transformative element in modern healthcare delivery, facilitating efficient case management and enhancing the quality of patient care.

2   Psychosocial Concepts & Support Systems:

Psychosocial concepts are integral to understanding the complex interplay between psychological and social factors that influence an individual's well-being and health outcomes. These concepts encompass a range of factors, including emotional, mental, social, and spiritual aspects of a person's life. They recognize the importance of relationships, community engagement, cultural influences, and personal beliefs in shaping health behaviors and outcomes.

Support systems refer to the network of individuals, groups, or organizations that provide emotional, informational, or practical assistance to individuals. These systems play a crucial role in enhancing resilience, coping strategies, and overall well-being. They include family members, friends, healthcare professionals, community services, and peer support groups. Effective support systems can mitigate the impact of stressors, promote recovery from illness or trauma, and improve adherence to treatment plans.

For case managers, understanding psychosocial concepts and support systems is essential for developing comprehensive care plans that address not only the physical but also the emotional and social needs of clients. This involves assessing the client's psychosocial status, identifying existing support systems, and facilitating access to additional resources as needed. By integrating these elements into care planning, case managers can promote holistic health outcomes and empower clients to achieve their health goals.

In summary, psychosocial concepts and support systems are foundational in case management practice. They provide a framework for understanding client needs beyond medical diagnoses and enable case managers to deliver person-centered care that supports overall well-being.

2.1 Abuse And Neglect:

Abuse and neglect are critical psychosocial issues that case managers must understand to effectively support their clients. Abuse refers to any intentional act that causes harm or potential harm to an individual. This can be physical, emotional, sexual, or financial in nature. Physical abuse involves inflicting bodily harm, while emotional abuse includes actions that damage an individual's self-esteem or emotional well-being. Sexual abuse is any non-consensual sexual contact, and financial abuse involves exploiting someone's financial resources for personal gain.

Neglect, on the other hand, is the failure to provide necessary care, assistance, or attention to someone who is unable to care for themselves. This can be physical, such as failing to provide food or medical care, or emotional, such as ignoring a person's need for social interaction or mental health support.

Case managers play a vital role in identifying signs of abuse and neglect, which may include unexplained injuries, changes in behavior, withdrawal from social activities, or sudden financial difficulties. They must assess the situation comprehensively and work collaboratively with other professionals to ensure the safety and well-being of their clients. This may involve creating a safety plan, connecting clients with appropriate resources, and reporting concerns to relevant authorities.

Understanding the complexities of abuse and neglect enables case managers to advocate effectively for their clients and contribute positively to their recovery and protection. It is essential for case managers to remain informed about legal obligations and ethical considerations related to reporting and addressing these issues.

2.1.1 Emotional:

Emotional abuse is a pattern of behavior that impairs a person's emotional development or sense of self-worth. This form of abuse can occur in various settings, including familial, romantic, and professional relationships. It involves the use of verbal and non-verbal communication to exert control, demean, isolate, or manipulate an individual, leading to psychological trauma and mental health issues.

Case managers must recognize the signs of emotional abuse, which can include constant criticism, threats, rejection, and withholding love or support. Victims may exhibit symptoms such as anxiety, depression, low self-esteem, and difficulties in forming trusting relationships. Emotional abuse can be subtle and challenging to identify because it often leaves no physical scars but rather inflicts deep psychological wounds.

Understanding the dynamics of emotional abuse is crucial for case managers as they work to develop effective intervention strategies. This involves creating a safe environment for clients to express their feelings and experiences without judgment. Case managers should be equipped with the skills to assess the extent of the abuse and provide appropriate referrals to mental health professionals or support groups.

Additionally, case managers should advocate for policies that protect individuals from emotional abuse and educate clients about healthy relationship dynamics. By fostering awareness and providing resources, case managers play a vital role in helping clients overcome the effects of emotional abuse and regain their autonomy and well-being. Effective case management requires empathy, active listening, and a commitment to empowering clients through informed decision-making processes.

2.1.2 Psychological:

The term 'psychological' pertains to the mental and emotional processes that influence an individual's behavior and well-being. In the context of abuse and neglect, psychological factors are crucial, as they encompass the cognitive and emotional impacts of such experiences on victims. Psychological abuse involves actions that harm an individual's mental health, such as manipulation, intimidation, or verbal aggression. It can lead to anxiety, depression, low self-esteem, and post-traumatic stress disorder (PTSD).

For case managers, understanding psychological aspects is vital in identifying signs of psychological abuse and neglect. Victims may exhibit symptoms such as withdrawal from social interactions, sudden changes in behavior or mood, or a reluctance to engage in previously enjoyed activities. It is essential for case managers to assess these signs accurately to provide appropriate interventions.

Intervention strategies may include counseling, psychotherapy, or support groups aimed at helping individuals process their experiences and develop coping mechanisms. Case managers should also be aware of the potential for re-victimization and work to create safe environments for recovery.

Moreover, psychological resilience—the ability to mentally or emotionally cope with a crisis—should be fostered in clients through empowerment and support. This involves promoting self-efficacy and encouraging positive relationships and self-care practices. By addressing psychological factors comprehensively, case managers can significantly contribute to the healing process of individuals affected by abuse and neglect, ultimately improving their quality of life and facilitating their reintegration into society as empowered individuals.

2.1.3 Physical Abuse:

Physical abuse refers to the intentional use of force against a person that results in bodily injury, physical pain, or impairment. It is a critical area of concern for case managers, who must recognize signs and intervene appropriately to ensure client safety. Physical abuse can manifest in various forms, including hitting, slapping, punching, kicking, burning, or using objects to inflict harm. It may also include actions such as restraining someone against their will or depriving them of necessary care.

For case managers, understanding the indicators of physical abuse is essential for effective intervention. These indicators may include unexplained bruises, fractures, burns, or other injuries that do not align with the given explanation. Additionally, victims may exhibit behavioral signs such as fearfulness around certain individuals, withdrawal from social interactions, or sudden changes in behavior.

Case managers play a pivotal role in assessing the risk and ensuring the safety of clients suspected of being physically abused. This involves conducting thorough assessments, documenting findings meticulously, and collaborating with multidisciplinary teams to develop and implement safety plans. Furthermore, they must be knowledgeable about mandatory reporting laws and procedures to report suspected abuse to the appropriate authorities.

In summary, physical abuse is a deliberate act that causes harm to an individual's body. Case managers must be adept at identifying signs of physical abuse and taking necessary steps to protect their clients while adhering to legal and ethical guidelines. Their role is crucial in advocating for the victims' rights and facilitating access to necessary support services.

2.1.4 Financial:

In the context of abuse and neglect, the term financial refers to the exploitation or improper use of an individual's financial resources, often involving manipulation or deceit to gain control over assets, funds, or property. Financial abuse is a critical concern for case managers, as it can significantly impact a client's well-being and quality of life. This type of abuse is most commonly seen in vulnerable populations, such as the elderly, disabled individuals, or those with cognitive impairments.

Financial abuse may manifest in various forms, including unauthorized access to bank accounts, forging signatures on financial documents, coercing individuals into signing legal papers, or misusing credit cards. It can also involve more subtle tactics, such as manipulating a person into making financial decisions that are not in their best interest or isolating them from trusted advisors who could provide guidance.

Case managers must be vigilant in identifying signs of financial abuse, which may include unexplained withdrawals from bank accounts, sudden changes in financial conditions, missing belongings or funds, and discrepancies in financial documents. They should also be aware of emotional cues from clients who may express fear or anxiety about their finances.

Addressing financial abuse requires a multidisciplinary approach involving legal intervention, social services support, and sometimes law enforcement. Case managers play a crucial role in advocating for their clients by coordinating these resources and ensuring that protective measures are put in place to safeguard their clients' financial assets and overall well-being.

2.2 Behavioral Change Theories & Stages:

Behavioral change theories and stages are essential frameworks that guide case managers in understanding and facilitating patient behavior modification. These theories provide a structured approach to assess readiness for change, tailor interventions, and support clients through the transformation process. One of the most prominent models is the Transtheoretical Model (TTM), which outlines five stages of change: precontemplation, contemplation, preparation, action, and maintenance.

In the precontemplation stage, individuals do not recognize the need for change and may resist discussing it. Case managers should focus on raising awareness and providing information to instigate reflection. During the contemplation stage, individuals acknowledge the problem but remain ambivalent about change. Here, motivational interviewing can be effective in resolving ambivalence and enhancing motivation.

The preparation stage involves a commitment to change and planning actionable steps. Case managers can assist by setting realistic goals and identifying resources. In the action stage, individuals actively modify their behavior. Supportive strategies include reinforcing positive behaviors and managing potential barriers.

Finally, maintenance is the stage where individuals sustain new behaviors over time. Case managers should focus on relapse prevention strategies and continuous encouragement to solidify changes. Understanding these stages allows case managers to apply appropriate interventions tailored to each client's specific needs and readiness level.

By utilizing behavioral change theories and stages, case managers can effectively guide clients through the complex journey of behavior modification, ultimately improving health outcomes and quality of life.

2.3 Understanding Behavioral Health: Concepts & Symptoms

Behavioral health encompasses the connection between behaviors and the well-being of the body, mind, and spirit. It involves the treatment and understanding of mental health disorders, substance use disorders, and other behaviors that impact health. Key concepts include the biopsychosocial model, which considers biological, psychological, and social factors affecting health. This holistic approach is essential for case managers to develop effective care plans.

Symptoms in behavioral health can vary widely but often include changes in mood, thought patterns, or behavior. Common symptoms may involve persistent sadness or anxiety, drastic mood swings, withdrawal from social activities, changes in eating or sleeping habits, and substance misuse. Recognizing these symptoms early is crucial for timely intervention and management.

Case managers must be adept at identifying these signs and understanding their impact on a client's overall health. They should also be familiar with diagnostic criteria from resources such as the DSM-5 (Diagnostic and Statistical Manual of Mental Disorders) to facilitate accurate assessments.

Understanding cultural competence is another vital aspect, as cultural beliefs can influence how individuals perceive symptoms and seek help. Effective communication skills are necessary for building trust with clients and coordinating with multidisciplinary teams to ensure comprehensive care.

In summary, behavioral health concepts and symptoms require a nuanced understanding of how various factors influence mental well-being. Case managers play a critical role in identifying symptoms, coordinating care, and advocating for clients within the healthcare system to improve outcomes.

2.3.1 Diagnosis:

Diagnosis is the process of identifying a disease, condition, or disorder based on a patient's symptoms and medical history. In the context of behavioral health, diagnosis involves a comprehensive assessment that includes clinical interviews, psychological testing, and observation to determine the presence of mental health disorders. For case managers, understanding the diagnostic process is crucial, as it forms the foundation for developing an effective care plan.

A correct diagnosis in behavioral health requires a thorough understanding of the Diagnostic and Statistical Manual of Mental Disorders (DSM-5), which provides standardized criteria for mental health conditions. The case manager must be familiar with these criteria to facilitate communication with healthcare providers and ensure that clients receive appropriate interventions.

The diagnostic process typically begins with gathering detailed information about the client's symptoms, duration, and impact on daily functioning. This includes evaluating both psychological and physical symptoms, as some medical conditions can mimic or exacerbate mental health issues. Collaboration with multidisciplinary teams is often necessary to rule out differential diagnoses and confirm the primary condition.

Accurate diagnosis is essential for determining the most effective treatment strategies, setting realistic goals, and monitoring progress. It also plays a critical role in securing insurance coverage for necessary services. Case managers must advocate for their clients by ensuring that diagnoses are accurate, up-to-date, and reflective of the client's current condition. This advocacy helps optimize resource allocation and enhances the overall quality of care provided to individuals with behavioral health needs.

2.3.2 Dual Diagnoses:

Dual diagnoses, also known as co-occurring disorders, refer to the simultaneous presence of both a mental health disorder and a substance use disorder in an individual. This complex condition requires integrated treatment approaches that address both disorders concurrently, as they often interact and exacerbate each other. For case managers, understanding dual diagnoses is crucial because clients with these conditions face unique challenges in achieving recovery.

The prevalence of dual diagnoses is significant; many individuals with mental health disorders such as depression, anxiety, or bipolar disorder also struggle with substance abuse issues like alcohol or drug dependency. The interplay between these disorders can complicate diagnosis and treatment, as symptoms of one can mask or mimic those of the other. Effective management involves comprehensive assessment to accurately identify all underlying conditions.

Treatment for dual diagnoses must be holistic and multidisciplinary, incorporating behavioral therapies, medication management, and support services tailored to the individual's needs. Collaboration among healthcare providers, mental health professionals, and substance abuse specialists is essential to create a cohesive treatment plan. Case managers play a pivotal role in coordinating care, advocating for clients, and ensuring access to necessary resources.

Understanding the complexities of dual diagnoses enables case managers to better support clients in navigating their recovery journey. By promoting integrated care strategies and fostering communication between various service providers, case managers can enhance treatment outcomes and improve the quality of life for individuals with co-occurring disorders.

2.3.3 Co-occurring Disorders:

Co-occurring disorders, also known as dual diagnosis, refer to the simultaneous presence of both a mental health disorder and a substance use disorder in an individual. This complex interplay can complicate diagnosis and treatment, as each disorder can exacerbate the symptoms of the other. For case managers, understanding co-occurring disorders is crucial because these conditions often require integrated treatment approaches that address both the mental health and substance use aspects concurrently.

Individuals with co-occurring disorders may present with a variety of symptoms, which can include mood swings, anxiety, depression, and impaired social functioning, alongside substance dependency or abuse. The presence of these disorders can lead to challenges in treatment adherence and recovery outcomes if not properly managed. Effective case management involves coordinating care across multiple healthcare providers and services to ensure a holistic approach.

Case managers must be adept at identifying signs of co-occurring disorders through comprehensive assessments that consider both psychiatric and substance use histories. By collaborating with multidisciplinary teams, they play a pivotal role in developing personalized care plans that incorporate evidence-based interventions such as cognitive-behavioral therapy (CBT), medication-assisted treatment (MAT), and motivational interviewing.

Furthermore, case managers should advocate for continuity of care, facilitating communication between mental health professionals and addiction specialists to optimize treatment efficacy. Understanding the complexities of co-occurring disorders empowers case managers to provide informed support, ultimately enhancing client outcomes and promoting sustained recovery.

2.3.4 Substance Use:

Substance use refers to the consumption of psychoactive substances, including alcohol, tobacco, and illicit drugs, which can alter mood, cognition, and behavior. It is a complex phenomenon that varies in severity from occasional use to substance use disorders (SUDs), which are characterized by compulsive drug-seeking and use despite harmful consequences. Substance use can significantly impact an individual's physical and mental health, social relationships, and occupational functioning.

Case managers must understand the biopsychosocial model of substance use, which considers genetic predispositions, psychological states, and environmental influences. Substance use disorders are chronic but treatable conditions that often require a comprehensive approach involving medical detoxification, behavioral therapies, medication-assisted treatment (MAT), and ongoing support systems such as counseling or peer support groups.

The assessment of substance use involves identifying the type of substance used, frequency, quantity, and context of usage. Screening tools such as the CAGE questionnaire or the Alcohol Use Disorders Identification Test (AUDIT) are commonly employed. Case managers should be adept at recognizing withdrawal symptoms and potential co-occurring mental health disorders, such as depression or anxiety, which often accompany substance use.

Effective intervention strategies include motivational interviewing to enhance readiness for change and cognitive-behavioral therapy to address maladaptive thought patterns. Case managers play a crucial role in coordinating care across multidisciplinary teams to ensure holistic treatment planning and facilitate access to community resources for sustained recovery.

2.4 Client Activation and Readiness:

Client activation and readiness to change are crucial components in the case management process, essential for facilitating successful client outcomes. Client activation refers to the level of a client's knowledge, skills, confidence, and willingness to manage their own health and healthcare. It is an indicator of how engaged a client is in their care process, which directly influences their ability to adhere to treatment plans and make informed health decisions.

Readiness to change, on the other hand, is a concept derived from the Transtheoretical Model of Change, which identifies the stages through which individuals progress when modifying behavior. These stages include precontemplation, contemplation, preparation, action, and maintenance. Understanding a client's readiness to change allows case managers to tailor interventions that align with the client's current stage, thus enhancing the likelihood of successful behavior modification.

For case managers, assessing both client activation and readiness to change involves evaluating psychological and behavioral factors that influence the client's motivation and ability to engage in health-related behaviors. Tools such as the Patient Activation Measure (PAM) can be employed to quantify activation levels.

By integrating these assessments into their practice, case managers can develop personalized care plans that empower clients to take an active role in their health management. This approach not only fosters independence but also improves overall health outcomes by ensuring that interventions are both relevant and achievable based on the client's current state of readiness and activation.

2.5 Client Empowerment:

Client empowerment in case management refers to the process of enabling clients to gain control over their own lives and make informed decisions about their healthcare and well-being. It involves equipping clients with the necessary knowledge, skills, resources, and support to actively participate in their care planning and decision-making processes. This concept is fundamental in fostering a collaborative partnership between case managers and clients, ensuring that care is tailored to meet the unique needs and preferences of each individual.

Empowerment is achieved through education, effective communication, and advocacy. Case managers play a crucial role in educating clients about their conditions, treatment options, and available resources. By providing clear and comprehensive information, clients are better positioned to understand their situations and make choices that align with their personal values and goals.

Effective communication is essential for building trust and rapport with clients. Case managers must listen actively, respect client autonomy, and encourage open dialogue. This approach helps clients feel valued and understood, promoting confidence in their ability to manage their health.

Advocacy involves supporting clients in navigating complex healthcare systems, addressing barriers to care, and ensuring access to necessary services. By advocating for their clients' needs, case managers help remove obstacles that may impede client empowerment.

Ultimately, client empowerment leads to improved health outcomes, increased satisfaction with care, and greater adherence to treatment plans. It transforms clients from passive recipients of care into active participants, fostering a sense of ownership over their health journey.

2.6 Client Engagement:
Client engagement in case management refers to the active involvement and participation of clients in their own care processes. It is a collaborative approach that emphasizes the importance of building a strong, trusting relationship between the case manager and the client. This engagement is crucial for ensuring that clients are motivated, informed, and empowered to make decisions about their healthcare and related services.

Effective client engagement involves clear communication, active listening, and empathy. Case managers must ensure that clients understand their care plans, the available resources, and the potential outcomes of different choices. By fostering an environment where clients feel respected and heard, case managers can enhance client satisfaction and adherence to care plans.

Engagement strategies may include setting realistic goals with the client, providing education tailored to the client's level of understanding, and regularly reviewing progress. It also involves addressing any barriers to engagement, such as cultural differences, language barriers, or health literacy issues.

Incorporating technology can further enhance client engagement. Tools like patient portals, mobile apps, and telehealth services can facilitate ongoing communication and support between visits. These tools help maintain continuity of care and keep clients informed and engaged.

Ultimately, successful client engagement leads to improved health outcomes, reduced healthcare costs, and increased client satisfaction. For case managers preparing for the CCM exam, understanding the principles of client engagement is essential for delivering high-quality care that meets both clinical objectives and client needs.

2.7 Client Self-care Management:
Client self-care management refers to the process by which individuals take an active role in their own healthcare, making informed decisions and engaging in behaviors that promote health and well-being. This concept is crucial in case management, as it empowers clients to manage their health conditions effectively, reduce dependency on healthcare providers, and improve overall health outcomes.

Effective client self-care management involves educating clients about their conditions, treatment options, and self-monitoring techniques. It requires case managers to assess the client's readiness to learn and implement self-care strategies, considering factors such as health literacy, cultural beliefs, and emotional readiness. By fostering a supportive environment, case managers can guide clients in setting realistic goals and developing personalized care plans.

Moreover, client self-care management includes teaching skills such as medication management, symptom monitoring, lifestyle modifications (diet and exercise), and stress management techniques. Encouraging regular follow-up and communication with healthcare providers also forms a critical component of this process.

Case managers play a pivotal role in facilitating access to resources and support systems that enhance self-care capabilities. They collaborate with interdisciplinary teams to ensure that clients receive comprehensive education and support tailored to their specific needs.

Ultimately, effective client self-care management leads to increased client autonomy, improved adherence to treatment plans, reduced hospitalizations, and enhanced quality of life. By empowering clients to take charge of their health, case managers contribute significantly to sustainable healthcare outcomes and the efficient utilization of healthcare resources.

2.7.1 Self Advocacy:
Self-advocacy refers to the process by which individuals actively communicate, convey, negotiate, or assert their own interests, desires, needs, and rights. It involves understanding one's own needs and making informed decisions about the support necessary to meet those needs. In the context of case management, self-advocacy is a critical component of client self-care management. It empowers clients to take an active role in their healthcare journey, ensuring they have a voice in the decision-making processes that affect their lives.

For case managers, fostering self-advocacy involves educating clients about their rights and responsibilities within the healthcare system. This includes helping them understand their medical conditions, treatment options, and potential outcomes. Case managers should encourage clients to ask questions and express their preferences regarding care plans. Additionally, they should provide tools and resources that enhance clients' confidence in advocating for themselves.

Effective self-advocacy can lead to improved health outcomes by promoting client engagement and adherence to care plans. It also helps in building a collaborative relationship between clients and healthcare providers, where communication is open and respectful. Case managers play a pivotal role in identifying barriers to self-advocacy, such as limited health literacy or cultural differences, and working to overcome these obstacles.

Ultimately, self-advocacy is about empowering clients to become active participants in their own care, ensuring that their voices are heard and respected throughout the healthcare continuum.

2.7.2 Self-directed Care:

Self-directed care is a model of care management that empowers clients to take control of their own healthcare decisions and resources. This approach emphasizes the client's autonomy and ability to make informed choices regarding their care, services, and support. It involves clients actively participating in the planning, budgeting, and management of their healthcare services, often with the assistance of a case manager who provides guidance and support.

In self-directed care, clients are encouraged to identify their own needs and preferences, select providers, and determine how their allocated funds will be spent to best meet their personal health goals. This model is particularly beneficial for individuals with chronic conditions or disabilities who require ongoing support but wish to maintain independence and control over their lives.

Case managers play a crucial role in facilitating self-directed care by helping clients understand their options, access necessary resources, and develop skills for effective decision-making. They ensure that clients have the information needed to make informed choices and provide ongoing support to address any challenges that may arise.

Self-directed care aligns with the principles of person-centered care by respecting client autonomy and promoting individualized care plans. It can lead to improved satisfaction, better health outcomes, and enhanced quality of life for clients. By fostering a collaborative partnership between clients and case managers, self-directed care supports a more personalized approach to healthcare management that respects each client's unique circumstances and preferences.

2.7.3 Informed Decision Making:

Informed decision-making is a critical component of client self-care management, empowering individuals to make choices about their health and care based on a comprehensive understanding of available options, potential outcomes, and associated risks. This process requires case managers to ensure that clients receive all necessary information in a clear, concise, and culturally sensitive manner, enabling them to weigh the benefits and drawbacks of different interventions.

For case managers, facilitating informed decision-making involves a multi-step approach. First, they must assess the client's ability to understand the information provided, taking into account any cognitive impairments or language barriers. Next, they must present evidence-based options tailored to the client's specific health conditions and personal preferences. This includes discussing potential side effects, costs, and the likelihood of success for each option.

Effective communication is paramount in this process. Case managers should use plain language and visual aids when necessary, ensuring that clients comprehend the information. They should also encourage questions and provide answers that enhance understanding.

Moreover, respecting client autonomy is essential. Clients should be supported in making decisions that align with their values and goals, even if these differ from medical recommendations. Documenting the decision-making process is also crucial for legal and ethical reasons.

Ultimately, informed decision-making fosters client empowerment and engagement in their own care, leading to improved satisfaction and health outcomes. By promoting this approach, case managers play a pivotal role in enhancing the quality of healthcare delivery.

2.7.4 Shared Decision Making:

Shared Decision Making (SDM) is a collaborative process that involves the active participation of both the patient and the healthcare provider in making healthcare decisions. This approach ensures that patients are fully informed about their options and the potential outcomes, allowing them to make decisions that align with their personal values and preferences. In the context of case management, SDM is pivotal as it empowers clients to take an active role in their care, fostering better adherence to treatment plans and enhancing overall satisfaction with care.

The process of SDM begins with open communication, where case managers provide clear, evidence-based information about the available options, including the benefits, risks, and uncertainties associated with each choice. It requires case managers to listen actively to the client's concerns, values, and preferences. This dialogue helps identify what matters most to the client, ensuring that the chosen healthcare path is not only clinically appropriate but also personally meaningful.

In practice, SDM can be facilitated through decision aids such as brochures, videos, or online tools that help clients understand their choices more clearly. Case managers play a crucial role in guiding clients through these resources and supporting them in weighing their options.

Ultimately, Shared Decision Making respects patient autonomy while promoting informed consent and personalized care. It aligns healthcare decisions with the client's lifestyle and goals, leading to improved health outcomes and a stronger patient-provider relationship.

2.7.5 Health Education:

Health education is a crucial component of client self-care management, focusing on empowering individuals with the knowledge and skills necessary to make informed health decisions. It involves a systematic approach to teaching clients about their health conditions, treatment options, and lifestyle modifications that can enhance their well-being. The primary goal is to foster autonomy and encourage active participation in health maintenance and disease prevention.

For case managers, effective health education requires an understanding of diverse learning styles and cultural backgrounds to tailor educational interventions accordingly. This process begins with assessing the client's current knowledge level and identifying any gaps or misconceptions. Once these areas are identified, case managers can develop personalized education plans that incorporate evidence-based information.

Communication is key in health education; thus, case managers must employ clear, concise language and utilize visual aids or demonstrations when necessary to enhance comprehension. They should also encourage questions and provide feedback to ensure that the client fully understands the information presented.

Moreover, health education extends beyond mere information dissemination; it involves motivating clients to adopt healthier behaviors and sustain them over time. This can be achieved by setting realistic goals, offering support, and celebrating small successes to boost confidence.

In summary, health education is an integral part of case management that equips clients with essential knowledge and skills for self-care. By fostering understanding and encouraging proactive health behaviors, case managers play a pivotal role in enhancing client outcomes and promoting long-term well-being.

2.8 Community Resources:

Community resources refer to the array of services, programs, and supports available within a community that assist individuals in meeting their health, social, and economic needs. These resources are crucial for case managers, as they facilitate comprehensive care planning and coordination, ensuring clients receive holistic support that extends beyond medical interventions.

Community resources encompass a wide range of services, including healthcare facilities, mental health services, housing assistance, food banks, transportation services, educational programs, employment assistance, and legal aid. They also include non-profit organizations, government agencies, and local community groups that provide specialized support tailored to diverse populations.

For case managers, understanding and effectively utilizing community resources is essential. This involves identifying appropriate resources that align with the client's specific needs and goals. Maintaining an up-to-date database of available resources and establishing strong networks with local service providers is crucial.

Effective use of community resources can enhance client outcomes by addressing social determinants of health, such as housing instability and food insecurity. It empowers clients by providing them access to necessary services that promote independence and improve their quality of life.

Moreover, leveraging community resources helps reduce healthcare costs by preventing unnecessary hospitalizations and promoting preventive care. Case managers play a pivotal role in bridging the gap between clients and these resources, advocating for their needs, and facilitating seamless transitions across different levels of care within the community setting.

2.8.1 Elder Care Services:

Elder Care Services encompass a broad range of support options designed to assist older adults in maintaining their independence and quality of life. These services are crucial in addressing the unique needs of the elderly, which may include physical, emotional, and social aspects. As case managers, understanding these services is vital to effectively coordinating care and resources for this demographic.

Elder Care Services typically include in-home care, adult day care, assisted living facilities, nursing homes, and hospice care. In-home care provides personal assistance with daily activities such as bathing, dressing, meal preparation, and medication management. Adult day care offers social interaction and health services during daytime hours for those who require supervision or companionship while family caregivers are at work.

Assisted living facilities provide a residential setting with support services like meals, housekeeping, and transportation, while allowing residents to maintain some level of independence. Nursing homes offer more intensive medical care for those with significant health issues or disabilities. Hospice care focuses on comfort and quality of life for individuals with terminal illnesses.

Additionally, elder care services often involve coordinating access to community resources such as transportation services, financial assistance programs, and legal aid for advance directives or estate planning. As case managers, it is essential to assess each client's specific needs and preferences to develop a personalized care plan that maximizes their well-being and autonomy while navigating the complexities of available elder care options.

2.8.2 Transportation:

Transportation is a critical component of community resources that case managers must understand and utilize effectively to ensure clients can access necessary services and maintain their quality of life. It encompasses a range of services designed to facilitate the movement of individuals from one location to another, particularly those who are elderly, disabled, or have limited mobility.

In the context of case management, transportation services may include public transit systems, paratransit services, non-emergency medical transportation (NEMT), volunteer driver programs, and specialized transport for individuals with specific needs. Public transit systems provide scheduled bus or train services that are accessible to the general public. Paratransit services offer door-to-door transportation for individuals who cannot use regular public transportation due to physical or cognitive limitations.

Non-emergency medical transportation is crucial for clients who need to attend medical appointments but lack reliable means of travel. This service ensures timely access to healthcare, which is essential for managing chronic conditions and preventing hospitalizations. Volunteer driver programs often involve community members providing rides to those in need, fostering a sense of community support.

Case managers must assess the transportation needs of their clients and coordinate appropriate services. This involves understanding eligibility criteria, scheduling requirements, and potential barriers such as cost or geographic limitations. Effective use of transportation resources can significantly enhance a client's ability to engage with healthcare providers, participate in social activities, and maintain independence, ultimately contributing to improved health outcomes and quality of life.

2.8.3 Fraternal/Religious Organizations:

Fraternal and religious organizations play a pivotal role in the community resource network, providing support and services that can be crucial for case management. These organizations are often founded on shared beliefs, values, or interests, and they aim to foster a sense of community and mutual aid among their members. Fraternal organizations, such as the Freemasons and the Knights of Columbus, typically focus on fellowship, moral development, and charitable activities. They often provide financial assistance, scholarships, and volunteer services that can benefit clients in need.

Religious organizations, including churches, synagogues, mosques, and temples, extend their support through spiritual guidance, counseling services, and community outreach programs. They often operate food banks, shelters, and health clinics that are accessible to both members and non-members. These organizations can be instrumental in addressing the social determinants of health by offering holistic support that encompasses emotional, spiritual, and physical well-being.

For case managers, understanding the resources available through fraternal and religious organizations is essential for comprehensive care planning. These organizations can serve as valuable partners in meeting the diverse needs of clients by providing resources that may not be available through traditional healthcare or social service systems. By fostering relationships with these entities, case managers can enhance their ability to connect clients with supportive networks that promote resilience and self-sufficiency. Engaging with fraternal and religious organizations requires cultural competence and sensitivity to ensure respectful collaboration and effective resource utilization.

2.8.4 Meal Delivery Services:

Meal delivery services are community resources that provide prepared meals directly to individuals who may have difficulty accessing or preparing nutritious food on their own. These services are particularly beneficial for elderly individuals, people with disabilities, and those recovering from illness or surgery. Meal delivery services can be tailored to meet specific dietary needs, including low-sodium, diabetic-friendly, vegetarian, and gluten-free options.

For case managers, understanding meal delivery services is crucial for developing comprehensive care plans that address clients' nutritional needs. These services help ensure that clients receive balanced meals, which are essential for maintaining health and preventing malnutrition. By coordinating with local meal delivery providers, case managers can facilitate access to these services for their clients.

Meal delivery programs often operate through non-profit organizations, government-funded initiatives like Meals on Wheels, or private companies. Eligibility criteria and availability may vary based on location and funding sources. Case managers should assess each client's eligibility and preferences to recommend the most suitable service.

Additionally, meal delivery services can offer more than just nutritional support; they provide opportunities for social interaction through regular visits by delivery personnel. This aspect can be particularly beneficial in reducing feelings of isolation among homebound individuals.

In summary, meal delivery services are a vital component of community resources that support the well-being of individuals who require assistance with their dietary needs. Case managers play a key role in connecting clients to these services as part of a holistic approach to care management.

2.8.5 Pharmacy Assistance Programs:

Pharmacy Assistance Programs are initiatives designed to help individuals, particularly those with limited financial resources, access necessary medications at reduced or no cost. These programs are often sponsored by pharmaceutical companies, non-profit organizations, and government agencies. They play a crucial role in ensuring that patients adhere to prescribed treatment regimens, thereby improving health outcomes and reducing the overall burden on healthcare systems.

For case managers, understanding Pharmacy Assistance Programs is essential for connecting clients with these valuable resources. These programs typically offer assistance to uninsured or underinsured individuals who meet specific income criteria. Eligibility requirements and the scope of assistance can vary significantly between programs, making it important for case managers to be well-versed in the options available within their community.

Case managers should guide clients through the application process, which may involve providing proof of income, residency, and prescription information. Additionally, they should educate clients about the potential benefits and limitations of each program, such as specifics regarding medication coverage and any associated costs like co-pays.

By effectively leveraging Pharmacy Assistance Programs, case managers can help reduce financial barriers to medication adherence, thus promoting better health management for their clients. This knowledge is vital for case managers preparing for the CCM exam, as it demonstrates their ability to integrate community resources into comprehensive care plans tailored to individual client needs.

2.9 Conflict Resolution Strategies:

Conflict resolution strategies are systematic approaches employed to address and manage disputes effectively within a professional setting. For case managers, mastering these strategies is crucial, as they often navigate complex interactions between clients, healthcare providers, and other stakeholders. Effective conflict resolution not only enhances collaboration but also ensures optimal client outcomes.

One primary strategy is active listening, which involves attentively hearing and understanding the concerns of all parties involved. This fosters an environment where individuals feel valued and understood, paving the way for constructive dialogue.

Another key strategy is negotiation, where case managers facilitate discussions to reach mutually beneficial agreements. This requires a balance of assertiveness and empathy, ensuring that all parties' needs are considered while maintaining focus on the client's best interests.

Mediation is also a valuable tool, where an impartial third party assists in resolving conflicts. Case managers may act as mediators or engage external mediators to help parties find common ground and develop solutions collaboratively.

Problem-solving techniques are essential, involving the identification of the root causes of conflicts and brainstorming potential solutions. This approach encourages creative thinking and collective decision-making.

Lastly, setting clear boundaries and expectations can preemptively reduce conflicts. By establishing transparent communication channels and defining roles and responsibilities, case managers can minimize misunderstandings and foster a cooperative atmosphere.

In summary, conflict resolution strategies are integral to case management, requiring a blend of communication skills, empathy, and strategic thinking to ensure effective collaboration and positive client outcomes.

2.10 Crisis Intervention Strategies:

Crisis intervention strategies are structured methods employed by case managers to address and mitigate the immediate psychological, emotional, and social distress experienced by individuals during a crisis. These strategies aim to stabilize the situation, provide support, and facilitate the individual's return to a pre-crisis level of functioning.

A comprehensive approach begins with assessment and triage to identify the severity of the crisis and prioritize interventions. This involves active listening, empathy, and establishing rapport to understand the individual's needs and concerns. The primary goal is to ensure safety by assessing risks such as self-harm or harm to others and implementing necessary protective measures.

Once safety is assured, case managers employ problem-solving techniques to help individuals regain control. This includes exploring coping mechanisms, identifying support systems, and setting realistic goals. Encouraging adaptive coping strategies over maladaptive ones is crucial for long-term resilience.

Case managers also provide psychoeducation about stress responses and normalize reactions to crises. This helps individuals understand their experiences and reduces feelings of isolation or stigma. Connecting clients with community resources or support networks can offer additional assistance and promote recovery.

Follow-up is an essential component of crisis intervention strategies. It involves monitoring progress, reassessing needs, and adjusting interventions as required. By maintaining communication, case managers ensure continuity of care and prevent potential relapse into crisis.

Overall, effective crisis intervention strategies require a compassionate, client-centered approach that empowers individuals to navigate through crises with confidence and support.

2.11 Client Support System Dynamics:

Client Support System Dynamics refers to the complex interplay of relationships and resources that surround a client, impacting their health outcomes and overall well-being. This system encompasses family members, friends, healthcare providers, community resources, and any other entities involved in the client's care network. Understanding these dynamics is crucial for case managers as they coordinate care and advocate for their clients.

The dynamics within a client support system can influence the effectiveness of case management interventions. For instance, a strong family support network can enhance adherence to treatment plans, while a lack of support may hinder progress. Case managers must assess the strengths and weaknesses of each client's support system to tailor interventions effectively.

Effective communication within the support system is vital. Case managers should facilitate open dialogue between the client and their support network to ensure that all parties are informed and aligned with care goals. Additionally, identifying potential conflicts or gaps in support allows case managers to proactively address issues that may arise.

Cultural, socioeconomic, and psychological factors also play significant roles in shaping support system dynamics. Case managers must be culturally competent and sensitive to these factors to provide equitable and effective care. By leveraging community resources and fostering collaborative relationships within the support network, case managers can optimize outcomes and enhance the client's quality of life.

In summary, understanding Client Support System Dynamics enables case managers to implement comprehensive care strategies that are responsive to the unique needs of each client within their social context.

2.12 Health Coaching And Counseling:

Health coaching and counseling are integral components of case management, aimed at empowering clients to achieve optimal health outcomes. Health coaching involves a collaborative partnership between the case manager and the client, focusing on developing personalized strategies to meet health-related goals. It is a client-centered process that emphasizes motivation, behavior change, and self-efficacy. The case manager acts as a facilitator, guiding clients through goal setting, action planning, and problem-solving while providing support and encouragement.

Counseling, on the other hand, involves providing emotional and psychological support to clients. It addresses mental health concerns, coping mechanisms, and emotional well-being. In the context of case management, counseling helps clients navigate stressors related to their medical conditions or life changes. It involves active listening, empathy, and the application of therapeutic techniques to foster resilience and adaptability.

Both health coaching and counseling require strong communication skills and an understanding of behavioral change theories. Case managers must be adept at building trusting relationships with clients, enabling open dialogue about challenges and aspirations. They employ motivational interviewing techniques to enhance client engagement and commitment to change.

In practice, effective health coaching and counseling lead to improved patient adherence to treatment plans, enhanced quality of life, and reduced healthcare costs. By empowering clients through education and support, case managers facilitate self-management skills that contribute to sustained health improvements. For the CCM exam, understanding these roles is crucial for demonstrating competency in comprehensive case management practices.

2.13 Health Literacy:

Health literacy is the degree to which individuals have the capacity to obtain, process, and understand basic health information and services needed to make appropriate health decisions. It encompasses a range of skills, including reading, writing, numeracy, communication, and critical thinking. For case managers, understanding health literacy is crucial, as it directly impacts patient outcomes and healthcare efficiency.

Patients with low health literacy may struggle to comprehend medical instructions, prescription labels, or appointment schedules. This can lead to medication errors, increased hospitalizations, and poor management of chronic conditions. As a case manager, it is vital to assess the health literacy levels of patients and tailor communication strategies accordingly. This might involve using plain language, visual aids, or interactive tools to enhance understanding.

Moreover, promoting health literacy involves empowering patients to ask questions and engage actively in their care. Case managers should encourage patients to voice concerns and seek clarification on medical advice. This not only fosters a more collaborative patient-provider relationship but also enhances patient autonomy.

In practice, improving health literacy can reduce healthcare costs by minimizing unnecessary tests and procedures while enhancing patient satisfaction. It is essential for case managers to advocate for organizational policies that support health literacy initiatives, such as staff training programs and the development of patient-centered materials. By prioritizing health literacy, case managers play a pivotal role in advancing health equity and improving overall healthcare delivery.

2.14 Interpersonal Communication:

Interpersonal communication is the process by which individuals exchange information, feelings, and meanings through verbal and non-verbal messages. It is a face-to-face communication method that is essential for building relationships, understanding, and trust between case managers and their clients. Effective interpersonal communication involves not only the words spoken but also the tone of voice, body language, facial expressions, and active listening.

For case managers, mastering interpersonal communication is crucial, as it directly impacts client outcomes. It involves demonstrating empathy, cultural sensitivity, and emotional intelligence to fully understand clients' needs and concerns. This communication skill enables case managers to convey complex information clearly, negotiate care plans effectively, and advocate for clients' best interests.

Key components include active listening, which requires fully concentrating on the speaker without interrupting; providing feedback that is constructive and supportive; and employing open-ended questions to encourage dialogue. Non-verbal cues such as eye contact, gestures, and posture play a significant role in conveying sincerity and understanding.

Barriers to effective interpersonal communication can include language differences, cultural misunderstandings, personal biases, and environmental distractions. Case managers must be adept at recognizing these barriers and employing strategies to overcome them to ensure clear and effective exchanges.

In summary, interpersonal communication is a foundational skill for case managers that facilitates successful interactions with clients, colleagues, and other healthcare professionals. Mastery of this skill enhances collaboration, improves client satisfaction, and ultimately contributes to the delivery of high-quality care.

2.14.1   Group Dynamics:

Group dynamics refers to the behavioral and psychological processes that occur within a social group or between social groups. It encompasses how individuals interact, communicate, and function together in a collective setting. For case managers, understanding group dynamics is crucial, as it aids in effectively managing and facilitating team-based healthcare delivery.

In the context of case management, group dynamics involves recognizing the roles and relationships among team members, which can include healthcare providers, patients, families, and other stakeholders. Effective group dynamics foster collaboration, enhance communication, and improve problem-solving capabilities within the team. This is achieved by understanding various elements such as leadership styles, group roles, decision-making processes, conflict resolution strategies, and group cohesion.

Case managers must be adept at identifying both positive and negative dynamics within a group. Positive dynamics can lead to increased productivity and improved patient outcomes, while negative dynamics may result in misunderstandings, reduced efficiency, and conflicts. By promoting open communication, mutual respect, and shared goals, case managers can harness the power of group dynamics to facilitate better care coordination.

Furthermore, case managers should be aware of the stages of group development—forming, storming, norming, performing, and adjourning—as these stages influence how a group functions over time. By understanding these processes, case managers can anticipate challenges and guide their teams through transitions effectively. Mastery of group dynamics ultimately contributes to a more cohesive healthcare team and better service delivery for patients.

2.14.2   Relationship Building:

Relationship building is a fundamental aspect of effective case management, emphasizing the creation and maintenance of positive, productive interactions between case managers, clients, and other stakeholders. It involves developing trust, understanding, and mutual respect to facilitate collaboration and achieve desired outcomes in the client's care journey.

A comprehensive definition of relationship building in the context of case management is the strategic process of establishing and nurturing professional connections that enhance communication, cooperation, and coordination among all parties involved in a client's care. This process is pivotal for understanding client needs, preferences, and goals while ensuring that all stakeholders are aligned toward achieving optimal health outcomes.

An in-depth explanation reveals that relationship building requires active listening skills, empathy, cultural competence, and effective communication strategies. Case managers must demonstrate a genuine interest in their clients' well-being, which fosters trust and openness. By engaging with clients on a personal level, case managers can better assess needs and tailor interventions accordingly.

Furthermore, relationship building extends to interdisciplinary team members and external partners. Establishing strong connections with healthcare providers, social services, and community resources ensures seamless transitions of care and comprehensive support for clients. Regular communication and feedback loops are vital to maintaining these relationships.

In summary, relationship building is an ongoing process that underpins successful case management by fostering collaborative environments where clients feel supported and empowered. By prioritizing strong relationships, case managers can effectively advocate for their clients and facilitate improved health outcomes

2.15 Interview Tools And Techniques:

Interview tools and techniques are essential components of the case management process, facilitating effective communication and information gathering. These tools help case managers assess clients' needs, develop care plans, and coordinate services. A comprehensive understanding of these tools is crucial for ensuring successful client outcomes.

Active listening is a fundamental technique that involves fully concentrating on, understanding, and responding to the client. It establishes trust and encourages open communication. Open-ended questions are another vital tool, prompting clients to share detailed information about their situations. These questions often begin with how, what, or tell me about, allowing clients to express themselves freely.

Reflective questioning is a technique used to clarify and confirm understanding by paraphrasing what the client has said. This ensures accurate comprehension and demonstrates empathy. Motivational interviewing is a client-centered approach that enhances motivation to change by exploring and resolving ambivalence. It involves expressing empathy, developing discrepancy, rolling with resistance, and supporting self-efficacy.

Structured interviews use standardized questions to ensure consistency and comprehensiveness in data collection. This tool is particularly useful in initial assessments or when specific information is required. Additionally, the use of technology, such as electronic health records (EHRs) and telehealth platforms, has become increasingly important in conducting interviews efficiently and effectively.

Overall, mastering interview tools and techniques enables case managers to gather critical information, build rapport with clients, and tailor interventions to meet individual needs, ultimately enhancing the quality of care provided.

2.15.1   Motivational Interviewing:

Motivational Interviewing (MI) is a client-centered, directive method for enhancing intrinsic motivation to change by exploring and resolving ambivalence. It is particularly useful in case management, as it empowers clients to take an active role in their own care, promoting lasting behavioral changes. Developed by clinical psychologists William R. Miller and Stephen Rollnick, MI is grounded in the principles of collaboration, evocation, and autonomy support.

The core of Motivational Interviewing lies in its empathetic and non-judgmental approach. Case managers utilize open-ended questions, affirmations, reflective listening, and summaries (OARS) to engage clients. This technique helps elicit the client's own motivations for change rather than imposing external reasons. By doing so, it respects the client's autonomy and fosters a sense of empowerment.

MI operates on the premise that ambivalence about change is a natural part of the process. Rather than confronting resistance directly, case managers guide clients to articulate their own reasons for change and explore potential barriers. This method encourages clients to voice their desire for change, thereby increasing their commitment to action.

In practice, MI involves establishing rapport, collaboratively setting agendas, exploring the importance of change from the client's perspective, and planning concrete steps forward. For case managers preparing for the CCM exam, mastering

Motivational Interviewing can significantly enhance their ability to facilitate effective client-centered interventions that lead to improved health outcomes and client satisfaction.

2.16 Impact of Multicultural and Spiritual Factors on Client Health:

Multicultural, spiritual, and religious factors play a crucial role in shaping an individual's health beliefs, practices, and outcomes. Understanding these elements is essential for case managers to provide culturally competent care that respects and integrates clients' diverse backgrounds.

Multicultural factors encompass the cultural norms, values, and practices that influence health perceptions and behaviors. These can include dietary habits, traditional healing practices, language barriers, and differing attitudes toward healthcare professionals. For instance, some cultures may prioritize natural remedies over pharmaceutical interventions or may have specific dietary restrictions that impact nutritional planning.

Spiritual factors involve an individual's beliefs about life's purpose, suffering, and healing. Spirituality can provide comfort and coping mechanisms during illness but may also lead to conflicts with medical advice if spiritual beliefs oppose certain treatments. For example, a client who believes in the power of prayer might prioritize spiritual interventions alongside or instead of medical treatments.

Religious factors are closely tied to spirituality but are more structured around specific doctrines and rituals. These can dictate healthcare decisions such as blood transfusions, end-of-life care, or surgical procedures. Case managers must be aware of these religious considerations to avoid conflicts and ensure compliance with clients' wishes.

In summary, acknowledging multicultural, spiritual, and religious factors allows case managers to tailor care plans effectively. This approach not only enhances client satisfaction but also improves health outcomes by fostering trust and collaboration between clients and healthcare providers.

2.17 Psychological And Neuropsychological Assessment:

Psychological and neuropsychological assessments are critical tools used in the evaluation of cognitive, emotional, and behavioral functioning. These assessments help case managers understand the mental health and cognitive status of clients, guiding treatment planning and intervention strategies. Psychological assessments typically involve standardized tests and clinical interviews to evaluate emotional and personality factors. They aim to identify conditions such as depression, anxiety, personality disorders, and other psychological issues that may impact a client's daily functioning.

Neuropsychological assessments, on the other hand, focus on understanding the relationship between brain function and behavior. These assessments involve a series of tests that measure various cognitive abilities, including memory, attention, language skills, problem-solving capabilities, and executive functions. They are particularly useful in diagnosing conditions like traumatic brain injuries, dementia, learning disabilities, and neurological disorders.

For case managers preparing for the CCM exam, it is essential to recognize the significance of these assessments in creating comprehensive care plans. Understanding the results of these evaluations can help case managers collaborate effectively with healthcare professionals to address clients' needs holistically. This includes advocating for appropriate therapies, supporting medication management, and facilitating access to community resources.

Overall, psychological and neuropsychological assessments provide invaluable insights into a client's mental health and cognitive functioning, enabling case managers to tailor interventions that promote optimal outcomes in their clients' health and well-being.

2.18 Psychosocial Impacts of Chronic Illness and Disability:

The psychosocial aspects of chronic illness and disability encompass the psychological and social dimensions that influence an individual's experience and management of long-term health conditions. These aspects are crucial for case managers to understand, as they significantly impact a patient's quality of life, adherence to treatment plans, and overall well-being.

Psychologically, chronic illness can lead to a range of emotional responses, such as anxiety, depression, and stress, due to the ongoing nature of the condition and its implications for daily life. Patients may experience a loss of identity or self-worth as they adjust to new limitations and changes in their roles within personal and professional settings. Understanding these emotional challenges allows case managers to provide appropriate support and interventions that promote mental health resilience.

Socially, chronic illness can alter relationships with family, friends, and colleagues. It may lead to social isolation or changes in social roles, impacting the individual's support network. Economic factors also play a role, as chronic conditions often result in financial strain due to medical expenses and potential loss of income. Case managers must assess these social determinants to facilitate access to resources, community support systems, and financial assistance programs.

In summary, addressing the psychosocial aspects involves a holistic approach that considers both the mental health needs and social circumstances of individuals with chronic illnesses or disabilities. This comprehensive understanding enables case managers to develop tailored care plans that enhance patient outcomes and improve their overall quality of life.

2.19 Support for the Uninsured and Underinsured:

Resources for the uninsured or underinsured are critical support systems designed to provide medical and financial assistance to individuals who lack adequate health insurance coverage. These resources aim to bridge the gap in healthcare access by offering affordable or free services, ensuring that all individuals receive necessary medical care regardless of their insurance status.

One key resource is community health centers, which provide comprehensive primary care services on a sliding fee scale based on income. These centers often offer preventive care, dental services, and mental health services. Additionally, many states have established Medicaid expansion programs to cover more low-income individuals, although eligibility varies by state.

Pharmaceutical assistance programs are another vital resource, offering discounted or free medications to those who qualify. These programs are often sponsored by pharmaceutical companies and require applications through healthcare providers.

Nonprofit organizations and charitable clinics also play a significant role in supporting the uninsured or underinsured. They offer various services ranging from routine check-ups to specialized care at reduced costs. Moreover, patient assistance programs help individuals navigate healthcare systems and connect them with available resources.

Case managers play an essential role in identifying these resources and guiding clients through the application processes. They assess individual needs, provide education on available options, and advocate for their clients' access to necessary healthcare services. By leveraging these resources effectively, case managers help mitigate barriers to healthcare access for uninsured and underinsured populations, promoting better health outcomes and equity in healthcare delivery.

2.20 Supportive Care Programs:

Supportive Care Programs are integral components of healthcare that focus on improving the quality of life for patients with chronic, progressive, or terminal illnesses. These programs are designed to provide comprehensive care that addresses not only the physical symptoms of a disease but also the emotional, social, and spiritual needs of patients and their families. The primary aim is to enhance comfort and support during all stages of illness, regardless of the prognosis.

Supportive care encompasses a wide range of services, including pain management, symptom control, psychological support, nutritional counseling, and assistance with daily living activities. It is delivered by a multidisciplinary team of healthcare professionals, including physicians, nurses, social workers, and chaplains, who collaborate to create personalized care plans tailored to individual patient needs.

Case Managers play a crucial role in coordinating supportive care by assessing patient needs, facilitating communication among caregivers, and ensuring access to necessary resources and services. They advocate for patients' preferences and goals, helping them navigate complex healthcare systems while maintaining dignity and autonomy.

Supportive Care Programs also extend to family members, offering respite care and bereavement support to help them cope with the challenges associated with their loved one's illness. By focusing on holistic care and quality of life, Supportive Care Programs empowerpatients and families to manage the impacts of illness more effectively, ultimately leading to improved patient satisfaction and outcomes.

2.20.1 Support Groups:

Support groups are structured gatherings of individuals who share common experiences, challenges, or conditions, providing a platform for mutual support and information exchange. These groups are essential components of supportive care programs and play a critical role in the holistic management of patients. They facilitate emotional support, practical advice, and coping strategies among participants, often led by a trained facilitator or peer leader.

For case managers, understanding the dynamics and benefits of support groups is crucial. These groups can significantly enhance the overall well-being of clients by reducing feelings of isolation and providing a sense of community. They offer a safe space for individuals to express emotions, share experiences, and learn from others who have faced similar challenges. This peer-to-peer interaction fosters empowerment and resilience, enabling participants to better manage their health conditions.

In the context of case management, recommending appropriate support groups can be an integral part of a comprehensive care plan. Case managers must assess the suitability of these groups based on the client's specific needs, preferences, and cultural considerations. Additionally, they should be knowledgeable about the various types of support groups available—such as those focused on chronic illness, mental health issues, caregiving responsibilities, or bereavement—to provide tailored recommendations.

Ultimately, support groups are valuable resources that complement clinical interventions by addressing the psychosocial aspects of health care. By facilitating access to these groups, case managers contribute to improved client outcomes and enhanced quality of life.

2.20.2 Pastoral Counseling:

Pastoral counseling is a form of therapy that integrates psychological principles with spiritual resources, often provided by trained clergy or certified pastoral counselors. It is designed to support individuals in addressing emotional and spiritual issues within the context of their faith and beliefs. This type of counseling recognizes the importance of spirituality in the healing process and seeks to offer guidance that aligns with the client's religious values.

In the context of case management, pastoral counseling can be a valuable supportive care program for clients who are experiencing life transitions, grief, moral dilemmas, or existential crises. It provides a safe space for individuals to explore their concerns while receiving empathetic listening and spiritual guidance. Pastoral counselors are equipped to address a range of issues, including anxiety, depression, relationship problems, and ethical conflicts, by incorporating theological insights and spiritual practices.

Case managers should recognize that pastoral counseling can complement other therapeutic approaches by offering a holistic perspective that considers the client's spiritual well-being alongside their mental and physical health. It is essential for case managers to assess the appropriateness of pastoral counseling based on the client's personal beliefs and preferences. Referrals to pastoral counselors should be made when clients express a desire for spiritually integrated care or when spiritual issues are identified as significant factors in their overall well-being.

By understanding the role of pastoral counseling in supportive care programs, case managers can better facilitate comprehensive care plans that respect and incorporate clients' spiritual dimensions.

2.20.3   Disease-based Organizations:

Disease-based organizations are specialized entities focused on specific illnesses or health conditions. These organizations play a crucial role in the healthcare ecosystem by providing resources, support, and advocacy for patients, families, and healthcare professionals dealing with particular diseases. They often operate as non-profit organizations and are dedicated to improving the quality of life for individuals affected by specific diseases.

These organizations offer a variety of services, including educational materials, support groups, and information on the latest research developments. They also advocate for public policies that benefit patients and fundraise for research initiatives aimed at finding cures or better treatments. By raising awareness about specific diseases, they help reduce stigma and promote early diagnosis and intervention.

For case managers, disease-based organizations are valuable partners in patient care management. They provide access to up-to-date information on disease management protocols and treatment options, which can enhance the case manager's ability to develop comprehensive care plans. Additionally, these organizations often offer training programs and workshops that can improve a case manager's skills in handling complex cases related to specific diseases.

Engagement with disease-based organizations allows case managers to connect patients with community resources that can provide emotional support and practical assistance. This collaboration ensures a holistic approach to patient care, addressing not only medical needs but also the social and psychological aspects of living with a chronic condition. Overall, disease-based organizations are integral to fostering an informed and supportive environment for both healthcare providers and patients.

2.20.4   Bereavement Counseling:

Bereavement counseling is a specialized form of support designed to help individuals cope with the emotional, psychological, and social impacts of losing a loved one. It is an integral component of supportive care programs, offering guidance and assistance throughout the grieving process. The aim of bereavement counseling is to provide a safe space for individuals to express their feelings, understand their grief, and develop coping strategies to navigate the challenges associated with loss.

The process involves trained professionals who utilize various therapeutic techniques tailored to the unique needs of the bereaved. Counselors may employ cognitive-behavioral therapy (CBT), narrative therapy, or other evidence-based practices to facilitate healing. They assist clients in acknowledging and accepting their loss, which is crucial for emotional adjustment and recovery.

Bereavement counseling addresses various aspects of grief, including denial, anger, bargaining, depression, and acceptance—commonly known as the stages of grief. It also considers the cultural, spiritual, and personal factors influencing an individual's grieving process. By providing empathetic support and understanding, counselors help individuals explore their emotions, reduce feelings of isolation, and find meaning in their loss.

For case managers preparing for the CCM exam, understanding bereavement counseling is essential as it equips them with the knowledge to refer clients to appropriate resources and integrate supportive care into comprehensive case management plans. This ensures that clients receive holistic care that addresses both their physical health needs and emotional well-being during times of profound loss.

2.21 Wellness & Illness Prevention Strategies:

Wellness and illness prevention programs are structured initiatives aimed at maintaining health and preventing disease. These programs incorporate various concepts and strategies designed to promote physical, mental, and social well-being while reducing the risk of illness. Key components include health education, lifestyle modification, and early detection screenings.

Health education focuses on increasing awareness about healthy behaviors and lifestyle choices. It empowers individuals with knowledge about nutrition, physical activity, stress management, and the importance of regular medical check-ups. Lifestyle modification strategies encourage the adoption of habits such as balanced diets, regular exercise, smoking cessation, and moderate alcohol consumption.

Preventive screenings are critical for the early detection and management of potential health issues. Regular screenings for blood pressure, cholesterol levels, cancer markers, and diabetes are essential components of these programs. Immunizations also play a vital role in preventing infectious diseases.

Case managers play a crucial role in coordinating wellness and prevention programs by assessing individual needs, developing personalized care plans, and facilitating access to necessary resources. They work collaboratively with healthcare providers to ensure that clients receive comprehensive care that addresses both current health concerns and future risks.

By focusing on prevention rather than treatment alone, these programs aim to reduce healthcare costs, improve quality of life, and enhance overall population health. Effective implementation requires a multidisciplinary approach involving healthcare professionals, community resources, and patient engagement to achieve sustainable health outcomes.

2.22 Social Determinants Of Health:

Social determinants of health (SDOH) refer to the non-medical factors that influence health outcomes. These are the conditions in which people are born, grow, live, work, and age. They encompass a broad range of socio-economic factors, including education, employment, income, family and social support, community safety, and access to healthcare services. SDOH are crucial for understanding the disparities in health outcomes among different populations.

For case managers preparing for the CCM exam, it is essential to recognize that these determinants can significantly impact a patient's ability to manage their health effectively. For instance, individuals with limited access to nutritious food or safe housing may struggle with chronic disease management. Similarly, those without stable employment or adequate income may face barriers to accessing necessary healthcare services.

Case managers must assess these determinants when developing care plans. By identifying and addressing SDOH, they can help mitigate barriers to care and improve overall health outcomes. This may involve coordinating with community resources to provide support in areas such as transportation, housing assistance, or educational programs.

Understanding SDOH also enables case managers to advocate for systemic changes that promote health equity. By addressing these broader social issues, case managers contribute to reducing health disparities and improving population health. In summary, social determinants of health are integral to effective case management and require a comprehensive approach to ensure positive patient outcomes.

2.23 Gender Health:

Gender health refers to the unique health needs and considerations associated with different genders, influenced by biological, social, and cultural factors. It encompasses a broad spectrum of issues that affect individuals based on their gender identity, including access to healthcare, the prevalence of certain diseases, and societal influences on health behaviors. Understanding gender health is crucial for case managers, as it ensures the delivery of personalized and equitable care.

Biologically, gender differences can manifest in susceptibility to certain diseases, responses to medications, and overall health outcomes. For instance, women may experience different symptoms of heart disease compared to men, requiring tailored diagnostic and treatment approaches. Socially and culturally, gender roles and expectations can impact mental health, access to healthcare services, and overall well-being. For example, transgender individuals often face significant barriers in accessing appropriate healthcare due to discrimination or a lack of provider knowledge.

Case managers must be adept at recognizing these disparities and advocating for inclusive practices that respect each individual's gender identity. This includes facilitating access to appropriate resources, coordinating care that considers gender-specific needs, and educating patients about their health risks and preventive measures. By integrating gender health into their practice, case managers contribute to reducing health inequities and improving outcomes for all genders. Understanding these dynamics is vital for effective case management and ensuring that all individuals receive comprehensive and compassionate care tailored to their specific needs.

2.23.1   Sexual Orientation:

Sexual orientation refers to an individual's enduring pattern of emotional, romantic, or sexual attraction to people of the same gender, the opposite gender, or multiple genders. It is a fundamental aspect of a person's identity and can include orientations such as heterosexuality, homosexuality, bisexuality, and more fluid identities like pansexuality. Understanding sexual orientation is crucial for case managers, as it impacts various aspects of healthcare delivery and patient interaction.

Case managers must recognize that sexual orientation is distinct from gender identity, which pertains to one's internal understanding of their own gender. Respecting and acknowledging a patient's sexual orientation is vital in creating an inclusive and supportive healthcare environment. This involves using appropriate language, avoiding assumptions about relationships or family structures, and providing resources that affirm diverse orientations.

In practice, case managers should be knowledgeable about the specific health risks and needs associated with different sexual orientations. For example, LGBTQ+ individuals may face unique challenges, such as higher rates of mental health issues due to societal stigma or discrimination. Additionally, they may encounter barriers to accessing healthcare services that are sensitive to their needs.

By fostering a respectful and informed approach to sexual orientation, case managers can enhance patient trust and engagement, ultimately improving health outcomes. This approach aligns with the ethical standards of promoting equity and advocating for the well-being of all individuals under their care.

2.23.2   Gender Expression:

Gender expression refers to the external manifestation of an individual's gender identity, which is expressed through behavior, clothing, hairstyle, voice, and other forms of presentation. It is important to note that gender expression is distinct from gender identity, which is an internal understanding of oneself as male, female, a blend of both, or neither. Gender expression can vary greatly among individuals and may not necessarily align with the societal norms traditionally associated with one's sex assigned at birth.

For case managers, understanding gender expression is crucial in providing comprehensive care and support to clients. Case managers should recognize that gender expression is a personal choice and respect each client's unique way of expressing their gender. This understanding aids in creating an inclusive and supportive environment that acknowledges and values diversity in gender expressions.

Case managers must also be aware of the potential challenges clients may face due to their gender expression, including discrimination, misunderstanding, or lack of access to appropriate services. By advocating for clients' rights and educating others about the importance of respecting diverse gender expressions, case managers can help reduce stigma and promote equality.

In practice, case managers should incorporate discussions about gender expression into their assessments and care plans, ensuring that services are tailored to meet the individual needs of each client. They should also stay informed about relevant policies and resources that support individuals with diverse gender expressions, facilitating better access to necessary services and support networks.

2.23.3   Gender Identity:

Gender identity is a deeply held sense of being male, female, a blend of both, or neither, and may not necessarily align with an individual's biological sex. It is an intrinsic aspect of a person's identity that encompasses the internal understanding and experience of gender. Unlike gender expression, which involves outward manifestations such as clothing and behavior, gender identity is a personal perception that may or may not be visible to others.

Case managers must recognize the importance of gender identity in delivering patient-centered care. Understanding that gender identity can differ from the assigned sex at birth is crucial for respecting clients' preferences and ensuring that care plans are inclusive and affirming. This awareness helps address healthcare disparities faced by transgender and non-binary individuals, who often encounter barriers such as discrimination or a lack of access to appropriate healthcare services.

Furthermore, case managers should be knowledgeable about the terminology associated with gender identity, including terms like cisgender, transgender, non-binary, and genderqueer. They should also be adept at using inclusive language and pronouns as preferred by the client. This respect for individual identity fosters trust and improves communication between clients and healthcare providers.

By integrating an understanding of gender identity into their practice, case managers can advocate effectively for their clients' needs, facilitate access to appropriate resources, and contribute to a healthcare environment that acknowledges and respects diverse gender identities.

3   Quality Outcomes Evaluation Metrics:

Quality and outcomes evaluation and measurement are essential components in the practice of case management, focusing on assessing the effectiveness, efficiency, and overall impact of healthcare services. This process involves systematic data collection, analysis, and interpretation to ensure that patient care meets established standards and achieves desired health outcomes.

In the context of case management, quality evaluation refers to assessing the processes and interventions used to deliver care. It involves examining whether these processes adhere to best practices and guidelines, ultimately ensuring that patients receive safe and effective treatment. Tools such as audits, peer reviews, and performance metrics are commonly employed to evaluate quality.

Outcomes measurement, on the other hand, focuses on the end results of healthcare interventions. It examines whether the care provided has led to improvements in patient health status, satisfaction, and quality of life. Commonly used outcome measures include patient-reported outcomes, clinical indicators (such as reduced hospital readmissions), and cost-effectiveness analyses.

Together, quality and outcomes evaluations provide a comprehensive view of the success of healthcare delivery. They enable case managers to identify areas for improvement, enhance patient satisfaction, and optimize resource utilization. By continuously monitoring and evaluating these parameters, case managers can implement evidence-based interventions that lead to better health outcomes and improved care quality.

In summary, quality and outcomes evaluation and measurement are critical for ensuring high standards of care in case management. They provide valuable insights into the effectiveness of healthcare services, guiding continuous improvement efforts to achieve optimal patient outcomes.

3.1 Accreditation Standards And Requirements:

Accreditation standards and requirements are established criteria that healthcare organizations must meet to ensure quality and safety in the delivery of care. These standards are developed by accrediting bodies to evaluate and recognize the competence of healthcare organizations in providing high-quality services. For case managers, understanding these standards is crucial, as they often play a pivotal role in ensuring that their organizations comply with these requirements.

Accreditation involves a rigorous process in which external agencies assess an organization's adherence to predefined standards. These standards typically cover various aspects, including patient care, safety protocols, organizational management, and performance improvement. Accreditation not only validates the quality of care provided but also enhances an organization's credibility and reputation.

For case managers, accreditation standards serve as a framework for evaluating and improving patient outcomes. They guide case managers in implementing best practices, developing effective care plans, and ensuring continuity of care.

Compliance with these standards requires thorough documentation, regular audits, and continuous quality improvement initiatives.

Moreover, accreditation requirements often mandate that case managers engage in ongoing education and professional development to stay updated with the latest industry practices. This ensures that case managers possess the necessary skills and knowledge to contribute effectively to their organization's accreditation efforts.

In summary, accreditation standards and requirements are essential for maintaining high-quality healthcare services. Case managers must be well-versed in these standards to facilitate compliance, enhance patient care, and support their organization's commitment to excellence in healthcare delivery.

3.2 Cost-benefit Analysis:

Cost-benefit analysis (CBA) is a systematic approach used to evaluate the economic worth of a project or decision by comparing its costs and benefits. In the context of case management, it serves as a critical tool for assessing the value of healthcare interventions and programs. The primary objective of CBA is to determine whether the benefits of a particular intervention outweigh its costs, thereby guiding decision-making processes.

To conduct a cost-benefit analysis, case managers first identify all potential costs associated with an intervention, including direct costs such as medical expenses and indirect costs like lost productivity. Next, they quantify the benefits, which may include improved patient outcomes, reduced hospital readmissions, and enhanced quality of life. These benefits are often converted into monetary terms to facilitate comparison with costs.

The results of a CBA are typically expressed as a benefit-cost ratio (BCR), where a ratio greater than one indicates that the benefits exceed the costs. A higher BCR suggests a more economically favorable intervention. Additionally, net present value (NPV) calculations may be used to account for the time value of money, providing further insight into long-term financial implications.

For case managers preparing for the CCM exam, understanding CBA is crucial for making informed decisions that optimize resource allocation and improve patient care outcomes. Mastery of this analytical tool enables case managers to advocate effectively for interventions that deliver maximum value to both patients and healthcare systems.

3.3 Data Interpretation And Reporting:

Data interpretation and reporting are critical components of the quality and outcomes evaluation process in case management. Data interpretation involves analyzing collected data to extract meaningful insights that inform decision-making and improve patient care. This process requires a thorough understanding of statistical methods and the ability to discern patterns, trends, and anomalies within datasets. Case managers must be adept at distinguishing between correlation and causation to ensure accurate conclusions.

Reporting involves presenting these findings in a clear, concise, and actionable manner to stakeholders, including healthcare providers, patients, and administrative staff. Effective reporting translates complex data into understandable formats such as charts, graphs, and executive summaries. The goal is to facilitate informed decision-making that enhances patient outcomes and optimizes resource utilization.

In the context of case management, data interpretation and reporting support continuous quality improvement initiatives by identifying areas for enhancement and tracking progress over time. They also aid in compliance with regulatory standards and accreditation requirements by providing evidence of effective case management practices.

Case managers must possess strong analytical skills and be proficient in using data analytics tools. They should also have excellent communication skills to convey findings accurately and persuasively. By mastering data interpretation and reporting, case managers can significantly contribute to the delivery of high-quality, cost-effective care that meets the needs of patients while aligning with organizational goals.

3.4 Health Care Analytics:

Health care analytics refers to the systematic use of data and related business insights developed through applied analytical disciplines such as statistical, contextual, quantitative, predictive, cognitive, and other models to drive fact-based decision-making for planning, management, measurement, and learning in health care. It encompasses a variety of techniques and processes designed to extract valuable insights from health-related data, which can be used to improve patient care, optimize operational efficiency, and reduce costs.

In the context of case management, health care analytics plays a crucial role in identifying trends and patterns that can inform care coordination and resource allocation. By analyzing data from electronic health records (EHRs), claims data, patient surveys, and other sources, case managers can gain a deeper understanding of patient needs and outcomes. This information supports the development of personalized care plans that enhance patient engagement and compliance.

Moreover, predictive analytics can forecast potential health events or complications, allowing case managers to proactively address issues before they escalate. This proactive approach not only improves patient outcomes but also contributes to cost savings by preventing unnecessary hospitalizations or interventions.

Additionally, health care analytics aids in evaluating the effectiveness of interventions and programs by providing evidence-based insights into their impact. This evaluation is essential for continuous improvement in case management practices. Overall, health care analytics empowers case managers with the tools needed to make informed decisions that enhance the quality of care provided to patients.

3.4.1 Health Risk Assessment:

A Health Risk Assessment (HRA) is a systematic approach used to evaluate an individual's health risks and quality of life. It involves collecting data through questionnaires, biometric screenings, and medical history to identify potential health issues and provide a basis for developing personalized interventions. HRAs are crucial tools in preventive healthcare, enabling case managers to proactively address health concerns and promote wellness among clients.

The process begins with the collection of demographic information, lifestyle behaviors, and personal medical history. This data helps identify risk factors such as smoking, physical inactivity, poor diet, and chronic conditions like hypertension or diabetes. Biometric screenings may include measurements of blood pressure, cholesterol levels, body mass index (BMI), and glucose levels, providing objective data to complement self-reported information.

Once the data is gathered, it is analyzed to assess the likelihood of future health problems. This analysis can highlight areas where lifestyle changes or medical interventions could reduce risks. For case managers, understanding these risks is essential for crafting individualized care plans that address specific needs and encourage healthier behaviors.

HRAs also serve as educational tools, increasing client awareness about their health status and motivating them to take proactive steps toward improvement. By integrating HRAs into their practice, case managers can enhance their ability to support clients in achieving better health outcomes, ultimately reducing healthcare costs and improving quality of life. Understanding HRAs is vital for case managers preparing for the CCM exam, as it underscores their role in preventive care and effective case management.

3.4.2 Predictive Modeling:

Predictive modeling is a statistical technique used in healthcare analytics to forecast future events or outcomes based on historical data. It involves creating a mathematical model that captures relationships within the data and utilizes these relationships to predict unknown outcomes. This approach is particularly valuable for case managers, as it aids in proactive decision-making and resource allocation.

In the context of healthcare, predictive modeling can be used to identify patients at high risk of hospital readmission, predict disease progression, or determine the likelihood of treatment success. By analyzing patterns from past patient data, such as demographics, medical history, and treatment plans, predictive models can provide insights into potential future health events.

For case managers, understanding predictive modeling is crucial because it enables them to prioritize interventions for patients who are most likely to benefit from additional care. This can lead to improved patient outcomes, reduced healthcare costs, and more efficient use of resources. For example, a predictive model might highlight a patient with chronic conditions who is likely to experience complications without timely intervention. Armed with this information, case managers can develop personalized care plans that address specific risks.

Moreover, predictive modeling supports evidence-based practice by providing quantifiable predictions that inform clinical decisions. As part of the CCM exam preparation, case managers should familiarize themselves with the principles of predictive modeling, including data collection, model selection, validation techniques, and ethical considerations related to patient data privacy and informed consent.

3.4.3 Adjusted Clinical Group (ACG):

The Adjusted Clinical Group (ACG) system is a risk adjustment and predictive modeling tool used in healthcare analytics to assess the health status and resource utilization of patient populations. Developed by researchers at Johns Hopkins University, the ACG system classifies individuals into distinct categories based on their medical diagnoses, demographics, and healthcare utilization patterns. This classification aids in predicting healthcare needs and costs, thereby facilitating effective resource allocation and management.

The ACG system operates by grouping patients with similar clinical characteristics into categories that reflect their expected healthcare resource consumption. It takes into account factors such as age, gender, diagnosis history, and healthcare service usage. By analyzing these variables, the ACG system provides a comprehensive picture of a population's health status and potential future healthcare needs.

For case managers, understanding the ACG system is crucial for developing care plans that are tailored to the specific needs of patients. It allows case managers to identify high-risk patients who may benefit from targeted interventions or more intensive management. Additionally, it supports decision-making processes related to cost management, quality improvement initiatives, and care coordination.

In summary, the Adjusted Clinical Group system is an essential tool in healthcare analytics that assists case managers in predicting patient needs and optimizing care delivery. By leveraging this system, case managers can enhance patient outcomes while efficiently managing healthcare resources.

3.5 Program Evaluation Methods:

Program evaluation methods are systematic approaches employed to assess the design, implementation, and outcomes of a program. For case managers, understanding these methods is crucial in determining the effectiveness and efficiency of healthcare interventions and services. The primary aim is to provide evidence-based insights that can guide decision-making, enhance program quality, and ensure optimal resource utilization.

There are several key methods used in program evaluation. Formative evaluation focuses on improving program design and delivery during its development phase. It involves collecting feedback to refine processes and ensure the program meets its objectives. Summative evaluation, on the other hand, assesses the overall impact and outcomes after program implementation. This method helps determine whether the goals were achieved and if the program should be continued, modified, or terminated.

Quantitative methods involve numerical data collection and statistical analysis to measure program outcomes objectively. Common techniques include surveys, experiments, and quasi-experimental designs. Qualitative methods, such as interviews, focus groups, and case studies, provide a deeper understanding of participant experiences and contextual factors influencing program success.

Mixed-methods evaluations integrate both quantitative and qualitative approaches to offer a comprehensive view of the program's effectiveness. This approach helps triangulate data to validate findings and provide robust conclusions.

For case managers preparing for the CCM exam, mastering these evaluation methods is essential for ensuring that healthcare programs effectively meet patient needs while maintaining accountability and transparency within healthcare systems.

3.6 Quality & Performance Improvement Concepts:
Quality and Performance Improvement (QPI) concepts are integral to the role of a case manager, focusing on enhancing healthcare delivery and patient outcomes. QPI involves systematic processes aimed at improving the quality of care, optimizing resource utilization, and ensuring patient satisfaction. These concepts are grounded in methodologies such as Plan-Do-Study-Act (PDSA), Six Sigma, and Lean Management, which provide structured frameworks for identifying inefficiencies and implementing effective solutions.

In the context of case management, QPI emphasizes the continuous assessment and refinement of care coordination processes. This includes evaluating the effectiveness of care plans, monitoring patient progress, and analyzing outcomes to identify areas for improvement. Data-driven decision-making is crucial, utilizing metrics such as readmission rates, patient satisfaction scores, and cost-effectiveness to guide improvements.

Case managers play a pivotal role in QPI by collaborating with interdisciplinary teams to develop evidence-based practices that enhance patient care. They must be adept at using performance data to advocate for necessary changes in protocols or resource allocation. Additionally, fostering a culture of quality improvement within healthcare settings is essential, encouraging all team members to contribute ideas and participate in initiatives aimed at enhancing service delivery.

Ultimately, mastering QPI concepts enables case managers to drive improvements that lead to better health outcomes, increased efficiency, and higher levels of patient satisfaction. Understanding these principles is critical for success in the CCM exam and in professional practice.

3.7 Quality Indicators And Applications:
Quality indicators are specific, measurable elements of healthcare that can be used to assess the quality of care provided by healthcare organizations. They serve as benchmarks for evaluating the effectiveness, efficiency, and safety of patient care services. In the context of case management, quality indicators are crucial for monitoring outcomes, identifying areas for improvement, and ensuring that care is patient-centered and evidence-based.

The application of quality indicators in case management involves using these metrics to guide decision-making processes and enhance service delivery. Case managers utilize quality indicators to track patient progress, evaluate the impact of interventions, and ensure compliance with established clinical guidelines. By analyzing data from quality indicators, case managers can identify trends, uncover gaps in care, and implement strategies to address them.

Furthermore, quality indicators facilitate communication among interdisciplinary teams by providing a common language for discussing patient outcomes and care processes. They also support accountability by enabling case managers to demonstrate the value of their services to stakeholders, including patients, healthcare providers, and payers.

In practice, case managers may apply quality indicators through tools such as performance dashboards and scorecards that visually represent key metrics. These tools help in setting targets for improvement and monitoring progress over time. Ultimately, the effective use of quality indicators in case management leads to enhanced patient satisfaction, improved health outcomes, and optimized resource utilization within healthcare systems.

3.8 Sources Of Quality Indicators:
Quality indicators are specific and measurable elements of healthcare that can be used to assess the quality of patient care and services. These indicators are essential for case managers to evaluate and improve healthcare outcomes. Sources of quality indicators include various organizations and systems that provide standardized metrics and benchmarks.

One primary source is the National Committee for Quality Assurance (NCQA), which develops quality measures known as the Healthcare Effectiveness Data and Information Set (HEDIS). HEDIS is widely used by health plans to measure performance on important dimensions of care and service.

The Centers for Medicare & Medicaid Services (CMS) also offer a wealth of quality indicators through programs like the Hospital Compare website, which provides data on hospital performance in areas such as patient satisfaction, readmission rates, and surgical complications.

Another vital source is The Joint Commission, which accredits healthcare organizations and sets performance standards. They offer the ORYX initiative, which integrates performance measurement into the accreditation process.

Additionally, the Agency for Healthcare Research and Quality (AHRQ) provides the Quality Indicators (QIs) toolkit, which includes measures for prevention, inpatient care, patient safety, and pediatric care.

Lastly, state health departments often develop region-specific quality indicators to address local health concerns. These sources collectively help case managers identify areas needing improvement, ensuring that high standards of care are maintained across healthcare settings. Understanding these sources allows case managers to effectively monitor performance and implement evidence-based interventions.

3.8.1 Overview of CMS:

The Centers for Medicare and Medicaid Services (CMS) is a federal agency within the United States Department of Health and Human Services (HHS) that administers the nation's major healthcare programs, including Medicare, Medicaid, and the Children's Health Insurance Program (CHIP). CMS plays a pivotal role in setting standards for quality care, ensuring healthcare access, and protecting beneficiary rights. It is instrumental in establishing healthcare policies and regulations that impact millions of Americans.

CMS is a critical source of quality indicators used by case managers to evaluate healthcare services. It develops and maintains various quality measurement programs, such as the Hospital Quality Initiative, which collects data on hospital performance to improve patient care. These indicators are essential for case managers to assess the effectiveness, safety, and efficiency of healthcare delivery systems.

Moreover, CMS is responsible for implementing value-based purchasing programs that incentivize providers to deliver high-quality care. Through initiatives like the Merit-based Incentive Payment System (MIPS), CMS encourages healthcare providers to focus on patient outcomes rather than service volume.

Case managers utilize CMS data to coordinate care effectively, ensuring that patients receive appropriate services at the right time. By understanding CMS guidelines and quality measures, case managers can advocate for patient-centered care while navigating complex healthcare systems. Consequently, proficiency in CMS regulations and quality indicators is imperative for case managers aiming to excel in their roles and contribute to improved healthcare outcomes.

3.8.2 URAC:

URAC, formerly known as the Utilization Review Accreditation Commission, is an independent, nonprofit organization that promotes healthcare quality through accreditation, education, and measurement. It establishes quality standards for the healthcare industry and provides a framework for organizations to demonstrate their commitment to quality and accountability. URAC accreditation is widely recognized as a symbol of excellence and compliance with industry best practices.

For case managers preparing for the CCM exam, understanding URAC's role is crucial. URAC develops rigorous standards across various healthcare sectors, including health plans, pharmacy benefits management, telehealth, and case management. These standards are designed to improve patient care by ensuring that healthcare organizations implement effective quality improvement processes and maintain high levels of service delivery.

URAC's accreditation process involves a comprehensive review of an organization's operations, policies, and procedures. This includes evaluating how an organization manages its case management services, ensuring they align with best practices for patient advocacy, care coordination, and resource utilization. By achieving URAC accreditation, organizations demonstrate their commitment to maintaining high-quality care standards and continuous improvement.

For case managers, familiarity with URAC standards is essential, as it underscores the importance of evidence-based practice and adherence to ethical guidelines in managing patient care. Understanding these principles helps case managers advocate effectively for patients while ensuring compliance with regulatory requirements. In essence, URAC serves as a benchmark for quality assurance in healthcare, guiding case managers in delivering optimal patient outcomes through structured and standardized processes.

3.8.3 NCQA Overview:

The National Committee for Quality Assurance (NCQA) is a pivotal organization in the healthcare sector, dedicated to improving the quality of healthcare delivered to patients. Established in 1990, NCQA is a non-profit entity that develops quality standards and performance measures for a broad range of healthcare entities. Its primary role is to evaluate and accredit health plans, ensuring they meet rigorous criteria related to quality management, utilization management, member satisfaction, and provider credentialing.

NCQA's Health Plan Accreditation is considered a benchmark for quality in the healthcare industry. It assesses health plans based on their ability to deliver high-quality care and services that meet the needs of their members. The accreditation process involves a comprehensive review of a health plan's operations and adherence to established standards.

Moreover, NCQA is renowned for its Healthcare Effectiveness Data and Information Set (HEDIS), which is one of the most widely used performance measurement tools in healthcare. HEDIS consists of over 90 measures across six domains of care, enabling consumers to compare the performance of health plans on an apples-to-apples basis.

For case managers preparing for the CCM exam, understanding NCQA's role is crucial, as it underscores the importance of quality indicators in evaluating and improving patient care. The NCQA's standards serve as a guide for case managers to ensure that their practices align with national benchmarks for quality and efficiency in healthcare delivery.

3.8.4 National Quality Forum:

The National Quality Forum (NQF) is a non-profit, nonpartisan organization dedicated to improving the quality of healthcare in the United States. It plays a critical role in setting national priorities and goals for performance improvement, endorsing standards for measuring and publicly reporting on performance, and promoting the attainment of national goals through education and outreach programs. Established in 1999, NQF brings together diverse stakeholders from across the healthcare spectrum, including consumers, providers, purchasers, and researchers, to foster consensus on performance measures that enhance healthcare quality.

NQF's endorsement process is rigorous and transparent, involving extensive review and input from its multi-stakeholder membership. This ensures that endorsed measures are evidence-based, reliable, and applicable across various healthcare settings. These measures cover a wide range of areas, such as patient safety, care coordination, and efficiency. For case managers, understanding NQF-endorsed measures is essential, as they directly influence care delivery models and reimbursement systems.

NQF also plays a pivotal role in shaping public policy by advising federal agencies like the Centers for Medicare & Medicaid Services (CMS) on quality measurement initiatives. Case managers should be well-versed in NQF's work to effectively advocate for quality care improvements within their organizations. By aligning care management practices with NQF-endorsed standards, case managers can enhance patient outcomes and contribute to the broader goal of achieving high-value healthcare.

3.8.5 AHRQ Overview:

The Agency for Healthcare Research and Quality (AHRQ) is a pivotal federal agency within the U.S. Department of Health and Human Services, dedicated to enhancing the quality, safety, efficiency, and effectiveness of healthcare for all Americans. AHRQ plays a crucial role in developing quality indicators that are essential for case managers to ensure optimal patient outcomes. These indicators serve as standardized measures that assess various aspects of healthcare quality, such as patient safety, clinical effectiveness, and patient-centered care.

AHRQ's mission is to produce evidence to make healthcare safer and improve quality by conducting research on healthcare systems, quality, costs, access, and outcomes. It provides tools and resources that help healthcare professionals and policymakers make informed decisions to improve care delivery. For case managers, understanding AHRQ's quality indicators is vital, as they provide benchmarks for evaluating the performance of healthcare services.

The agency supports the development of evidence-based guidelines and disseminates research findings to facilitate the implementation of best practices in healthcare settings. AHRQ also funds projects that aim to reduce medical errors and promote patient safety initiatives. By leveraging data from AHRQ's quality indicators, case managers can identify areas needing improvement and implement strategies to enhance care coordination and patient satisfaction.

In summary, AHRQ serves as a cornerstone in the landscape of healthcare quality improvement, providing essential resources that empower case managers to deliver high-quality care while effectively navigating the complexities of the healthcare system.

3.8.6 National Quality Strategy:

The National Quality Strategy (NQS) is a pivotal framework established by the U.S. Department of Health and Human Services (HHS) to guide and coordinate efforts to improve the quality of healthcare across the nation. It was developed in response to the Affordable Care Act's mandate to enhance healthcare delivery, patient outcomes, and overall system efficiency. The NQS serves as a blueprint for aligning public and private sector initiatives around three broad aims: better care, healthy people/healthy communities, and affordable care.

At its core, the NQS identifies six priorities that address the most common challenges in healthcare quality: making care safer by reducing harm caused in the delivery of care; ensuring that each person and family is engaged as partners in their care; promoting effective communication and coordination of care; promoting the most effective prevention and treatment practices for the leading causes of mortality; working with communities to promote the widespread use of best practices to enable healthy living; and making quality care more affordable for individuals, families, employers, and governments by developing and spreading new healthcare delivery models.

For case managers, understanding the NQS is crucial, as it influences policy-making, funding, and the implementation of quality improvement programs. By aligning with these priorities, case managers can effectively contribute to enhancing patient safety, improving care coordination, and optimizing resource utilization. This alignment ensures that case management practices are not only compliant with national standards but also actively contribute to transforming the healthcare landscape toward achieving higher quality care for all patients.

3.9 Types Of Quality Indicators:

Quality indicators are standardized, evidence-based measures of healthcare quality that can be used to gauge the performance of healthcare services. These indicators are crucial for case managers as they assess and improve patient care outcomes. There are three primary types of quality indicators: structure, process, and outcome indicators.

Structure indicators assess the attributes of the settings in which care occurs. They include the physical and organizational infrastructure, such as staffing levels, facility accreditation, and the availability of resources. These indicators help ensure that the necessary conditions for providing quality care are in place.

Process indicators measure the methods by which healthcare is provided. They focus on whether the services offered are consistent with current professional knowledge and guidelines. Examples include adherence to clinical guidelines, timely administration of medications, and the frequency of follow-up visits. Process indicators help identify areas where clinical practices can be improved.

Outcome indicators evaluate the results of healthcare services on patient health status. These include changes in health status attributable to healthcare, such as mortality rates, infection rates, and patient satisfaction scores. Outcome indicators provide direct evidence of the effectiveness of care and are critical in determining the ultimate impact on patients.

For case managers, understanding these types of quality indicators is essential for assessing healthcare delivery, identifying areas for improvement, and ensuring that patients receive high-quality care. Mastery of these concepts enables case managers to contribute effectively to enhancing healthcare systems and patient outcomes.

3.9.1 Clinical Quality Indicators:

Clinical quality indicators are measurable elements of healthcare services that reflect the quality of care provided to patients. These indicators are essential tools for case managers, as they help assess the effectiveness, safety, and efficiency of clinical interventions. They serve as benchmarks for evaluating clinical performance and ensuring that patient care meets established standards.

Clinical indicators typically focus on patient outcomes, processes of care, and adherence to clinical guidelines. For instance, they may include rates of hospital-acquired infections, readmission rates, or adherence to evidence-based protocols for managing chronic conditions such as diabetes or heart disease. These indicators provide valuable insights into the quality of clinical care delivered by healthcare providers.

For case managers, understanding and utilizing clinical quality indicators is crucial for coordinating care that is both effective and patient-centered. By analyzing these indicators, case managers can identify areas where improvements are needed, develop strategies to enhance care delivery, and monitor the impact of interventions over time. Moreover, clinical quality indicators facilitate communication among interdisciplinary teams by providing a common framework for discussing patient outcomes and care processes.

In preparation for the Certified Case Manager (CCM) exam, it is important for candidates to comprehend how clinical quality indicators are developed, measured, and applied in practice. This knowledge enables case managers to advocate for high-quality patient care and contribute to continuous improvement initiatives within healthcare organizations. Understanding these indicators is pivotal in ensuring that patients receive optimal clinical care aligned with best practice standards.

3.9.2 Financial Quality Indicators:

Financial quality indicators are metrics used to assess the economic efficiency and effectiveness of healthcare services. These indicators help case managers evaluate how well resources are being utilized to deliver patient care while maintaining financial viability. In the context of case management, financial indicators are crucial for ensuring that healthcare organizations can provide sustainable, high-quality care without unnecessary expenditures.

A comprehensive understanding of financial quality indicators involves analyzing cost-effectiveness, budget adherence, and resource allocation. Cost-effectiveness measures the balance between the costs incurred and the outcomes achieved, ensuring that interventions provide value for money. Budget adherence focuses on whether healthcare services are delivered within the allocated financial resources, preventing overspending that could jeopardize other aspects of patient care.

Resource allocation examines how effectively resources such as staff, equipment, and facilities are distributed to meet patient needs. Efficient resource allocation ensures that patients receive timely and appropriate care without wasteful practices.

Case managers must be adept at interpreting these indicators to make informed decisions that align with both clinical goals and financial constraints. This involves collaborating with financial departments to understand budgeting processes and identify areas where cost savings can be achieved without compromising care quality.

In summary, financial quality indicators are essential tools for case managers to ensure that healthcare delivery is both economically sustainable and clinically effective. Mastery of these indicators enables case managers to contribute to the strategic planning and operational efficiency of healthcare organizations, ultimately enhancing patient outcomes while maintaining fiscal responsibility.

3.9.3 Productivity:

Productivity in the context of case management refers to the efficiency with which case managers use their time and resources to achieve desired outcomes for clients. It is a measure of how effectively case managers can manage their caseloads, coordinate care, and facilitate client progress toward their health and wellness goals. High productivity implies that a case manager can maximize outputs (such as successful client outcomes) with minimal inputs (such as time and resources).

To enhance productivity, case managers need to employ effective time management strategies, prioritize tasks based on urgency and importance, and utilize technology to streamline processes. For instance, using electronic health records (EHRs) can reduce the time spent on documentation and allow for more focus on client interactions. Additionally, productivity can be improved through continuous professional development, which equips case managers with the latest skills and knowledge to handle complex cases efficiently.

Measuring productivity involves assessing both quantitative and qualitative indicators. Quantitative measures may include the number of cases managed per day or the average time spent per client. Qualitative measures might involve client satisfaction levels or the quality of care coordination. Balancing these measures ensures that increased productivity does not compromise the quality of care provided.

Ultimately, high productivity in case management contributes to better resource utilization, enhanced client satisfaction, and improved overall outcomes. It is a crucial quality indicator that reflects the effectiveness and efficiency of case management services within healthcare systems.

3.9.4 Utilization:

Utilization, in the context of case management and healthcare, refers to the efficient and effective use of healthcare services and resources to ensure optimal patient outcomes while maintaining cost-effectiveness. It involves assessing the necessity, appropriateness, and efficiency of medical services provided to patients. Utilization is a critical quality indicator, as it helps identify areas where healthcare services can be optimized, reducing unnecessary procedures and ensuring that patients receive the right care at the right time.

In practice, utilization encompasses several key activities. These include utilization review, which evaluates the medical necessity of proposed treatments or ongoing care; utilization management, which involves planning and coordinating care to ensure that resources are used effectively; and utilization control, which aims to prevent the overuse or misuse of healthcare services. Case managers play a pivotal role in these processes by collaborating with healthcare providers, insurers, and patients to develop care plans that align with evidence-based guidelines and individual patient needs.

Effective utilization management can lead to improved patient outcomes by ensuring timely access to appropriate care while minimizing wasteful spending. It requires a thorough understanding of healthcare systems, clinical guidelines, and patient advocacy. By focusing on utilization as a quality indicator, case managers contribute to the sustainability of healthcare systems by balancing cost containment with high-quality patient care. This ensures that healthcare resources are allocated efficiently, promoting both economic efficiency and patient satisfaction within the healthcare continuum.

3.9.5 Client Experience Of Care:

Client Experience of Care refers to clients' perceptions and interactions with the healthcare system, encompassing all aspects of care from the initial contact through follow-up. It is a vital quality indicator that reflects the degree to which care is patient-centered, respectful, and responsive to individual client preferences, needs, and values. This indicator assesses various dimensions, such as communication with healthcare providers, ease of access to services, physical comfort, emotional support, and involvement in decision-making.

For case managers, understanding Client Experience of Care is crucial, as it directly impacts client satisfaction, adherence to treatment plans, and overall health outcomes. Effective case management involves actively listening to clients' concerns, facilitating clear communication between clients and providers, and ensuring that care plans are tailored to meet individual needs. Moreover, case managers play a pivotal role in coordinating services across different sectors of the healthcare system to ensure seamless care transitions.

To evaluate Client Experience of Care, surveys such as the Consumer Assessment of Healthcare Providers and Systems (CAHPS) are commonly used. These tools provide valuable insights into areas where improvements are needed. By focusing on enhancing the client experience, healthcare organizations can foster trust, improve client engagement, and ultimately achieve better clinical outcomes.

In summary, Client Experience of Care is a comprehensive measure of how well healthcare services align with client expectations and contribute to positive health experiences. For case managers preparing for the CCM exam, mastering this concept is essential for delivering high-quality, patient-centered care.

3.10 Evidence-Based Case Management Guidelines:

Evidence-based care guidelines in case management refer to systematically developed protocols and recommendations that are derived from the best available clinical evidence, expert consensus, and patient preferences. These guidelines aim to optimize patient outcomes by integrating clinical expertise with the most current research findings. For case managers, adherence to evidence-based guidelines ensures that they provide care that is both effective and efficient while aligning with the latest standards of practice.

The process of implementing evidence-based care involves several critical steps. Firstly, case managers must stay informed about the latest research and updates in their field through continuous education and professional development. This knowledge allows them to critically appraise and apply relevant studies to their practice. Secondly, these guidelines require adaptation to individual patient needs, considering factors such as comorbidities, cultural preferences, and personal values. This patient-centered approach ensures that care plans are tailored and relevant.

Additionally, case managers play a pivotal role in coordinating interdisciplinary teams to ensure that all aspects of patient care adhere to these evidence-based standards. They act as liaisons between healthcare providers, patients, and families to facilitate communication and ensure compliance with treatment protocols.

Overall, evidence-based care guidelines serve as a foundation for decision-making in case management. By consistently applying these principles, case managers can enhance the quality of care delivered, improve patient satisfaction, and contribute to more favorable health outcomes.

4 Rehabilitation Concepts And Strategies:

Rehabilitation Concepts and Strategies encompass a systematic approach aimed at restoring, maintaining, and enhancing the physical, cognitive, and emotional well-being of individuals who have experienced illness or injury. This process is integral to helping patients achieve optimal functionality and independence, tailored to their unique needs and goals. Rehabilitation is multidisciplinary, involving collaboration among healthcare professionals such as physicians, nurses, physical therapists, occupational therapists, speech-language pathologists, and social workers.

The core concept of rehabilitation is patient-centered care, which emphasizes personalized treatment plans that consider the patient's preferences, goals, and social context. Strategies employed in rehabilitation are diverse and depend on the specific condition being addressed. They may include therapeutic exercises to improve strength and mobility, cognitive-behavioral therapy to enhance mental health resilience, or adaptive technologies to support daily living activities.

Effective rehabilitation strategies also involve goal setting and continuous evaluation. Goals should be Specific, Measurable, Achievable, Relevant, and Time-bound (SMART) to ensure that progress can be tracked effectively. Regular assessments allow for adjustments in the treatment plan to address any emerging challenges or changes in the patient's condition.

Additionally, education plays a pivotal role in rehabilitation by empowering patients with knowledge about their conditions and self-management techniques. This fosters autonomy and encourages active participation in their recovery journey. Overall, successful rehabilitation requires an integrated approach that bridges medical treatment with supportive care to facilitate holistic recovery and improve quality of life.

4.1 Adaptive Technologies:

Adaptive technologies refer to specialized devices or software designed to assist individuals with disabilities in performing tasks that might otherwise be challenging or impossible. These technologies aim to enhance the functional capabilities of individuals, allowing them to live more independently and participate fully in various aspects of life, including work, education, and social activities.

Adaptive technologies encompass a wide range of tools tailored to meet diverse needs. For instance, mobility aids such as wheelchairs and walkers facilitate movement for individuals with physical impairments. Communication devices, like speech-generating devices or text-to-speech software, support those with speech or language difficulties. For individuals with visual impairments, screen readers and braille displays convert text into audible speech or tactile feedback.

In the realm of rehabilitation, adaptive technologies are crucial for fostering recovery and improving quality of life. They are often integrated into personalized care plans by case managers who assess individual needs and recommend suitable technologies. This process involves collaboration with interdisciplinary teams to ensure that selected tools align with therapeutic goals and client preferences.

Moreover, adaptive technologies are continually evolving with advancements in technology, leading to more innovative solutions such as smart home systems and wearable devices that monitor health metrics. Case managers must stay informed about these developments to effectively advocate for their clients and facilitate access to appropriate resources.

Understanding adaptive technologies is essential for case managers, as they play a pivotal role in empowering clients to overcome barriers and achieve greater autonomy in their daily lives.

4.1.1 Text Telephone Device: Adaptive Technology

Adaptive Technologies: Text Telephone Device

A Text Telephone Device (TTY), also known as a Telecommunication Device for the Deaf (TDD), is a specialized piece of equipment that enables individuals with hearing or speech impairments to communicate over the telephone network. This device is essential for ensuring accessibility and inclusivity in communication, particularly for those who are deaf, hard of hearing, or have speech difficulties.

The TTY operates by converting typed text into signals that can be transmitted over standard telephone lines. When a TTY user types a message on the device's keyboard, it is sent as an audio signal to another TTY device, where it appears on the display screen for the recipient to read. Conversely, incoming messages are received and displayed in text form, allowing for two-way communication without the need for spoken words.

Case managers should understand the significance of TTY devices in facilitating independence and equal access to communication for clients with disabilities. Familiarity with how these devices function is crucial for recommending appropriate adaptive technologies that align with clients' needs. Additionally, case managers must be aware of related services like Telecommunications Relay Services (TRS), which provide intermediary assistance between TTY users and standard voice telephone users.

In conclusion, TTY devices represent a vital component of adaptive technology strategies within rehabilitation contexts. By enabling effective communication, they empower individuals with hearing and speech challenges to engage more fully in personal and professional interactions, thereby enhancing their quality of life and participation in society.

4.1.2 Teletypewriter (TTY):

A Teletypewriter (TTY) is an assistive communication device that facilitates written communication over telephone lines for individuals who are deaf, hard of hearing, or speech-impaired. This technology translates typed text into electrical signals that are transmitted via phone lines and then converted back into text on the receiving end, allowing users to engage in real-time conversations.

The TTY consists of a keyboard and a display screen. Users type messages on the keyboard, which are then sent as signals through the phone line. The recipient's TTY converts these signals back into text, which appears on their display screen, enabling two-way communication. Some TTY devices also include a printer to provide a hard copy of the conversation.

For case managers, understanding the role and functionality of TTY is crucial when coordinating care for clients with communication impairments. It ensures that these individuals have equitable access to telecommunication services, thereby enhancing their ability to communicate with healthcare providers, emergency services, and support networks.

Moreover, TTY devices are often integrated with relay services, where an operator assists in translating spoken words into text and vice versa, bridging communication between TTY users and those using standard telephones. This integration underscores the importance of adaptive technologies in promoting inclusivity and accessibility within healthcare settings.

In summary, the Teletypewriter is a vital adaptive technology that empowers individuals with hearing or speech disabilities by providing them with a reliable means of communication over telephone networks. Understanding its application is essential for case managers in delivering comprehensive and inclusive care.

4.1.3 Telecommunication Devices for the Deaf:
A Telecommunication Device for the Deaf (TDD), also known as a text telephone (TTY) or telecommunications device for the deaf, is an assistive technology that enables individuals with hearing impairments to communicate over telephone lines. This device is essential for facilitating effective communication for those who are deaf or hard of hearing, ensuring they have equal access to telecommunication services.

The TDD operates by converting typed messages into electrical signals that can be transmitted over phone lines. The recipient's TDD then translates these signals back into text, which appears on a display screen. This allows users to read and type responses in real-time, mimicking a conversation. TDDs often include a keyboard and a small display screen, and some models may also have printers to produce a hard copy of the conversation.

In contemporary practice, TDDs are increasingly integrated with other technologies, such as computers and smartphones, allowing for more versatile communication options. With advancements in digital communication, video relay services (VRS) and real-time text (RTT) have also become popular alternatives, offering enhanced accessibility features.

For case managers, understanding the functionality and application of TDDs is crucial when developing care plans for clients with hearing impairments. Ensuring that clients have access to appropriate telecommunication devices supports their autonomy and facilitates better engagement with healthcare providers and support networks. Familiarity with adaptive technologies like TDDs underscores the commitment to inclusive care practices and enhances case management effectiveness.

4.1.4 Orientation and Mobility Services:
Orientation and Mobility (O&M) services are specialized services designed to assist individuals with visual impairments in navigating their environments safely and independently. These services are crucial for promoting autonomy and enhancing the quality of life for those who are blind or have low vision. O&M services involve teaching skills that enable individuals to understand their spatial environment and move through it effectively.

A key component of O&M services is orientation, which involves understanding one's position in space relative to other objects and landmarks. This skill is critical for developing a mental map of the surroundings, which aids in navigation. Mobility refers to the physical movement through an environment, often using techniques such as trailing, protective techniques, and the use of mobility aids like white canes or guide dogs.

O&M specialists work with clients to develop personalized training programs that address specific needs and goals. Training may include learning how to use public transportation, crossing streets safely, or navigating complex indoor environments such as shopping malls or office buildings. The ultimate goal is to foster confidence and independence, enabling individuals to engage fully in daily activities.

For case managers, understanding the scope and benefits of O&M services is essential when coordinating care for clients with visual impairments. They play a pivotal role in ensuring access to these services, advocating for necessary resources, and collaborating with O&M specialists to support the client's rehabilitation journey. Through comprehensive planning and support, case managers help clients achieve greater independence and an improved quality of life.

4.2 Functional Capacity Evaluation (FCE):
A Functional Capacity Evaluation (FCE) is a comprehensive assessment process used to determine an individual's capacity to perform work-related tasks. It is a critical tool for case managers, particularly in the context of rehabilitation and return-to-work planning. The FCE evaluates an individual's physical and functional abilities, identifying both strengths and limitations in relation to specific job demands.

The evaluation typically involves a series of standardized tests and observations that assess various physical functions, such as lifting, carrying, pushing, pulling, and other job-specific tasks. Additionally, it may include assessments of endurance, flexibility, balance, and coordination. The FCE aims to provide objective data regarding the individual's ability to safely perform work activities over a sustained period.

Case managers utilize FCE results to make informed decisions about an individual's readiness to return to work or the need for workplace modifications or accommodations. The evaluation helps establish baseline functional abilities and set realistic goals for rehabilitation. It also plays a role in determining eligibility for disability benefits or workers' compensation claims.

In practice, FCEs are conducted by trained professionals, such as occupational therapists or physical therapists, who have expertise in evaluating functional performance. The results are documented in a detailed report that outlines the individual's capabilities and any identified limitations. This information is crucial for developing personalized rehabilitation plans aimed at maximizing the individual's potential for safe and productive employment.

4.3 Post-Hospitalization Rehabilitation:

Rehabilitation following hospitalization or an acute health condition refers to the coordinated process of recovery and therapy designed to restore a patient's functional ability and quality of life after a hospital stay or acute health event. This process is crucial for patients who have experienced significant medical events, such as surgeries, strokes, or severe injuries, which may impair their physical, cognitive, or emotional abilities.

The primary goal of rehabilitation is to assist patients in regaining independence and returning to their daily activities as safely and efficiently as possible. It involves a multidisciplinary approach that includes physical therapy, occupational therapy, speech-language therapy, and sometimes psychological counseling. Case managers play a vital role in coordinating these services to ensure a seamless transition from the hospital to home or another care setting.

Effective rehabilitation requires the development of an individualized care plan based on the patient's specific needs, goals, and potential for improvement. This plan should be regularly reviewed and adjusted as the patient progresses. Case managers must also consider the patient's social support system, financial resources, and potential barriers to accessing care.

Furthermore, case managers are responsible for educating patients and their families about the rehabilitation process, expected outcomes, and self-management strategies. They must also facilitate communication among healthcare providers to optimize care continuity and prevent readmissions. By effectively managing the rehabilitation process, case managers contribute significantly to improving patient outcomes and enhancing their quality of life following hospitalization or an acute health condition.

4.4 Vocational & Rehabilitation Service Systems:

Vocational and Rehabilitation Service Delivery Systems are structured frameworks designed to assist individuals with disabilities or impairments in achieving their optimal level of independence and employment. These systems encompass a range of services, including assessment, counseling, training, job placement, and support services tailored to meet the unique needs of each client.

The primary goal is to facilitate the integration or reintegration of individuals into the workforce by addressing barriers to employment. This involves a comprehensive evaluation of the individual's skills, interests, and limitations to develop a personalized rehabilitation plan. Services often include physical therapy, occupational therapy, job coaching, and adaptive technology training.

Case managers play a crucial role in coordinating these services, ensuring that clients receive appropriate interventions and support throughout the rehabilitation process. They work collaboratively with healthcare providers, employers, and community resources to create an inclusive environment that promotes successful employment outcomes.

Effective service delivery systems emphasize client-centered approaches, empowering individuals to actively participate in their rehabilitation journey. This includes setting realistic goals, monitoring progress, and adjusting plans as necessary to accommodate changes in the client's condition or circumstances.

Understanding the intricacies of these systems is vital for case managers preparing for the Certified Case Manager (CCM) exam. Mastery of this topic ensures that they can effectively advocate for their clients' needs, navigate complex service networks, and contribute to positive rehabilitation outcomes.

4.5 Vocational Aspects of Disability and Illness:

The vocational aspects of disabilities and illnesses pertain to how these conditions impact an individual's ability to engage in work-related activities. Case managers must understand these aspects to effectively support clients in achieving optimal employment outcomes. Disabilities and illnesses can affect work capacity, productivity, and the ability to perform specific job functions, necessitating accommodations or modifications in the workplace.

A comprehensive evaluation of a client's vocational potential involves assessing their physical, cognitive, and emotional capabilities in relation to their job requirements. This assessment helps identify any barriers to employment and facilitates the development of a tailored vocational rehabilitation plan. The plan may include job training, skill enhancement, or education to align the client's abilities with suitable employment opportunities.

Furthermore, case managers must be knowledgeable about legal frameworks such as the Americans with Disabilities Act (ADA), which mandates reasonable accommodations for employees with disabilities. Understanding these regulations ensures that clients receive appropriate support and protection in the workplace.

Case managers also play a critical role in coordinating with employers, vocational rehabilitation specialists, and other stakeholders to foster an inclusive work environment. They advocate for necessary adjustments and provide resources to both clients and employers, enhancing job retention and satisfaction.

In summary, addressing the vocational aspects of disabilities and illnesses involves a holistic approach that considers individual capabilities, workplace accommodations, and legal protections. This ensures that clients can achieve meaningful and sustainable employment despite their health challenges.

4.5.1 Job Analysis And Accommodation:

Job analysis is a systematic process of gathering, documenting, and analyzing information about the responsibilities, necessary skills, outcomes, and work environment of a particular job. For case managers, understanding job analysis is crucial in assessing how disabilities or illnesses impact an individual's ability to perform their job functions. This involves identifying essential job duties and determining the physical, mental, and emotional requirements needed to perform these tasks effectively.

Accommodation refers to modifications or adjustments to a job or work environment that enable an individual with a disability or illness to perform essential job functions. Under the Americans with Disabilities Act (ADA), employers are required to provide reasonable accommodations unless doing so would cause undue hardship on the operation of the business. Examples of accommodations include modifying work schedules, altering workstations, providing assistive technology, or reassigning non-essential tasks.

Case managers play a pivotal role in facilitating communication between employees and employers to ensure that appropriate accommodations are implemented. They assess the individual's capabilities and limitations, collaborate with medical professionals for recommendations, and advocate for the necessary changes within the workplace. By doing so, they help maintain employment continuity and enhance the quality of life for individuals with disabilities or illnesses.

Understanding job analysis and accommodations allows case managers to effectively support clients in overcoming barriers to employment. This knowledge ensures that individuals can achieve their vocational goals while complying with legal standards and promoting an inclusive work environment.

4.5.2 Life Care Planning:

Life Care Planning is a comprehensive process aimed at developing a detailed, individualized plan that addresses the future medical and supportive care needs of individuals with chronic health conditions or disabilities. It serves as a roadmap for managing the long-term care of patients, ensuring that their medical, psychological, and social needs are met throughout their lifetime. This plan is typically created by a certified life care planner, who collaborates with various healthcare professionals to assess the patient's current and anticipated needs.

The process begins with a thorough evaluation of the patient's medical history, current condition, and prognosis. The life care planner considers all aspects of the patient's life, including daily living activities, mobility, therapies, medications, assistive devices, and potential complications. The goal is to anticipate future needs and provide recommendations for interventions that can enhance the patient's quality of life.

Life Care Planning also involves financial planning to estimate the costs associated with ongoing care and to identify funding sources such as insurance benefits or government programs. By providing a structured approach to long-term care management, life care plans help patients and their families make informed decisions about treatment options and resource allocation.

For case managers preparing for the CCM exam, understanding Life Care Planning is crucial, as it underscores the importance of interdisciplinary collaboration in creating sustainable care strategies that align with patients' goals and preferences while optimizing resource use.

4.6 Rehabilitation Concepts:

Rehabilitation concepts encompass a range of strategies and interventions designed to assist individuals in recovering, maintaining, or enhancing their physical, mental, and social capabilities following illness, injury, or disability. The primary goal of rehabilitation is to enable individuals to achieve optimal functioning and independence in daily activities. This involves a holistic approach that considers the physical, emotional, psychological, and social aspects of a person's health.

Key components of rehabilitation include assessment, goal setting, therapeutic interventions, and evaluation. Assessment involves identifying the individual's needs, strengths, and limitations. Goal setting is collaborative, involving both the patient and the healthcare team in establishing realistic and achievable objectives. Therapeutic interventions may include physical therapy to improve mobility and strength, occupational therapy to enhance daily living skills, speech therapy for communication challenges, and psychological support to address mental health needs.

Case managers play a crucial role in coordinating these services, ensuring that care plans are tailored to individual needs and that resources are utilized efficiently. They facilitate communication among healthcare providers, patients, and families to promote continuity of care.

Rehabilitation also emphasizes patient education and self-management strategies to empower individuals in their recovery journey. By fostering an environment of support and encouragement, rehabilitation aims to improve quality of life and promote reintegration into the community. Understanding these concepts is vital for case managers as they navigate complex healthcare systems to advocate for their clients' best interests.

4.6.1 Medical Rehabilitation:

Medical rehabilitation is a comprehensive, patient-centered process aimed at restoring individuals to their highest possible level of function and independence following illness, injury, or surgery. It encompasses a wide range of interventions designed to address physical, mental, and social impairments. The primary goal of medical rehabilitation is to enhance the quality of life for patients by improving their functional abilities and promoting self-sufficiency.

Rehabilitation involves a multidisciplinary team approach, typically including physicians, nurses, physical therapists, occupational therapists, speech-language pathologists, and social workers. Each team member contributes specialized expertise to develop a personalized rehabilitation plan tailored to the patient's unique needs and goals. This plan focuses on maximizing the patient's strengths while addressing any limitations.

Key components of medical rehabilitation include assessment, goal setting, therapeutic interventions, education, and evaluation. Assessment involves identifying the patient's current level of function and potential for improvement. Goal setting establishes realistic and achievable objectives for recovery. Therapeutic interventions may include exercises to improve strength and mobility, techniques to enhance communication skills, and strategies to adapt daily activities for greater independence. Education empowers patients and their families with knowledge about managing their condition and preventing complications.

Evaluation is an ongoing process that measures progress toward goals and adjusts the rehabilitation plan as needed. Successful medical rehabilitation requires active participation from the patient and collaboration among healthcare providers. By facilitating recovery and adaptation, medical rehabilitation plays a crucial role in helping individuals regain control over their lives and reintegrate into their communities.

4.6.2 Substance Use Rehabilitation:
Substance use rehabilitation refers to a structured program aimed at helping individuals who are struggling with substance use disorders achieve and maintain sobriety. This rehabilitation process is comprehensive, addressing not only the physical aspects of addiction but also the psychological, social, and behavioral components. It often involves a combination of medical detoxification, counseling, therapy, and support groups.

The primary goal of substance use rehabilitation is to enable individuals to stop using substances, manage withdrawal symptoms, and develop coping strategies to prevent relapse. Medical detoxification is usually the first step, during which healthcare professionals supervise the safe elimination of substances from the body. This is followed by various forms of therapy, such as cognitive-behavioral therapy (CBT), which helps patients identify and change negative thought patterns and behaviors associated with substance use.

Case managers play a crucial role in coordinating care during rehabilitation by assessing individual needs, developing personalized treatment plans, and connecting clients with appropriate resources. They also provide ongoing support and monitor progress throughout the recovery journey. Additionally, case managers educate clients about the importance of lifestyle changes and help them build a supportive network to sustain long-term recovery.

Understanding the complexities of substance use rehabilitation is essential for case managers as they guide clients through their recovery process. This knowledge ensures that they can effectively advocate for their clients' needs and facilitate access to comprehensive care services tailored to each individual's unique circumstances.

4.6.3 Vocational Rehabilitation:
Vocational Rehabilitation is a process designed to enable individuals with disabilities or impairments to attain and maintain employment. This service is crucial in helping clients overcome barriers that hinder their ability to work, thereby enhancing their independence and quality of life. It involves a comprehensive evaluation of the individual's skills, interests, and limitations, followed by the development of a tailored plan that addresses their specific needs.

The process begins with an assessment conducted by a vocational rehabilitation counselor. This assessment evaluates the client's physical, emotional, and cognitive abilities in relation to potential job opportunities. Based on these findings, a personalized rehabilitation plan is created, which may include job training, career counseling, resume preparation, and assistance with job placement.

Case Managers play a pivotal role in coordinating these services. They collaborate with healthcare providers, employers, and educational institutions to ensure that the client receives comprehensive support. Additionally, they advocate for reasonable workplace accommodations under the Americans with Disabilities Act (ADA) to facilitate successful employment outcomes.

Vocational Rehabilitation also emphasizes skill development and education. Clients may be enrolled in courses or workshops that enhance their employability skills. Moreover, it includes ongoing support and follow-up to address any challenges that arise during employment.

Overall, Vocational Rehabilitation is an essential component of case management that empowers individuals to achieve economic self-sufficiency and social integration through meaningful employment. Case Managers must be adept at navigating this process to effectively support their clients' vocational goals.

4.6.4 Return To Work Strategies:
Return to Work (RTW) strategies are comprehensive plans designed to facilitate the reintegration of an individual into the workplace after an injury, illness, or disability. These strategies aim to optimize the recovery process while ensuring that the employee can safely perform their job duties. A successful RTW strategy is a collaborative effort involving case managers, employers, healthcare providers, and the employee.

Key components of RTW strategies include a thorough assessment of the employee's medical condition and functional capabilities. This involves understanding any limitations or accommodations needed to support a safe return to work. Case managers play a crucial role in coordinating communication between all parties, ensuring that everyone is informed and aligned on the employee's progress and needs.

RTW strategies often involve transitional work programs or modified duties that allow the employee to gradually resume their responsibilities without compromising their health. These programs are tailored to match the employee's current abilities and may include reduced hours, altered tasks, or ergonomic adjustments.

Effective RTW strategies also incorporate ongoing monitoring and evaluation to address any emerging issues promptly. This ensures that adjustments can be made as necessary to support the employee's continued recovery and work performance.

Ultimately, RTW strategies aim not only to reduce absenteeism and associated costs but also to promote a supportive work environment that values employee well-being and productivity. By implementing these strategies, case managers help facilitate a smoother transition back to work, benefiting both the employee and the employer.

4.7 Job Analysis and Accommodation Strategies:

Job analysis involves a systematic process to identify and determine the duties, responsibilities, necessary skills, outcomes, and work environment of a particular job. It is crucial for case managers to understand job analysis, as it forms the foundation for hiring, training, performance evaluation, and compensation. By conducting a thorough job analysis, case managers can ensure that job descriptions accurately reflect the requirements and expectations of a position, which is essential for matching clients with suitable employment opportunities.

Job accommodation refers to adjustments or modifications made to a job or work environment that enable individuals with disabilities to perform their job duties effectively. Case managers must be adept at identifying reasonable accommodations that comply with the Americans with Disabilities Act (ADA). This may include modifying work schedules, altering physical workspaces, providing assistive technology, or restructuring job tasks. Understanding job accommodation helps case managers advocate for their clients' needs while ensuring compliance with legal standards.

Job modification involves altering specific aspects of a job to better fit an employee's capabilities or limitations. This can include changing the way tasks are performed or redistributing job duties among team members. For case managers, understanding job modification is essential in developing return-to-work plans for clients recovering from illness or injury. Effective job modification strategies help maintain productivity while supporting an individual's health and well-being.

In summary, proficiency in job analysis, accommodation, and modification allows case managers to effectively support clients in achieving sustainable employment outcomes tailored to their unique needs and abilities.

4.8 Life Care Planning:

Life Care Planning is a comprehensive, dynamic process utilized by case managers to project the lifelong needs and associated costs for individuals with catastrophic injuries or chronic health conditions. It involves a multidisciplinary approach that integrates medical, psychological, vocational, and social aspects to ensure that the patient receives optimal care throughout their lifetime.

The primary objective of Life Care Planning is to create a detailed plan that outlines current and future needs, including medical treatments, therapies, equipment, and support services. This plan serves as a roadmap for managing the patient's condition effectively while maximizing their quality of life. It requires collaboration among healthcare providers, patients, families, and, at times, legal representatives to ensure that all aspects of the individual's care are addressed comprehensively.

A Life Care Plan is typically developed after a thorough assessment of the individual's medical history, current health status, and potential future complications. The plan also considers the financial implications of long-term care and may include cost projections for various services and interventions. This financial component is crucial for securing necessary funding from insurance companies or legal settlements.

Case managers play a pivotal role in Life Care Planning by coordinating assessments, facilitating communication among stakeholders, and continuously updating the plan as the patient's condition evolves. Their expertise ensures that all elements of care are aligned with best practices and tailored to meet the unique needs of each patient. Through effective Life Care Planning, case managers help optimize resource utilization while enhancing patient outcomes over time.

4.9 Work Adjustment & Transitional Employment Strategies:

Work adjustment refers to the process of helping individuals develop the necessary skills and behaviors to meet the demands of the workplace. This includes enhancing interpersonal skills, time management, and adapting to workplace norms. The goal is to facilitate a smoother transition into employment for those who may have been out of work due to illness, injury, or other personal challenges.

Transitional employment is a strategy used to provide individuals with temporary work opportunities that serve as a bridge to permanent employment. These positions are often part-time or short-term and are designed to help individuals gain work experience, build confidence, and develop job-specific skills. Transitional employment can be particularly beneficial for those re-entering the workforce after a significant absence or for those with disabilities seeking to integrate into competitive employment settings.

Work hardening is a highly structured program designed to help individuals regain their physical and functional capabilities following an injury or illness. It involves simulated or real work tasks that are progressively more demanding and tailored to the individual's job requirements. The focus is on improving strength, endurance, and work-related skills in a controlled environment. Work hardening aims to prepare individuals for a safe return to their previous employment or similar roles by ensuring they can meet the physical demands of their job.

Together, these concepts form a comprehensive approach to vocational rehabilitation, aiding individuals in achieving successful and sustainable employment outcomes.

5   Ethical and Legal Practice Standards:

Ethical, legal, and practice standards are foundational elements that guide case managers in their professional roles, ensuring accountability, integrity, and excellence in practice. Ethical standards involve adhering to a set of moral principles that prioritize the welfare and rights of clients. These principles include maintaining confidentiality, obtaining informed consent, and demonstrating respect for client autonomy. Case managers must act with honesty and transparency, avoiding conflicts of interest to uphold trust.

Legal standards encompass adherence to laws and regulations relevant to case management practice. This includes understanding healthcare laws such as the Health Insurance Portability and Accountability Act (HIPAA), which safeguards patient information, and being aware of state-specific licensure requirements. Legal compliance ensures that case managers practice within the boundaries of the law, protecting both clients and practitioners from legal repercussions.

Practice standards refer to the professional guidelines established by governing bodies like the Commission for Case Manager Certification (CCMC). These standards outline the competencies necessary for effective case management, including assessment, planning, facilitation, care coordination, evaluation, and advocacy. Adhering to these standards promotes consistency in service delivery and enhances the quality of care provided.

Together, these standards create a framework that supports ethical decision-making and professional conduct. Case managers must continuously educate themselves on evolving ethical dilemmas and legal mandates while striving to meet practice standards. This commitment not only enhances their professional credibility but also ensures optimal outcomes for clients.

5.1 Case Recording And Documentation:

Case recording and documentation are critical components of case management, serving as the backbone for effective communication, continuity of care, and legal protection. In the context of case management, recording refers to the systematic process of capturing relevant client information, interventions, and outcomes. Documentation encompasses the accurate and detailed written records that reflect the assessment, planning, implementation, coordination, monitoring, and evaluation activities conducted by case managers.

Effective documentation ensures that all team members have access to consistent and comprehensive client information, facilitating coordinated care and informed decision-making. It includes client demographics, medical history, psychosocial assessments, care plans, progress notes, and any changes in client status or interventions. Documentation should be clear, concise, objective, and timely to maintain its utility and relevance.

From a legal standpoint, proper documentation serves as evidence of the services provided and decisions made throughout the case management process. It is essential for compliance with regulatory requirements and ethical standards. Inadequate or inaccurate documentation can lead to misunderstandings among care providers, potential harm to clients, and legal liabilities.

Moreover, documentation supports quality assurance and improvement efforts by providing data for evaluating the effectiveness of interventions and identifying areas for enhancement. Case managers must adhere to confidentiality standards while ensuring that records are accessible only to authorized personnel. Mastery of case recording and documentation is vital for case managers to uphold professional practice standards and deliver high-quality, client-centered care.

5.2 Ethics in Care Delivery:

Ethics related to care delivery encompasses the moral principles and standards that guide case managers in their professional duties. It involves ensuring that all actions and decisions prioritize patient welfare, respect autonomy, maintain confidentiality, and promote justice. Case managers must adhere to ethical codes, such as those outlined by the Commission for Case Manager Certification (CCMC), which emphasize integrity, accountability, and advocacy.

An essential aspect of ethics in care delivery is informed consent. Case managers must ensure that patients receive comprehensive information about their treatment options, enabling them to make informed decisions. This approach respects the patient's autonomy and right to self-determination.

Confidentiality is another critical component. Case managers are entrusted with sensitive patient information and must protect this data from unauthorized access or disclosure, adhering to legal standards such as HIPAA.

Advocacy plays a significant role in ethical care delivery. Case managers must act in the best interest of their clients, advocating for necessary services and resources while navigating complex healthcare systems.

Justice involves ensuring equitable access to care and resources, regardless of a patient's background or socioeconomic status. Case managers should work to eliminate disparities in healthcare delivery.

Finally, professional boundaries must be maintained to avoid conflicts of interest and ensure objectivity. Ethical dilemmas may arise, requiring case managers to engage in reflective practice and seek guidance from ethical frameworks or committees when necessary.

In summary, ethics in care delivery requires a balanced approach that respects patient rights while adhering to professional standards and legal requirements.

5.2.1 Principles:

The principles of ethics related to care delivery are foundational guidelines that ensure case managers uphold the highest standards of professional conduct and patient care. These principles include autonomy, beneficence, non-maleficence, justice, fidelity, and veracity.

Autonomy emphasizes respecting the client's right to make informed decisions about their own care. Case managers must ensure that clients are fully informed and supported in their decision-making processes. Beneficence involves acting in the best interest of the client, promoting their well-being, and providing beneficial interventions.

Non-maleficence requires case managers to avoid causing harm. This principle underscores the importance of risk assessment and mitigation strategies in care delivery. Justice relates to fairness and equality in providing care, ensuring that resources are distributed equitably and that all clients have access to necessary services, regardless of their background or circumstances.

Fidelity refers to being faithful to commitments made to clients and maintaining trust through honesty and integrity. This includes confidentiality and honoring agreements made with clients. Veracity involves truthfulness and transparency in communication with clients, ensuring they have accurate information to make informed choices.

These ethical principles guide case managers in navigating complex care scenarios, balancing client needs with available resources, and addressing ethical dilemmas. Adherence to these principles fosters trust, enhances client satisfaction, and upholds the integrity of the case management profession. Understanding and applying these principles is crucial for case managers preparing for the CCM exam, as they form the ethical backbone of effective care delivery.

5.2.2 Advocacy:

Advocacy in case management is the process of supporting and promoting the interests and rights of clients to ensure they receive optimal care and services. It involves acting as a liaison between clients and healthcare providers, payers, and other stakeholders to facilitate access to necessary resources, services, and information. Advocacy is rooted in the ethical obligation of case managers to uphold client autonomy, dignity, and respect while navigating complex healthcare systems.

Case managers must be adept at identifying client needs, understanding their preferences, and effectively communicating these to relevant parties. This requires a comprehensive understanding of healthcare policies, community resources, and legal rights pertinent to the client's situation. Advocacy extends beyond securing medical treatment; it includes addressing social determinants of health, such as housing, education, and employment, that impact overall well-being.

Effective advocacy involves building trusting relationships with clients, empowering them to voice their concerns, and educating them about their rights and options. Case managers must remain objective and unbiased, ensuring that personal beliefs do not interfere with the client's best interests. They should also be skilled in negotiation and conflict resolution to address any barriers or disputes that may arise during care coordination.

Ultimately, advocacy in case management aims to enhance client outcomes by ensuring equitable access to quality care while respecting individual values and choices. It is a dynamic process that requires vigilance, empathy, and a commitment to ethical practice in all interactions.

5.2.3 Experimental Treatments:

Experimental treatments refer to medical interventions that are in the investigational phase and have not yet been approved by regulatory bodies such as the FDA for general use. These treatments are typically part of clinical trials designed to evaluate their safety, efficacy, and potential benefits compared to standard therapies. For case managers, understanding the ethical implications of experimental treatments is crucial, as these interventions often involve unproven methods with unknown risks and benefits.

In the context of care delivery, case managers must ensure that patients are fully informed about the nature of experimental treatments. This includes discussing potential risks, benefits, and alternatives, as well as obtaining informed consent. Case managers play a pivotal role in coordinating communication between patients, healthcare providers, and research teams to ensure that patient autonomy and rights are respected throughout the trial process.

Moreover, case managers should be aware of regulatory requirements and institutional review board (IRB) guidelines governing experimental treatments. They must advocate for patient safety and ethical standards while facilitating access to potentially life-saving interventions. Balancing hope with realism is essential, as patients may view experimental treatments as their last resort.

Overall, case managers must possess a thorough understanding of the ethical considerations surrounding experimental treatments to guide patients effectively through complex decision-making processes. By doing so, they uphold the integrity of care delivery while supporting innovative medical advancements.

5.2.4 End Of Life:

End-of-life refers to the phase in a patient's life when they are living with a terminal condition and death is imminent. This period can vary significantly in duration and is characterized by the need for comprehensive care that addresses physical, emotional, social, and spiritual needs. For case managers, understanding end-of-life care is essential, as it involves coordinating a multidisciplinary approach to ensure quality of life for patients and support for their families.

During this phase, ethical considerations become paramount. Case managers must facilitate discussions about advance directives, ensuring that patients' wishes regarding treatment preferences are respected. This includes decisions about life-sustaining treatments such as resuscitation, mechanical ventilation, and artificial nutrition and hydration.

Communication is a critical component of end-of-life care. Case managers must ensure clear, compassionate communication between healthcare providers, patients, and families to navigate complex emotions and decisions. They should also be adept at recognizing signs of distress or discomfort in patients who may not be able to verbalize their needs.

Moreover, case managers play a vital role in coordinating palliative or hospice care services, which focus on symptom management and enhancing the quality of life rather than curative treatment. They must advocate for appropriate pain management and psychosocial support while respecting cultural and individual differences in end-of-life practices.

Ultimately, the goal of end-of-life care is to provide dignity, comfort, and peace to patients while supporting their loved ones through the transition.

5.2.5 Advance Directives:

Advance directives are legal documents that allow individuals to convey their preferences regarding medical treatment and care in the event that they become incapacitated and unable to communicate their decisions. These directives serve as a crucial component of patient autonomy, ensuring that an individual's healthcare choices are respected even when they cannot actively participate in decision-making processes.

There are two primary types of advance directives: the living will and the durable power of attorney for healthcare. A living will specifies the types of medical treatments and life-sustaining measures an individual desires or wishes to avoid, such as mechanical ventilation or resuscitation efforts. The durable power of attorney for healthcare designates a trusted person, often referred to as a healthcare proxy or agent, to make medical decisions on behalf of the individual if they are unable to do so themselves.

For case managers, understanding advance directives is essential for facilitating patient-centered care and ensuring compliance with ethical and legal standards. Case managers play a pivotal role in educating patients and families about the importance of advance directives, assisting in their completion, and ensuring that these documents are readily accessible within the patient's medical records.

Furthermore, case managers must advocate for the patient's stated wishes during care planning discussions, especially when conflicts arise between family members or healthcare providers. By upholding the principles outlined in advance directives, case managers contribute to ethical care delivery that honors patient autonomy and respects their end-of-life preferences.

5.2.6 Refusal Of Treatment/services:

Refusal of treatment or services is a fundamental patient right, grounded in the ethical principle of autonomy, which asserts that individuals have the right to make decisions about their own healthcare. This includes the right to refuse medical treatment or services, even if such refusal may result in harm or death. Case managers must respect and uphold this right while ensuring that patients are fully informed about the consequences of their decisions.

When a patient refuses treatment, it is essential for case managers to engage in thorough and empathetic dialogue to understand the underlying reasons for the refusal. This may involve exploring cultural beliefs, personal values, previous experiences with healthcare, or fear of side effects. Case managers should provide clear and comprehensive information about the proposed treatment, including potential benefits, risks, and alternatives.

Documentation of the refusal is crucial and should include details of the discussion, the patient's understanding of the consequences, and any alternatives offered. In situations where refusal may lead to significant harm, case managers should collaborate with the healthcare team to ensure that all ethical and legal considerations are addressed. This may include consulting with ethics committees or legal counsel when necessary.

Ultimately, case managers play a pivotal role in balancing respect for patient autonomy with advocacy for optimal care outcomes. They must navigate these complex situations with sensitivity and professionalism, ensuring that patients' rights are honored while promoting informed decision-making.

5.3 Ethics in Professional Practice:

Ethics in professional practice refers to the moral principles and standards that guide behavior and decision-making within the case management profession. These ethical guidelines ensure that case managers act with integrity, fairness, and respect for all individuals involved in the care process. At the core of professional ethics is the commitment to uphold the dignity and rights of clients while ensuring confidentiality, informed consent, and advocacy.

Case managers must navigate complex situations where ethical dilemmas may arise, such as conflicts of interest, allocation of resources, or balancing client autonomy with safety. Adhering to a code of ethics helps professionals resolve these challenges by providing a framework for evaluating actions and making decisions that align with ethical standards.

Key ethical principles in case management include beneficence (promoting the well-being of clients), non-maleficence (avoiding harm), autonomy (respecting clients' rights to make their own decisions), justice (ensuring fair treatment), and fidelity (maintaining trust through honesty and loyalty). Case managers must also recognize cultural diversity and demonstrate cultural competence by respecting differences in values, beliefs, and practices.

Professional ethics require ongoing education and self-reflection to stay informed about evolving standards and best practices. Case managers are encouraged to engage in peer consultations and seek guidance from ethics committees when faced with challenging situations. By adhering to ethical principles, case managers foster trust, enhance professional credibility, and contribute to positive outcomes for clients and the healthcare system as a whole.

5.3.1 Cultural And Linguistic Sensitivity:

Cultural and linguistic sensitivity is a critical component of effective case management, requiring professionals to acknowledge and respect the diverse cultural backgrounds and languages of their clients. This sensitivity involves understanding and appreciating cultural differences, including beliefs, values, practices, and communication styles that may influence a client's health behaviors and decision-making processes. Case managers must be adept at recognizing these differences to provide personalized care that aligns with the client's cultural context.

Linguistic sensitivity entails the ability to communicate effectively with clients who may have limited proficiency in the dominant language. This includes using interpreters or translation services when necessary, ensuring that communication is clear, accurate, and respectful. It also involves being mindful of non-verbal cues and body language, which can vary significantly across cultures.

Cultural and linguistic sensitivity enhances the therapeutic relationship by building trust and rapport between the case manager and the client. It fosters an environment where clients feel understood and respected, which can lead to improved adherence to care plans and better health outcomes. Additionally, this sensitivity helps identify potential barriers to care, such as cultural stigmas or language obstacles, allowing for tailored interventions.

For case managers preparing for the CCM exam, demonstrating cultural and linguistic sensitivity is essential not only for ethical practice but also for delivering high-quality, equitable care. It underscores a commitment to diversity and inclusion within healthcare settings, ensuring that all clients receive compassionate and competent support.

5.3.2 Code Of Professional Conduct:

The Code of Professional Conduct serves as a fundamental framework guiding case managers in ethical and professional behavior. It outlines the principles and standards that ensure integrity, accountability, and respect in the practice of case management. This code is pivotal in maintaining public trust and upholding the dignity of the profession.

A comprehensive understanding of the Code of Professional Conduct involves recognizing its key components: confidentiality, competence, informed consent, and professional boundaries. Confidentiality mandates that case managers protect client information, sharing it only with authorized individuals or entities. Competence requires continuous professional development to maintain and enhance the skills necessary for effective case management. Informed consent emphasizes the importance of clear communication with clients regarding their rights, treatment options, and potential outcomes, ensuring that they make well-informed decisions.

Professional boundaries are crucial to preventing conflicts of interest and maintaining an objective relationship with clients. Case managers must avoid dual relationships that could impair their judgment or exploit client vulnerability. Adherence to these principles fosters a professional environment where clients feel respected and supported.

Moreover, the code encourages advocacy for client rights and equitable access to resources while promoting cultural competence and diversity awareness. By adhering to this code, case managers demonstrate their commitment to ethical practice, ultimately enhancing the quality of care provided to clients.

Understanding and implementing the Code of Professional Conduct is essential for case managers preparing for the CCM exam, as it forms the ethical foundation upon which all professional interactions are built.

5.3.3 Veracity:

Veracity refers to the ethical principle of truthfulness and honesty in professional practice, which is fundamental for case managers. It involves providing accurate and complete information to clients, colleagues, and other stakeholders. This principle is crucial for building trust and maintaining professional integrity within the healthcare system.

For case managers, veracity means ensuring that clients are fully informed about their care options, potential outcomes, and any risks associated with treatment plans. It requires transparent communication, where the case manager must not withhold or distort information that could influence a client's decision-making process. This transparency empowers clients to make informed choices regarding their health and well-being.

Furthermore, veracity extends to the documentation and reporting processes. Case managers must ensure that all records are truthful, precise, and reflect the actual circumstances of a client's situation. Inaccurate documentation can lead to misinformed decisions, impacting client care and potentially resulting in ethical violations or legal consequences.

In practice, upholding veracity may sometimes present challenges, such as when delivering unfavorable news or managing complex cases with uncertain outcomes. However, maintaining honesty is essential for fostering a collaborative relationship between case managers and clients. It also supports ethical decision-making by ensuring that all parties have access to the same factual information.

Ultimately, veracity is a cornerstone of ethical practice for case managers. It underpins the trust necessary for effective client advocacy and supports the broader goal of promoting client autonomy and empowerment within the healthcare system.

5.4 Health Care & Disability Legislation:

Health care and disability-related legislation encompasses a range of laws designed to ensure access to medical services, protect patient rights, and promote the well-being of individuals with disabilities. Key legislation includes the Americans with

Disabilities Act (ADA), which prohibits discrimination against individuals with disabilities in all areas of public life, including jobs, schools, transportation, and all public and private places open to the general public. The ADA ensures that individuals with disabilities have the same rights and opportunities as everyone else.

The Affordable Care Act (ACA) is another crucial piece of legislation that expanded access to health insurance, prohibited the denial of coverage due to pre-existing conditions, and established essential health benefits. It also emphasizes preventive care and aims to reduce healthcare costs.

The Rehabilitation Act of 1973, particularly Section 504, mandates that no qualified individual with a disability should be excluded from, denied benefits of, or subjected to discrimination under any program or activity receiving federal financial assistance. This act laid the groundwork for later disability rights legislation.

Medicare and Medicaid programs are governed by federal statutes that provide healthcare coverage to eligible populations, including low-income individuals, families, children, pregnant women, the elderly, and people with disabilities. These programs are crucial in ensuring that vulnerable populations receive necessary medical care.

Understanding these laws is essential for case managers as they navigate the complexities of healthcare delivery and advocate for their clients' rights and access to services. This legislation forms the backbone of policies that guide equitable healthcare practices and support for individuals with disabilities.

5.4.1 Understanding the Americans With Disabilities Act (ADA):
Americans With Disabilities Act (ADA):

The Americans With Disabilities Act (ADA) is a pivotal civil rights law enacted in 1990, designed to prohibit discrimination against individuals with disabilities in all areas of public life, including jobs, schools, transportation, and all public and private places open to the general public. As case managers, understanding the ADA is crucial for ensuring compliance and advocating for clients' rights.

The ADA is divided into five titles that address different areas of public life. Title I focuses on employment, requiring employers with 15 or more employees to provide reasonable accommodations to qualified applicants or employees with disabilities unless doing so would cause undue hardship. Title II mandates that state and local governments provide equal access to programs, services, and activities. Title III requires public accommodations and commercial facilities to be accessible and non-discriminatory. Title IV addresses telecommunications, ensuring services for individuals with hearing and speech impairments. Lastly, Title V contains miscellaneous provisions, including prohibitions against retaliation or coercion.

For case managers, the ADA underscores the importance of facilitating access to necessary resources and services for clients with disabilities. This includes ensuring that workplace accommodations are met and advocating for accessible environments in various settings. Familiarity with ADA provisions enables case managers to effectively support clients in navigating potential barriers and securing their legal rights to equal opportunities. Understanding the ADA helps case managers not only comply with legal standards but also promote inclusivity and empowerment for individuals with disabilities.

5.4.2 OSHA Regulations Overview:
The Occupational Safety and Health Administration (OSHA) regulations are a critical component of workplace safety and health standards in the United States. Established under the Occupational Safety and Health Act of 1970, OSHA's primary mission is to ensure safe and healthful working conditions by setting and enforcing standards, as well as providing training, outreach, education, and assistance. These regulations apply to most private sector employers and their workers, as well as some public sector employers.

OSHA regulations encompass a wide range of workplace hazards, including chemical exposure, mechanical dangers, unsanitary conditions, excessive noise levels, heat or cold stress, and hazardous atmospheres. Case Managers should be knowledgeable about these regulations, as they often intersect with patient care environments where safety protocols must be adhered to in order to prevent workplace injuries and illnesses.

In healthcare settings specifically, OSHA has guidelines addressing bloodborne pathogens, emergency preparedness, ergonomic risks, and more. Compliance with these regulations is mandatory to minimize occupational hazards for healthcare workers. Case Managers play a pivotal role in ensuring that these standards are met by coordinating safety training sessions, conducting risk assessments, and implementing corrective actions when necessary.

Understanding OSHA regulations is essential for Case Managers to effectively advocate for safe work environments. Their role includes monitoring compliance with these standards to protect both healthcare providers and patients from potential harm. Adherence to OSHA regulations not only fosters a safer workplace but also enhances the quality of care provided in healthcare settings.

5.4.3 HIPAA Overview and Significance:
The Health Insurance Portability and Accountability Act (HIPAA) is pivotal U.S. legislation enacted in 1996, primarily designed to safeguard patients' medical information and ensure data privacy. As case managers, understanding HIPAA's implications is crucial for maintaining compliance and protecting patient confidentiality. HIPAA comprises several key provisions: the Privacy Rule, the Security Rule, and the Breach Notification Rule.

The Privacy Rule establishes national standards for the protection of individually identifiable health information, known as Protected Health Information (PHI). This rule mandates that healthcare providers, health plans, and clearinghouses implement safeguards to protect the privacy of PHI and sets limits on the use and disclosure of such information without patient authorization.

The Security Rule complements the Privacy Rule by setting standards for securing electronic Protected Health Information (ePHI). It requires covered entities to implement administrative, physical, and technical safeguards to ensure the confidentiality, integrity, and availability of ePHI.

The Breach Notification Rule requires covered entities to notify individuals, the Department of Health and Human Services (HHS), and, in some cases, the media, of any breaches of unsecured PHI. This ensures transparency and accountability in managing data breaches.

For case managers, adherence to HIPAA is essential in daily operations to ensure compliance with legal requirements while fostering trust with patients. Understanding HIPAA's provisions helps case managers navigate complex healthcare environments while prioritizing patient privacy and security.

5.4.4 Affordable Care Act (ACA):
The Affordable Care Act (ACA), enacted in 2010, is a comprehensive health care reform law aimed at expanding access to health insurance, improving the quality of care, and reducing health care costs. It represents one of the most significant overhauls of the U.S. health care system since the introduction of Medicare and Medicaid in 1965. For case managers, understanding the ACA is crucial, as it directly impacts patient care coordination and resource allocation.

The ACA mandates that most Americans obtain health insurance and provides subsidies to make coverage more affordable for low- and middle-income individuals. It expands Medicaid eligibility for low-income adults, although this expansion varies by state. The law also establishes Health Insurance Marketplaces where individuals can compare and purchase insurance plans.

A critical feature of the ACA is its emphasis on preventive care, requiring most insurance plans to cover preventive services without cost-sharing. This shift aims to reduce long-term health care costs by addressing health issues early. Additionally, the ACA prohibits insurance companies from denying coverage due to pre-existing conditions and removes lifetime limits on essential health benefits.

For case managers, the ACA necessitates an understanding of these provisions to effectively navigate patient care options and ensure compliance with regulations. By facilitating patient access to necessary services and coordinating comprehensive care plans, case managers play a pivotal role in achieving the ACA's goals of improved health outcomes and cost efficiency.

5.4.5 HITECH Act:
The Health Information Technology for Economic and Clinical Health (HITECH) Act was enacted as part of the American Recovery and Reinvestment Act of 2009. It aims to promote the adoption and meaningful use of health information technology, particularly electronic health records (EHRs), across the United States. The HITECH Act addresses privacy and security concerns associated with the electronic transmission of health information, primarily by strengthening the enforcement of the Health Insurance Portability and Accountability Act (HIPAA) rules.

Under the HITECH Act, healthcare providers are incentivized to demonstrate meaningful use of EHRs, which involves using certified EHR technology to improve quality, safety, efficiency, and reduce health disparities. This includes maintaining the privacy and security of patient information, engaging patients and families, improving care coordination, and ensuring adequate public health reporting.

For case managers, understanding the HITECH Act is crucial, as it directly impacts how patient data is managed and shared. Compliance with HITECH not only ensures legal adherence but also enhances patient care coordination by facilitating seamless access to comprehensive patient information. Additionally, case managers must be aware of the penalties for non-compliance with HIPAA rules strengthened by HITECH, which include significant fines and potential criminal charges.

Overall, the HITECH Act represents a pivotal shift towards a more integrated healthcare system, where technology plays a central role in improving patient outcomes while safeguarding sensitive health information.

5.5 Case Management: Legal & Regulatory Framework
Legal and regulatory requirements in case management practice encompass the rules, standards, and laws that govern the professional conduct and operations of case managers. These requirements are designed to ensure ethical practice, protect client rights, and maintain the integrity of the healthcare system. Key components include compliance with federal and state laws, such as the Health Insurance Portability and Accountability Act (HIPAA), which mandates the protection of patient health information. Case managers must also adhere to the Americans with Disabilities Act (ADA), ensuring non-discriminatory practices in service delivery.

In addition to legal statutes, regulatory guidelines from bodies such as the Centers for Medicare & Medicaid Services (CMS) provide frameworks for case management services within their programs. Case managers must be knowledgeable about these regulations to navigate funding, eligibility criteria, and service provision effectively.

Professional standards set by organizations like the Commission for Case Manager Certification (CCMC) outline ethical guidelines and best practices that case managers must follow. This includes maintaining confidentiality, obtaining informed consent, and advocating for clients' needs while balancing resource limitations.

Understanding these legal and regulatory requirements is crucial for case managers to avoid legal liabilities, ensure compliance, and provide quality care. Continuous education and staying informed about changes in laws and regulations are essential responsibilities for certified case managers to uphold professional standards and deliver competent services.

5.6 Privacy And Confidentiality:

Privacy and confidentiality are fundamental principles in case management, ensuring that clients' personal information is protected and shared appropriately. Privacy refers to an individual's right to control access to their personal information, while confidentiality involves the obligation of professionals to protect this information from unauthorized disclosure.

In the context of case management, maintaining privacy and confidentiality is crucial for building trust between clients and case managers. It requires adherence to legal standards such as the Health Insurance Portability and Accountability Act (HIPAA) in the United States, which sets national standards for the protection of health information. Case managers must ensure that they collect only necessary information, store it securely, and share it solely with authorized individuals or entities involved in the client's care.

Confidentiality extends beyond mere compliance with legal requirements; it also involves ethical considerations. Case managers should be aware of the ethical implications of disclosing client information, even when such disclosure is legally permissible. They must obtain informed consent from clients before sharing their information and ensure that clients understand the potential consequences of such disclosures.

Furthermore, case managers should be vigilant about potential breaches of confidentiality in various settings, including digital communications and electronic health records. Implementing robust security measures and regularly reviewing privacy policies can help mitigate risks.

Ultimately, respecting privacy and confidentiality not only complies with legal mandates but also fosters a therapeutic relationship grounded in trust, respect, and professionalism, which are essential for effective case management.

5.7 Risk Management:

Risk management in case management is a systematic process of identifying, assessing, and mitigating potential risks that could negatively impact patient care outcomes, financial stability, or operational efficiency. It involves proactive strategies to minimize the likelihood and impact of adverse events while enhancing the quality of care provided to patients.

In the context of case management, risk management begins with risk identification, where case managers evaluate potential risks related to patient safety, legal liabilities, and resource allocation. This includes assessing patient conditions, treatment plans, and potential barriers to effective care delivery. Once risks are identified, they are analyzed to determine their potential impact and likelihood. This analysis helps prioritize risks based on their severity and probability.

The next step involves developing risk mitigation strategies. These strategies may include creating contingency plans, implementing safety protocols, or coordinating with interdisciplinary teams to ensure comprehensive care. Effective communication with patients and healthcare providers is crucial in this phase to ensure that everyone is aware of potential risks and the steps being taken to mitigate them.

Continuous monitoring and evaluation are integral components of risk management. Case managers must regularly review outcomes and adjust strategies as needed to address new or evolving risks. Documentation is essential throughout this process to maintain transparency and accountability.

Ultimately, effective risk management enhances patient safety, ensures compliance with legal and regulatory standards, and optimizes resource utilization. By incorporating risk management into their practice, case managers can significantly contribute to improved healthcare delivery and patient satisfaction.

5.8 Professional Self-Care and Safety:

Self-care, safety, and well-being are critical components of a case manager's professional life, ensuring not only personal health but also the ability to provide optimal care to clients. Self-care involves proactive measures taken by individuals to maintain their physical, mental, and emotional health. For case managers, this means engaging in activities that reduce stress, such as regular exercise, adequate sleep, healthy eating, and mindfulness practices like meditation or yoga. These activities help mitigate burnout and compassion fatigue, which are common in high-stress healthcare environments.

Safety, in a professional context, refers to creating a work environment that minimizes the risks of physical harm and ensures psychological security. This includes adhering to organizational policies and procedures designed to protect staff from occupational hazards, maintaining awareness of surroundings when conducting home visits or working in potentially volatile situations, and utilizing personal protective equipment when necessary.

Well-being extends beyond mere self-care and safety; it encompasses a holistic approach to maintaining balance between work and personal life. This involves setting boundaries to prevent work from encroaching on personal time, seeking support from colleagues or supervisors when needed, and engaging in continuous professional development to enhance job satisfaction.

For case managers preparing for the CCM exam, understanding the importance of self-care, safety, and well-being is essential not only for personal health but also for sustaining a long-term career in case management. Prioritizing these elements ensures resilience and effectiveness in navigating the complexities of client care.

5.9 Standards Of Practice:

Standards of Practice in case management are a set of guidelines and principles that define the responsibilities and expected conduct of case managers in their professional roles. These standards ensure that case managers provide high-quality, ethical, and effective services to clients, healthcare providers, and other stakeholders. They serve as a benchmark for evaluating the performance and accountability of case managers.

The Standards of Practice encompass several key areas: assessment, planning, implementation, coordination, monitoring, and evaluation. During the assessment, case managers collect comprehensive information to understand clients' needs. In planning, they develop individualized care plans that outline goals and necessary resources. Implementation involves executing the care plan by coordinating with healthcare providers and community resources.

Coordination is crucial as it ensures seamless communication among all parties involved in the client's care. Monitoring involves regularly reviewing the client's progress toward goals and adjusting the care plan as needed. Evaluation is the final step, where outcomes are assessed to determine the effectiveness of interventions and overall client satisfaction.

Ethical practice is integral to these standards, emphasizing confidentiality, advocacy, and respect for client autonomy. Case managers must adhere to legal regulations and maintain professional competence through continuous education. The Standards of Practice serve not only as a guide for daily operations but also as a framework for professional development and improvement in case management practice. Adhering to these standards ensures that case managers deliver consistent, client-centered care that meets industry benchmarks.

5.9.1 CMSA Standards of Practice for Case Management:

The Case Management Society of America (CMSA) Standards of Practice for Case Management serve as a foundational framework for case managers, ensuring quality and consistency in the delivery of case management services. These standards are designed to guide case managers in their professional roles and responsibilities, emphasizing the importance of ethical practice, client-centered care, and interdisciplinary collaboration.

The CMSA Standards outline key principles such as advocacy, communication, and resource management. Advocacy involves supporting clients' rights and needs, ensuring they receive appropriate care and services. Effective communication is crucial for coordinating with healthcare providers, clients, and families to develop comprehensive care plans. Resource management entails the efficient use of healthcare resources to achieve optimal client outcomes while controlling costs.

Furthermore, the standards emphasize the necessity of continuous professional development and adherence to legal and ethical guidelines. Case managers are encouraged to engage in lifelong learning to stay updated on the latest practices and regulations in healthcare.

The CMSA Standards also highlight the importance of cultural competence, urging case managers to respect and understand diverse client backgrounds to provide equitable care. By following these standards, case managers can enhance their practice, improve client satisfaction, and contribute positively to the healthcare system.

In summary, the CMSA Standards of Practice for Case Management provide a comprehensive framework that supports case managers in delivering high-quality, ethical, and client-focused care across various healthcare settings.

5.9.2 NASW Standards for Case Management:

The National Association of Social Workers (NASW) Standards for Case Management provide a structured framework for social workers engaged in case management. These standards ensure that case managers deliver consistent, high-quality care and services to clients. The standards emphasize the importance of ethical practice, client-centered approaches, and professional competence.

Case management involves assessing clients' needs, developing comprehensive care plans, coordinating services, and monitoring progress. The NASW standards outline essential competencies such as advocacy, cultural competence, and ethical decision-making. They stress the need for case managers to advocate for clients' rights and access to resources while maintaining confidentiality and respecting client autonomy.

Cultural competence is a critical standard, requiring case managers to understand and respect diverse backgrounds and perspectives. This ensures that services are tailored to meet the unique needs of each client, promoting inclusivity and equity in service delivery.

Additionally, the standards highlight the importance of continuous professional development. Case managers are encouraged to engage in ongoing education and training to stay updated with best practices and emerging trends in the field.

Ethical practice is central to the NASW standards, guiding case managers in navigating complex situations with integrity. This includes adhering to professional codes of ethics, maintaining boundaries, and avoiding conflicts of interest.

Overall, the NASW Standards for Case Management serve as a vital tool for ensuring that social workers provide effective, ethical, and client-focused care throughout their practice.

CCM Practice
Questions
[SET 1]

Question 1: Tom, a 40-year-old man, reports experiencing neglect in his childhood, leading to trust issues in adulthood. As his case manager, which psychological approach should be prioritized to help him build healthier relationships?
A) Attachment-Based Therapy
B) Solution-Focused Brief Therapy
C) Rational Emotive Behavior Therapy (REBT)
D) Dialectical Behavior Therapy (DBT)

Question 2: Which of the following theories best explains the impact of chronic illness on an individual's self-identity and role within society?
A) Social Learning Theory
B) Biopsychosocial Model
C) Social Role Theory
D) Cognitive Behavioral Theory

Question 3: Maria, a 30-year-old woman with opioid use disorder, is considering treatment options. She expresses concerns about withdrawal symptoms and relapse. As her case manager, which treatment approach would you recommend to effectively manage withdrawal symptoms while minimizing relapse risk?
A) Cold turkey cessation with supportive counseling
B) Methadone maintenance therapy
C) Detoxification followed by naltrexone administration
D) Buprenorphine-naloxone combination therapy

Question 4: Which of the following strategies is most effective for a case manager to facilitate client empowerment in decision-making processes?
A) Providing clients with comprehensive educational materials
B) Encouraging clients to independently research their conditions
C) Collaborating with clients to set achievable goals
D) Directly advising clients on the best course of action

Question 5: Which psychosocial theory emphasizes the role of personal control and self-efficacy in managing chronic illness and disability?
A) Social Cognitive Theory
B) Health Belief Model
C) Transtheoretical Model
D) Biopsychosocial Model

Question 6: During a case management team meeting, the group is tasked with developing a new protocol for patient discharge planning. Despite having several experienced members, the group struggles to reach a consensus. Which of the following is most likely hindering their decision-making process?
A) Groupthink
B) Social loafing
C) Role ambiguity
D) Group polarization

Question 7: In a multidisciplinary healthcare team meeting, Case Manager John observes tension arising due to differing opinions on patient treatment plans. What group dynamic strategy should John employ to effectively manage this conflict?
A) Compromise
B) Collaboration
C) Avoidance
D) Competition

Question 8: John, a case manager, needs to help a client navigate their pharmacy benefits plan, which includes tiered drug coverage. The client is concerned about high out-of-pocket costs for a non-preferred brand-name medication. What approach should John prioritize to minimize these costs?
A) Advise appealing for an exception for coverage at a preferred rate.
B) Recommend using manufacturer coupons for temporary relief.
C) Suggest exploring therapeutic alternatives within the same tier.
D) Encourage adherence to prescribed therapy regardless of cost.

Question 9: Maria, a case manager in a rehabilitation center, is reviewing the center's adherence to accreditation standards concerning patient care plans. She notices variability in how care plans are updated across different departments. Which strategy should she prioritize to ensure consistent compliance with these standards?
A) Standardize care plan templates across all departments.
B) Increase frequency of interdisciplinary team meetings.
C) Introduce electronic health records for real-time updates.
D) Perform monthly reviews of care plan updates.

Question 10: John, a case manager, is tasked with coding for an outpatient clinic visit where multiple services were provided, including an X-ray and a blood test. What coding methodology should John use to ensure accurate billing for each service provided during the visit?
A) ICD-10-CM
B) CPT
C) DRG
D) LOINC

Question 11: Which model of care delivery is most effective in coordinating chronic care management for patients with multiple chronic conditions, emphasizing a team-based approach and integrated services?
A) Patient-Centered Medical Home (PCMH)
B) Disease Management Programs
C) Traditional Fee-for-Service Model
D) Accountable Care Organizations (ACO)

Question 12: John, a case manager in a rural community hospital, needs to implement a healthcare delivery system that maximizes resource utilization while maintaining high-quality patient outcomes. Which system should John implement to achieve these goals?
A) Patient-Centered Medical Home (PCMH)
B) Integrated Delivery System (IDS)
C) Capitation Payment Model
D) Bundled Payments

Question 13: As a case manager, Sarah is reviewing the reimbursement options for a patient undergoing a complex surgical procedure. The hospital is considering adopting a bundled payment model to streamline costs and improve care coordination. Which of the following best describes the bundled payment model?
A) Payments are made for each individual service rendered during the patient's care.
B) A single payment is made for all services provided during an episode of care.
C) Payment is based on the patient's diagnosis and expected resource use.
D) Providers receive a fixed amount per patient, regardless of services provided.

Question 14: In the context of transitions of care, which factor is most critical in reducing hospital readmission rates for elderly patients?
A) Comprehensive medication reconciliation at discharge
B) Timely communication between hospital and primary care provider

C) Utilization of telehealth services post-discharge
D) Patient education on disease management

Question 15: Sarah, a case manager, is tasked with optimizing hospital reimbursement for patients undergoing hip replacement surgeries. She notices discrepancies in DRG assignments. Which action should she prioritize to ensure accurate DRG coding?
A) Review patient's discharge summary
B) Verify surgical procedure codes
C) Analyze hospital length of stay trends
D) Assess post-operative complications

Question 16: A case manager, Sarah, is working with a multidisciplinary team to develop a care plan for a patient, Mr. Johnson, who has recently been diagnosed with a chronic illness. During the meeting, there is a disagreement between the social worker and the nurse regarding the prioritization of Mr. Johnson's psychosocial needs versus his immediate medical interventions. Which conflict resolution strategy should Sarah employ to effectively address this situation?
A) Compromise
B) Collaboration
C) Avoidance
D) Accommodation

Question 17: In the context of dual diagnoses, which strategy is most effective in reducing relapse rates in individuals with co-occurring anxiety and alcohol use disorders?
A) Sequentially treating anxiety before addressing alcohol use
B) Utilizing motivational interviewing exclusively for alcohol cessation
C) Employing cognitive-behavioral therapy (CBT) tailored to address both conditions
D) Administering anxiolytics without concurrent addiction therapy

Question 18: During a home visit, case manager John notices that Mrs. Lee, an elderly client with dementia, has poor hygiene and appears malnourished despite living with her son who claims she refuses care. What should John do first in response to suspected neglect?
A) Arrange for Mrs. Lee to be temporarily placed in a care facility.
B) Educate Mrs. Lee's son on proper caregiving techniques and nutrition.
C) Conduct an immediate risk assessment to evaluate Mrs. Lee's safety at home.
D) Schedule regular follow-up visits to monitor Mrs. Lee's condition.

Question 19: Which of the following strategies is most effective for enhancing a patient's adherence to a self-care management plan in chronic disease management, according to contemporary health education theories?
A) Providing detailed written instructions
B) Utilizing motivational interviewing techniques
C) Conducting group educational sessions
D) Offering regular follow-up phone calls

Question 20: In the context of case management for individuals experiencing physical abuse, which of the following is the most critical initial step a case manager should take to ensure client safety?
A) Develop a long-term care plan
B) Establish a therapeutic alliance
C) Conduct a comprehensive risk assessment
D) Refer to community resources

Question 21: John, a 60-year-old smoker with chronic obstructive pulmonary disease (COPD), expresses interest in quitting smoking after a recent hospitalization. As his case manager, how would you categorize his current stage of readiness according to the Transtheoretical Model if he has started gathering information on cessation programs?
A) Precontemplation
B) Contemplation
C) Preparation
D) Maintenance

Question 22: John, a case manager at a healthcare facility, must determine the most suitable reimbursement method for managing chronic disease patients under value-based care initiatives. Which reimbursement model aligns with incentivizing improved health outcomes and cost efficiency in this context?
A) Fee-for-service model
B) Capitation model
C) Pay-for-performance model
D) Retrospective cost-based reimbursement

Question 23: In the context of health insurance principles, which of the following best describes the concept of "moral hazard"?
A) The risk that an insured individual may take greater risks because they have coverage
B) The likelihood that an insurer will deny a claim based on policy exclusions
C) The probability that a provider will offer unnecessary services to increase reimbursement
D) The chance that a patient will switch providers due to dissatisfaction with care

Question 24: In assessing the impact of social determinants on mental health outcomes, which factor is most likely to exacerbate stress and anxiety in individuals?
A) Housing instability
B) Access to recreational facilities
C) Availability of healthy food options
D) Neighborhood safety

Question 25: In the context of SSDI, what is the significance of the "Substantial Gainful Activity" (SGA) threshold?
A) It determines the amount of benefits a recipient will receive.
B) It indicates whether a disability claimant is able to engage in competitive employment.
C) It assesses the severity of the claimant's medical condition.
D) It evaluates the claimant's need for vocational rehabilitation services.

Question 26: What is a critical factor in assessing a client's readiness to make informed decisions about their self-care management?
A) The client's previous experience with similar medical decisions.
B) The client's understanding of medical terminology used during consultations.
C) The client's emotional state and its impact on decision-making capacity.
D) The client's willingness to comply with prescribed treatments.

Question 27: John, a 75-year-old man with early-stage dementia, is being evaluated for a new assisted living facility. What life span consideration should be prioritized by the case manager in this scenario?
A) Ensuring the facility has a robust cognitive stimulation program.

B) Confirming the facility offers personalized meal plans.
C) Verifying the availability of on-site medical staff 24/7.
D) Evaluating the accessibility of the facility for family visits.

Question 28: John, a 75-year-old man with chronic heart failure, lives alone and frequently misses medical appointments due to transportation issues. As his case manager, you need to implement a supportive care strategy that ensures continuity of care. Which option should be prioritized?
A) Arrange for telehealth consultations
B) Schedule regular visits from a community health worker
C) Coordinate transportation services for medical appointments
D) Enroll him in an adult day care program

Question 29: John, a case manager, is assisting a client whose employer offers multiple health coverage plans. The client wants to maximize their benefits while minimizing out-of-pocket costs. Which factor should John prioritize when advising the client on selecting an employer-sponsored health plan?
A) The network of providers included in the plan
B) The premium cost of the plan
C) The deductible and co-payment amounts
D) The wellness programs offered by the plan

Question 30: Which of the following is a primary focus of URAC's accreditation standards in the context of quality and outcomes evaluation and measurements?
A) Financial performance metrics
B) Patient-centered care indicators
C) Staffing ratios and qualifications
D) Facility infrastructure improvements

Question 31: John, a case manager, is helping his client Lisa navigate self-directed care options after a recent diagnosis requiring long-term support. What should be John's primary focus to ensure Lisa's successful transition into self-directed care?
A) Encourage Lisa to independently research all available services without guidance.
B) Assist Lisa in developing a comprehensive plan that includes setting realistic goals.
C) Advise Lisa to choose services based solely on recommendations from peers.
D) Suggest that Lisa prioritize convenience over cost when selecting services.

Question 32: Mr. Thompson, a 72-year-old patient with advanced heart failure, is admitted to a hospice program. His family is concerned about managing his symptoms effectively while ensuring quality of life. As a case manager, what is the most appropriate initial step in creating his care plan?
A) Focus on aggressive treatment options to prolong life
B) Develop a comprehensive symptom management plan tailored to his needs
C) Prioritize family counseling sessions over symptom management
D) Initiate discussions about potential surgical interventions

Question 33: Sarah, a 32-year-old woman, has been experiencing emotional distress and isolation due to her partner's controlling behavior. As her case manager, you need to assess her situation and provide appropriate support. Which intervention should be prioritized to address Sarah's psychosocial needs effectively?
A) Encourage Sarah to attend couples therapy with her partner.
B) Facilitate Sarah's access to a women's support group.
C) Advise Sarah to discuss her feelings with close family members.
D) Recommend Sarah seek individual therapy for personal growth.

Question 34: In the context of performance improvement in healthcare, which strategy primarily focuses on reducing variability and enhancing consistency in clinical processes?
A) Total Quality Management (TQM)
B) Lean Management
C) Statistical Process Control (SPC)
D) Balanced Scorecard

Question 35: Emily, a case manager in a hospital setting, is coordinating the discharge plan for Mr. Johnson, a patient with complex medical needs and limited family support. Which of the following roles is most critical for Emily to ensure a smooth transition from hospital to home care?
A) Advocate for additional home health services
B) Arrange transportation for follow-up appointments
C) Educate Mr. Johnson on medication management
D) Coordinate with community resources for ongoing support

Question 36: Maria, a 60-year-old woman with diabetes and limited mobility, relies heavily on her daughter for daily activities. As her case manager, you need to evaluate potential stressors within her support system. Which factor is most likely to create stress within this dynamic?
A) The daughter's lack of knowledge about diabetes management
B) The daughter's work commitments limiting her availability
C) Maria's reluctance to accept help from outside caregivers
D) The financial burden of managing diabetes-related expenses

Question 37: Sarah, a case manager, is working with Mrs. Jenkins, who has limited health literacy and needs to understand her new medication regimen post-surgery. Which approach should Sarah prioritize to enhance Mrs. Jenkins' understanding and adherence?
A) Schedule multiple follow-up appointments for reinforcement.
B) Simplify the medication regimen by using color-coded charts.
C) Encourage family involvement in medication management discussions.
D) Provide detailed written instructions emphasizing medication side effects.

Question 38: Which strategy best supports shared decision making by enhancing client engagement in their healthcare decisions?
A) Delivering complex medical jargon without simplification
B) Utilizing decision aids tailored to individual client needs
C) Relying on verbal communication only during consultations
D) Limiting client participation to avoid overwhelming them

Question 39: According to the Transtheoretical Model of Change, which stage is characterized by an individual's intention to take action within the next six months, but no immediate plans for change?
A) Precontemplation
B) Contemplation
C) Preparation
D) Action

Question 40: Maria, a case manager, is assisting a 45-year-old patient named John who has recently lost his job and health insurance. John requires ongoing medication for his chronic condition but cannot afford it.

Which resource should Maria prioritize to help John access his medication at a reduced cost?
A) Medicaid
B) Pharmaceutical Assistance Program
C) Community Health Clinic
D) Emergency Room Services

Question 41: In the context of psychosocial support systems, which transportation strategy is most likely to promote social engagement among individuals with mobility challenges?
A) Subsidized taxi vouchers for medical appointments only
B) Community shuttle services with fixed routes and schedules
C) Personalized door-to-door transport services for social activities
D) Public transit accessibility improvements focused on infrastructure

Question 42: Sarah, a case manager, is advising a client who has been offered multiple health plans by their new employer. The client is interested in minimizing out-of-pocket costs while managing a chronic condition. Which type of employer-sponsored plan should Sarah suggest?
A) High-Deductible Health Plan (HDHP) with Health Savings Account (HSA).
B) Preferred Provider Organization (PPO).
C) Health Maintenance Organization (HMO).
D) Exclusive Provider Organization (EPO).

Question 43: Sarah, a case manager, is working with John, a patient struggling with adherence to his medication regimen. During their session, John expresses ambivalence about taking his medication regularly. Which strategy should Sarah employ as part of Motivational Interviewing to help John resolve this ambivalence?
A) Provide direct advice on the benefits of adherence.
B) Explore John's values and how they align with taking medication.
C) Emphasize the negative consequences of non-adherence.
D) Encourage John to make a decision immediately.

Question 44: John is a case manager tasked with designing a reimbursement model for a new clinic focused on value-based care. Which payment methodology should John consider implementing to best support this model?
A) Fee-for-service reimbursement
B) Capitation payment system
C) Pay-for-performance incentives
D) Retrospective cost-based reimbursement

Question 45: Emily, a 30-year-old woman with cerebral palsy, requires ongoing support to maintain her independence in the community. As her case manager, what is the most appropriate action to enhance her access to necessary resources?
A) Refer Emily to local community support groups for social interaction.
B) Develop an individualized service plan focusing on assistive technology needs.
C) Encourage Emily to participate in vocational training programs.
D) Schedule regular meetings with her family to discuss progress and challenges.

Question 46: In the context of reimbursement methods for virtual care services at alternative care sites, which factor is most critical for ensuring financial sustainability?

A) Patient satisfaction scores
B) Accurate coding and billing practices
C) Volume of virtual consultations
D) Integration with electronic health records (EHRs)

Question 47: Which of the following is a primary goal of supportive care programs in the context of case management for patients with chronic illnesses?
A) To cure the underlying disease
B) To improve quality of life and manage symptoms
C) To provide financial assistance
D) To ensure adherence to medication regimens

Question 48: In evaluating the success of a support group integrated into a client's care plan, what key indicator should a case manager prioritize to assess its impact on the client's psychosocial well-being?
A) The frequency of client attendance at the support group meetings.
B) The increase in client's social network size due to group participation.
C) The improvement in client-reported quality of life measures.
D) The number of new coping strategies learned by the client.

Question 49: In case management, which tool is most effective in identifying potential barriers to a patient's care plan and facilitating timely interventions?
A) SWOT Analysis
B) Risk Stratification Tool
C) Root Cause Analysis
D) Gantt Chart

Question 50: In the context of psychological and neuropsychological assessments, which test is primarily used to evaluate executive functions, such as planning and problem-solving, in adults?
A) Wechsler Adult Intelligence Scale (WAIS)
B) Minnesota Multiphasic Personality Inventory (MMPI)
C) Wisconsin Card Sorting Test (WCST)
D) Beck Depression Inventory (BDI)

Question 51: Sarah, a case manager, is working with a client who has recently been diagnosed with a chronic illness. The client expresses feelings of isolation and anxiety. Sarah considers recommending a support group. Which factor should Sarah prioritize when selecting an appropriate support group for her client?
A) The group's proximity to the client's home
B) The group's focus on the specific illness
C) The frequency of the group's meetings
D) The size of the group

Question 52: In the context of health education for promoting self-management among clients with diabetes, which approach is considered most effective based on current research?
A) Structured educational workshops
B) Interactive digital platforms with personalized feedback
C) Distribution of informational pamphlets
D) Traditional lecture-based seminars

Question 53: Sarah, a 68-year-old woman with multiple chronic conditions, is considering a new treatment plan that involves significant lifestyle changes. As her case manager, you need to ensure she makes an informed decision. Which approach is most effective in facilitating Sarah's informed decision-making process?
A) Provide Sarah with detailed medical literature and ask her to review it independently.
B) Discuss the treatment options with Sarah, including risks, benefits, and alternatives, and encourage questions.

C) Recommend Sarah to consult with another healthcare professional for a second opinion.
D) Schedule a meeting with Sarah's family to discuss the treatment plan on her behalf.

Question 54: In the context of interpersonal communication, which approach should a case manager prioritize to enhance client engagement and rapport building?
A) Authoritative guidance
B) Empathetic understanding
C) Structured feedback
D) Transactional analysis

Question 55: John, a case manager at a hospital, is tasked with evaluating the effectiveness of a new discharge planning process aimed at reducing readmission rates. Which of the following methods would best allow John to determine the quality and outcomes of this process?
A) Conducting patient satisfaction surveys post-discharge
B) Analyzing readmission rates within 30 days post-discharge
C) Reviewing staff compliance with discharge protocols
D) Monitoring length of stay for discharged patients

Question 56: John, a patient with an indemnity insurance plan, received treatment from an out-of-network provider due to an emergency situation: As his case manager, you need to explain how indemnity plans typically handle such situations regarding reimbursement. What should you tell John?
A) Indemnity plans do not cover out-of-network services under any circumstances.
B) Indemnity plans will cover out-of-network services only if pre-approved by the insurer.
C) Indemnity plans often reimburse out-of-network services based on standard rates but may require higher co-payments or deductibles from John.
D) Indemnity plans automatically cover all costs associated with out-of-network services at full rate.

Question 57: In the context of self-directed care, which of the following principles is most essential for empowering clients to manage their own health effectively?
A) Autonomy in decision-making
B) Frequent supervision by healthcare professionals
C) Structured care pathways
D) Regular assessment of client satisfaction

Question 58: John, a case manager, is assisting a client named Sarah who recently lost her job and is concerned about maintaining her health insurance coverage. She was employed at a company with 25 employees. Under the Consolidated Omnibus Budget Reconciliation Act (COBRA), what should John advise Sarah regarding her eligibility for continued health coverage?
A) Sarah is not eligible for COBRA because the company has fewer than 50 employees.
B) Sarah is eligible for COBRA regardless of the number of employees in the company.
C) Sarah can only apply for COBRA if she finds another job within 60 days.
D) Sarah is eligible for COBRA because the company has more than 20 employees.

Question 59: Emily, a 45-year-old patient with chronic pain, is considering several treatment options. As her case manager, you aim to implement shared decision making. Which approach best embodies the principles of shared decision making in this context?
A) Presenting all treatment options and letting Emily choose independently.
B) Discussing only the most effective treatment based on clinical evidence.
C) Exploring Emily's values and preferences before discussing treatment options.
D) Recommending the treatment option with the least side effects.

Question 60: John, a 60-year-old diabetic patient, is overwhelmed by multiple management strategies suggested by his healthcare team. As his case manager, how should you facilitate shared decision making to enhance his self-care management?
A) Prioritize strategies that align with John's lifestyle and goals after a comprehensive discussion.
B) Focus on the strategy with the highest success rate in clinical trials.
C) Encourage John to follow the most cost-effective strategy recommended by insurance.
D) Select a strategy for John based on your professional judgment.

Question 61: When managing reimbursement for clients with disabilities, which strategy is most effective in optimizing financial resources while maintaining quality of care?
A) Utilization review processes
B) Capitated payment models
C) Fee-for-service billing
D) Value-based purchasing

Question 62: How does the Veterans Health Administration (VHA) prioritize veterans for healthcare services?
A) VHA prioritizes based on the veteran's rank at discharge from service.
B) VHA uses an income-based means test to determine priority levels.
C) VHA prioritizes veterans with service-connected disabilities first, followed by those with lower incomes.
D) VHA provides equal access to all veterans regardless of service history or income level.

Question 63: In the context of indemnity insurance plans, which of the following best describes the primary responsibility of a case manager when coordinating care for a patient?
A) Ensuring that all services are pre-approved by the insurance provider.
B) Facilitating communication between providers to ensure seamless care delivery.
C) Monitoring patient outcomes to ensure compliance with treatment plans.
D) Negotiating lower rates with healthcare providers on behalf of the patient.

Question 64: In the context of client support system dynamics, which of the following best describes the concept of "reciprocal determinism" in influencing client behavior and outcomes?
A) The client's behavior is solely determined by their environment.
B) The client's personal factors, behavior, and environment interact to influence outcomes.
C) The client's environment is influenced only by their personal factors.
D) The client's behavior is determined by external support systems alone.

Question 65: Sarah, a case manager, is evaluating the needs of Mr. Thompson, a 78-year-old patient with mild cognitive impairment and limited mobility, who is considering transitioning to an assisted living facility.

Which factor should Sarah prioritize to ensure Mr. Thompson's successful adjustment to the new environment?
A) Proximity to family members
B) Availability of specialized memory care services
C) Cost of the facility
D) Social activity programs

Question 66: John, a 45-year-old male with a history of substance abuse, presents with frequent injuries and inconsistent explanations about their causes. As his case manager, what would be the most effective approach to assess for potential physical abuse?
A) Refer John for a psychological evaluation to assess mental health status.
B) Interview John's family members separately about his injuries.
C) Create a safe environment for John to disclose information voluntarily.
D) Monitor John's injury patterns over several months before taking action.

Question 67: Sarah, a case manager, is assessing a new patient, Mr. Thompson, who has been admitted with congestive heart failure. To accurately determine Mr. Thompson's acuity level for appropriate resource allocation, which factor should Sarah prioritize?
A) Length of hospital stay
B) Frequency of emergency department visits
C) Complexity of the patient's medication regimen
D) Patient's socioeconomic status

Question 68: Sarah, a 45-year-old woman with chronic health conditions, is enrolled in a self-directed care program. She is responsible for managing her own care budget to hire personal care assistants. Which strategy should Sarah prioritize to ensure effective self-management and optimal use of her resources?
A) Focus on hiring the least expensive care providers to maximize her budget.
B) Invest in training for her personal care assistants to improve service quality.
C) Allocate most of her budget towards medical treatments rather than personal care.
D) Use her budget primarily for assistive devices instead of personal assistance.

Question 69: Maria, a 30-year-old woman with bipolar disorder and opioid dependence, is experiencing severe mood swings and withdrawal symptoms. As her case manager, what is the best approach to ensure successful management of her dual diagnosis?
A) Stabilize her mood with medication before addressing opioid dependence.
B) Address opioid dependence first through detoxification and rehabilitation.
C) Implement an integrated treatment plan that includes psychotherapy and pharmacotherapy for both conditions.
D) Focus on behavioral therapy to manage mood swings before tackling opioid dependence.

Question 70: Tom is a case manager working with an elderly client transitioning from hospital discharge to long-term care. To effectively manage this transition within the continuum of care framework, which strategy should he prioritize?
A) Arranging transportation services for future medical appointments.
B) Developing a comprehensive discharge plan involving multidisciplinary teams.
C) Providing educational materials about chronic disease management.
D) Scheduling regular phone check-ins post-discharge.

Question 71: What is a primary consideration for case managers when evaluating a patient's eligibility for a pharmaceutical assistance program?
A) The patient's current insurance coverage.
B) The patient's income relative to the federal poverty level.
C) The patient's adherence to medication regimens.
D) The patient's medical history.

Question 72: John, a patient under your care, often misses appointments and seems disengaged during consultations. To build a stronger therapeutic relationship and improve his engagement, which approach should you prioritize?
A) Implement stricter appointment policies to ensure attendance.
B) Develop personalized care plans that align with John's interests and goals.
C) Increase the frequency of reminders about upcoming appointments.
D) Offer incentives for attending scheduled consultations.

Question 73: In the context of reimbursement methods for chronic care management, which payment model incentivizes providers to deliver high-quality care while managing the costs associated with chronic conditions?
A) Capitation Payment Model
B) Pay-for-Performance Model
C) Bundled Payments Model
D) Global Budget Payment Model

Question 74: Under the Consolidated Omnibus Budget Reconciliation Act (COBRA), which of the following scenarios would allow an employee to qualify for continued health coverage?
A) Voluntary resignation from employment
B) Termination due to gross misconduct
C) Reduction in working hours resulting in loss of benefits
D) Reaching retirement age

Question 75: Sarah, a case manager, is assisting Emily, who has been diagnosed with ALS and is exploring viatical settlements as an option to manage her care expenses. Which factor should Sarah emphasize as crucial when explaining the potential downsides of entering into a viatical settlement?
A) The possibility of outliving the estimated life expectancy used in the settlement offer calculation.
B) The fees and commissions charged by the viatical settlement company.
C) The inability to retain any portion of her life insurance policy after the settlement.
D) The requirement to disclose personal health information during the process.

Question 76: Which case management model is primarily focused on the integration of services across the continuum of care to ensure seamless transitions and optimal resource utilization?
A) Broker Model
B) Integrated Care Model
C) Client-Centered Model
D) Collaborative Care Model

Question 77: Which of the following community resources is most effective in providing comprehensive support for individuals with chronic mental health conditions, focusing on both medical and social needs?
A) Outpatient psychiatric clinics
B) Integrated care networks
C) Support groups
D) Emergency shelters

Question 78: As a case manager, you are tasked with developing a virtual care plan for Maria, a patient with chronic heart failure who requires frequent monitoring. Which approach would best utilize virtual care technologies to enhance Maria's health outcomes?
A) Schedule regular video check-ins with her cardiologist without additional monitoring tools.
B) Implement an app-based symptom tracker alongside video consultations for comprehensive management.
C) Use email updates as the primary method of communication about her condition.
D) Depend on automated phone reminders for medication adherence without direct interaction.

Question 79: Which of the following methods is most effective in evaluating the quality of care through patient outcomes in a healthcare setting?
A) Process mapping
B) Root cause analysis
C) Outcome measurement
D) Benchmarking

Question 80: When managing a client with dual diagnoses of substance use disorder and major depressive disorder, which intervention is most crucial for ensuring effective treatment outcomes?
A) Prioritizing the treatment of substance use disorder first
B) Coordinating simultaneous treatment for both disorders
C) Focusing on pharmacotherapy for the depressive disorder
D) Emphasizing psychotherapy for substance use disorder

Question 81: In promoting self-advocacy among clients with chronic conditions, which approach should a case manager prioritize to ensure effective self-care management?
A) Educate clients on medication adherence only.
B) Develop personalized care plans with client input.
C) Monitor clients' health outcomes closely without their involvement.
D) Focus solely on crisis intervention strategies.

Question 82: Which of the following is a primary advantage of individually purchased insurance compared to employer-sponsored insurance in terms of coverage flexibility?
A) Individually purchased insurance allows for customization of benefits to suit personal needs.
B) Individually purchased insurance typically offers lower premiums than employer-sponsored plans.
C) Individually purchased insurance provides better network access to healthcare providers.
D) Individually purchased insurance mandates comprehensive coverage for all policyholders.

Question 83: Which stage of the Transtheoretical Model of Change is characterized by a client's acknowledgment of the need for change but with no immediate plans to take action?
A) Precontemplation
B) Contemplation
C) Preparation
D) Action

Question 84: Sarah, a 68-year-old patient with advanced cancer, is enrolled in a supportive care program. Her case manager is evaluating the effectiveness of the program in addressing her psychosocial needs. Which of the following interventions is most likely to enhance Sarah's emotional well-being within this supportive care framework?
A) Regular physical therapy sessions
B) Weekly group counseling sessions
C) Nutritional supplements tailored to her needs

D) Scheduled medication reviews

Question 85: Emily, a 45-year-old freelance graphic designer, has decided to purchase individual health insurance. She is concerned about the potential for high out-of-pocket costs. Which feature should Emily prioritize in her individually purchased insurance plan to minimize her financial burden in case of major medical expenses?
A) Low monthly premiums
B) High deductible
C) Low out-of-pocket maximum
D) Wide network of providers

Question 86: Which of the following is a primary source of quality indicators in healthcare that provides comprehensive data on patient outcomes and hospital performance?
A) National Quality Forum (NQF)
B) Hospital Consumer Assessment of Healthcare Providers and Systems (HCAHPS)
C) Centers for Medicare & Medicaid Services (CMS)
D) Agency for Healthcare Research and Quality (AHRQ)

Question 87: In employer-based health and wellness programs, what is considered a key factor that influences the effectiveness of these programs in reducing healthcare costs?
A) Comprehensive health assessments
B) Employee engagement levels
C) Availability of fitness facilities
D) Incentive-based participation

Question 88: John is tasked with designing a managed care plan for a population with diverse healthcare needs. Which strategy should he employ to ensure cost-effectiveness while maintaining high-quality care?
A) Gatekeeping
B) Open Access Plans
C) Retrospective Payment System
D) High Deductible Health Plans

Question 89: In an interdisciplinary/interprofessional care team, what is the most critical factor for ensuring effective communication among team members?
A) Regular meetings with all team members present.
B) Use of standardized communication tools like SBAR (Situation-Background-Assessment-Recommendation).
C) Establishment of a clear hierarchy within the team.
D) Frequent email updates summarizing patient progress.

Question 90: Which healthcare provider's role includes assessing patients' functional abilities to facilitate discharge planning in a hospital setting?
A) Occupational Therapist
B) Physical Therapist
C) Speech-Language Pathologist
D) Clinical Nurse Specialist

Question 91: What is a primary benefit of integrating virtual care platforms in the management of chronic diseases, particularly in alternative care sites?
A) Reduced need for in-person specialist consultations
B) Enhanced patient data security and privacy
C) Improved patient adherence to treatment plans
D) Increased healthcare provider workload

Question 92: In the context of client engagement, which approach best supports sustained behavioral change by integrating psychosocial support systems?
A) Goal setting with periodic assessments
B) Offering incentives for compliance with care plans
C) Building a supportive community network around the

client
D) Providing comprehensive health education sessions

Question 93: In the context of case rate reimbursement methodologies, which of the following best describes a primary advantage of using case rates for healthcare providers?
A) Encourages overutilization of services
B) Provides predictable revenue streams
C) Increases administrative burden
D) Reduces focus on patient outcomes

Question 94: As a case manager, you are tasked with developing a care plan for Maria, a 65-year-old patient with multiple chronic conditions. Considering the principles of population health, which strategy should you prioritize to effectively manage her health outcomes while optimizing resources?
A) Implementing personalized care plans focusing solely on Maria's immediate health needs
B) Establishing community-based programs to address social determinants of health affecting Maria
C) Coordinating frequent hospital visits to monitor Maria's condition closely
D) Focusing on medication adherence through regular pharmaceutical consultations

Question 95: In the context of value-based care, which reimbursement method is most likely to promote integrated care delivery among healthcare providers?
A) Fee-for-service
B) Shared savings programs
C) Capitation models
D) Direct primary care

Question 96: Maria, a 60-year-old woman with rheumatoid arthritis, feels isolated due to her physical limitations and frequent pain. Which of the following strategies should a case manager prioritize to improve her social interaction and quality of life?
A) Encourage participation in online support groups
B) Refer to a pain management specialist
C) Suggest mindfulness meditation practices
D) Recommend physical therapy sessions

Question 97: Sarah, a 40-year-old woman, has been experiencing anxiety and depression due to ongoing emotional abuse from her partner. As a case manager, which psychological intervention is most effective in empowering Sarah to regain control over her life?
A) Cognitive Behavioral Therapy (CBT)
B) Psychoanalysis
C) Supportive Counseling
D) Mindfulness-Based Stress Reduction (MBSR)

Question 98: In the context of DSM-5, which disorder is characterized by excessive worry occurring more days than not for at least six months?
A) Panic Disorder
B) Generalized Anxiety Disorder
C) Obsessive-Compulsive Disorder
D) Social Anxiety Disorder

Question 99: John, a case manager, is tasked with developing a care plan for a patient with multiple chronic conditions. His primary goal is to ensure the patient receives coordinated and efficient care. Which of the following objectives best aligns with this goal?
A) Minimize hospital readmissions through regular follow-ups.
B) Reduce medication costs by suggesting generic alternatives.
C) Enhance patient satisfaction by conducting routine surveys.
D) Increase provider engagement through team meetings.

Question 100: How do case managers contribute to effective reimbursement processes in diverse healthcare settings?
A) By negotiating payment terms directly with patients.
B) By documenting clinical outcomes to support billing claims.
C) By setting prices for healthcare services provided.
D) By solely focusing on reducing service costs.

Question 101: Sarah, a 45-year-old female with Type 2 Diabetes Mellitus, presents with frequent hypoglycemic episodes despite adherence to her medication regimen. As her case manager, what should be your primary focus to manage her condition effectively?
A) Adjust her medication dosage in consultation with her endocrinologist.
B) Provide dietary counseling focusing on carbohydrate counting and meal planning.
C) Refer her to a diabetes support group for peer support and shared experiences.
D) Schedule more frequent blood glucose monitoring sessions.

Question 102: Which of the following is a primary advantage of private benefit programs in healthcare for case managers when coordinating patient care?
A) Flexibility in coverage options
B) Uniformity in reimbursement rates
C) Governmental oversight and regulation
D) Limited network of providers

Question 103: Jane, a 35-year-old woman, presents to the clinic with signs of anxiety and depression. She reveals a history of emotional abuse from her partner. As a case manager, which psychological intervention is most effective in addressing her current symptoms and promoting long-term recovery?
A) Cognitive Behavioral Therapy (CBT)
B) Psychoanalytic Therapy
C) Supportive Group Therapy
D) Mindfulness-Based Stress Reduction (MBSR)

Question 104: Sarah, a case manager, is assisting a client who recently lost their job and is seeking Medicaid coverage. The client is concerned about maintaining access to necessary medical services during this transition. Which of the following factors should Sarah prioritize to ensure the client qualifies for Medicaid under their state's eligibility criteria?
A) The client's current employment status
B) The client's household income relative to the Federal Poverty Level (FPL)
C) The client's previous health insurance coverage
D) The client's age and disability status

Question 105: In the context of identifying signs of physical neglect in a child, which indicator is most likely to be overlooked by case managers due to its subtlety?
A) Frequent unexplained injuries
B) Consistent hunger and malnutrition
C) Poor hygiene and unkempt appearance
D) Delayed physical development

Question 106: John, a 60-year-old man with chronic heart failure, expresses feelings of hopelessness and withdrawal from social activities. As his case manager, what is the most effective strategy to address his psychosocial needs?
A) Facilitate sessions with a clinical psychologist specializing in chronic illness.

B) Encourage him to volunteer in community service activities.
C) Introduce him to online forums for patients with similar conditions.
D) Suggest he keep a daily gratitude journal.

Question 107: John, a case manager working with Medicaid beneficiaries, encounters a patient who requires specialized medical equipment that is not covered under standard Medicaid benefits in their state. What should John explore as an option to secure coverage for this equipment?
A) Apply for a waiver program specific to home and community-based services
B) Seek assistance through Medicare Part B
C) Request an exception through the patient's primary care physician
D) Explore private insurance options as supplementary coverage

Question 108: In Motivational Interviewing, what technique involves helping clients explore their own motivations for change by highlighting inconsistencies between their current behavior and broader life goals?
A) Reflective Listening
B) Developing Discrepancy
C) Affirmation
D) Eliciting Change Talk

Question 109: Which of the following is considered the most effective integrated treatment approach for individuals with co-occurring disorders, according to contemporary research?
A) Sequential Treatment
B) Parallel Treatment
C) Integrated Dual Disorder Treatment (IDDT)
D) Collaborative Care Model

Question 110: How does the Federal Medical Assistance Percentage (FMAP) influence state funding under the Medicaid program?
A) FMAP provides states with a fixed dollar amount annually.
B) FMAP varies inversely with state per capita income.
C) FMAP matches state spending at a constant rate regardless of state wealth.
D) FMAP reduces federal contributions as state spending increases.

Question 111: Which of the following is a key advantage of using predictive analytics in health care management for improving patient outcomes?
A) Retrospective data analysis
B) Real-time decision support
C) Descriptive statistical reporting
D) Manual data collection

Question 112: Which negotiation technique is most effective for a case manager aiming to balance patient care needs with cost constraints in a healthcare setting?
A) Integrative Negotiation
B) Distributive Negotiation
C) Compromise Strategy
D) Competitive Bargaining

Question 113: In the context of substance use disorder treatment, which approach primarily focuses on enhancing an individual's motivation to change behavior?
A) Twelve-Step Facilitation Therapy
B) Motivational Interviewing
C) Cognitive Behavioral Therapy (CBT)
D) Dialectical Behavior Therapy (DBT)

Question 114: In the context of promoting self-advocacy among clients, which approach best aligns with recognized theories of client-centered care?
A) Prioritizing interventions based on clinical guidelines over client preferences.
B) Involving clients in decision-making processes about their care plans.
C) Implementing standardized care protocols universally for all clients.
D) Encouraging clients to follow expert recommendations without question.

Question 115: Which model of chronic care delivery emphasizes patient empowerment through self-management and collaborative goal setting with healthcare providers?
A) Patient-Centered Medical Home (PCMH)
B) Chronic Care Model (CCM)
C) Integrated Care Model (ICM)
D) Disease Management Program (DMP)

Question 116: Sarah, a case manager, is evaluating eligibility for public benefit programs for Mr. Thompson, a 68-year-old retiree with limited income who requires prescription medications. Which program should Sarah consider first to assist Mr. Thompson with his medication costs?
A) Medicare Part A
B) Medicare Part B
C) Medicare Part D
D) Social Security Disability Insurance (SSDI)

Question 117: In your role as a case manager, you need to identify potential areas for improvement in post-operative care for patients like Ms. Lee, who recently underwent knee replacement surgery. Which source of quality indicators is most relevant for identifying trends in post-operative complications?
A) National database registries
B) Peer-reviewed clinical studies
C) Patient-reported outcome measures (PROMs)
D) Local hospital incident reports

Question 118: In the context of case management, which principle is essential for ensuring successful negotiation outcomes when dealing with multiple stakeholders?
A) Positional Bargaining
B) Interest-Based Approach
C) Zero-Sum Game Theory
D) Fixed-Pie Perception

Question 119: Maria is evaluating her employer-sponsored health coverage options during open enrollment. She has chronic medical conditions requiring regular specialist visits and prescriptions. What should be her primary consideration in choosing a plan?
A) Access to a wide range of specialists
B) Lower monthly premiums
C) Comprehensive prescription drug coverage
D) High annual maximum out-of-pocket limit

Question 120: Jamie, a case manager, is working with Alex, a 17-year-old who has recently come out as bisexual. Alex expresses feeling isolated at school due to their sexual orientation. Which of the following strategies should Jamie prioritize to support Alex's psychosocial well-being?
A) Encourage Alex to join a local LGBTQ+ youth group.
B) Suggest Alex focus on academic achievements to distract from feelings of isolation.
C) Advise Alex to avoid discussing their sexual orientation at

school.
D) Recommend that Alex seek individual therapy to address feelings of isolation.

Question 121: Sarah, a case manager, is coordinating the care for John, a patient with multiple chronic conditions. In this scenario, which healthcare provider is primarily responsible for ensuring medication reconciliation to prevent adverse drug interactions during John's transition from hospital to home?
A) Primary Care Physician
B) Pharmacist
C) Nurse Practitioner
D) Social Worker

Question 122: What is the primary purpose of establishing a Special Needs Trust for an individual with disabilities?
A) To provide supplemental income without affecting eligibility for government benefits
B) To manage all financial aspects of the individual's life independently
C) To ensure the individual receives maximum Social Security benefits
D) To transfer all assets to family members to avoid taxes

Question 123: Sarah, a 72-year-old woman with limited mobility and a recent diagnosis of diabetes, is struggling to maintain a balanced diet. As her case manager, you are considering meal delivery services to support her dietary needs. Which factor is most crucial when selecting an appropriate meal delivery service for Sarah?
A) The variety of meal options available
B) The cost-effectiveness of the service
C) The nutritional content tailored to diabetic needs
D) The delivery schedule flexibility

Question 124: In the context of private benefit programs, what is the main advantage of Preferred Provider Organizations (PPOs) over Health Maintenance Organizations (HMOs)?
A) Lower premiums
B) Comprehensive coverage without network restrictions
C) Flexibility to see specialists without referrals
D) Higher reimbursement rates for providers

Question 125: Sarah, a 75-year-old diabetic patient, is transitioning from hospital to home after surgery. What is the most critical component of her transitional care plan to reduce the risk of complications?
A) Ensuring Sarah has sufficient medication supply for two weeks post-discharge.
B) Coordinating a multidisciplinary team meeting before discharge.
C) Arranging transportation for follow-up appointments.
D) Providing Sarah with dietary guidelines tailored to her condition.

Question 126: Which of the following symptoms is most indicative of Major Depressive Disorder (MDD) according to the DSM-5 criteria?
A) Persistent elevated mood
B) Anhedonia
C) Compulsive behaviors
D) Rapid speech

Question 127: In the context of hospice and palliative care, which of the following best describes the primary goal of palliative care?
A) To prolong life at all costs
B) To manage pain and symptoms while improving quality of life

C) To provide curative treatment for terminal illnesses
D) To focus solely on emotional support for patients and families

Question 128: John, a case manager, is working with a multidisciplinary team to coordinate care for a patient with multiple chronic conditions. The team aims to improve the patient's health outcomes by integrating various services. Which model of care delivery should John implement to ensure seamless coordination and comprehensive care for the patient?
A) Patient-Centered Medical Home (PCMH)
B) Accountable Care Organization (ACO)
C) Transitional Care Model (TCM)
D) Chronic Care Model (CCM)

Question 129: Emily is a case manager assisting Tom, who struggles with managing his diabetes due to low motivation. Which approach should Emily adopt to effectively empower Tom and improve his adherence to the treatment plan?
A) Implement strict monitoring of Tom's glucose levels and dietary intake.
B) Facilitate motivational interviewing sessions to explore Tom's ambivalence towards change.
C) Provide Tom with a detailed list of dietary restrictions and exercise regimes.
D) Arrange for frequent visits from healthcare professionals for supervision.

Question 130: Which of the following strategies is most effective in ensuring a successful transition of care from hospital to home for a patient with complex medical needs?
A) Providing a comprehensive discharge summary to the patient
B) Scheduling a follow-up appointment within two weeks of discharge
C) Implementing a transitional care nurse to coordinate post-discharge care
D) Offering educational materials about medication management

Question 131: Sarah, a case manager in a community clinic, is working with Ms. Lee, who has been recently diagnosed with diabetes and struggles to manage her condition due to financial constraints. What should be Sarah's priority action to fulfill her role effectively?
A) Referring Ms. Lee to a diabetes support group
B) Assisting Ms. Lee in applying for financial assistance programs
C) Monitoring Ms. Lee's blood glucose levels regularly
D) Providing nutritional education tailored to Ms. Lee's cultural preferences

Question 132: Sarah, a case manager, is tasked with evaluating the healthcare utilization of a patient population using the Adjusted Clinical Group (ACG) system. She notices that two patients with similar chronic conditions have different resource utilizations. What is the primary factor in the ACG system that could explain this variation?
A) Socioeconomic status
B) Diagnosis-based risk adjustment
C) Age and gender differences
D) Comorbidity levels

Question 133: David, a Medicaid beneficiary with diabetes and depression, is enrolled in a Health Home. His case manager notices that he frequently misses appointments due to transportation issues. What aspect of the Health Home model should the case manager prioritize to address this barrier?

A) Comprehensive Transitional Care
B) Care Coordination
C) Individual and Family Support Services
D) Referral to Community and Social Support Services

Question 134: Lisa, a case manager, has a client named Sarah who recently lost her spouse. Sarah expresses interest in joining a bereavement support group but fears it might increase her distress by reliving painful memories. How should Lisa address Sarah's concern about the potential impact of joining such a group?
A) Emphasize that sharing painful memories leads to immediate emotional relief.
B) Explain that discussing grief can initially be distressing but often leads to long-term healing through mutual understanding and empathy.
C) Assure her that all members focus on positive topics only to avoid distress.
D) Suggest that attending sessions without speaking will prevent distress.

Question 135: John, a case manager, is reviewing an indemnity insurance policy for a patient named Sarah. Sarah's policy allows her to choose any healthcare provider without restrictions. However, she is concerned about the reimbursement process and potential out-of-pocket expenses. Which aspect of indemnity insurance should John emphasize to address Sarah's concerns?
A) Deductibles and Co-payments
B) Network Limitations
C) Pre-authorization Requirements
D) Capitation Fees

Question 136: Which of the following strategies is most effective in promoting client empowerment within a psychosocial support system?
A) Providing clients with detailed instructions and guidelines for managing their care.
B) Encouraging clients to participate actively in decision-making processes regarding their care.
C) Offering clients access to a wide range of educational resources and materials.
D) Establishing a structured routine for clients to follow in their daily activities.

Question 137: John, a case manager in a Health Home, needs to select an appropriate strategy for integrating behavioral health services for a client with diabetes and depression. Which strategy aligns best with the principles of the Health Home model?
A) Referring the client to external mental health specialists
B) Coordinating care through telehealth consultations only
C) Embedding behavioral health providers within primary care teams
D) Scheduling separate appointments for medical and behavioral health

Question 138: Sarah, a case manager, is assessing a patient, Mr. Johnson, who requires ongoing rehabilitation after a stroke. Considering his need for intensive therapy and monitoring, which alternative care site would be most appropriate for Mr. Johnson to achieve optimal recovery?
A) Home Health Care
B) Skilled Nursing Facility
C) Long-Term Acute Care Hospital
D) Outpatient Rehabilitation Center

Question 139: During a home visit, case manager Alex assesses Mrs. Jenkins' medication management following her recent hospital discharge for heart failure. Mrs. Jenkins reports taking her diuretics only when she feels swollen due to leg edema. What should Alex

prioritize in his management plan?
A) Educating on daily diuretic adherence
B) Monitoring blood pressure regularly
C) Adjusting diuretic dosage based on symptoms
D) Scheduling frequent follow-up visits

Question 140: Sarah, a case manager, is reviewing a patient's pharmacy benefits to ensure cost-effective medication management. The patient is prescribed a brand-name drug that has a generic equivalent. Which strategy should Sarah consider first to optimize the patient's pharmacy benefits while maintaining therapeutic efficacy?
A) Encourage the use of mail-order pharmacies for cost savings.
B) Recommend switching to the generic equivalent of the medication.
C) Suggest enrolling in a patient assistance program for the brand-name drug.
D) Propose splitting higher-dose tablets to reduce costs.

Question 141: John, a case manager at an acute care hospital, is developing a discharge plan for an elderly patient who requires ongoing wound care at home. Which healthcare provider should he primarily involve to ensure continuity of wound care management post-discharge?
A) Occupational Therapist
B) Dietitian
C) Home Health Nurse
D) Speech-Language Pathologist

Question 142: John, a 60-year-old male, is under your care as a case manager. He reports feeling isolated and has visible signs of malnutrition. Which factor should you consider most indicative of potential neglect?
A) Lack of social support
B) Poor personal hygiene
C) Financial instability
D) Recent bereavement

Question 143: How do disease-based organizations primarily enhance supportive care programs for patients with complex medical conditions?
A) By advocating for policy changes in healthcare legislation
B) By coordinating multidisciplinary care teams to manage patient care
C) By developing personalized treatment plans based on genetic profiling
D) By funding large-scale epidemiological studies

Question 144: What is a primary advantage of group homes in the context of care delivery for individuals with chronic mental health conditions?
A) They provide personalized one-on-one therapy sessions.
B) They offer a structured environment promoting social interaction and support.
C) They ensure access to advanced medical technologies.
D) They reduce the need for professional healthcare staff.

Question 145: John, a 45-year-old male with a history of alcohol use disorder, has been abstinent for six months. He is now experiencing heightened anxiety and insomnia. As his case manager, what would be the most appropriate initial intervention to address these symptoms while considering his substance use history?
A) Prescribe benzodiazepines for immediate relief
B) Suggest cognitive behavioral therapy (CBT)
C) Recommend over-the-counter sleep aids
D) Initiate antidepressant therapy

Question 146: Emily, a case manager, is assisting a client named Robert who has difficulty adhering to his

medication regimen due to a lack of social support. Which intervention should Emily prioritize to improve Robert's engagement and adherence?

A) Educating Robert about the importance of medication adherence
B) Connecting Robert with community support groups
C) Monitoring Robert's medication intake closely
D) Scheduling frequent check-ins with Robert

Question 147: Which of the following Medicaid eligibility groups is primarily determined by income level and family size, rather than specific medical conditions or disabilities?

A) Medically Needy
B) Pregnant Women
C) Disabled Individuals
D) Aged Individuals

Question 148: As a case manager, you are negotiating with a rehabilitation facility for the care of Mr. Johnson, a post-stroke patient. The facility has proposed a higher rate than usual due to specialized services. Which negotiation technique should you employ to achieve a fair rate while ensuring quality care for Mr. Johnson?

A) Anchoring
B) BATNA (Best Alternative to a Negotiated Agreement)
C) Interest-based negotiation
D) Compromise

Question 149: In the context of employer-based health and wellness programs, which strategy is most effective in increasing employee participation rates?

A) Offering gym memberships at a discounted rate
B) Implementing personalized wellness plans
C) Providing free healthy meals at work
D) Organizing monthly wellness challenges

Question 150: Sarah, a case manager at a large corporation, is tasked with evaluating the effectiveness of the company's new health and wellness program. The program includes biometric screenings, health coaching, and fitness challenges. Which outcome measure would most accurately assess the program's success in improving employee health?

A) Employee participation rates
B) Reduction in healthcare claims costs
C) Employee satisfaction surveys
D) Number of fitness challenge participants

ANSWER WITH DETAILED EXPLANATION SET [1]

Question 1: Correct Answer: A) Attachment-Based Therapy

Rationale: Attachment-Based Therapy focuses on understanding and improving relationship dynamics rooted in early attachment experiences, making it ideal for addressing trust issues stemming from childhood neglect. Solution-Focused Brief Therapy emphasizes solutions rather than underlying issues. Rational Emotive Behavior Therapy targets irrational beliefs but may not address deep-seated relational patterns. Dialectical Behavior Therapy is effective for emotional regulation but not specifically tailored for attachment-related trust issues like Attachment-Based Therapy is.

Question 2: Correct Answer: C) Social Role Theory

Rationale: Social Role Theory explains how chronic illness can alter an individual's self-identity by impacting their roles and interactions within society. Unlike the Biopsychosocial Model, which considers biological, psychological, and social factors but doesn't focus solely on identity, or Cognitive Behavioral Theory, which addresses thought patterns rather than societal roles, Social Role Theory specifically addresses changes in societal roles and expectations. Social Learning Theory focuses on behavior learned through observation, not directly on role change due to illness.

Question 3: Correct Answer: D) Buprenorphine-naloxone combination therapy

Rationale: Buprenorphine-naloxone is recommended due to its efficacy in managing withdrawal symptoms and reducing relapse risk by blocking opioid effects. Methadone (Option B), while effective, requires strict regulation and carries a higher risk of dependency. Naltrexone (Option C), post-detoxification, does not alleviate withdrawal symptoms effectively. Cold turkey cessation (Option A) often results in severe withdrawal symptoms and high relapse rates, making it less suitable for managing opioid use disorder effectively.

Question 4: Correct Answer: C) Collaborating with clients to set achievable goals

Rationale: Collaborating with clients to set achievable goals fosters empowerment by actively involving them in their care plan, enhancing their autonomy and confidence. While providing educational materials (A) and encouraging independent research (B) are beneficial, they may not directly engage the client in decision-making. Directly advising (D) limits client involvement, reducing empowerment. Collaborative goal-setting aligns with contemporary theories emphasizing shared decision-making as a cornerstone of empowerment.

Question 5: Correct Answer: A) Social Cognitive Theory

Rationale: Social Cognitive Theory focuses on self-efficacy and personal control as crucial factors in managing chronic illness. It highlights how beliefs in one's capabilities influence motivation and behavior. The Health Belief Model centers on perceived threats and benefits, while the Transtheoretical Model addresses stages of change. The Biopsychosocial Model integrates biological, psychological, and social factors but does not specifically emphasize self-efficacy. Therefore, Social Cognitive Theory is most aligned with the question's focus on personal control.

Question 6: Correct Answer: C) Role ambiguity

Rationale: Role ambiguity occurs when there is a lack of clarity in team roles and responsibilities, leading to confusion and inefficiency. In this scenario, despite having experienced members, unclear roles can hinder decision-making. Groupthink (A) involves conformity

leading to poor decisions, which isn't described here. Social loafing (B) refers to reduced effort by individuals in a group, not necessarily affecting decision consensus. Group polarization (D) describes groups making more extreme decisions, not struggling with consensus.

Question 7: Correct Answer: B) Collaboration

Rationale: Collaboration focuses on finding win-win solutions by integrating diverse perspectives, making it ideal for resolving conflicts in a multidisciplinary setting. Compromise might lead to partial satisfaction but doesn't fully utilize the team's potential. Avoidance ignores the issue, risking unresolved tension. Competition may exacerbate conflict rather than resolve it. By promoting collaboration, John can harness the team's collective expertise for optimal patient care outcomes.

Question 8: Correct Answer: A) Advise appealing for an exception for coverage at a preferred rate.

Rationale: Appealing for an exception can potentially lower out-of-pocket costs by reclassifying the drug into a more favorable tier, thus reducing copayments significantly if successful. Option B offers temporary financial relief but doesn't solve long-term cost issues. Option C might not be feasible if no alternatives exist or are ineffective for the client's condition. Option D does not address financial concerns and may lead to non-adherence due to cost barriers, making option A the most comprehensive solution.

Question 9: Correct Answer: A) Standardize care plan templates across all departments.

Rationale: Standardizing care plan templates (Option A) ensures uniformity and consistency in documentation, directly aligning with accreditation requirements for standardization and quality assurance. While Option B enhances communication, it doesn't ensure uniform documentation; Option C focuses on technology rather than standardization; Option D provides oversight but doesn't inherently standardize processes. Standardization directly addresses variability and supports consistent compliance across departments.

Question 10: Correct Answer: B) CPT

Rationale: CPT (Current Procedural Terminology) codes are used to describe medical procedures and services provided in outpatient settings. They ensure each service, like an X-ray or blood test, is billed accurately. ICD-10-CM codes diagnoses rather than services; DRG is for inpatient care; LOINC standardizes lab results reporting but isn't used for billing purposes. Thus, CPT is the correct choice for coding outpatient services in this scenario.

Question 11: Correct Answer: A) Patient-Centered Medical Home (PCMH)

Rationale: The PCMH model focuses on a team-based approach and integrated services, making it effective for managing multiple chronic conditions. It emphasizes comprehensive care coordination, patient engagement, and continuous improvement. Disease Management Programs focus on specific diseases rather than multiple conditions. The Traditional Fee-for-Service Model lacks coordination incentives. ACOs do promote integration but are more focused on cost reduction than patient-centered comprehensive care, unlike PCMH which prioritizes holistic management.

Question 12: Correct Answer: A) Patient-Centered Medical Home (PCMH)

Rationale: PCMH emphasizes comprehensive primary care through team-based approaches, enhancing resource utilization and patient outcomes. While IDS also integrates services, it may not focus as intensely on primary care as PCMH does. Capitation incentivizes cost control but might compromise quality without careful management. Bundled payments align with specific episodes of care rather than continuous management. PCMH provides a structured framework for resource optimization in rural settings like John's hospital by focusing on holistic and continuous patient-centered care.

Question 13: Correct Answer: B) A single payment is made for all services provided during an episode of care.
Rationale: The bundled payment model involves a single comprehensive payment for all services related to a specific treatment or condition over a set period, encouraging coordinated care and cost efficiency. Option A describes fee-for-service, where payments are made per service, not as a bundle. Option C refers to diagnosis-related groups (DRGs), which are based on diagnosis and resource use but not necessarily bundled payments. Option D outlines capitation, where providers are paid per patient rather than per episode of care.

Question 14: Correct Answer: B) Timely communication between hospital and primary care provider
Rationale: Timely communication between hospital and primary care providers is critical as it ensures continuity and consistency in treatment plans, reducing readmissions. Although medication reconciliation (A), telehealth (C), and patient education (D) are vital components, they do not directly address the need for synchronized healthcare provider collaboration. Medication reconciliation prevents errors but doesn't ensure follow-up. Telehealth can support ongoing monitoring but lacks personal interaction. Education empowers patients but may not suffice without professional guidance and coordination.

Question 15: Correct Answer: B) Verify surgical procedure codes
Rationale: Verifying surgical procedure codes is crucial as inaccuracies directly impact DRG assignment and subsequent reimbursement. While reviewing discharge summaries and assessing complications provide valuable information, they are secondary to ensuring correct procedure coding. Analyzing length of stay trends helps in resource management but does not directly influence DRG accuracy. Proper coding ensures that the hospital receives appropriate payment for services rendered, reflecting true clinical activity and resource use.

Question 16: Correct Answer: B) Collaboration
Rationale: Collaboration is the most effective strategy as it involves all parties working together to find a mutually beneficial solution, ensuring both psychosocial and medical needs are addressed. Compromise might lead to partial satisfaction, Avoidance ignores the issue, and Accommodation may prioritize one need over another without fully addressing both. Collaboration fosters open communication and integrates diverse perspectives, crucial for developing a comprehensive care plan that meets all of Mr. Johnson's needs.

Question 17: Correct Answer: C) Employing cognitive-behavioral therapy (CBT) tailored to address both conditions
Rationale:CBT tailored to both anxiety and alcohol use disorders effectively reduces relapse by targeting underlying cognitive patterns contributing to both conditions. Option A's sequential approach may leave one disorder untreated temporarily, increasing relapse risk. Option B's exclusive focus on motivational interviewing may not adequately address anxiety. Option D risks dependency without addressing alcohol issues. Tailored CBT integrates coping strategies for both

disorders, promoting sustained recovery.

Question 18: Correct Answer: C) Conduct an immediate risk assessment to evaluate Mrs. Lee's safety at home.
Rationale: Conducting an immediate risk assessment prioritizes evaluating Mrs. Lee's current safety and well-being, which is critical in cases of suspected neglect. Option A could be considered if the risk assessment indicates immediate danger but requires further evaluation first. Option B addresses potential knowledge gaps but does not assess urgency or severity of neglect signs. Option D ensures ongoing monitoring but lacks immediacy in addressing potential harm or neglect risks present during the initial visit.

Question 19: Correct Answer: B) Utilizing motivational interviewing techniques
Rationale: Motivational interviewing (MI) is recognized for its effectiveness in enhancing patient adherence by addressing ambivalence and fostering intrinsic motivation. While providing detailed instructions (A) and offering follow-up calls (D) can support adherence, they lack the personalized approach of MI. Group sessions (C) offer peer support but may not address individual concerns. MI's strength lies in its person-centered approach, which aligns with contemporary theories emphasizing patient empowerment and engagement.

Question 20: Correct Answer: C) Conduct a comprehensive risk assessment
Rationale: Conducting a comprehensive risk assessment (Option C) is crucial as it allows the case manager to understand the immediate dangers and prioritize interventions. While developing a care plan (Option A) and establishing a therapeutic alliance (Option B) are essential, they follow after assessing risks. Referring to community resources (Option D) is supportive but secondary to understanding immediate threats. The risk assessment ensures the client's immediate safety and informs further actions.

Question 21: Correct Answer: C) Preparation
Rationale: The preparation stage involves taking small steps towards change and gathering information, as seen in John's actions. He is beyond contemplation (B), where he would only be considering change without action. Precontemplation (A) involves no intention to change, while maintenance (D) occurs post-change when sustaining efforts. His active information-gathering indicates preparation readiness.

Question 22: Correct Answer: C) Pay-for-performance model
Rationale: The pay-for-performance model rewards providers for meeting specific quality and efficiency benchmarks, aligning with value-based care by promoting improved outcomes and cost-effectiveness. Option A, fee-for-service, incentivizes volume over value without focusing on outcomes. Option B, capitation, provides fixed payments per patient but lacks direct outcome incentives. Option D, retrospective cost-based reimbursement, reimburses based on incurred costs rather than outcomes or performance metrics.

Question 23: Correct Answer: A) The risk that an insured individual may take greater risks because they have coverage
Rationale: Moral hazard refers to the tendency of individuals to engage in riskier behavior when they are insulated from the consequences, such as having health insurance coverage. Option A is correct as it captures this essence. Option B relates to insurer practices, not insured behavior. Option C involves provider incentives rather than insured behavior. Option D pertains to patient satisfaction, not risk-taking behavior. Thus, A correctly

identifies moral hazard in health insurance.

Question 24: Correct Answer: A) Housing instability
Rationale: Housing instability significantly exacerbates stress and anxiety due to uncertainty and potential homelessness, directly impacting mental health. While neighborhood safety also affects stress levels, housing instability creates a more immediate threat to an individual's well-being. Access to recreational facilities and healthy food options contribute positively to mental health but do not have the same immediate negative impact as housing insecurity. The chronic stress from unstable housing situations can lead to severe mental health issues compared to other factors.

Question 25: Correct Answer: B) It indicates whether a disability claimant is able to engage in competitive employment.
Rationale: The SGA threshold is used to assess if a disability claimant can perform substantial work despite their impairment, impacting SSDI eligibility. Option A pertains to benefit calculations, C relates to medical evaluations, and D concerns rehabilitation needs, which are distinct from SGA's purpose. Understanding SGA helps case managers evaluate clients' ability to maintain employment under SSDI guidelines, crucial for proper case management.

Question 26: Correct Answer: C) The client's emotional state and its impact on decision-making capacity.
Rationale: A client's emotional state significantly affects their cognitive processing and ability to make rational decisions, aligning with psychosocial theories on decision making. Previous experience (A), understanding terminology (B), and willingness to comply (D) are relevant but secondary; they do not directly address the cognitive-emotional interplay critical for informed decisions. Emotional readiness ensures clients can process information effectively and engage in meaningful discussions about their care, making C the valid choice based on contemporary psychosocial concepts.

Question 27: Correct Answer: A) Ensuring the facility has a robust cognitive stimulation program.
Rationale: For John's early-stage dementia, cognitive stimulation programs are vital as they can slow progression and enhance quality of life. While personalized meals (B), on-site medical staff (C), and family visit accessibility (D) contribute to overall well-being, cognitive engagement directly addresses his primary health challenge. Cognitive programs foster mental activity that can help maintain cognitive function longer than focusing solely on physical health or convenience factors alone.

Question 28: Correct Answer: C) Coordinate transportation services for medical appointments
Rationale: Coordinating transportation services directly addresses John's primary barrier to accessing medical care—his inability to attend appointments due to transportation issues. Telehealth consultations (A), while convenient, may not be feasible if John lacks technology access or comfort. Community health worker visits (B) provide support but don't solve the appointment attendance issue. Adult day care programs (D) offer socialization but don't ensure medical follow-up. Transportation ensures John can maintain regular contact with healthcare providers, crucial for managing his condition effectively.

Question 29: Correct Answer: C) The deductible and co-payment amounts
Rationale: While all options are relevant, focusing on deductibles and co-payments (Option C) is crucial as they directly impact out-of-pocket costs. Premiums (Option B) are fixed costs, but high deductibles can lead to unexpected expenses. Provider networks (Option A) are important for access but do not directly affect cost efficiency. Wellness programs (Option D) offer long-term benefits but do not immediately reduce expenses. Thus, understanding deductible and co-payment structures helps optimize financial planning for healthcare needs.

Question 30: Correct Answer: B) Patient-centered care indicators
Rationale: URAC emphasizes patient-centered care indicators as a critical component of its accreditation standards. This focus ensures that healthcare organizations prioritize patient outcomes, satisfaction, and engagement in care processes. While financial performance metrics (A), staffing ratios (C), and facility infrastructure (D) are important, they do not directly align with URAC's primary emphasis on enhancing patient-centered care. Patient-centered care involves personalized treatment plans and active patient participation, which are central to URAC's quality measurement approach.

Question 31: Correct Answer: B) Assist Lisa in developing a comprehensive plan that includes setting realistic goals.
Rationale: Developing a comprehensive plan with realistic goals empowers Lisa and provides structure for effective self-management. Option A may overwhelm her without guidance; C limits decision-making based on others' experiences; D could lead to unsustainable choices. By focusing on goal-setting and planning, John aligns with self-directed care principles, fostering autonomy while ensuring informed decisions tailored to Lisa's unique needs.

Question 32: Correct Answer: B) Develop a comprehensive symptom management plan tailored to his needs
Rationale: Developing a comprehensive symptom management plan (Option B) is crucial in hospice care to ensure Mr. Thompson's comfort and quality of life. Unlike Option A, hospice care emphasizes comfort rather than aggressive treatments. Option C overlooks the immediate need for symptom control, and Option D contradicts hospice principles by suggesting surgical interventions. The correct approach aligns with palliative care principles focusing on symptom relief and patient-centered care.

Question 33: Correct Answer: B) Facilitate Sarah's access to a women's support group.
Rationale: Facilitating access to a women's support group provides immediate peer support, fostering empowerment and understanding among individuals in similar situations. While couples therapy (Option A) could be beneficial, it may not address the power imbalance effectively. Discussing feelings with family (Option C) might not offer the necessary professional guidance, and individual therapy (Option D), while helpful for personal growth, may not provide the immediate community support needed in cases of controlling behavior.

Question 34: Correct Answer: C) Statistical Process Control (SPC)
Rationale: Statistical Process Control (SPC) uses statistical methods to monitor and control a process, aiming to reduce variability and improve consistency. TQM emphasizes overall organizational quality culture, Lean Management targets waste elimination, and Balanced Scorecard measures performance across multiple perspectives. SPC's unique focus on data-driven decision-making through control charts allows for precise tracking of process variations, ensuring consistent clinical outcomes by addressing inconsistencies in real-time.

Question 35: Correct Answer: D) Coordinate with community resources for ongoing support
Rationale: Coordinating with community resources ensures Mr. Johnson receives comprehensive care post-discharge, addressing his complex needs and limited support. While advocating for services (A), arranging transportation (B), and educating on medication (C) are important, they do not encompass the broader scope of ensuring continuous support through community resources, which is crucial for his long-term well-being.

Question 36: Correct Answer: B) The daughter's work commitments limiting her availability
Rationale: The daughter's work commitments can significantly limit her availability and create stress in Maria's support system due to potential conflicts between caregiving and professional responsibilities. Although lack of knowledge (A), reluctance to accept help (C), and financial burdens (D) are stressors, they can be mitigated through education, gradual acceptance of external aid, and financial planning. However, balancing work and caregiving demands directly impacts time management and care consistency, making it a primary stressor in this scenario.

Question 37: Correct Answer: B) Simplify the medication regimen by using color-coded charts.
Rationale: Simplifying complex information through visual aids like color-coded charts can significantly aid individuals with limited health literacy in understanding and adhering to medication regimens. Option A may help reinforce information but doesn't specifically address comprehension barriers. Option C is beneficial but relies on family availability and involvement rather than empowering Mrs. Jenkins directly. Option D might overwhelm or confuse her further due to her limited ability to process detailed written information independently.

Question 38: Correct Answer: B) Utilizing decision aids tailored to individual client needs
Rationale: Option B is correct as it highlights the use of personalized decision aids, which facilitate understanding and active participation in healthcare decisions. This approach is supported by research indicating that tailored aids improve client engagement and outcomes. Option A can confuse clients, hindering understanding. Option C limits engagement by not considering diverse communication methods. Option D contradicts the goal of shared decision making by restricting client involvement.

Question 39: Correct Answer: B) Contemplation
Rationale: The contemplation stage involves individuals recognizing the need for change and intending to take action within the next six months. Unlike preparation, where plans are imminent, contemplation lacks immediate action. Precontemplation involves no intention to change, while action involves active modification of behavior. Understanding these subtle distinctions is crucial for effective case management.

Question 40: Correct Answer: B) Pharmaceutical Assistance Program
Rationale: Pharmaceutical Assistance Programs are designed to help individuals like John access medications at reduced or no cost, making them an ideal resource for the uninsured or underinsured. Medicaid (A) may not be immediately available due to eligibility requirements. Community Health Clinics (C) provide general healthcare but might not cover specific medications. Emergency Room Services (D) are not intended for ongoing medication management and are costly. Thus, option B is the most suitable choice.

Question 41: Correct Answer: C) Personalized door-to-door transport services for social activities

Rationale: Personalized door-to-door transport for social activities significantly enhances social engagement by addressing specific mobility needs and fostering independence. While subsidized taxis (A) focus on medical needs, they overlook broader social engagement. Fixed-route shuttles (B) may not align with individual schedules or locations. Infrastructure improvements (D), though important, do not provide immediate personal support. Thus, option C uniquely combines personalization and accessibility to promote active participation in social life.

Question 42: Correct Answer: C) Health Maintenance Organization (HMO).
Rationale: An HMO typically offers lower out-of-pocket costs with fixed copayments and no deductible for network services, which benefits clients managing chronic conditions. While HDHPs offer HSAs for savings, they involve higher initial costs. PPOs provide flexibility but often come with higher premiums and out-of-network costs. EPOs limit provider choice without referral requirements but can be costly if out-of-network care is needed. Therefore, an HMO provides cost-effective management for chronic conditions within its network structure.

Question 43: Correct Answer: B) Explore John's values and how they align with taking medication.
Rationale: Exploring John's values helps him connect personal beliefs with behavior change, fostering intrinsic motivation—a core principle of Motivational Interviewing. Option A lacks patient-centeredness, Option C may increase resistance by focusing on negatives, and Option D pressures decision-making without resolving ambivalence. Each incorrect option fails to address the underlying ambivalence effectively, unlike option B, which aligns with Motivational Interviewing's empathetic and collaborative approach.

Question 44: Correct Answer: C) Pay-for-performance incentives
Rationale: Pay-for-performance aligns financial incentives with quality outcomes, central to value-based care. Option A encourages volume over quality, B offers fixed payments potentially leading to under-service, and D reimburses based on past costs without incentivizing improved future performance. Pay-for-performance effectively balances cost control and quality improvement.

Question 45: Correct Answer: B) Develop an individualized service plan focusing on assistive technology needs.
Rationale: An individualized service plan tailored to assistive technology addresses Emily's specific functional needs, enhancing independence and resource access. A), while beneficial socially, doesn't address practical needs directly. C) is valuable but not as immediate in impact as assistive technology. D) involves family but lacks direct action on Emily's resource access. The focus on assistive technology aligns with contemporary research emphasizing personalized interventions for individuals with disabilities.

Question 46: Correct Answer: B) Accurate coding and billing practices
Rationale: Accurate coding and billing practices are crucial for financial sustainability in virtual care services because they ensure appropriate reimbursement. While patient satisfaction scores (A), volume of consultations (C), and integration with EHRs (D) are important, they do not directly impact reimbursement processes. Proper coding ensures compliance with payer requirements, directly affecting revenue flow. In contrast, high volumes or satisfied patients without accurate billing may lead to

revenue loss due to denied claims or audits.

Question 47: Correct Answer: B) To improve quality of life and manage symptoms

Rationale: The primary goal of supportive care programs is to enhance the quality of life and manage symptoms for patients with chronic illnesses. While curing the disease (Option A) is ideal, it is not always possible, making symptom management crucial. Financial assistance (Option C) may be part of supportive care but is not its primary goal. Ensuring medication adherence (Option D) is important but secondary to overall quality of life improvement. Supportive care focuses on holistic well-being, encompassing physical, emotional, and social health.

Question 48: Correct Answer: C) The improvement in client-reported quality of life measures.

Rationale: Improvement in client-reported quality of life measures is a direct indicator of enhanced psychosocial well-being, reflecting meaningful change beyond mere participation or social expansion. Option A focuses on attendance rather than outcomes. Option B may not correlate directly with well-being improvements. Option D, while beneficial, does not necessarily equate to overall quality of life enhancement. Thus, option C provides a comprehensive measure of the group's impact on the client's psychosocial health.

Question 49: Correct Answer: B) Risk Stratification Tool

Rationale: The Risk Stratification Tool is crucial for identifying patients at high risk for adverse outcomes, allowing for proactive interventions. While SWOT Analysis assesses strengths and weaknesses broadly, it lacks specificity in patient care contexts. Root Cause Analysis focuses on problem-solving post-incident rather than preemptive identification. A Gantt Chart aids in project timelines but doesn't directly identify patient-specific barriers. Hence, the Risk Stratification Tool is most aligned with preemptive care planning needs.

Question 50: Correct Answer: C) Wisconsin Card Sorting Test (WCST)

Rationale: The Wisconsin Card Sorting Test (WCST) is specifically designed to assess executive functions like planning, cognitive flexibility, and problem-solving. While the WAIS measures overall intelligence, the MMPI assesses personality structure and psychopathology, and the BDI evaluates depressive symptoms. The WCST's focus on executive functioning makes it the correct choice for evaluating these cognitive processes in adults.

Question 51: Correct Answer: B) The group's focus on the specific illness

Rationale: Selecting a support group focused on the client's specific illness ensures that members share relevant experiences and resources, fostering better understanding and support. While proximity (A), meeting frequency (C), and group size (D) are important, they are secondary to ensuring that the group can address specific concerns related to the illness. This alignment enhances emotional support and practical advice tailored to the client's condition.

Question 52: Correct Answer: B) Interactive digital platforms with personalized feedback

Rationale: Interactive digital platforms provide personalized feedback, enhancing engagement and learning retention, which are crucial for self-management in diabetes. While structured workshops (A) and lecture-based seminars (D) offer valuable information, they lack interactivity and personalization. Pamphlets (C), though informative, do not engage users actively. Current research supports digital platforms as they cater to individual learning needs and preferences, fostering

better understanding and adherence to self-care practices.

Question 53: Correct Answer: B) Discuss the treatment options with Sarah, including risks, benefits, and alternatives, and encourage questions.

Rationale: Option B is correct because it involves direct communication with Sarah about her treatment options, ensuring she understands the implications and can make an informed choice. This approach aligns with patient-centered care principles and empowers Sarah in her decision-making process. Option A lacks interactive engagement; Option C may be helpful but doesn't directly involve the case manager; Option D bypasses Sarah's autonomy by involving her family without her input.

Question 54: Correct Answer: B) Empathetic understanding

Rationale: Empathetic understanding is crucial for building rapport and engaging clients, as it involves recognizing and responding to their emotions. Authoritative guidance (A) might create distance, structured feedback (C) focuses on task-oriented interactions, and transactional analysis (D), while useful, can be too analytical in initial rapport-building stages. Empathy helps establish a connection by showing genuine care and understanding, which is fundamental in interpersonal communication according to contemporary research on emotional intelligence.

Question 55: Correct Answer: B) Analyzing readmission rates within 30 days post-discharge

Rationale: Analyzing readmission rates within 30 days post-discharge directly measures the effectiveness of the discharge planning process in preventing unnecessary readmissions, which is a key quality outcome. While patient satisfaction surveys (A) provide subjective feedback, they do not directly measure clinical outcomes. Reviewing staff compliance (C) focuses on process adherence rather than outcomes. Monitoring length of stay (D) can indicate efficiency but not necessarily quality in terms of preventing readmissions.

Question 56: Correct Answer: C) Indemnity plans often reimburse out-of-network services based on standard rates but may require higher co-payments or deductibles from John.

Rationale: Indemnity plans typically reimburse out-of-network care at standard rates while imposing higher cost-sharing measures like increased deductibles or co-payments to deter non-preferred provider use. Option A inaccurately suggests complete exclusion of coverage; Option B misleads about pre-approval necessity during emergencies; and Option D falsely claims full cost coverage without additional expense to the insured party.

Question 57: Correct Answer: A) Autonomy in decision-making

Rationale: Autonomy in decision-making is central to self-directed care as it allows clients to make informed choices about their health, fostering independence and empowerment. While frequent supervision (B) and structured care pathways (C) can support care, they may limit autonomy. Regular assessment of client satisfaction (D) is important but does not directly empower clients. The focus on autonomy aligns with contemporary research emphasizing patient-centered approaches that enhance self-efficacy and engagement in personal health management.

Question 58: Correct Answer: D) Sarah is eligible for COBRA because the company has more than 20 employees.

Rationale: Under COBRA, employers with 20 or more employees must offer continuation of group health coverage when it would otherwise be lost due to specific events like job loss. Option A is incorrect as the threshold is not 50 employees; Option B is incorrect as eligibility depends on the size of the company; Option C is incorrect as finding another job isn't a requirement for applying to COBRA.

Question 59: Correct Answer: C) Exploring Emily's values and preferences before discussing treatment options.

Rationale: Shared decision making involves understanding the patient's values and preferences to guide discussions about treatment options, fostering collaboration and informed choices. Option A lacks guidance; B limits patient involvement by focusing solely on clinical evidence; D prioritizes side effects without considering personal values. Option C ensures that Emily's preferences are central to the decision-making process, aligning with contemporary research emphasizing patient-centered care.

Question 60: Correct Answer: A) Prioritize strategies that align with John's lifestyle and goals after a comprehensive discussion.

Rationale: Shared decision making requires integrating patient lifestyle and goals into care planning, promoting adherence and satisfaction. Option A aligns with this by emphasizing personalized care through dialogue. Option B disregards individualization in favor of statistical success; C might compromise care quality due to cost considerations; D overlooks patient autonomy. Acknowledging John's unique circumstances ensures meaningful engagement in his self-care management plan, consistent with recognized theories of shared decision making.

Question 61: Correct Answer: D) Value-based purchasing

Rationale: Value-based purchasing aligns reimbursement with quality outcomes, incentivizing providers to deliver high-quality, cost-effective care. It emphasizes efficiency and patient satisfaction over volume, optimizing resources. Utilization review processes (A), while important for monitoring service use, do not directly link payment to outcomes. Capitated payment models (B) offer fixed payments but may risk underutilization of services. Fee-for-service billing (C) encourages volume over value, potentially increasing costs without improving quality, making D the optimal strategy for balancing finances and care quality.

Question 62: Correct Answer: C) VHA prioritizes veterans with service-connected disabilities first, followed by those with lower incomes.

Rationale: The Veterans Health Administration prioritizes veterans with service-connected disabilities first, as these individuals often have greater healthcare needs related to their service. Following this, income levels are considered to ensure accessibility for those with financial constraints. Option A is incorrect since rank does not influence priority; Option B is partially correct but lacks the disability component; and Option D inaccurately suggests equal access without prioritization criteria.

Question 63: Correct Answer: B) Facilitating communication between providers to ensure seamless care delivery.

Rationale: The primary responsibility of a case manager in an indemnity insurance plan is to facilitate communication between providers to ensure seamless care delivery. Unlike managed care plans, indemnity plans often lack a network structure, requiring case managers to coordinate among diverse providers. Option A focuses on pre-approval, more relevant in managed care. Option C is important but secondary to coordination. Option D involves negotiation, which is not typically within a case manager's role in indemnity contexts.

Question 64: Correct Answer: B) The client's personal factors, behavior, and environment interact to influence outcomes.

Rationale: Reciprocal determinism, a concept from social cognitive theory, emphasizes the dynamic interplay between personal factors, behavior, and environmental influences. Unlike option A and D, which suggest unidirectional influence, reciprocal determinism (option B) acknowledges mutual interaction. Option C incorrectly limits the interaction to just personal factors and the environment. Understanding this concept helps case managers design interventions that consider all three elements for effective client support.

Question 65: Correct Answer: B) Availability of specialized memory care services

Rationale: The availability of specialized memory care services is crucial for Mr. Thompson due to his mild cognitive impairment, ensuring he receives appropriate support and management. While proximity to family (Option A), cost (Option C), and social activities (Option D) are important, they do not directly address his cognitive needs. Specialized memory care can provide tailored interventions that enhance his quality of life and potentially slow cognitive decline, making it the most critical factor for his successful transition.

Question 66: Correct Answer: C) Create a safe environment for John to disclose information voluntarily.

Rationale: The correct answer is C. Establishing trust and safety encourages disclosure of sensitive information like abuse. Psychological evaluations (Option A) focus on mental health rather than immediate safety concerns. Interviewing family members (Option B) might breach confidentiality or worsen John's situation without his consent. Monitoring injury patterns (Option D) delays intervention and can endanger John's safety if abuse is occurring. Creating a supportive space prioritizes John's autonomy and well-being.

Question 67: Correct Answer: C) Complexity of the patient's medication regimen

Rationale: The complexity of the patient's medication regimen is crucial in determining acuity because it reflects the intricacy and intensity of care needed. While length of stay (A) and emergency visits (B) are important, they are outcomes rather than direct indicators of current acuity. Socioeconomic status (D), although significant for overall care planning, does not directly measure clinical acuity. Medication complexity directly impacts daily management needs and potential complications, making it a primary factor in assessing severity levels.

Question 68: Correct Answer: B) Invest in training for her personal care assistants to improve service quality.

Rationale: Investing in training enhances the quality of care, leading to better health outcomes and more efficient use of resources. Option A may compromise care quality, while C and D overlook the importance of personalized assistance in daily living activities. Training ensures that assistants are well-equipped to meet Sarah's needs, aligning with principles of self-directed care that emphasize empowerment and informed decision-making.

Question 69: Correct Answer: C) Implement an integrated treatment plan that includes psychotherapy and pharmacotherapy for both conditions.

Rationale: An integrated treatment plan combining psychotherapy and pharmacotherapy is vital for managing dual diagnoses like Maria's, as it addresses both mental health and substance use issues simultaneously. Option A may neglect immediate substance-related risks; B fails to consider mental health stabilization needs; D focuses too narrowly on behavioral aspects without comprehensive care. Integrated approaches ensure balanced attention to both conditions, promoting better long-term outcomes.

Question 70: Correct Answer: B) Developing a comprehensive discharge plan involving multidisciplinary teams.
Rationale:A comprehensive discharge plan ensures coordinated efforts across disciplines, addressing complex needs during transitions. Option A is supportive but not comprehensive enough alone. Option C aids self-management but lacks immediate transitional focus. Option D offers ongoing contact but doesn't ensure initial coordination essential for seamless transition.

Question 71: Correct Answer: B) The patient's income relative to the federal poverty level.
Rationale: Pharmaceutical assistance programs often determine eligibility based on financial need, typically using the federal poverty level as a benchmark. While insurance coverage (Option A), adherence (Option C), and medical history (Option D) are important in managing care, they do not primarily determine eligibility for these programs. Income assessment ensures resources are allocated to those who most need financial support, making it the key criterion.

Question 72: Correct Answer: B) Develop personalized care plans that align with John's interests and goals.
Rationale: Developing personalized care plans tailored to John's interests fosters engagement by making him an active participant in his care, enhancing motivation and commitment. Stricter policies (A) or reminders (C), while potentially helpful in ensuring attendance, do not address the underlying disengagement issue. Incentives (D) might temporarily increase attendance but fail to build intrinsic motivation or strengthen the therapeutic relationship like personalized care planning does through mutual respect and collaboration.

Question 73: Correct Answer: B) Pay-for-Performance Model
Rationale: The Pay-for-Performance Model incentivizes providers to improve quality by linking payments to performance metrics related to patient outcomes and cost management. Capitation provides a fixed amount per patient regardless of services, potentially neglecting quality. Bundled Payments focus on episodes of care rather than ongoing chronic management. Global Budget Payments set a total budget for all services, lacking specific quality incentives. Thus, Pay-for-Performance aligns financial incentives with the goal of high-quality chronic care management.

Question 74: Correct Answer: C) Reduction in working hours resulting in loss of benefits
Rationale:COBRA provides continued health coverage when an employee loses benefits due to reduced work hours. While voluntary resignation (A) qualifies, termination for gross misconduct (B) does not. Retirement age (D) may offer other coverage options like Medicare but isn't a COBRA trigger. Reduction in hours directly impacts benefit eligibility, making it a valid COBRA qualifying event, unlike the other options where eligibility is either conditional or not applicable.

Question 75: Correct Answer: A) The possibility of outliving the estimated life expectancy used in the settlement offer calculation.
Rationale: Option A is correct because if Emily outlives her projected life expectancy, she may face financial challenges without insurance coverage or additional

funds from future settlements. Options B and C are valid concerns but do not directly affect long-term financial security like Option A does. Option D involves privacy issues but doesn't impact financial outcomes significantly. This highlights why understanding longevity risks is vital for Emily's decision-making process regarding viatical settlements.

Question 76: Correct Answer: B) Integrated Care Model
Rationale: The Integrated Care Model emphasizes seamless service delivery across various healthcare settings, ensuring continuity and efficient use of resources. Unlike the Broker Model, which focuses on linking clients to services, or the Client-Centered Model, which prioritizes individual needs, the Integrated Care Model aims for systemic coordination. The Collaborative Care Model involves teamwork but may not emphasize integration across all service levels as extensively as the Integrated Care Model.

Question 77: Correct Answer: B) Integrated care networks
Rationale: Integrated care networks are designed to address both medical and social needs, offering a holistic approach to managing chronic mental health conditions. They combine healthcare services with social support systems, which is crucial for comprehensive management. Outpatient psychiatric clinics (A) primarily focus on medical treatment, while support groups (C) provide social support but lack medical integration. Emergency shelters (D) offer temporary housing and basic services but are not specialized for chronic mental health management.

Question 78: Correct Answer: B) Implement an app-based symptom tracker alongside video consultations for comprehensive management.
Rationale: Option B is correct as it integrates multiple technologies—symptom tracking apps and video consultations—providing a holistic approach to managing chronic conditions like heart failure. Option A lacks continuous monitoring; C is insufficient for real-time updates; D doesn't offer personalized engagement necessary for complex health management.

Question 79: Correct Answer: C) Outcome measurement
Rationale: Outcome measurement directly assesses the results of healthcare services, providing clear insights into patient health improvements and overall care quality. While process mapping (A) and root cause analysis (B) focus on understanding and improving processes, they do not directly evaluate patient outcomes. Benchmarking (D), though useful for comparing standards, does not specifically measure patient outcomes. Therefore, outcome measurement is the most effective method for evaluating care quality through patient outcomes.

Question 80: Correct Answer: B) Coordinating simultaneous treatment for both disorders
Rationale: Coordinating simultaneous treatment is crucial as both disorders can exacerbate each other. Addressing them concurrently can improve overall outcomes and reduce relapse rates. While prioritizing one disorder (Option A) or focusing solely on pharmacotherapy (Option C) or psychotherapy (Option D) might seem logical, these approaches may not address the complex interplay between the disorders effectively. Contemporary research supports integrated treatment plans as the most effective strategy for dual diagnoses.

Question 81: Correct Answer: B) Develop personalized care plans with client input.
Rationale: Personalized care plans foster ownership and engagement in self-care, crucial for chronic condition management. Option A is too narrow, neglecting broader

advocacy skills. C excludes clients from decision-making, hindering empowerment. D addresses immediate issues but not long-term advocacy skills development. Involving clients in planning aligns with holistic, client-centered approaches that contemporary research supports for sustainable self-management.

Question 82: Correct Answer: A) Individually purchased insurance allows for customization of benefits to suit personal needs.

Rationale: The primary advantage of individually purchased insurance is the ability to tailor coverage options to fit individual preferences and needs, unlike employer-sponsored plans which often have predetermined benefits. Option B is incorrect as individually purchased plans usually have higher premiums due to lack of group discounts. Option C is misleading because network access depends on the specific plan, not the purchase method. Option D is incorrect since individually purchased plans do not mandate comprehensive coverage; they offer varying levels based on choice.

Question 83: Correct Answer: B) Contemplation

Rationale: In the Contemplation stage, clients recognize the need for change but are not yet ready to take action. This distinguishes it from Precontemplation, where there is no recognition of the need to change. Preparation involves planning to take action soon, while Action refers to actively making changes. Understanding these nuances helps case managers tailor interventions according to client readiness.

Question 84: Correct Answer: B) Weekly group counseling sessions

Rationale: Weekly group counseling sessions are crucial for enhancing emotional well-being by providing social support and reducing feelings of isolation. While physical therapy (A), nutritional supplements (C), and medication reviews (D) contribute to overall health, they do not directly address emotional support like counseling does. Counseling facilitates sharing experiences and coping strategies, which are essential in managing psychosocial aspects of chronic illness.

Question 85: Correct Answer: C) Low out-of-pocket maximum

Rationale: A low out-of-pocket maximum limits the total amount Emily would need to pay in a year, reducing her financial burden during major medical events. While low premiums (Option A) reduce monthly costs, they often accompany higher out-of-pocket expenses. A high deductible (Option B) increases initial costs before insurance coverage kicks in. A wide network (Option D) offers provider flexibility but doesn't directly address cost concerns. Thus, Option C best aligns with minimizing Emily's potential financial burden.

Question 86: Correct Answer: C) Centers for Medicare & Medicaid Services (CMS)

Rationale: CMS is a primary source of quality indicators, offering extensive data on patient outcomes and hospital performance through programs like the Hospital Compare website. NQF endorses standards but doesn't directly collect data. HCAHPS provides patient satisfaction surveys, not comprehensive performance data. AHRQ focuses on research to improve quality but does not directly provide performance metrics like CMS.

Question 87: Correct Answer: B) Employee engagement levels

Rationale: Employee engagement levels are crucial for the success of wellness programs in reducing healthcare costs. Engaged employees are more likely to participate actively, leading to better health outcomes and cost reductions. While comprehensive health assessments (A), availability of fitness facilities (C), and incentive-based participation (D) contribute to program success, they depend heavily on engagement. Research indicates that without high engagement, even well-designed programs may not achieve significant cost savings or desired health improvements.

Question 88: Correct Answer: A) Gatekeeping

Rationale: Gatekeeping is effective in managing costs by requiring primary care physician referrals for specialist services, ensuring appropriate and necessary use of resources. Open Access Plans (B) allow direct access to specialists, potentially increasing costs without improving quality. Retrospective Payment System (C), where providers are paid after services are delivered, can lead to overutilization. High Deductible Health Plans (D) may reduce initial costs but can deter necessary care due to high out-of-pocket expenses, unlike gatekeeping which balances cost and quality effectively.

Question 89: Correct Answer: B) Use of standardized communication tools like SBAR (Situation-Background-Assessment-Recommendation).

Rationale: Standardized communication tools like SBAR are crucial for effective communication in interdisciplinary teams, providing a structured method to convey information clearly and consistently. While regular meetings (A) and frequent updates (D) support communication, they lack the standardization that prevents misunderstandings. Establishing a hierarchy (C) may hinder open communication by creating power dynamics that discourage input from all team members. Therefore, using standardized tools ensures clarity and precision in exchanges among diverse professionals, enhancing overall teamwork efficiency.

Question 90: Correct Answer: A) Occupational Therapist

Rationale: Occupational Therapists assess patients' functional abilities to aid discharge planning by evaluating activities of daily living. While Physical Therapists focus on mobility, Speech-Language Pathologists address communication/swallowing disorders, and Clinical Nurse Specialists provide advanced nursing care, none are primarily tasked with assessing functional abilities for discharge planning. Occupational Therapists uniquely evaluate how physical, cognitive, and emotional factors impact daily functioning, making them integral to developing effective discharge plans that ensure safe transitions from hospital to home.

Question 91: Correct Answer: C) Improved patient adherence to treatment plans

Rationale: Virtual care platforms enhance patient adherence by facilitating regular monitoring and communication, allowing for timely interventions and support. While A) reduced need for in-person consultations is a benefit, it doesn't directly impact adherence. B) enhanced data security is crucial but not unique to virtual care. D) increased workload is typically a challenge rather than a benefit. The key advantage lies in improved adherence through consistent engagement and personalized care management.

Question 92: Correct Answer: C) Building a supportive community network around the client

Rationale: Building a supportive community network around the client is essential for sustained behavioral change as it provides ongoing psychosocial support and encouragement from peers and family. Option A focuses on individual progress but may lack external reinforcement. Option B might motivate short-term compliance but doesn't ensure long-term engagement or address deeper psychosocial needs. Option D increases knowledge but doesn't inherently provide the ongoing support that a community network offers, which is crucial for lasting change.

Question 93: Correct Answer: B) Provides predictable revenue streams

Rationale: Case rates offer predictable revenue streams as they provide a fixed payment per case, enabling healthcare providers to forecast financial outcomes more accurately. Unlike option A, which suggests overutilization, case rates discourage unnecessary services due to fixed payments. Option C is incorrect as case rates often reduce administrative tasks by simplifying billing processes. Option D is incorrect because while focus on outcomes can vary, case rates generally do not inherently reduce outcome focus.

Question 94: Correct Answer: B) Establishing community-based programs to address social determinants of health affecting Maria

Rationale: Option B is correct because addressing social determinants of health is crucial in population health management, impacting long-term outcomes and resource optimization. Option A focuses narrowly on immediate needs, missing broader determinants. Option C may increase costs without addressing root causes. Option D, while important, doesn't encompass broader community and environmental factors influencing health.

Question 95: Correct Answer: B) Shared savings programs

Rationale: Shared savings programs incentivize integrated care by allowing providers to share in cost savings achieved through coordinated efforts. Unlike fee-for-service (A), which encourages fragmented services, shared savings promote collaboration. Capitation models (C) provide fixed payments but may not incentivize integration specifically. Direct primary care (D), while promoting access, does not inherently foster provider integration across systems. Thus, shared savings programs effectively drive integrated delivery by aligning financial incentives with collaborative patient-centered approaches in value-based frameworks.

Question 96: Correct Answer: A) Encourage participation in online support groups

Rationale: Online support groups provide social interaction without requiring physical presence, crucial for someone like Maria who has mobility issues. While pain management (B), mindfulness (C), and physical therapy (D) can improve her condition, they do not directly address her isolation.

Question 97: Correct Answer: A) Cognitive Behavioral Therapy (CBT)

Rationale: Cognitive Behavioral Therapy (CBT) is the most effective intervention for Sarah as it focuses on identifying and changing negative thought patterns and behaviors, which are crucial in dealing with emotional abuse. While psychoanalysis delves into unconscious conflicts, supportive counseling provides general support, and MBSR helps manage stress, CBT specifically empowers individuals by addressing the cognitive distortions that contribute to anxiety and depression. This makes CBT particularly suited for helping Sarah regain control over her life.

Question 98: Correct Answer: B) Generalized Anxiety Disorder

Rationale: Generalized Anxiety Disorder (GAD) is defined by excessive worry occurring more days than not for at least six months, according to DSM-5. Option A (Panic Disorder) involves recurrent unexpected panic attacks. Option C (Obsessive-Compulsive Disorder) involves obsessions and compulsions, not generalized worry.

Option D (Social Anxiety Disorder) focuses on fear in social situations, rather than pervasive worry. The chronic nature and focus on excessive worry distinguish GAD from other anxiety-related disorders.

Question 99: Correct Answer: A) Minimize hospital readmissions through regular follow-ups.

Rationale: The primary goal of case management in this scenario is to ensure coordinated and efficient care, which is best achieved by minimizing hospital readmissions through regular follow-ups (Option A). This directly addresses the need for continuity and efficiency in care delivery. Option B focuses on cost reduction, which is important but not central to coordination. Option C aims at patient satisfaction, which may not directly impact care efficiency. Option D enhances provider engagement but does not necessarily ensure coordinated patient care.

Question 100: Correct Answer: B) By documenting clinical outcomes to support billing claims.

Rationale: Case managers contribute to reimbursement processes by meticulously documenting clinical outcomes, which supports accurate billing claims and ensures appropriate reimbursement. Option A is incorrect as negotiations with patients are not typically within their purview. Option C is inaccurate because pricing is generally determined by administrative or financial departments. Option D oversimplifies their role, as cost reduction is part of a broader strategy involving quality and outcome documentation for reimbursement purposes.

Question 101: Correct Answer: B) Provide dietary counseling focusing on carbohydrate counting and meal planning.

Rationale: Dietary counseling focusing on carbohydrate counting is essential for managing Sarah's hypoglycemic episodes as it directly impacts blood glucose levels. While adjusting medication (A), peer support (C), and increased monitoring (D) are beneficial, understanding dietary impacts through education provides immediate tools for managing fluctuations effectively, supported by research advocating nutritional education as a cornerstone in diabetes management.

Question 102: Correct Answer: A) Flexibility in coverage options

Rationale: Private benefit programs often provide flexibility in coverage options, allowing case managers to tailor care plans to individual patient needs. This flexibility contrasts with uniformity (B), which limits customization. Governmental oversight (C) is more typical of public programs, not private ones. A limited network (D) restricts choices, contrary to the flexibility offered by private benefits. The adaptability of private programs supports personalized care strategies, enhancing patient outcomes.

Question 103: Correct Answer: A) Cognitive Behavioral Therapy (CBT)

Rationale: Cognitive Behavioral Therapy (CBT) is the most effective intervention for addressing anxiety and depression due to its structured approach in changing negative thought patterns and behaviors. While psychoanalytic therapy delves into past experiences, it may not provide immediate relief for current symptoms. Supportive group therapy offers peer support but lacks individualized focus on cognitive restructuring. Mindfulness-Based Stress Reduction aids stress management but doesn't directly address cognitive distortions like CBT does.

Question 104: Correct Answer: B) The client's household income relative to the Federal Poverty Level (FPL)

Rationale: Medicaid eligibility primarily hinges on household income relative to the FPL. While employment status (A), previous insurance (C), and age/disability (D) may influence eligibility, income is crucial in determining access. States use FPL percentages to assess Medicaid qualification, making it vital for Sarah to focus on this aspect. Employment status can affect income but is not directly used in eligibility criteria. Previous coverage does not determine Medicaid eligibility, and age/disability are specific criteria but not universally applicable.

Question 105: Correct Answer: D) Delayed physical development

Rationale: Delayed physical development can be subtle and often attributed to other causes, making it easily overlooked. While frequent injuries, hunger, and poor hygiene are more overt signs of neglect, developmental delays require careful observation over time. They may result from chronic neglect affecting nutrition and health. Understanding these nuances helps case managers identify less obvious indicators that could signify ongoing neglect.

Question 106: Correct Answer: A) Facilitate sessions with a clinical psychologist specializing in chronic illness.

Rationale: Facilitating sessions with a clinical psychologist (Option A) provides professional guidance tailored to managing hopelessness and withdrawal associated with chronic illness. This approach is grounded in contemporary therapeutic practices. Volunteering (Option B), while beneficial for engagement, may not directly address underlying psychological issues. Online forums (Option C) offer peer support but lack professional intervention. A gratitude journal (Option D), though helpful for mindset shifts, may not adequately tackle deep-seated feelings of hopelessness compared to professional therapy.

Question 107: Correct Answer: A) Apply for a waiver program specific to home and community-based services

Rationale: Waiver programs allow states to provide additional services not typically covered by Medicaid, including specialized equipment. While Medicare Part B (B) covers some equipment, it's separate from Medicaid. Exceptions via physicians (C) are unlikely for non-standard items without waiver support. Private insurance (D) may supplement but doesn't address Medicaid's limitations directly. Waivers are designed precisely for such gaps in standard coverage, making them the most viable solution within the Medicaid framework.

Question 108: Correct Answer: B) Developing Discrepancy

Rationale: Developing discrepancy involves highlighting the gap between a client's current behaviors and their broader goals or values, which can motivate change. This technique encourages clients to recognize the personal importance of change. Reflective listening focuses on understanding and mirroring client statements, affirmation supports positive reinforcement, and eliciting change talk involves prompting clients to verbalize reasons for change. The distinction lies in discrepancy's specific role in creating internal motivation by aligning actions with values, unlike other techniques that support different aspects of motivation.

Question 109: Correct Answer: C) Integrated Dual Disorder Treatment (IDDT)

Rationale: Integrated Dual Disorder Treatment (IDDT) is recognized as the most effective approach because it addresses both mental health and substance use disorders concurrently, leading to better outcomes. Unlike Sequential Treatment, which treats one disorder at a time, or Parallel Treatment, which treats disorders separately but simultaneously, IDDT provides a cohesive strategy. The Collaborative Care Model focuses on general mental health and primary care integration rather than specific co-occurring disorder treatments.

Question 110: Correct Answer: B) FMAP varies inversely with state per capita income.

Rationale: The Federal Medical Assistance Percentage (FMAP) varies inversely with a state's per capita income, meaning poorer states receive a higher federal match rate for their Medicaid programs than wealthier states. Option A misrepresents FMAP as providing fixed amounts rather than percentage-based matches. Option C incorrectly suggests a constant rate irrespective of state wealth, while D inaccurately implies decreased federal contributions with increased spending, misrepresenting FMAP's purpose to equitably support states based on need.

Question 111: Correct Answer: B) Real-time decision support

Rationale: Real-time decision support is a significant advantage of predictive analytics, enabling timely interventions that improve patient outcomes. Unlike retrospective data analysis and descriptive reporting, which provide insights after events occur, real-time support allows proactive management. Manual data collection lacks the efficiency and immediacy required for dynamic decision-making. Predictive analytics leverages current data to inform immediate clinical decisions, enhancing patient care quality by anticipating potential issues before they arise.

Question 112: Correct Answer: A) Integrative Negotiation

Rationale: Integrative Negotiation focuses on collaboration and finding mutually beneficial solutions, which is crucial in balancing patient care and cost constraints. Unlike Distributive Negotiation (B), which views resources as fixed, Integrative Negotiation seeks win-win outcomes. The Compromise Strategy (C) may lead to suboptimal solutions by splitting differences rather than maximizing value. Competitive Bargaining (D) often results in one party winning at the expense of the other, unsuitable for healthcare settings where ongoing relationships are key.

Question 113: Correct Answer: B) Motivational Interviewing

Rationale: Motivational Interviewing is a client-centered approach specifically designed to enhance an individual's intrinsic motivation to change behavior by exploring and resolving ambivalence. Unlike Twelve-Step Facilitation Therapy, CBT, and DBT, which focus on structured frameworks or cognitive restructuring, Motivational Interviewing emphasizes empathetic communication and collaboration. This approach effectively engages individuals in the process of change by aligning treatment goals with personal values and readiness for change, making it distinctively powerful in addressing substance use disorders.

Question 114: Correct Answer: B) Involving clients in decision-making processes about their care plans.

Rationale: Involving clients in decision-making aligns with client-centered care theories, emphasizing respect for individual preferences and shared decision-making. This approach enhances self-advocacy by valuing client input and fostering collaboration. Options A), C), and D) undermine autonomy by prioritizing standardized practices or expert opinions over personalized care, thereby limiting opportunities for clients to advocate for their unique needs and preferences within their healthcare journey.

Question 115: Correct Answer: B) Chronic Care Model (CCM)
Rationale: The Chronic Care Model (CCM) focuses on empowering patients by involving them in their care through self-management and collaborative goal setting, which is central to effective chronic care management. While the Patient-Centered Medical Home (PCMH) also emphasizes patient-centered approaches, it is broader in scope. The Integrated Care Model (ICM) focuses more on coordination across various healthcare sectors. Disease Management Programs (DMPs) target specific diseases rather than fostering overall patient empowerment. CCM uniquely integrates these elements to enhance patient self-efficacy and provider collaboration.

Question 116: Correct Answer: C) Medicare Part D
Rationale: Medicare Part D specifically covers prescription drug costs for eligible individuals, making it the appropriate choice for Mr. Thompson's medication needs. Medicare Part A covers hospital services, and Part B covers outpatient care; neither directly addresses prescription drugs. SSDI provides income support for disabled individuals under retirement age and does not cover medication costs for retirees like Mr. Thompson. Therefore, Medicare Part D is the correct option to assist with his prescription expenses.

Question 117: Correct Answer: A) National database registries
Rationale: National database registries compile extensive data on surgical outcomes across multiple institutions, offering comprehensive trends and benchmarks for post-operative complications. Peer-reviewed clinical studies (B) provide evidence-based insights but may not reflect current institutional trends. PROMs (C) focus on patient perspectives rather than clinical complications. Local hospital incident reports (D), while useful, are limited to single-institution data and may not capture broader trends. Registries offer large-scale, comparative data essential for identifying improvement areas.

Question 118: Correct Answer: B) Interest-Based Approach
Rationale: The Interest-Based Approach emphasizes understanding and addressing the underlying interests of all parties, leading to more sustainable and satisfactory outcomes. Positional Bargaining (A), focusing on fixed positions, often results in stalemates. Zero-Sum Game Theory (C) assumes one party's gain is another's loss, not conducive to collaborative healthcare environments. Fixed-Pie Perception (D) limits creativity by assuming resources are limited, whereas Interest-Based Approach encourages exploring options that expand the pie for all stakeholders.

Question 119: Correct Answer: C) Comprehensive prescription drug coverage
Rationale: For Maria's situation, comprehensive prescription drug coverage (Option C) is vital due to her ongoing medication needs. While access to specialists (Option A) is necessary, inadequate drug coverage could lead to significant expenses. Lower premiums (Option B) might initially seem attractive but could result in higher overall costs if medication needs aren't met. A high annual out-of-pocket limit (Option D) doesn't address immediate costs related to prescriptions. Therefore, ensuring robust drug coverage aligns best with Maria's healthcare requirements.

Question 120: Correct Answer: A) Encourage Alex to join a local LGBTQ+ youth group.
Rationale: Encouraging participation in an LGBTQ+ youth group provides Alex with peer support and acceptance, crucial for reducing isolation and fostering a sense of belonging. Option B might neglect the emotional aspect, while Option C could reinforce feelings of shame. Option D is helpful but lacks the peer connection that Option A offers. Social support from peers who share similar experiences is vital for mental health and well-being, making Option A the most comprehensive approach.

Question 121: Correct Answer: B) Pharmacist
Rationale: The pharmacist is primarily responsible for medication reconciliation, ensuring accurate and complete transfer of medication information during transitions of care. This role involves reviewing all medications the patient is taking to prevent adverse interactions. While the primary care physician (A) and nurse practitioner (C) may prescribe medications, and the social worker (D) supports social aspects of care, it is the pharmacist who specializes in medication management and safety.

Question 122: Correct Answer: A) To provide supplemental income without affecting eligibility for government benefits
Rationale: The primary purpose of a Special Needs Trust is to provide supplemental income and resources to individuals with disabilities without jeopardizing their eligibility for government benefits like Medicaid and Supplemental Security Income (SSI). Option B is incorrect as it does not solely manage all financial aspects. Option C is incorrect because it focuses on Social Security, which isn't the sole purpose. Option D is incorrect as it misrepresents tax avoidance, which isn't the trust's intent.

Question 123: Correct Answer: C) The nutritional content tailored to diabetic needs
Rationale: For Sarah, who has diabetes, the most critical factor is ensuring the meal delivery service provides meals specifically tailored to her dietary needs. While variety (A), cost-effectiveness (B), and delivery flexibility (D) are important, they are secondary to ensuring that meals support her health condition. Nutritional content directly impacts her blood sugar management and overall health, making it paramount in her situation.

Question 124: Correct Answer: C) Flexibility to see specialists without referrals
Rationale: PPOs offer greater flexibility than HMOs by allowing members to see specialists without needing referrals, enhancing patient autonomy and convenience. Option A is incorrect as PPOs often have higher premiums than HMOs. Option B is misleading since PPOs still have network considerations, though less restrictive. Option D does not highlight the consumer advantage but rather a provider perspective, making C the correct choice.

Question 125: Correct Answer: B) Coordinating a multidisciplinary team meeting before discharge.
Rationale: A multidisciplinary team meeting ensures all aspects of Sarah's care are addressed collaboratively, reducing complication risks through integrated planning. Option A focuses on medication supply but lacks holistic care coordination. Option C addresses logistics but not clinical needs directly impacting outcomes. Option D offers dietary advice but misses broader care integration. The correct answer emphasizes teamwork in addressing Sarah's complex needs post-surgery, which is crucial in transitional care management.

Question 126: Correct Answer: B) Anhedonia
Rationale: Anhedonia, or the loss of interest or pleasure in almost all activities, is a core symptom of Major Depressive Disorder as per DSM-5. Persistent elevated mood (A) is more characteristic of bipolar disorder.

Compulsive behaviors (C) are associated with obsessive-compulsive disorder, and rapid speech (D) is often seen in manic episodes. Understanding these distinctions helps in accurate diagnosis and treatment planning.

Question 127: Correct Answer: B) To manage pain and symptoms while improving quality of life

Rationale: The primary goal of palliative care is to manage pain and symptoms while enhancing the quality of life for patients with serious illnesses. Unlike option A, it does not aim to prolong life at all costs. Option C is incorrect as it does not focus on curative treatment. Option D, while important, does not encompass the comprehensive approach of symptom management and quality improvement that defines palliative care.

Question 128: Correct Answer: A) Patient-Centered Medical Home (PCMH)

Rationale: The PCMH model emphasizes coordinated, comprehensive care through primary care teams, making it ideal for managing patients with multiple chronic conditions. It ensures seamless integration of services and improved health outcomes. While ACOs focus on cost-efficiency across a network, TCM targets transitions between care settings, and CCM focuses on self-management support and community resources. Each incorrect option lacks the comprehensive integration of services that PCMH provides.

Question 129: Correct Answer: B) Facilitate motivational interviewing sessions to explore Tom's ambivalence towards change.

Rationale: Motivational interviewing (B) is an effective strategy for empowering clients by addressing ambivalence and enhancing intrinsic motivation for behavior change, crucial for adherence. Strict monitoring (A), though ensuring compliance, may not empower or motivate Tom intrinsically. Providing lists of restrictions (C) might overwhelm rather than empower him without addressing underlying motivational issues. Frequent supervision (D) focuses on external control rather than fostering internal motivation necessary for empowerment and sustainable adherence.

Question 130: Correct Answer: C) Implementing a transitional care nurse to coordinate post-discharge care

Rationale: Implementing a transitional care nurse is most effective as it provides personalized coordination, addressing the unique needs of complex patients. While A, B, and D are important, they lack the comprehensive oversight that a dedicated nurse offers. A discharge summary (A) is informational but not proactive. A follow-up appointment (B) might be delayed or insufficiently coordinated. Educational materials (D) are supportive but not interactive. The nurse ensures seamless communication and continuity of care, crucial for complex cases.

Question 131: Correct Answer: B) Assisting Ms. Lee in applying for financial assistance programs

Rationale: The correct answer is B because addressing financial barriers directly impacts Ms. Lee's ability to manage her diabetes effectively, aligning with Sarah's role in facilitating access to resources. Option A provides emotional support but doesn't address immediate financial needs. Option C involves clinical monitoring rather than resource facilitation, while option D offers valuable education but doesn't solve the financial constraint issue critical for accessing necessary care and supplies.

Question 132: Correct Answer: D) Comorbidity levels

Rationale: The ACG system primarily uses comorbidity levels to explain variations in healthcare utilization among patients with similar conditions. While socioeconomic status and age can influence health outcomes, the ACG focuses on the number and severity of comorbid conditions to predict resource use. Diagnosis-based risk adjustment is part of the process but does not capture the full complexity of comorbidities. Thus, comorbidity levels are crucial for understanding differences in resource utilization.

Question 133: Correct Answer: D) Referral to Community and Social Support Services

Rationale: Referral to Community and Social Support Services is crucial for addressing social determinants of health like transportation barriers. This aspect of the Health Home model helps connect patients with resources that can mitigate such obstacles. While Comprehensive Transitional Care (A), Care Coordination (B), and Individual and Family Support Services (C) play roles in managing health care delivery, they do not directly address external factors like transportation, making D the correct choice for David's situation.

Question 134: Correct Answer: B) Explain that discussing grief can initially be distressing but often leads to long-term healing through mutual understanding and empathy.

Rationale: Option B is correct because research supports that while discussing grief can be initially distressing, it often results in long-term healing through empathy and understanding from peers who have similar experiences. Option A oversimplifies the process of emotional relief, which isn't always immediate. Option C misrepresents the nature of bereavement groups where difficult emotions are addressed rather than avoided. Option D overlooks the benefit of active participation in processing grief within supportive environments.

Question 135: Correct Answer: A) Deductibles and Co-payments

Rationale: Indemnity insurance typically allows patients to choose any healthcare provider, but it often involves deductibles and co-payments, which are out-of-pocket expenses that the patient must pay before the insurer reimburses the remaining costs. Unlike network limitations or pre-authorization requirements, which are more common in managed care plans, indemnity plans do not restrict provider choice. Capitation fees are associated with provider payment models rather than patient expenses. Therefore, understanding deductibles and co-payments is crucial for managing potential costs under an indemnity plan.

Question 136: Correct Answer: B) Encouraging clients to participate actively in decision-making processes regarding their care.

Rationale: Encouraging active participation in decision-making empowers clients by fostering autonomy and self-efficacy, key components of empowerment theories. Option A, while informative, does not involve the client in decisions. Option C provides resources but lacks engagement in personal choices. Option D imposes structure without considering individual preferences or involvement. Active participation uniquely aligns with empowerment by valuing client input and promoting ownership of health outcomes.

Question 137: Correct Answer: C) Embedding behavioral health providers within primary care teams

Rationale: The integration of behavioral health into primary care teams (C) aligns with the Health Home model's emphasis on coordinated, comprehensive care. This approach fosters collaboration among providers, enhancing communication and treatment outcomes. Options A and D segregate services, which can hinder integrated care delivery. Option B limits interaction modes, potentially affecting service accessibility. Thus, embedding providers ensures seamless coordination essential for managing co-occurring conditions like diabetes and depression in a holistic manner.

Question 138: Correct Answer: B) Skilled Nursing Facility

Rationale: A Skilled Nursing Facility (SNF) is ideal for Mr. Johnson as it offers comprehensive rehabilitation services and 24-hour medical supervision necessary for post-stroke recovery. Home Health Care lacks the intensive resources; Long-Term Acute Care Hospitals are suited for medically complex patients needing prolonged hospital-level care, not primarily rehabilitation; and Outpatient Rehabilitation Centers do not provide the residential support needed for intensive therapy. Thus, SNF is the most appropriate choice for his condition.

Question 139: Correct Answer: A) Educating on daily diuretic adherence

Rationale: Consistent daily diuretic use is crucial for managing heart failure and preventing fluid overload, unlike symptom-based intake which can lead to exacerbations. Option B is important but secondary to proper medication adherence. Option C could worsen fluid retention issues due to irregular dosing, while option D supports monitoring but does not address the root issue of non-adherence directly. Education ensures understanding and compliance with prescribed regimens.

Question 140: Correct Answer: B) Recommend switching to the generic equivalent of the medication.

Rationale: Switching to a generic equivalent is typically the most cost-effective strategy as generics are usually cheaper than brand-name drugs while maintaining similar efficacy and safety profiles. Option A might save costs but doesn't address immediate medication expense reduction. Option C helps with costs but is not always applicable or immediate. Option D can be effective but isn't universally applicable due to dosage accuracy concerns. Therefore, recommending a generic equivalent directly impacts cost and maintains therapeutic efficacy.

Question 141: Correct Answer: C) Home Health Nurse

Rationale: A home health nurse specializes in providing medical care at home, including wound care management, ensuring continuity of care post-discharge. An occupational therapist focuses on improving daily living skills, while a dietitian addresses nutritional needs. A speech-language pathologist works on communication and swallowing disorders. Thus, involving a home health nurse is essential for managing ongoing wound care effectively after hospital discharge.

Question 142: Correct Answer: B) Poor personal hygiene

Rationale: Poor personal hygiene is a direct physical sign of neglect, indicating that basic needs are not being met. While lack of social support (A), financial instability (C), and recent bereavement (D) can contribute to neglect, they are more indirect factors. Contemporary theories emphasize observable physical conditions like hygiene as primary indicators of neglect, making this the most relevant choice for identifying potential issues in John's care situation.

Question 143: Correct Answer: B) By coordinating multidisciplinary care teams to manage patient care

Rationale: Coordinating multidisciplinary care teams enhances supportive care by ensuring comprehensive management of complex medical conditions through collaboration among various healthcare professionals. This approach integrates different perspectives to address diverse patient needs effectively. While advocating for policy changes (A), developing personalized treatment plans (C), and funding epidemiological studies (D) contribute to overall healthcare improvements, they do not directly provide the immediate, integrated support that multidisciplinary coordination offers in managing patient care.

Question 144: Correct Answer: B) They offer a structured environment promoting social interaction and support.

Rationale: Group homes are designed to create a structured environment that fosters social interaction and mutual support among residents, which is crucial for individuals with chronic mental health conditions. Option A is incorrect because personalized one-on-one therapy is not typically the focus in group homes. Option C is misleading as group homes do not prioritize advanced medical technologies. Option D is incorrect since professional staff are essential to manage and support residents' needs effectively.

Question 145: Correct Answer: B) Suggest cognitive behavioral therapy (CBT)

Rationale: CBT is the most appropriate initial intervention as it addresses both anxiety and insomnia without the risk of substance dependency. Benzodiazepines (Option A), though effective for anxiety, carry a risk of dependency. Over-the-counter sleep aids (Option C) may not adequately address underlying issues and can lead to misuse. Antidepressants (Option D) may help long-term but are not the first-line treatment for immediate anxiety and insomnia in patients with a history of substance use disorder.

Question 146: Correct Answer: B) Connecting Robert with community support groups

Rationale: Connecting Robert with community support groups addresses the root issue—lack of social support—enhancing engagement through peer encouragement and shared experiences. Option A provides knowledge but not support; Option C focuses on surveillance rather than empowerment; Option D increases contact but doesn't address underlying social needs.

Question 147: Correct Answer: B) Pregnant Women

Rationale: Pregnant Women are eligible for Medicaid primarily based on income and family size, aligning with the program's aim to support low-income families. While the Medically Needy group can include those with high medical expenses, eligibility isn't solely based on income. Disabled and Aged Individuals are typically qualified through disability or age criteria, not just income. The focus on income and family size for pregnant women distinguishes this group from others in Medicaid eligibility.

Question 148: Correct Answer: C) Interest-based negotiation

Rationale: Interest-based negotiation focuses on understanding the underlying needs and interests of both parties to find mutually beneficial solutions. This approach ensures that Mr. Johnson receives quality care while addressing the facility's need for adequate compensation. Unlike anchoring, which sets an initial offer point, or BATNA, which involves having an alternative plan, interest-based negotiation fosters collaboration and understanding. Compromise might lead to suboptimal outcomes as it often involves splitting differences rather than addressing core interests.

Question 149: Correct Answer: B) Implementing personalized wellness plans

Rationale: Personalized wellness plans are most effective as they cater to individual needs, fostering higher engagement by addressing personal health goals. While discounted gym memberships (A) and free healthy meals (C) are attractive, they may not suit everyone's preferences or schedules.

Question 150: Correct Answer: B) Reduction in healthcare claims costs

Rationale: Reduction in healthcare claims costs directly reflects improved employee health and reduced medical expenses, making it a key indicator of program success. While participation rates (A) and satisfaction surveys (C) provide insight into engagement and perception, they do not measure health outcomes. The number of fitness challenge participants (D) indicates activity involvement but not overall health improvement. Therefore, option B is the most comprehensive measure of the program's impact on health.

CCM Exam Practice Questions [SET 2]

Question 1: Sarah, a single mother who was recently diagnosed with a chronic illness, is seeking SSDI benefits. She has worked part-time over the past decade while caring for her children. What aspect of her work history will most impact her eligibility for SSDI?
A) The number of hours she worked each week.
B) The total amount of money she earned annually.
C) The number of work credits she has accumulated.
D) The type of job she held during her employment.

Question 2: In the context of self-care management, which approach is most likely to enhance a client's adherence to a prescribed health regimen?
A) Providing a list of potential health complications
B) Emphasizing the consequences of non-adherence
C) Encouraging self-monitoring and reflective practices
D) Offering incentives for compliance

Question 3: Case Manager John is working with a 10-year-old child, Alex, who shows signs of neglect such as poor hygiene and frequent absenteeism from school. When questioned, Alex mentions that his parents are often absent due to work commitments. What is John's best initial action?
A) Arrange for Alex to attend a school counseling session.
B) Contact Child Protective Services (CPS) immediately.
C) Schedule a meeting with Alex's parents to discuss his needs.
D) Provide resources for after-school care programs.

Question 4: How might a case manager effectively address spiritual beliefs when planning care for a client from a diverse cultural background?
A) Focus solely on medical interventions, as spirituality is not directly related to health outcomes.
B) Encourage the client to participate in religious practices that align with the case manager's beliefs.
C) Integrate the client's spiritual beliefs into the care plan after discussing them with the client.
D) Avoid discussing spiritual beliefs to prevent potential conflicts or misunderstandings.

Question 5: In the context of Health Homes, which of the following best describes a key function that differentiates it from traditional care models?
A) Provision of acute care services
B) Coordination of comprehensive care across different providers
C) Focus on disease-specific interventions
D) Emphasis on episodic treatment

Question 6: Which of the following approaches best exemplifies holistic case management services in improving patient outcomes?
A) Focusing primarily on the patient's medical treatment plan.
B) Coordinating care among multiple healthcare providers to address all aspects of a patient's needs.
C) Emphasizing cost-efficiency over patient-centered care.
D) Prioritizing short-term goals over long-term health management.

Question 7: Mr. Thompson, a 65-year-old patient with newly diagnosed diabetes, is struggling to manage his condition due to low health literacy. As a case manager, which strategy would most effectively improve his health literacy and support self-management?
A) Provide him with printed educational materials in simple language.
B) Refer him to a diabetes support group for peer learning.
C) Use the teach-back method to confirm understanding of self-care instructions.
D) Recommend online resources for independent learning.

Question 8: In the context of value-based care, which reimbursement model ties payments to the quality of care provided, rewarding providers for meeting specific performance metrics?
A) Prospective Payment System (PPS)
B) Pay-for-performance (P4P)
C) Global Budgeting
D) Resource-Based Relative Value Scale (RBRVS)

Question 9: In the context of care delivery and reimbursement methods, which negotiation technique is most effective for ensuring a win-win outcome between case managers and healthcare providers?
A) Competitive Bargaining
B) Integrative Negotiation
C) Positional Bargaining
D) Distributive Negotiation

Question 10: During a case management meeting, Emily discusses with her team about coordinating care for a patient with complex needs under an HMO plan. Which principle of insurance is most critical in ensuring that Emily can effectively manage and coordinate care within this framework?
A) Adverse selection
B) Moral hazard
C) Network adequacy
D) Risk pooling

Question 11: In the context of informed decision-making, which principle is most crucial for ensuring that a client's autonomy is respected when they are making self-care management decisions?
A) Beneficence
B) Non-maleficence
C) Informed consent
D) Paternalism

Question 12: Which of the following best describes a primary function of a Health Home under the Patient Protection and Affordable Care Act (PPACA)?
A) Providing acute care services to patients.
B) Coordinating comprehensive care across the healthcare continuum.
C) Offering financial assistance for medical expenses.
D) Delivering specialized surgical interventions.

Question 13: In the context of private benefit programs, what is a significant challenge that case managers face when ensuring comprehensive patient care?
A) Navigating complex eligibility criteria
B) Accessing a wide range of specialists
C) High levels of transparency in benefits
D) Consistent policy updates and changes

Question 14: John, a 45-year-old construction worker, has been diagnosed with a severe back injury that prevents him from working for at least a year. He is considering applying for Social Security Disability Insurance (SSDI). As his case manager, what is the most crucial factor in determining his eligibility for SSDI benefits?
A) His current income level
B) The severity and expected duration of his disability
C) His past work history and contributions to Social Security
D) Availability of other insurance benefits

Question 15: Which of the following strategies is most

effective in integrating psychosocial support within wellness and illness prevention programs for chronic disease management?
A) Regular physical activity sessions
B) Cognitive-behavioral therapy (CBT) interventions
C) Nutritional counseling
D) Medication adherence reminders

Question 16: In the context of interpersonal communication, which principle best describes the idea that individuals adjust their communication styles based on their perception of others' behaviors?
A) Reciprocity Principle
B) Expectancy Violations Theory
C) Interaction Adaptation Theory
D) Social Exchange Theory

Question 17: Maria, a case manager, is assisting her client Lisa who is experiencing a family crisis due to sudden illness in the family. What critical step should Maria take first to ensure effective crisis intervention?
A) Provide Lisa with resources for long-term family therapy.
B) Establish rapport and actively listen to Lisa's concerns.
C) Immediately contact social services for emergency support.
D) Encourage Lisa to focus on maintaining her daily routine.

Question 18: John, a factory employee, has sustained an injury at work and is now unable to perform his regular duties. As his case manager, you need to develop a return-to-work plan. What should be your primary consideration in creating this plan?
A) The employer's need to fill John's position quickly.
B) The financial impact of John's absence on his family.
C) John's current physical limitations and recovery progress.
D) The availability of temporary disability benefits.

Question 19: Sarah, a 45-year-old female with chronic back pain and depression, requires an integrated approach for her care plan. As her case manager, which strategy should you prioritize to effectively address both her physical and behavioral health needs?
A) Refer her to a pain management specialist only
B) Coordinate joint sessions with a physiotherapist and psychologist
C) Focus solely on prescribing antidepressants
D) Schedule regular follow-ups with her primary care physician

Question 20: John, who recently retired at age 62 from a large corporation, wants to maintain his employer-sponsored health insurance through COBRA until he qualifies for Medicare at age 65. What should John consider regarding his COBRA continuation coverage?
A) John can maintain his COBRA coverage until he turns 65 with no additional conditions.
B) John's COBRA coverage will automatically terminate when he becomes eligible for Medicare at age 65.
C) John must apply for Medicare immediately upon retirement to retain any healthcare benefits.
D) John can extend his COBRA coverage beyond Medicare eligibility by paying an additional premium.

Question 21: Which of the following is considered a key factor in determining the effectiveness of a group in achieving its goals according to Tuckman's model of group development?
A) Group Size
B) Norming Stage
C) Leadership Style
D) Communication Patterns

Question 22: Emily, a 45-year-old woman, presents with persistent sadness, lack of interest in daily activities, and feelings of hopelessness for over six months. As a case manager, which diagnosis is most appropriate considering the chronicity and severity of her symptoms?
A) Major Depressive Disorder
B) Adjustment Disorder with Depressed Mood
C) Dysthymia (Persistent Depressive Disorder)
D) Bipolar II Disorder

Question 23: In the context of client self-care management, which strategy is most effective in promoting long-term adherence to a self-care regimen for patients with chronic illnesses?
A) Providing detailed educational materials about the illness
B) Encouraging the use of smartphone apps to track symptoms
C) Facilitating regular follow-up appointments with healthcare providers
D) Empowering clients through motivational interviewing techniques

Question 24: During a family meeting about discharge planning for Mrs. Lee, who has experienced frequent hospitalizations due to heart failure, her daughter insists on home care services while her son believes she should be transferred to a rehabilitation facility. As the case manager facilitating this meeting, what conflict resolution approach should be prioritized to ensure Mrs. Lee's best interests are met?
A) Mediation
B) Competing
C) Negotiation
D) Compromise

Question 25: John is a 45-year-old patient living in an underserved area with limited access to healthcare services. As his case manager, how can you apply population health principles to improve his care delivery?
A) Encouraging John to participate in telehealth services for routine check-ups
B) Recommending frequent emergency room visits for comprehensive care
C) Suggesting relocation to an area with better healthcare facilities
D) Coordinating home visits by healthcare professionals for continuous monitoring

Question 26: Sarah, a 78-year-old woman living alone, has been experiencing increasing forgetfulness and difficulty managing her daily tasks. As her case manager, you are considering the best community resource to support her independence while ensuring her safety. Which of the following options is most appropriate for Sarah's situation?
A) Adult Day Care Services
B) In-Home Health Aide
C) Assisted Living Facility
D) Memory Care Unit

Question 27: Which principle is fundamental to the success of a Health Home model in improving patient outcomes?
A) Exclusively using electronic health records for communication
B) Prioritizing cost reduction over patient engagement
C) Integrating behavioral health into primary care
D) Limiting patient access to specialist consultations

Question 28: Sarah, a case manager, is assessing her client, John, who is applying for Supplemental Security Income (SSI). John has a disability and limited

resources. Which of the following factors is most likely to affect John's eligibility for SSI benefits?
A) The value of John's primary residence
B) John's monthly earned income
C) The number of dependents John has
D) John's age at the time of application

Question 29: John, a 30-year-old male with a history of substance abuse, exhibits extreme mood swings from euphoria to deep depression within days. He often engages in risky behavior during his euphoric states. What is the most likely behavioral health diagnosis for John?
A) Borderline Personality Disorder
B) Cyclothymic Disorder
C) Bipolar I Disorder
D) Schizoaffective Disorder

Question 30: Which of the following interventions is considered most effective in preventing relapse in individuals with substance use disorders, according to contemporary cognitive-behavioral therapy (CBT) approaches?
A) Psychoeducation sessions
B) Mindfulness-based stress reduction
C) Motivational interviewing
D) Skills training for coping with high-risk situations

Question 31: Which factor is most critical for a case manager to consider when assessing the physical impact of abuse on an elderly client?
A) The client's financial resources
B) The client's level of physical mobility
C) The client's support network
D) The client's medical history

Question 32: Sarah, a 40-year-old professional, reports stress-related symptoms impacting her daily life. Her case manager aims to assess her psychological state comprehensively. Which assessment tool would best evaluate Sarah's overall psychological well-being?
A) Hamilton Anxiety Rating Scale (HAM-A)
B) Minnesota Multiphasic Personality Inventory (MMPI-2)
C) Trail Making Test Part B (TMT-B)
D) Stroop Color and Word Test

Question 33: Jamie, a 25-year-old seeking case management support, has recently begun hormone therapy as part of their transition. What should be the primary focus for the case manager in supporting Jamie's ongoing care?
A) Monitor only physical changes due to hormone therapy.
B) Ensure regular psychological assessments are conducted.
C) Discourage further exploration of gender identity until therapy stabilizes.
D) Advocate for discontinuation of therapy if any side effects occur.

Question 34: Sarah, a 30-year-old woman with a history of opioid use disorder, is seeking help to maintain sobriety after detoxification. As her case manager, which strategy should you prioritize to support her recovery according to current behavioral health concepts?
A) Encouraging participation in a peer support group
B) Initiating methadone maintenance therapy
C) Recommending mindfulness-based stress reduction (MBSR)
D) Scheduling regular family therapy sessions

Question 35: Which of the following approaches is most effective in facilitating behavior change in clients during health coaching sessions?
A) Directive advice-giving
B) Motivational interviewing
C) Prescriptive goal-setting
D) Structured educational sessions

Question 36: John, a 60-year-old diabetic patient, has been advised to incorporate regular exercise into his routine. He has joined a gym and exercises three times a week for the past two months. Which stage of the Transtheoretical Model does John's behavior exemplify?
A) Maintenance
B) Action
C) Preparation
D) Contemplation

Question 37: Which of the following measures is best suited to evaluate patient satisfaction as an outcome in healthcare quality assessments?
A) Clinical Outcome Measures
B) Patient-Reported Outcome Measures (PROMs)
C) Process Measures
D) Structural Measures

Question 38: What is a primary advantage of utilizing alternative care sites for patient management in terms of healthcare delivery?
A) Reduced administrative costs
B) Increased patient engagement
C) Enhanced access to specialized care
D) Improved coordination with primary care providers

Question 39: Sarah, a case manager at a healthcare facility participating in bundled payments for cardiac procedures, must develop strategies to manage financial risks associated with this model. Which strategy should Sarah prioritize to effectively manage these risks?
A) Negotiate lower prices for all medical supplies used during cardiac procedures.
B) Implement standardized clinical pathways to minimize variability in treatment outcomes.
C) Focus solely on reducing staff salaries to cut down on operational costs.
D) Delay elective procedures until reimbursement rates increase.

Question 40: In the context of non-traditional sites of care, which model is primarily focused on providing comprehensive primary care services to underserved populations in community settings?
A) Ambulatory surgical centers
B) Federally Qualified Health Centers (FQHCs)
C) Concierge medicine practices
D) Retail clinics

Question 41: As a case manager, you are assisting Ms. Garcia, who has been prescribed an expensive specialty medication not covered by her insurance plan. Which approach should you take first to help her obtain this medication through Pharmacy Assistance Programs?
A) Contact the drug manufacturer directly to inquire about their patient assistance program.
B) Advise Ms. Garcia to seek financial aid from local community organizations.
C) Suggest Ms. Garcia switch to a generic alternative if available.
D) Recommend applying for state pharmaceutical assistance programs.

Question 42: John, a case manager, is assisting a client named Emily who is dealing with grief after losing her spouse. Emily is hesitant about joining a support group.

What should John emphasize as the primary benefit of joining such a group?
A) Access to professional counseling services
B) Opportunities for social interaction
C) Learning coping strategies from peers
D) Distraction from personal grief

Question 43: Tom, a 50-year-old patient recovering from a stroke, expresses frustration about his rehabilitation plan. As his case manager, how can you best support Tom's self-advocacy in this situation?
A) Tell Tom to trust the expertise of his rehabilitation team without question.
B) Encourage Tom to communicate his concerns and preferences directly to his rehabilitation team.
C) Suggest Tom research alternative therapies online without professional consultation.
D) Advise Tom to accept the current plan as is due to the team's experience.

Question 44: In the context of elder care services, which strategy is most effective in addressing the psychosocial needs of elderly clients through community resources?
A) Implementing telehealth consultations
B) Establishing senior peer support groups
C) Providing transportation services
D) Offering nutritional meal programs

Question 45: When evaluating potential financial neglect in a case management scenario, which situation most accurately reflects this issue?
A) A client has unpaid bills despite having sufficient funds due to their cognitive decline.
B) A client chooses to allocate funds primarily towards leisure activities rather than essentials.
C) A client has set up automatic payments for all their bills but occasionally forgets minor expenses.
D) A client receives regular financial advice from a trusted family member without any reported issues.

Question 46: In a situation where immediate action is required to resolve a conflict in patient care, which strategy should be prioritized to ensure swift decision-making?
A) Accommodating
B) Competing
C) Collaborating
D) Avoiding

Question 47: David, a case manager at a healthcare facility participating in a bundled payment program for cardiac procedures, notices a discrepancy in patient outcomes. What should be David's primary focus to improve patient outcomes under this payment model?
A) Enhancing pre-operative education while neglecting follow-up care
B) Monitoring and reducing unnecessary tests and procedures
C) Increasing reliance on specialist consultations regardless of necessity
D) Emphasizing only on reducing hospital stay duration

Question 48: Sarah, a case manager, encounters Mike, a patient struggling with stress due to his recent diagnosis of diabetes. Mike expresses a strong religious faith and seeks guidance that aligns with his beliefs. Which aspect of pastoral counseling should Sarah emphasize when discussing its potential benefits with Mike?
A) The focus on cognitive-behavioral techniques to manage stress effectively.
B) The opportunity for Mike to explore his faith in relation to

his health challenges.
C) The emphasis on medication adherence as the primary method of coping.
D) The reliance on group therapy sessions without individual spiritual guidance.

Question 49: Mrs. Lee, an 85-year-old patient with metastatic cancer, expresses her wish to remain at home during her final days. As her case manager, which strategy best supports her preference while ensuring appropriate care delivery?
A) Arrange for frequent hospital visits for monitoring
B) Set up a home-based palliative care team for ongoing support
C) Encourage relocation to a skilled nursing facility for better supervision
D) Schedule weekly telehealth consultations with her oncologist

Question 50: Which conflict resolution strategy is most effective in ensuring long-term collaboration among healthcare team members when addressing complex patient care issues?
A) Competing
B) Avoiding
C) Collaborating
D) Accommodating

Question 51: John, a case manager in a PCMH model, aims to optimize outcomes for patients with diabetes through team-based care. Which approach best exemplifies the collaborative nature of a PCMH?
A) Assigning all responsibility for diabetes education solely to the physician
B) Engaging a multidisciplinary team including dietitians and educators in patient management
C) Limiting communication between team members to written reports only
D) Focusing exclusively on glycemic control without addressing lifestyle factors

Question 52: Which version of the International Classification of Diseases (ICD) introduced the concept of "clinical modifications" to better capture detailed health information for case management and reimbursement purposes?
A) ICD-9
B) ICD-10
C) ICD-11
D) ICD-8

Question 53: What is a key benefit of telehealth in managing chronic conditions from the perspective of care delivery and reimbursement methods?
A) Reduced need for in-person visits
B) Increased patient data privacy
C) Enhanced face-to-face communication
D) Simplified insurance claim processes

Question 54: Which of the following is a primary role of disease-based organizations in the context of supportive care programs for chronic illness management?
A) Conducting clinical trials for new drug therapies
B) Providing emotional support and education to patients and families
C) Developing new surgical techniques for disease treatment
D) Offering medical equipment at subsidized rates

Question 55: Sarah, a 68-year-old patient with advanced cancer, is experiencing significant emotional distress and anxiety related to her prognosis. As her case manager, you are tasked with coordinating supportive

care programs to address her psychosocial needs. Which intervention is most appropriate to prioritize for Sarah's situation?
A) Referral to a palliative care specialist
B) Enrollment in a cognitive-behavioral therapy program
C) Coordination of home health nursing services
D) Facilitation of family counseling sessions

Question 56: In managing cases of elder neglect, which psychosocial intervention is considered most effective in ensuring long-term safety and well-being?
A) Implementing regular home visits by healthcare professionals
B) Increasing family involvement in caregiving activities
C) Placing the elder in a long-term care facility
D) Providing financial management assistance

Question 57: Which principle is central to integrated case management services in enhancing patient outcomes within a holistic framework?
A) Prioritizing acute interventions over preventive measures
B) Emphasizing patient autonomy and self-management
C) Standardizing treatment protocols across all cases
D) Limiting provider involvement to reduce complexity

Question 58: In health coaching, which counseling technique is most aligned with enhancing a client's self-efficacy?
A) Providing direct solutions
B) Reflective listening
C) Emphasizing past failures
D) Focusing on barriers

Question 59: John, a 45-year-old man diagnosed with schizophrenia and opioid use disorder, struggles with adherence to his medication regimen. As his case manager, what strategy should you employ to enhance his adherence?
A) Educate John about the importance of medication adherence for schizophrenia only.
B) Focus solely on behavioral therapies for opioid use disorder.
C) Use motivational interviewing techniques to address barriers to adherence in both conditions.
D) Schedule frequent check-ins to monitor medication intake for schizophrenia alone.

Question 60: John, a healthcare analyst, is using the Adjusted Clinical Group (ACG) system to assess quality outcomes in a hospital setting. He finds that two departments report significantly different ACG scores despite serving similar patient demographics. Which aspect of the ACG system should John investigate to understand this discrepancy?
A) Variability in provider practice patterns
B) Patient adherence to treatment plans
C) Differences in data coding accuracy
D) Frequency of emergency room visits

Question 61: In the context of public benefit programs, which of the following is a key characteristic of the Supplemental Security Income (SSI) program?
A) Provides benefits based on past work history
B) Offers financial assistance regardless of age or disability status
C) Requires recipients to have limited income and resources
D) Is funded entirely by payroll taxes

Question 62: Which of the following elements is essential for a successful Patient-centered Medical Home (PCMH) model to enhance care coordination and improve patient outcomes?
A) Integration of electronic health records (EHRs)

B) Regular patient satisfaction surveys
C) Implementation of telemedicine services
D) Comprehensive care management plans

Question 63: During a case management meeting, Sarah, a case manager, is discussing the impact of the Prospective Payment System (PPS) on hospital discharge planning. Which of the following best describes how PPS influences discharge planning?
A) It encourages longer hospital stays to maximize reimbursement.
B) It promotes early discharge to reduce hospital costs.
C) It focuses on increasing the number of inpatient procedures to boost revenue.
D) It eliminates the need for post-discharge follow-up care.

Question 64: Sarah, a case manager, is reviewing the insurance policy of a patient, Mr. Thompson, who requires long-term rehabilitation services. The policy includes a clause about "stop-loss" provisions. Which of the following best describes how the "stop-loss" provision benefits Mr. Thompson's coverage?
A) It limits the total amount the insurance company will pay for Mr. Thompson's rehabilitation services.
B) It ensures that once Mr. Thompson reaches his deductible, all services are covered at 100%.
C) It caps Mr. Thompson's out-of-pocket expenses after reaching a certain threshold.
D) It provides additional coverage for services not initially covered by his plan.

Question 65: During a crisis intervention session, a case manager is working with John, who has recently lost his job and is experiencing severe anxiety about his financial future. Which of the following strategies should the case manager prioritize to help John effectively manage his current crisis?
A) Encourage John to immediately start applying for new jobs to regain financial stability.
B) Focus on helping John develop a short-term action plan to address immediate financial concerns.
C) Suggest that John engage in mindfulness exercises to reduce anxiety levels.
D) Advise John to seek support from family and friends for emotional reassurance.

Question 66: Which of the following symptoms is most indicative of Major Depressive Disorder according to the DSM-5 criteria?
A) Persistent elevated mood
B) Anhedonia
C) Increased energy
D) Hyperactivity

Question 67: Which type of Special Needs Trust is typically established by a parent or guardian for a child with disabilities?
A) First-Party Special Needs Trust
B) Third-Party Special Needs Trust
C) Pooled Special Needs Trust
D) Revocable Living Trust

Question 68: Sarah, a case manager, is working with a patient named John who has multiple chronic conditions. She needs to select the most appropriate case management model to ensure comprehensive care and cost-effectiveness. Which model should Sarah choose to best integrate services across various healthcare settings while focusing on John's unique needs?
A) Brokerage Model
B) Primary Care Case Management Model
C) Intensive Case Management Model

D) Interdisciplinary Team Model

Question 69: John, a 55-year-old man with a history of substance abuse, is at risk of neglect due to isolation and lack of social support. As his case manager, which psychological approach should you prioritize to enhance his social integration and reduce neglect risk?
A) Motivational Interviewing
B) Solution-Focused Brief Therapy
C) Interpersonal Therapy (IPT)
D) Dialectical Behavior Therapy (DBT)

Question 70: Sarah, a 67-year-old woman with multiple chronic conditions, has been hospitalized several times in the past year. Her case manager is evaluating the most appropriate level of care to minimize hospital readmissions while ensuring comprehensive management of her conditions. Which level of care should be prioritized for Sarah to achieve these goals?
A) Acute Care
B) Long-term Acute Care
C) Home Health Care
D) Skilled Nursing Facility

Question 71: Sarah, a case manager, is coordinating care for a patient transitioning from acute care to home health services. Which of the following actions best demonstrates her understanding of the continuum of care in optimizing patient outcomes?
A) Scheduling follow-up appointments with the primary care physician only.
B) Ensuring the patient has access to necessary medical equipment and medications at home.
C) Conducting a one-time home visit to assess the patient's living conditions.
D) Referring the patient to community resources without ongoing monitoring.

Question 72: John, a newly appointed case manager, is evaluating the effectiveness of the Patient-Centered Medical Home model at his clinic. Which outcome measure would most accurately reflect successful implementation of PCMH principles?
A) Increased number of patient visits per year
B) Higher patient satisfaction scores related to care coordination
C) Reduction in healthcare staff turnover rates
D) Decreased use of advanced imaging services

Question 73: Which of the following is the most significant benefit of support groups in enhancing the psychosocial well-being of patients with chronic illnesses?
A) Providing medical advice tailored to individual cases
B) Offering a platform for emotional expression and shared experiences
C) Facilitating direct access to healthcare professionals
D) Delivering educational materials on disease management

Question 74: In the context of crisis intervention, which approach best supports empowering clients to regain control during a crisis?
A) Directive counseling techniques
B) Collaborative problem-solving
C) Providing informational resources
D) Emotional validation

Question 75: Which of the following criteria must be met for an individual to qualify for Supplemental Security Income (SSI) benefits under the Social Security Administration's guidelines?
A) The individual must have a disability and limited income and resources.

B) The individual must be over 65 years old, regardless of income or resources.
C) The individual must have a disability, but income and resources are not considered.
D) The individual must be a U.S. citizen with any income level.

Question 76: Which factor is most critical in developing an effective case management plan that addresses the psychosocial aspects of gender health?
A) Cultural competence training for case managers
B) Inclusion of family members in decision-making
C) Comprehensive assessment of social determinants of health
D) Regular updates to medical treatment protocols

Question 77: Which of the following approaches is most effective in helping a bereaved individual process grief according to the Dual Process Model of Coping with Bereavement?
A) Encouraging continuous expression of emotions
B) Fostering oscillation between loss-oriented and restoration-oriented activities
C) Promoting avoidance of reminders of the deceased
D) Supporting complete immersion in daily routines

Question 78: Sarah is a case manager working with a team to optimize resource utilization for patients covered by the Prospective Payment System. A new patient, Mr. Lee, has been admitted with multiple chronic conditions. What strategy should Sarah prioritize to ensure efficient use of resources while maintaining compliance with PPS guidelines?
A) Early discharge planning
B) Comprehensive medication review
C) Utilization of outpatient services
D) Coordination of post-discharge follow-up

Question 79: Sarah, a case manager at a large urban hospital, is tasked with managing her caseload effectively while considering diverse patient needs and resource allocation. Which strategy should Sarah prioritize to ensure optimal outcomes for her patients?
A) Focus on patients with the highest acuity levels only.
B) Allocate more time to patients with complex social determinants of health.
C) Prioritize patients based on their potential for quick discharge.
D) Balance her time equally among all patients regardless of their needs.

Question 80: When considering caseload management for a case manager, which factor is most critical in determining the appropriate number of clients per case manager to ensure effective care delivery?
A) The average length of stay of clients
B) The complexity and acuity of client conditions
C) The geographical distribution of clients
D) The availability of community resources

Question 81: John, a healthcare administrator, is analyzing how the Prospective Payment System affects hospital financial performance. Which of the following statements accurately reflects this impact?
A) PPS guarantees higher revenue by increasing service prices annually.
B) PPS aligns payments with actual service costs incurred during treatment.
C) PPS creates financial risk if patient care exceeds DRG payment limits.
D) PPS allows hospitals to bill separately for each service provided.

Question 82: John, a newly certified case manager, is developing a strategy to improve patient outcomes in his hospital. He wants to align his strategy with NCQA's standards. Which initiative should John prioritize to enhance patient-centered care according to NCQA guidelines?
A) Patient-Centered Medical Home (PCMH) Recognition
B) Utilization Management Accreditation
C) Long-Term Services and Supports (LTSS) Distinction
D) Health Plan Accreditation

Question 83: In the context of managing financial resources, which approach should a case manager prioritize to enhance cost-effectiveness in patient care?
A) Implementing a fee-for-service model
B) Establishing capitated payment agreements
C) Encouraging overutilization of services for higher reimbursement
D) Adopting bundled payment systems for specific conditions

Question 84: In the context of wellness programs focused on mental health prevention, which strategy is considered most comprehensive for reducing stress-related disorders?
A) Yoga and meditation classes
B) Time management workshops
C) Mindfulness-based stress reduction (MBSR) programs
D) Social support groups

Question 85: Sarah, a case manager, is working with a patient-centered medical home (PCMH) to improve care coordination for a patient with multiple chronic conditions. Which of the following strategies is most aligned with the principles of PCMH to enhance care delivery and reimbursement methods?
A) Implementing regular telehealth check-ins to monitor the patient's condition
B) Referring the patient to multiple specialists without coordinating their care
C) Encouraging the patient to utilize emergency services for urgent needs
D) Prioritizing medication management over comprehensive care planning

Question 86: John, a 45-year-old patient, has been admitted to the hospital for alcohol withdrawal. He reports experiencing intense cravings and anxiety. As a case manager, you need to develop a comprehensive care plan. Which intervention is most critical to address John's immediate needs based on contemporary research in substance use management?
A) Implementing a daily exercise regimen
B) Providing cognitive-behavioral therapy (CBT) sessions
C) Administering benzodiazepines for withdrawal symptoms
D) Enrolling in a long-term residential treatment program

Question 87: Which of the following strategies is most effective for a case manager to use when addressing a client's resistance during an interpersonal communication session?
A) Assertive confrontation
B) Reflective listening
C) Direct persuasion
D) Information overload

Question 88: Sarah, a 45-year-old patient with a history of obesity and hypertension, expresses interest in starting a healthier lifestyle. As her case manager, you need to assess her readiness to change. Which of the following strategies would be most effective in activating Sarah's readiness to change?
A) Provide Sarah with detailed educational materials about healthy eating and exercise.

B) Engage Sarah in setting small, achievable health goals that align with her interests.
C) Encourage Sarah to join a support group for individuals with similar health conditions.
D) Suggest that Sarah consults with a nutritionist for personalized dietary advice.

Question 89: Maria, a case manager, is working with Mr. Lee, a patient who adheres to traditional Chinese medicine practices. Mr. Lee believes in balancing the body's energy (Qi) and often uses herbal remedies. How should Maria incorporate Mr. Lee's beliefs into his care plan to ensure effective case management?
A) Encourage Mr. Lee to solely rely on Western medicine for treatment
B) Integrate Mr. Lee's use of herbal remedies with his prescribed medications after consulting with his healthcare provider
C) Advise Mr. Lee to discontinue herbal remedies due to potential interactions
D) Focus only on educating Mr. Lee about potential risks of alternative therapies

Question 90: Which of the following is a primary objective of Medicaid Home and Community-Based Services (HCBS) waiver programs?
A) To provide funding for hospital-based acute care services
B) To support long-term institutional care in nursing facilities
C) To enable individuals to receive care in their own homes or communities
D) To prioritize emergency medical services over preventive care

Question 91: John, a case manager, is working with Emily, a patient who has been diagnosed with a chronic illness. Emily expresses feelings of hopelessness and questions the purpose of her suffering. John considers referring Emily to pastoral counseling. What is the primary benefit of pastoral counseling in this context?
A) It provides specific medical advice related to her illness.
B) It offers emotional support by integrating spiritual beliefs into coping strategies.
C) It focuses solely on psychological techniques without spiritual considerations.
D) It encourages complete reliance on religious practices for healing.

Question 92: In the context of gender identity development, which concept refers to the internalization of societal expectations regarding behaviors and roles typically associated with one's assigned sex at birth?
A) Gender Role Socialization
B) Gender Fluidity
C) Gender Dysphoria
D) Gender Constancy

Question 93: John, a 75-year-old patient with multiple chronic conditions, is transitioning from acute care to a skilled nursing facility. As his case manager, what is the most effective strategy to ensure continuity of care during this transition?
A) Conducting a comprehensive medication reconciliation prior to transfer
B) Arranging transportation to the skilled nursing facility
C) Facilitating a detailed handover meeting between hospital and facility staff
D) Providing John with contact information for his new care team

Question 94: Under the Medicare program, which of the following services is covered by Medicare Part B but not by Part A?
A) Inpatient hospital stays.

B) Outpatient physician visits.
C) Skilled nursing facility care.
D) Hospice care.

Question 95: During a health coaching session, Maria, a case manager, notices that her client, John, frequently expresses feelings of being overwhelmed by his chronic illness management. Which of the following strategies should Maria prioritize to effectively support John's psychosocial needs in this scenario?
A) Encourage John to set multiple ambitious health goals to boost motivation.
B) Facilitate a discussion on John's personal values and how they relate to his health goals.
C) Provide John with detailed educational materials about his illness.
D) Suggest that John join a peer support group for individuals with similar conditions.

Question 96: When assessing a client with co-occurring disorders, which screening tool is most recommended for identifying both mental health and substance use issues simultaneously?
A) CAGE Questionnaire
B) Beck Depression Inventory (BDI)
C) Addiction Severity Index (ASI)
D) Modified Mini Screen (MMS)

Question 97: As a case manager, you are reviewing the healthcare analytics data for a patient named John, who has been readmitted multiple times due to heart failure. Which analytical approach would best help identify patterns in John's readmissions to improve care outcomes?
A) Predictive analytics using historical data
B) Descriptive analytics summarizing current readmission rates
C) Prescriptive analytics suggesting interventions
D) Diagnostic analytics identifying causes of readmissions

Question 98: What is a significant psychosocial benefit of utilizing meal delivery services for individuals with limited mobility?
A) Increased independence by reducing reliance on family members for meals
B) Enhanced social interaction through regular visits from delivery personnel
C) Improved financial savings due to bulk purchasing by the service provider
D) Greater access to diverse cuisines promoting cultural awareness

Question 99: John, a case manager in a rural community clinic, must decide how to manage his caseload given limited resources and increasing patient demands. What approach should John take to ensure equitable access to care?
A) Implement a first-come, first-served policy for all appointments.
B) Use a triage system based on medical urgency alone.
C) Integrate both medical urgency and socio-economic factors into his triage system.
D) Prioritize long-term patients over new ones due to established relationships.

Question 100: Which financial risk model primarily focuses on evaluating the potential impact of rare but severe financial losses in healthcare reimbursement systems?
A) Value at Risk (VaR)
B) Conditional Value at Risk (CVaR)
C) Monte Carlo Simulation
D) Scenario Analysis

Question 101: John, a hospital administrator, is considering switching from fee-for-service to a case rate model for cardiac surgeries. What is a significant challenge he might face with this transition?
A) Increased administrative burden due to detailed billing requirements.
B) Difficulty in predicting costs due to variable patient needs and outcomes.
C) Enhanced ability to track specific service costs and allocate resources accurately.
D) Greater flexibility in adjusting payments based on individual patient outcomes.

Question 102: Sarah, a case manager, is working with a client named John who has experienced emotional abuse. John's self-esteem is severely affected, and he struggles with trust issues. Which of the following interventions should Sarah prioritize to address John's emotional needs effectively?
A) Encourage John to join a support group for emotional abuse survivors.
B) Suggest that John write a daily journal about his feelings.
C) Focus on developing coping strategies for stress management.
D) Refer John to a psychiatrist for medication evaluation.

Question 103: In the context of quality and outcomes evaluation, which method is most effective for identifying areas of improvement in a healthcare setting by comparing performance metrics with established benchmarks?
A) Process Mapping
B) Root Cause Analysis
C) Benchmarking
D) SWOT Analysis

Question 104: Which stage of the Transtheoretical Model of Change is characterized by a client recognizing the need for change but not yet ready to take action, often seeking information to understand their behavior better?
A) Precontemplation
B) Contemplation
C) Preparation
D) Action

Question 105: In the context of shared decision making, which of the following is considered a critical component to ensure effective client self-care management?
A) Providing clients with multiple treatment options without guidance
B) Ensuring clients have access to evidence-based information about their conditions
C) Encouraging clients to rely solely on their intuition for decision making
D) Allowing healthcare providers to make decisions on behalf of clients

Question 106: In the context of relationship building, which communication technique is most likely to enhance rapport between a case manager and a client?
A) Using technical jargon to demonstrate knowledge
B) Employing reflective listening to validate feelings
C) Focusing on problem-solving from the outset
D) Maintaining a formal tone throughout interactions

Question 107: John, a 45-year-old patient with chronic kidney disease, is struggling to communicate his needs during medical appointments. As his case manager, how can you best support John's self-advocacy skills?
A) Encourage John to write down his questions and concerns before each appointment.

B) Provide John with pamphlets about kidney disease management.
C) Advise John to rely on family members to communicate his needs.
D) Suggest that John attend all appointments with a healthcare advocate.

Question 108: Maria, a case manager, is assessing the implementation of a new medication management system in her facility. During the cost-benefit analysis, which outcome should she focus on to justify the system's adoption?
A) Increased time spent by nurses on documentation
B) Decreased medication errors
C) Cost of software licensing
D) Improved staff morale

Question 109: In the context of pastoral counseling within supportive care programs, which of the following approaches best integrates spiritual assessment into a comprehensive case management plan?
A) Focusing solely on religious rituals and practices
B) Incorporating spiritual history taking as part of the initial assessment
C) Relying exclusively on a patient's expressed religious beliefs
D) Utilizing standardized psychological assessments without spiritual components

Question 110: Jamie, a case manager, is assisting Sarah, a female client diagnosed with coronary artery disease. Considering gender-specific health risks, what should Jamie emphasize during health education sessions?
A) Focus on general dietary changes applicable to all genders.
B) Highlight the atypical presentation of heart attack symptoms in women.
C) Emphasize smoking cessation as the primary preventive measure.
D) Discuss routine exercise plans without gender considerations.

Question 111: Which approach is most aligned with contemporary theories of client self-care management in enhancing a patient's ability to manage their health condition independently?
A) Implementing a strict routine for medication adherence
B) Encouraging participation in peer support groups
C) Using a reward system for achieving health goals
D) Developing personalized care plans incorporating patient preferences

Question 112: Which of the following initiatives by the Centers for Medicare and Medicaid Services (CMS) focuses on incentivizing hospitals to improve patient care quality through financial rewards based on performance metrics?
A) Hospital Readmissions Reduction Program (HRRP)
B) Hospital Value-Based Purchasing (VBP) Program
C) Medicare Shared Savings Program (MSSP)
D) Inpatient Quality Reporting (IQR) Program

Question 113: Sarah, a case manager, is tasked with finding a suitable living arrangement for a 30-year-old client with mild schizophrenia who is stable on medication but requires social support and supervision to ensure adherence to treatment. Which option best aligns with her client's requirements?
A) Psychiatric Hospital
B) Group Home
C) Homeless Shelter
D) Independent Apartment

Question 114: When conducting a cost-benefit analysis in healthcare, which factor is most critical in determining whether a case management intervention should be implemented?
A) The intervention's alignment with current healthcare policies
B) The net monetary benefit after comparing costs and savings
C) The potential for reducing hospital readmission rates
D) The degree of innovation presented by the intervention

Question 115: What is a significant challenge faced by case managers when coordinating services under Medicaid Waiver Programs?
A) Ensuring adequate hospital bed availability
B) Navigating complex eligibility criteria for clients
C) Prioritizing surgical interventions over preventive measures
D) Reducing inpatient readmission rates

Question 116: Sarah, a case manager at a large hospital, is reviewing the billing process for a patient who underwent a knee replacement surgery. The hospital uses a case rate payment method. Which of the following best describes how the case rate would impact the hospital's reimbursement for this procedure?
A) The hospital will be reimbursed based on the number of days the patient stays in the hospital.
B) The hospital will receive a fixed amount regardless of actual costs incurred during the patient's stay.
C) The hospital will be reimbursed based on individual services provided to the patient.
D) The hospital will be paid according to the total cost of all resources used during treatment.

Question 117: Sarah, a 45-year-old patient, has been smoking for over 20 years. She expresses a desire to quit and has started researching nicotine replacement therapies but hasn't taken any concrete steps yet. According to the Transtheoretical Model of Change, which stage is Sarah currently in?
A) Precontemplation
B) Contemplation
C) Preparation
D) Action

Question 118: Which of the following characteristics most accurately distinguishes a skilled nursing facility (SNF) from other types of alternative care facilities?
A) Provides long-term custodial care for chronic conditions.
B) Offers intensive rehabilitation services and 24-hour medical supervision.
C) Primarily focuses on palliative and end-of-life care.
D) Specializes in short-term post-acute care with a focus on recovery.

Question 119: John, a case manager, needs to evaluate the long-term impact of a chronic disease management program on patient quality of life. He chooses an evaluation method that collects data from the same participants over several years. What evaluation method is John employing?
A) Longitudinal Study
B) Cross-Sectional Study
C) Cohort Study
D) Time-Series Analysis

Question 120: Emily, a case manager, is assisting a low-income family in understanding their Medicaid benefits. The family is concerned about potential out-of-pocket costs for services not covered under Medicaid. Which of the following services is most likely to be covered by

Medicaid without additional out-of-pocket expenses?
A) Cosmetic surgery
B) Routine dental check-ups for children
C) Over-the-counter medications
D) Experimental treatments

Question 121: Which of the following best describes the concept of "gender expression" in contemporary gender studies?
A) The biological differences between males and females.
B) The internal sense of being male, female, both, or neither.
C) The external manifestation of gender through behavior, clothing, and other expressions.
D) The legal recognition of an individual's gender identity.

Question 122: Mark, a case manager, is assisting a client named Linda in selecting a private benefit program after her employer discontinued their group health plan. Linda wants to ensure her new plan offers comprehensive coverage similar to her previous one. What private benefit program should Mark suggest that aligns closely with Linda's requirements?
A) Marketplace Insurance Plan
B) Health Maintenance Organization (HMO) Plan
C) Preferred Provider Organization (PPO) Plan
D) Catastrophic Health Insurance

Question 123: Sarah, a veteran with service-connected disabilities, needs long-term care services. She has access to VA benefits but is unsure if she qualifies for additional financial support through the Aid and Attendance program. As her case manager, what criteria should you consider to determine her eligibility?
A) Sarah must have a disability rating of at least 50% from the VA.
B) Sarah must be receiving VA pension benefits to qualify.
C) Sarah must require assistance with activities of daily living (ADLs).
D) Sarah must have served during wartime.

Question 124: Sarah, a case manager, is working with John, who has been smoking for over 20 years. John expresses a strong desire to quit smoking but has not yet taken any concrete steps. According to the Transtheoretical Model of Change, which stage is John most likely in?
A) Precontemplation
B) Contemplation
C) Preparation
D) Action

Question 125: Alex, a case manager, is developing a care plan for Taylor, a non-binary individual facing discrimination at work due to their gender expression. What key strategy should Alex include in Taylor's care plan?
A) Suggest Taylor dress more traditionally at work.
B) Advocate for workplace sensitivity training on gender diversity.
C) Recommend Taylor keep their non-binary status private.
D) Encourage Taylor to change jobs for a more accepting environment.

Question 126: In the context of chronic care, which reimbursement method incentivizes improved health outcomes by linking payment to the quality of care provided?
A) Fee-for-Service
B) Capitation
C) Pay-for-Performance
D) Bundled Payments

Question 127: What is the primary benefit of utilizing an
interdisciplinary/interprofessional care team approach in managing chronic conditions within a healthcare setting?
A) Enhanced patient satisfaction due to multiple perspectives.
B) Increased efficiency through task delegation.
C) Improved patient outcomes through collaborative decision-making.
D) Reduced healthcare costs by minimizing resource utilization.

Question 128: In the context of reimbursement methods, which model incentivizes healthcare providers to deliver efficient and high-quality care by rewarding them with shared savings?
A) Capitation
B) Pay-for-Performance (P4P)
C) Accountable Care Organizations (ACOs)
D) Diagnosis-Related Groups (DRGs)

Question 129: During an interdisciplinary team meeting, case manager John is tasked with identifying clients with high acuity levels to ensure proper allocation of resources. Which assessment criterion should John focus on to identify high-acuity clients effectively?
A) Patient's age
B) Number of comorbid conditions
C) Recent changes in functional status
D) Family support availability

Question 130: Emily, a case manager, is assisting Tom, who has recently lost his job and health insurance. Tom needs ongoing medication for his mental health condition. Which strategy should Emily prioritize to ensure Tom receives his medication through a pharmacy assistance program?
A) Encourage Tom to apply for Medicaid immediately
B) Assist Tom in enrolling in a State Health Insurance Exchange plan
C) Help Tom access manufacturer-sponsored PAPs
D) Refer Tom to community health clinics under the 340B program

Question 131: John, a 45-year-old patient recovering from surgery, requires follow-up care through telehealth services. As his case manager, which reimbursement model should you prioritize to ensure sustainable telehealth service delivery?
A) Fee-for-service model for each telehealth visit
B) Capitation model including telehealth services
C) Bundled payments covering post-operative care
D) Pay-for-performance based on patient outcomes

Question 132: In Motivational Interviewing, what is the primary purpose of using open-ended questions during a session?
A) To gather specific information quickly
B) To encourage detailed client responses
C) To provide direct advice to clients
D) To confront clients about their behaviors

Question 133: John, a case manager, is reviewing the hospital stay of a patient who underwent a coronary artery bypass graft (CABG). He needs to ensure accurate reimbursement through Diagnosis-Related Groups (DRGs). Which factor most significantly influences the DRG assignment for this procedure?
A) Length of hospital stay
B) Primary diagnosis
C) Patient's age
D) Presence of comorbidities

Question 134: Which of the following social

determinants of health most directly influences an individual's ability to access healthcare services?
A) Employment status
B) Educational attainment
C) Transportation availability
D) Social support networks

Question 135: In the context of psychological support systems, which approach is considered most effective for addressing complex trauma resulting from prolonged abuse?
A) Cognitive Behavioral Therapy (CBT)
B) Dialectical Behavior Therapy (DBT)
C) Trauma-Focused Cognitive Behavioral Therapy (TF-CBT)
D) Eye Movement Desensitization and Reprocessing (EMDR)

Question 136: Maria, a case manager, is reviewing a patient's medical records for coding purposes. The patient was admitted for acute bronchitis but also has a history of chronic obstructive pulmonary disease (COPD). Which ICD-10-CM code should Maria prioritize to ensure accurate reimbursement and reflect the complexity of care?
A) J20.9 - Acute bronchitis, unspecified
B) J44.0 - COPD with acute lower respiratory infection
C) J44.1 - COPD with acute exacerbation
D) J45.909 - Unspecified asthma, uncomplicated

Question 137: In the context of reporting outcomes for a case management program, what is the primary benefit of using a control chart?
A) It provides a snapshot of current performance levels.
B) It helps identify variations due to special causes.
C) It predicts future performance based on historical data.
D) It compares outcomes across different programs.

Question 138: In the context of cost-benefit analysis for case management, which of the following best describes the primary objective when evaluating healthcare interventions?
A) Maximizing patient satisfaction while minimizing treatment costs
B) Balancing clinical outcomes with resource allocation efficiency
C) Achieving the highest quality of care regardless of cost implications
D) Ensuring all stakeholders have equitable access to healthcare services

Question 139: Sarah is a case manager assessing the eligibility for expanded home care benefits for her patient, Mrs. Lee, who has complex post-surgical needs. Which criterion would most likely qualify Mrs. Lee for additional coverage under her private insurance plan?
A) Demonstrated improvement in health outcomes with home care
B) Proximity to a major hospital facility
C) A high level of family support at home
D) A recent increase in hospital readmissions

Question 140: In the context of Workers Compensation, which principle primarily dictates that an injured worker must be compensated for lost wages and medical expenses without proving employer negligence?
A) No-Fault Liability
B) Comparative Negligence
C) Assumption of Risk
D) Contributory Negligence

Question 141: In the context of social determinants of health, which factor most significantly contributes to disparities in mental health outcomes among different populations?
A) Access to nutritious food
B) Social support networks
C) Housing stability
D) Educational opportunities

Question 142: When negotiating reimbursement rates with insurance companies, what strategy should a case manager prioritize to maintain a sustainable partnership?
A) Hard Bargaining
B) Interest-Based Negotiation
C) Zero-Sum Tactics
D) Adversarial Approach

Question 143: Which of the following is a critical component of the Joint Commission's accreditation standards for case management that directly impacts quality and outcomes evaluation?
A) Patient-centered care planning
B) Financial resource allocation
C) Staff credentialing requirements
D) Technology integration

Question 144: Maria is a case manager tasked with improving client engagement for John, who has been non-compliant with his treatment regimen for diabetes. Which approach should Maria prioritize to effectively engage John in managing his condition?
A) Implementing a strict monitoring system for John's medication intake
B) Educating John on the potential complications of unmanaged diabetes
C) Exploring John's beliefs and attitudes towards diabetes management
D) Providing John with regular updates on his glucose levels

Question 145: Sarah, a case manager, is working with John, a 65-year-old diabetic patient who has recently been discharged from the hospital. John expresses difficulty in managing his medication regimen and maintaining a healthy diet. What is the most effective self-care management strategy that Sarah should prioritize to support John's independence and adherence?
A) Provide John with a detailed written schedule of his medications and dietary plan.
B) Arrange for a home health nurse to administer John's medications daily.
C) Educate John on using a pill organizer and involve him in meal planning.
D) Schedule weekly check-ins to monitor John's progress and make necessary adjustments.

Question 146: In the context of care delivery and reimbursement methods, which model is most effective in predicting financial risks associated with patient population variability?
A) Predictive Modeling
B) Retrospective Cost Analysis
C) Prospective Payment System
D) Risk Adjustment Model

Question 147: John, a case manager, is working with a veteran named Mark who is transitioning from active duty to civilian life. Mark is concerned about his healthcare coverage under TRICARE and wants to know which plan would best suit his needs as a retiree. Which TRICARE plan should John recommend to Mark that provides the most comprehensive coverage for retirees?
A) TRICARE Prime
B) TRICARE Select
C) TRICARE for Life

D) TRICARE Reserve Select

Question 148: John, a 60-year-old patient recovering from a stroke, expresses doubt about regaining his independence. As his case manager, which counseling approach would best support John's psychosocial needs and encourage his active participation in rehabilitation?
A) Person-Centered Counseling
B) Psychoeducational Counseling
C) Gestalt Therapy
D) Narrative Therapy

Question 149: Lisa is managing her diabetes through a self-directed care plan. She has identified her dietary habits as an area needing improvement. As her case manager, what strategy should you recommend Lisa focus on first to enhance her self-directed care plan?
A) Encourage Lisa to research various dietary plans online independently.
B) Assist Lisa in creating a personalized meal plan based on her preferences and nutritional needs.
C) Suggest Lisa consults with multiple dietitians to gather diverse opinions.
D) Advise Lisa to join an online community for individuals managing diabetes.

Question 150: What role do Diagnosis-Related Groups (DRGs) play in influencing hospital coding practices?
A) DRGs require detailed patient history documentation for accurate classification
B) DRGs necessitate precise coding to ensure proper reimbursement rates
C) DRGs demand comprehensive discharge summaries for payment processing
D) DRGs encourage frequent updates to electronic health records for complianc

ANSWER WITH DETAILED EXPLANATION SET [2]

Question 1: Correct Answer: C) The number of work credits she has accumulated.
Rationale: SSDI eligibility is primarily based on the number of work credits earned through employment, which are determined by annual earnings (Option C). Options A and B are related but not directly impactful; hours worked and total earnings contribute to credits but aren't sole determinants. Option D is irrelevant as job type doesn't affect eligibility unless it pertains to specific disability criteria under SSA guidelines.

Question 2: Correct Answer: C) Encouraging self-monitoring and reflective practices
Rationale: Encouraging self-monitoring and reflection helps clients understand their health patterns, fostering greater awareness and control over their behaviors. This method promotes intrinsic motivation, which is more sustainable than extrinsic incentives (D). Listing complications (A) or focusing on negative consequences (B) may induce fear rather than proactive engagement. Self-monitoring aligns with behavior change theories that prioritize self-efficacy and personal insight as key drivers for adherence.

Question 3: Correct Answer: C) Schedule a meeting with Alex's parents to discuss his needs.
Rationale: Engaging with parents helps identify underlying issues and offers solutions without prematurely involving CPS (B), which might not be warranted initially. Counseling (A) or after-school programs (D) can support Alex but do not address parental involvement or awareness directly, which is critical for sustainable change in neglect situations.

Question 4: Correct Answer: C) Integrate the client's spiritual beliefs into the care plan after discussing them with the client.
Rationale: Integrating a client's spiritual beliefs into their care plan acknowledges their holistic needs and can improve health outcomes. This approach respects cultural diversity and supports personalized care. Option A overlooks spirituality's role in well-being; B imposes external beliefs, violating ethical standards; D ignores an essential aspect of culturally competent care. Thus, C is correct, as it involves collaboration and respect for the client's values, aligning with contemporary research on culturally sensitive healthcare.

Question 5: Correct Answer: B) Coordination of comprehensive care across different providers
Rationale: Health Homes are designed to provide integrated and coordinated care for individuals with chronic conditions, emphasizing comprehensive care coordination across various providers. Unlike traditional models, which may focus on specific diseases or episodic treatments (Options C and D), Health Homes aim to address all health needs collectively. Acute care services (Option A) are generally part of broader healthcare but not a defining feature of Health Homes. The emphasis on coordination is crucial for effective management and improved outcomes.

Question 6: Correct Answer: B) Coordinating care among multiple healthcare providers to address all aspects of a patient's needs.
Rationale: Holistic case management involves addressing the physical, emotional, social, and financial needs of patients by coordinating care among various providers. Option A is incorrect as it focuses only on medical treatment without considering other factors. Option C is misleading because holistic care prioritizes patient-centered approaches rather than cost alone.

Option D is incorrect as it neglects the importance of long-term health management, which is crucial in holistic care.

Question 7: Correct Answer: C) Use the teach-back method to confirm understanding of self-care instructions.
Rationale: The teach-back method ensures that patients understand their care instructions by asking them to repeat the information in their own words, directly addressing comprehension issues associated with low health literacy. Option A may not be effective if Mr. Thompson struggles with reading comprehension. Option B offers peer support but doesn't guarantee understanding of medical instructions. Option D assumes digital literacy, which might not be applicable for all patients, especially those with low health literacy.

Question 8: Correct Answer: B) Pay-for-performance (P4P)
Rationale: Pay-for-performance (P4P) aligns reimbursement with quality metrics, rewarding providers for achieving specific outcomes and efficiency benchmarks. Unlike PPS, which offers pre-determined rates based on diagnosis-related groups, P4P directly links compensation to performance. Global budgeting allocates fixed budgets for healthcare entities, focusing on cost control rather than individual performance metrics. RBRVS assigns value units to medical services based on resource costs but does not inherently tie payments to quality outcomes as P4P does.

Question 9: Correct Answer: B) Integrative Negotiation
Rationale: Integrative negotiation focuses on collaboration to achieve mutually beneficial outcomes, making it ideal for case managers working with healthcare providers. Unlike competitive bargaining and distributive negotiation, which focus on winning over the other party, integrative negotiation seeks to understand both parties' needs and create value. Positional bargaining often leads to stalemates due to rigid positions. Therefore, integrative negotiation is preferred for fostering long-term relationships and ensuring comprehensive care solutions.

Question 10: Correct Answer: C) Network adequacy
Rationale: Network adequacy is crucial in an HMO plan as it ensures there are sufficient providers within the network to meet patient needs effectively, facilitating coordinated care management. Option A refers to risk selection issues rather than care coordination. Option B deals with behavioral changes due to insurance coverage and does not directly impact care coordination within an HMO framework. Option D relates to spreading risk across insured individuals but doesn't address provider network sufficiency needed for effective case management within an HMO plan.

Question 11: Correct Answer: C) Informed consent
Rationale: Informed consent is essential for respecting a client's autonomy as it ensures that they have all necessary information to make voluntary and educated decisions about their self-care. Beneficence and non-maleficence focus on doing good and avoiding harm, respectively, but do not directly address client autonomy. Paternalism involves overriding a client's wishes for their perceived benefit, which contradicts the principle of autonomy. Thus, informed consent directly supports clients' rights to make autonomous decisions.

Question 12: Correct Answer: B) Coordinating comprehensive care across the healthcare continuum.
Rationale: Health Homes, as outlined in the PPACA, primarily focus on coordinating comprehensive care

across various healthcare settings to ensure that all patient needs are met efficiently. This involves integrating physical and behavioral health services, which is not covered by options A), C), or D). Acute care services (A) and surgical interventions (D) are specific treatments rather than coordination efforts, while financial assistance (C) pertains to cost management, not care coordination.

Question 13: Correct Answer: A) Navigating complex eligibility criteria

Rationale: Case managers often struggle with complex eligibility criteria (A), which can hinder access to necessary services for patients. While accessing specialists (B) might seem challenging, private programs generally offer broad networks. High transparency (C) is an advantage rather than a challenge. Policy updates (D), though frequent, are manageable compared to deciphering intricate eligibility rules. Understanding these criteria is crucial for effective patient advocacy and resource allocation within private benefit frameworks.

Question 14: Correct Answer: C) His past work history and contributions to Social Security

Rationale: Eligibility for SSDI primarily depends on the applicant's work history and their contributions to the Social Security system, as this program is funded by payroll taxes. While the severity and duration of the disability (Option B) are important, they are secondary to having sufficient work credits. Current income level (Option A) and availability of other insurance benefits (Option D) do not directly determine SSDI eligibility. Therefore, Option C is correct as it focuses on the foundational requirement for SSDI.

Question 15: Correct Answer: B) Cognitive-behavioral therapy (CBT) interventions

Rationale: Cognitive-behavioral therapy (CBT) interventions are most effective as they address the psychological aspects of chronic disease management, promoting behavior change and emotional well-being. While regular physical activity, nutritional counseling, and medication adherence are important, CBT specifically targets mental health issues, enhancing coping mechanisms. Physical activity (A), nutritional counseling (C), and medication reminders (D) focus on physical or routine aspects rather than directly addressing psychological barriers to managing chronic illness.

Question 16: Correct Answer: C) Interaction Adaptation Theory

Rationale: Interaction Adaptation Theory posits that individuals modify their communication behavior based on their perceptions of others' actions. While Reciprocity Principle involves mutual exchanges and Expectancy Violations Theory focuses on unexpected behavior, they do not specifically address adaptation. Social Exchange Theory is more about cost-benefit analysis in relationships. Thus, Interaction Adaptation Theory best explains the adjustment of communication styles based on perceived behaviors in interpersonal interactions.

Question 17: Correct Answer: B) Establish rapport and actively listen to Lisa's concerns.

Rationale: The first step in effective crisis intervention is establishing rapport and actively listening, as it builds trust and allows the client to express their feelings openly (Option B). This sets the foundation for further interventions. Option A addresses long-term needs rather than immediate crisis management. Option C may be necessary but should follow after understanding Lisa's specific needs through active listening. Option D might help with stability but does not address the immediate emotional support required in a crisis situation like establishing rapport does.

Question 18: Correct Answer: C) John's current physical limitations and recovery progress.

Rationale: The primary consideration in developing a return-to-work plan should be John's current physical limitations and recovery progress to ensure safety and prevent further injury. While options A and B are important factors, they do not prioritize John's health and recovery needs. Option D relates to financial support but does not directly address the suitability of returning to work based on health status. Therefore, option C is essential for crafting a safe and effective return-to-work strategy.

Question 19: Correct Answer: B) Coordinate joint sessions with a physiotherapist and psychologist

Rationale: Coordinating joint sessions with both a physiotherapist and psychologist ensures an integrated approach addressing Sarah's physical pain and mental health simultaneously. Option A focuses narrowly on physical pain without addressing behavioral health. Option C overlooks the need for physical therapy. Option D lacks the interdisciplinary approach necessary for comprehensive care. Thus, option B offers a holistic strategy aligning with contemporary practices in managing co-occurring physical and behavioral health issues.

Question 20: Correct Answer: B) John's COBRA coverage will automatically terminate when he becomes eligible for Medicare at age 65.

Rationale: According to COBRA regulations, an individual's continuation coverage generally ends when they become entitled to Medicare benefits, which typically occurs at age 65. Therefore, John's COBRA will terminate upon his Medicare eligibility. Option A overlooks this automatic termination condition. Option C misrepresents the relationship between retirement and immediate Medicare application—Medicare enrollment timing does not affect initial retirement status under COBRA. Option D falsely suggests an option that does not exist in standard regulations without specific provisions or exceptions.

Question 21: Correct Answer: B) Norming Stage

Rationale: The Norming Stage is crucial in Tuckman's model as it involves the establishment of group norms and cohesion, which significantly impact group effectiveness. While Group Size (A) can influence dynamics, it is not a primary determinant in Tuckman's theory. Leadership Style (C) and Communication Patterns (D) are important but are more directly related to how the group functions rather than its developmental stages. Thus, the Norming Stage is pivotal for setting standards and fostering collaboration.

Question 22: Correct Answer: C) Dysthymia (Persistent Depressive Disorder)

Rationale: Dysthymia is characterized by chronic depression lasting at least two years in adults, aligning with Emily's six-month history of persistent symptoms. Major Depressive Disorder involves more severe symptoms but typically occurs in episodes. Adjustment Disorder with Depressed Mood is related to a specific stressor and is short-term. Bipolar II Disorder includes hypomanic episodes, which are not present in Emily's case. Therefore, the chronic nature of her symptoms best fits Dysthymia.

Question 23: Correct Answer: D) Empowering clients through motivational interviewing techniques

Rationale: Motivational interviewing (MI) effectively enhances long-term adherence by addressing ambivalence and enhancing intrinsic motivation. While educational materials (A) and smartphone apps (B)

support self-management, they lack the personalized engagement MI offers. Regular follow-ups (C) are essential but may not address underlying motivational issues. MI focuses on client autonomy and readiness to change, making it superior in fostering sustained self-care behaviors.

Question 24: Correct Answer: A) Mediation
Rationale: Mediation involves the case manager acting as a neutral facilitator to help both parties understand each other's perspectives and reach an agreement that serves Mrs. Lee's best interests. Competing could escalate tensions, Negotiation without mediation may not address underlying concerns fully, and Compromise might not result in the optimal solution for Mrs. Lee's care needs. Mediation encourages understanding and collaboration towards an agreed-upon solution that considers all aspects of Mrs. Lee's health and well-being.

Question 25: Correct Answer: A) Encouraging John to participate in telehealth services for routine check-ups
Rationale: Option A is correct as telehealth expands access and continuity of care in underserved areas, aligning with population health goals. Option B is inefficient and costly. Option C is impractical and ignores systemic issues. Option D provides support but lacks scalability and may not address all barriers John faces.

Question 26: Correct Answer: B) In-Home Health Aide
Rationale: An In-Home Health Aide can provide personalized support tailored to Sarah's needs, allowing her to remain in her home while receiving assistance with daily tasks. This option supports independence and safety without requiring a move to a facility. Adult Day Care Services (A) offer daytime supervision but do not address in-home needs. Assisted Living (C) and Memory Care Units (D) involve relocation, which may not be necessary at this stage of forgetfulness.

Question 27: Correct Answer: C) Integrating behavioral health into primary care
Rationale: Integrating behavioral health into primary care is fundamental to the Health Home model, as it addresses both physical and mental health needs comprehensively, leading to improved patient outcomes. While electronic health records (Option A) enhance communication, they alone do not define success. Prioritizing cost reduction (Option B) without patient engagement can undermine quality care. Limiting access to specialists (Option D) contradicts the holistic approach essential in Health Homes, where comprehensive and integrated care is prioritized.

Question 28: Correct Answer: B) John's monthly earned income
Rationale: John's monthly earned income directly impacts his eligibility for SSI because SSI is designed to assist individuals with limited income and resources. Unlike earned income, the value of the primary residence (Option A) is not considered a countable resource. The number of dependents (Option C) does not directly affect SSI eligibility, as it primarily depends on individual financial need. While age (Option D) can be relevant in certain cases, it is not a primary factor unless related to specific age-based criteria.

Question 29: Correct Answer: C) Bipolar I Disorder
Rationale: John's symptoms suggest Bipolar I Disorder due to the presence of extreme mood swings from euphoria (mania) to deep depression and risky behavior during manic episodes. Borderline Personality Disorder (A) involves emotional instability but lacks distinct manic episodes. Cyclothymic Disorder (B) features milder mood swings without full-blown manic or depressive episodes. Schizoaffective Disorder (D) includes psychotic symptoms along with mood disorder features, which are not described here. Thus, Bipolar I Disorder best explains John's condition based on his symptoms and behavior patterns.

Question 30: Correct Answer: D) Skills training for coping with high-risk situations
Rationale: Skills training for coping with high-risk situations is a core component of CBT and is specifically designed to equip individuals with strategies to handle triggers and prevent relapse. While psychoeducation (A) provides valuable information, it lacks the practical application focus of skills training. Mindfulness-based stress reduction (B) aids in stress management but doesn't directly address relapse prevention.

Question 31: Correct Answer: B) The client's level of physical mobility
Rationale: Physical mobility is crucial as it directly affects the client's ability to escape or report abuse and impacts their vulnerability. While financial resources, support network, and medical history are important, they do not directly determine the immediate physical risks or barriers faced by the client. Mobility issues can exacerbate the effects of abuse and hinder access to assistance, making it a primary concern in physical assessments.

Question 32: Correct Answer: B) Minnesota Multiphasic Personality Inventory (MMPI-2)
Rationale: The MMPI-2 provides a comprehensive evaluation of psychological well-being and personality structure, making it ideal for Sarah's case. Option A, HAM-A, focuses solely on anxiety levels. Option C, TMT-B, assesses attention and task-switching abilities rather than overall psychological health. Option D, Stroop Test, evaluates cognitive flexibility but lacks depth in assessing broad psychological states like the MMPI-2 does.

Question 33: Correct Answer: B) Ensure regular psychological assessments are conducted.
Rationale: Regular psychological assessments are vital for monitoring Jamie's mental well-being and ensuring comprehensive support throughout their transition process. Option A neglects emotional and psychological aspects critical in transitions. Option C can hinder personal growth and self-understanding by discouraging exploration. Option D lacks nuance; side effects should be managed carefully rather than abruptly stopping therapy, aligning with best practices in gender health management.

Question 34: Correct Answer: A) Encouraging participation in a peer support group
Rationale: Peer support groups are vital in sustaining recovery by providing social support and accountability, aligning with behavioral health principles. Methadone (Option B), while effective for some, isn't suitable post-detox if Sarah seeks abstinence. MBSR (Option C) complements recovery but isn't standalone. Family therapy (Option D) aids recovery but doesn't directly address personal accountability like peer groups do. Therefore, Option A is prioritized as it directly supports Sarah's sobriety maintenance through community engagement and support.

Question 35: Correct Answer: B) Motivational interviewing
Rationale: Motivational interviewing is a client-centered approach that enhances motivation by exploring and resolving ambivalence, making it highly effective for behavior change. Unlike directive advice-giving (A), which can lead to resistance, motivational interviewing fosters collaboration. Prescriptive goal-setting (C) may not address underlying motivations, and structured educational sessions (D) lack personalized engagement.

Thus, motivational interviewing is preferred for its ability to empower clients through intrinsic motivation.

Question 36: Correct Answer: B) Action

Rationale: John is in the Action stage as he has actively started exercising regularly for two months. The Maintenance stage (Option A) involves sustaining behavior change for six months or more. Preparation (Option C) would involve planning but not yet taking consistent action. Contemplation (Option D) refers to considering change without action.

Question 37: Correct Answer: B) Patient-Reported Outcome Measures (PROMs)

Rationale: Patient-Reported Outcome Measures (PROMs) are specifically designed to evaluate patient satisfaction as they capture patients' perspectives on their health status and care experience. Clinical outcome measures focus on health results rather than satisfaction. Process measures assess how healthcare services are delivered, not patient experiences. Structural measures evaluate facility resources, not individual satisfaction. PROMs provide direct insights into patients' views on care quality, making them the best choice for assessing patient satisfaction outcomes.

Question 38: Correct Answer: C) Enhanced access to specialized care

Rationale: Alternative care sites, such as urgent care centers and telemedicine platforms, enhance access to specialized care by providing services outside traditional hospital settings. This advantage allows patients to receive timely interventions from specialists without the constraints of hospital availability. While options A, B, and D are beneficial, they do not primarily focus on the accessibility aspect that alternative sites offer. Reduced costs (A), increased engagement (B), and improved coordination (D) are secondary benefits but do not directly address the specialization access like option C does.

Question 39: Correct Answer: B) Implement standardized clinical pathways to minimize variability in treatment outcomes.

Rationale: Option B is correct because standardized clinical pathways help ensure consistent outcomes and reduce unnecessary variations that can drive up costs in bundled payments. Option A does not address clinical outcome consistency, which is crucial for managing financial risk. Option C could affect staff morale and patient care quality negatively. Option D is not viable as delaying procedures can affect patient satisfaction and health outcomes, contrary to the goals of bundled payments.

Question 40: Correct Answer: B) Federally Qualified Health Centers (FQHCs)

Rationale: Federally Qualified Health Centers (FQHCs) are designed to deliver comprehensive primary care services to underserved populations in community settings. They differ from ambulatory surgical centers, which focus on outpatient surgical procedures, and concierge medicine practices, which cater to individuals who can afford personalized services. Retail clinics offer limited scope services mainly for minor illnesses. FQHCs receive federal funding to ensure access to essential healthcare services regardless of patients' ability to pay, emphasizing their community-centered mission.

Question 41: Correct Answer: A) Contact the drug manufacturer directly to inquire about their patient assistance program.

Rationale: Drug manufacturers often offer patient assistance programs specifically for their medications, providing significant financial relief (A). While local

organizations (B), generic alternatives (C), and state programs (D) can be helpful, they may not address specialty medication costs as effectively as direct manufacturer programs designed for these situations, ensuring Ms. Garcia receives the exact prescribed treatment without switching or waiting for external aid processes.

Question 42: Correct Answer: C) Learning coping strategies from peers

Rationale: Support groups primarily offer members the chance to learn coping strategies through shared experiences, which can be particularly beneficial in managing grief. While professional counseling (A), social interaction (B), and distraction (D) may occur within support groups, they are not their primary purpose. Peer learning provides practical insights and emotional validation, aiding in personal healing processes more effectively than other aspects.

Question 43: Correct Answer: B) Encourage Tom to communicate his concerns and preferences directly to his rehabilitation team.

Rationale: Option B is correct as it promotes direct communication, a key element of self-advocacy, enabling Tom to voice concerns and influence his care plan. Option A discourages self-advocacy by silencing patient input. Option C could lead to misinformation without professional guidance. Option D dismisses patient involvement, contrary to advocacy principles promoting active participation in decision-making processes.

Question 44: Correct Answer: B) Establishing senior peer support groups

Rationale: Establishing senior peer support groups effectively addresses the psychosocial needs of elderly clients by fostering a sense of belonging and mutual understanding. These groups facilitate emotional support and shared experiences among peers. Telehealth consultations (A), while useful for medical advice, lack the interpersonal connection. Transportation services (C) and nutritional meal programs (D), although beneficial for physical needs, do not directly address emotional or social aspects. Therefore, peer support groups uniquely cater to the psychosocial dimensions of elder care.

Question 45: Correct Answer: A) A client has unpaid bills despite having sufficient funds due to their cognitive decline.

Rationale: Option A indicates financial neglect because it highlights a failure to manage finances due to cognitive issues, leading to unmet needs despite available resources. Option B reflects personal choice rather than neglect. Option C shows proactive financial management, albeit with minor lapses. Option D suggests positive involvement without neglect indicators. Only Option A directly ties unmet essential needs to an inability to manage finances effectively due to health-related factors, characteristic of neglect.

Question 46: Correct Answer: B) Competing

Rationale: Competing is prioritized for swift decision-making in urgent situations as it involves assertiveness and quick action. Unlike accommodating, which prioritizes others' needs over quick resolutions, competing ensures decisive outcomes. Collaborating may delay decisions due to its focus on consensus-building. Avoiding postpones action altogether, making it unsuitable for urgent scenarios requiring immediate resolution.

Question 47: Correct Answer: B) Monitoring and reducing unnecessary tests and procedures

Rationale: Monitoring and reducing unnecessary tests aligns with bundled payment goals by minimizing costs without compromising quality. Option A neglects follow-up care, essential for comprehensive management. Option C might increase costs without adding value if consultations are unwarranted. Option D focuses narrowly on hospital stay duration, potentially overlooking other critical factors affecting outcomes. Thus, option B effectively balances cost control with quality care delivery.

Question 48: Correct Answer: B) The opportunity for Mike to explore his faith in relation to his health challenges.
Rationale: Pastoral counseling allows patients like Mike to align their faith with their health journey, offering a personalized approach that integrates spirituality into coping mechanisms. Option A focuses on secular techniques; option C emphasizes medication over personal beliefs; and option D overlooks individualized spiritual guidance. The correct choice highlights how pastoral counseling can enhance Mike's resilience by connecting his faith with his health management strategies.

Question 49: Correct Answer: B) Set up a home-based palliative care team for ongoing support
Rationale: Establishing a home-based palliative care team (Option B) aligns with Mrs. Lee's desire to stay at home while providing necessary medical support. Unlike Option A, which increases hospital visits contrary to her wishes, and Option C, which disregards her preference for remaining at home, this option ensures comprehensive care in the desired setting. Option D offers limited interaction and lacks the continuous support needed in end-of-life care scenarios.

Question 50: Correct Answer: C) Collaborating
Rationale: Collaborating involves open communication and a cooperative approach, ensuring all parties' needs are addressed, which is essential for long-term collaboration. Competing focuses on individual goals, often neglecting team cohesion. Avoiding may delay resolution and exacerbate issues. Accommodating sacrifices one's own needs for others, potentially leading to resentment. Collaborating balances diverse perspectives and fosters mutual respect, making it the most effective strategy for complex patient care.

Question 51: Correct Answer: B) Engaging a multidisciplinary team including dietitians and educators in patient management
Rationale: Engaging a multidisciplinary team embodies PCMH's collaborative approach by leveraging diverse expertise for comprehensive care. Option A isolates responsibility, hindering teamwork. Option C restricts dynamic interaction vital for effective collaboration. Option D narrows focus, neglecting holistic management crucial in PCMH. Multidisciplinary engagement ensures diverse inputs, addressing both medical and lifestyle aspects of diabetes management, aligning with the integrative principles of PCMH.

Question 52: Correct Answer: A) ICD-9
Rationale: The concept of "clinical modifications" was first introduced with ICD-9, specifically as ICD-9-CM (Clinical Modification), to provide more detailed coding for clinical and billing purposes. While ICD-10 and ICD-11 have their own versions, they were designed after the initial introduction of clinical modifications in ICD-9. ICD-8 did not include this feature. The introduction of clinical modifications allowed for more precise data collection, which is crucial for effective case management and accurate reimbursement.

Question 53: Correct Answer: A) Reduced need for in-person visits
Rationale: Telehealth allows for remote monitoring and management of chronic conditions, reducing the necessity for frequent in-person visits. This is particularly beneficial in managing resources and lowering costs, aligning with reimbursement strategies. While increased data privacy (B) is important, it is not a direct benefit related to care delivery. Enhanced communication (C) refers to traditional settings, and simplified claims (D) are more about administrative efficiency than direct care benefits.

Question 54: Correct Answer: B) Providing emotional support and education to patients and families
Rationale: Disease-based organizations primarily focus on providing emotional support and education to patients and their families, which is crucial for managing chronic illnesses. While conducting clinical trials (A) or developing surgical techniques (C) may involve collaboration with these organizations, they are not their primary role. Offering medical equipment (D) is more aligned with healthcare providers or insurance programs. Emotional support and education empower patients, enhancing self-management and adherence to treatment plans.

Question 55: Correct Answer: B) Enrollment in a cognitive-behavioral therapy program
Rationale: Cognitive-behavioral therapy (CBT) is particularly effective in addressing emotional distress and anxiety, making it the most appropriate intervention for Sarah. While palliative care (A) addresses physical symptoms and quality of life, it may not specifically target psychological distress. Home health nursing (C) focuses on medical needs, not psychosocial aspects. Family counseling (D) supports family dynamics but may not directly alleviate Sarah's individual anxiety. CBT offers targeted strategies to help manage Sarah's emotional responses effectively.

Question 56: Correct Answer: A) Implementing regular home visits by healthcare professionals
Rationale: Regular home visits by healthcare professionals are crucial as they allow for continuous monitoring and early detection of neglect signs. This intervention ensures direct assessment and timely intervention. Increasing family involvement (Option B), while beneficial, may not address underlying neglect issues if family dynamics are part of the problem. Long-term care placement (Option C) might ensure safety but can be disruptive and isn't always necessary. Financial management assistance (Option D) addresses only one aspect of neglect, lacking comprehensive oversight provided by professional visits.

Question 57: Correct Answer: B) Emphasizing patient autonomy and self-management
Rationale: Emphasizing patient autonomy and self-management is crucial in integrated case management, as it empowers patients to actively participate in their care, leading to improved outcomes. Prioritizing acute interventions (Option A) neglects long-term wellness. Standardizing protocols (Option C) fails to address individual needs, while limiting provider involvement (Option D) reduces comprehensive support. The focus on autonomy aligns with holistic principles, promoting tailored interventions and fostering collaboration between patients and providers for optimal health outcomes.

Question 58: Correct Answer: B) Reflective listening
Rationale: Reflective listening supports self-efficacy by validating clients' feelings and thoughts, encouraging them to articulate their goals and solutions. Providing direct solutions (A) can undermine autonomy, while emphasizing past failures (C) may decrease confidence. Focusing on barriers (D), without addressing strengths, can be demotivating. Reflective listening builds trust and empowers clients to believe in their capacity to change,

aligning with self-efficacy principles.

Question 59: Correct Answer: C) Use motivational interviewing techniques to address barriers to adherence in both conditions.

Rationale: Motivational interviewing is effective in enhancing adherence by exploring and resolving ambivalence in patients with dual diagnoses. It addresses both conditions simultaneously, unlike options A and D that focus solely on schizophrenia or scheduling without addressing underlying issues. Option B overlooks the need for pharmacological management in schizophrenia. Research supports motivational interviewing as it empowers patients, promoting engagement and sustained adherence across co-occurring disorders.

Question 60: Correct Answer: C) Differences in data coding accuracy

Rationale: Data coding accuracy significantly impacts ACG scores as it determines how patient information is categorized and analyzed. While variability in practice patterns and patient adherence can affect outcomes, they do not directly alter ACG scores like coding accuracy does. Emergency room visit frequency may reflect utilization but not necessarily score discrepancies between departments. Thus, ensuring accurate data coding is vital for consistent and reliable ACG assessments across departments.

Question 61: Correct Answer: C) Requires recipients to have limited income and resources

Rationale: SSI provides financial assistance to individuals who are aged, blind, or disabled and have limited income and resources. Unlike Social Security benefits, which are based on work history (Option A), SSI does not require recipients to have a work history. It specifically targets those with limited means (Option C). Option B is incorrect because SSI eligibility is contingent upon age or disability status. Option D is incorrect as SSI is funded by general tax revenues, not payroll taxes.

Question 62: Correct Answer: D) Comprehensive care management plans

Rationale: Comprehensive care management plans are vital in a PCMH as they ensure coordinated and continuous care, addressing all aspects of a patient's health. While EHRs (Option A) support information sharing, they alone don't ensure comprehensive care. Patient satisfaction surveys (Option B) provide feedback but don't directly enhance care coordination. Telemedicine services (Option C) facilitate access but aren't central to the holistic approach of PCMH. Thus, comprehensive care management plans are crucial for integrating services and improving outcomes.

Question 63: Correct Answer: B) It promotes early discharge to reduce hospital costs.

Rationale: The Prospective Payment System incentivizes hospitals to manage resources efficiently by providing a fixed payment based on diagnosis-related groups (DRGs). This encourages hospitals to discharge patients as soon as medically appropriate to minimize costs and avoid exceeding the predetermined payment amount. Option A is incorrect as longer stays increase costs without additional reimbursement. Option C is misleading because PPS emphasizes cost control, not procedure volume. Option D is incorrect as post-discharge care remains crucial for patient outcomes.

Question 64: Correct Answer: C) It caps Mr. Thompson's out-of-pocket expenses after reaching a certain threshold.

Rationale: The "stop-loss" provision is designed to protect policyholders from excessive out-of-pocket costs by capping them after reaching a predetermined limit. Option A is incorrect as it refers to insurance company limits, not patient protection. Option B is misleading; deductibles and stop-loss are different concepts. Option D incorrectly suggests additional coverage beyond the policy terms, which is not related to stop-loss provisions.

Question 65: Correct Answer: B) Focus on helping John develop a short-term action plan to address immediate financial concerns.

Rationale: Prioritizing a short-term action plan (Option B) addresses immediate needs, stabilizing John's situation and reducing anxiety. While applying for jobs (Option A) is important, it does not address urgent financial stress. Mindfulness (Option C) helps manage anxiety but doesn't solve immediate practical issues. Emotional support (Option D) is beneficial but secondary to immediate financial planning. The correct option focuses on practical solutions aligned with crisis intervention strategies emphasizing immediate stabilization.

Question 66: Correct Answer: B) Anhedonia

Rationale: Anhedonia, the inability to feel pleasure, is a core symptom of Major Depressive Disorder per DSM-5. While options A, C, and D suggest elevated mood or increased energy, these are more aligned with manic episodes seen in Bipolar Disorder. The key difference lies in the nature of mood disturbances: Major Depressive Disorder involves pervasive low mood and loss of interest or pleasure in activities, whereas manic symptoms involve heightened mood and activity levels.

Question 67: Correct Answer: B) Third-Party Special Needs Trust

Rationale: A Third-Party Special Needs Trust is typically established by parents or guardians for a child with disabilities, using their own assets. Option A, First-Party Trusts, are funded with the beneficiary's own assets. Option C, Pooled Trusts, are managed by nonprofit organizations and combine resources from multiple beneficiaries. Option D, Revocable Living Trusts, do not specifically address special needs considerations and can be altered or revoked by the grantor.

Question 68: Correct Answer: D) Interdisciplinary Team Model

Rationale: The Interdisciplinary Team Model is best for integrating services across healthcare settings, focusing on the patient's unique needs through collaboration among diverse healthcare professionals. Unlike the Brokerage Model, which primarily coordinates services without deep integration, and the Primary Care Case Management Model, which centers around primary care providers, the Intensive Case Management Model is more suitable for high-risk patients requiring frequent interventions. The interdisciplinary approach ensures comprehensive and cost-effective care for patients like John with complex conditions.

Question 69: Correct Answer: C) Interpersonal Therapy (IPT)

Rationale: Interpersonal Therapy (IPT) is the best approach for John as it focuses on improving interpersonal relationships and social functioning, directly addressing his isolation and lack of support. Motivational Interviewing targets motivation for change rather than social integration. Solution-Focused Brief Therapy emphasizes solutions but not specifically social aspects. DBT is more suited for emotion regulation rather than enhancing social connections. IPT's focus on relationships makes it ideal for reducing John's neglect risk by fostering social integration.

Question 70: Correct Answer: C) Home Health Care

Rationale: Home Health Care offers ongoing monitoring and management of chronic conditions in a patient's home, reducing hospital readmissions by providing personalized care plans and regular follow-ups. While Long-term Acute Care and Skilled Nursing Facilities provide intensive services, they may not be necessary for Sarah's condition stabilization at home. Acute Care is primarily for short-term treatment during severe episodes, not for ongoing management. Home Health Care effectively balances comprehensive care with the comfort of being at home.

Question 71: Correct Answer: B) Ensuring the patient has access to necessary medical equipment and medications at home.
Rationale: Ensuring access to necessary medical equipment and medications demonstrates an understanding of continuity in care, addressing immediate needs for effective recovery. Option A, while important, is limited without comprehensive support. Option C lacks ongoing engagement crucial for adapting to changing needs. Option D misses continuous assessment, vital for holistic care management.

Question 72: Correct Answer: B) Higher patient satisfaction scores related to care coordination
Rationale: PCMH aims to enhance care coordination and patient-centeredness, making higher patient satisfaction scores regarding coordination (Option B) a direct measure of success. Increased visits (Option A) could indicate more issues rather than improvement. Staff turnover rates (Option C), while important, don't directly measure PCMH success. Reduced imaging use (Option D), though cost-effective, doesn't specifically relate to the core PCMH principle of coordinated, comprehensive care delivery.

Question 73: Correct Answer: B) Offering a platform for emotional expression and shared experiences
Rationale: Support groups primarily enhance psychosocial well-being by offering a platform for emotional expression and shared experiences, allowing participants to connect with others facing similar challenges. This sense of community reduces feelings of isolation, which is critical for mental health. Option A is incorrect as medical advice should come from healthcare professionals, not support groups. Option C is incorrect as support groups are not typically led by healthcare professionals. Option D focuses on education rather than emotional support, which is secondary in this context.

Question 74: Correct Answer: B) Collaborative problem-solving
Rationale: Collaborative problem-solving empowers clients by involving them in decision-making, fostering autonomy and control. Directive counseling techniques (A), while useful in guiding clients, may limit their sense of empowerment. Providing informational resources (C) and emotional validation (D) are supportive but do not actively engage clients in regaining control over their situation. The correct answer emphasizes partnership and shared decision-making as key to empowerment.

Question 75: Correct Answer: A) The individual must have a disability and limited income and resources.
Rationale: To qualify for SSI, individuals must meet specific criteria, including having a disability or being over 65, coupled with limited income and resources. Option A is correct as it captures both the disability requirement and financial limitations necessary for eligibility. Option B is incorrect because age alone does not suffice without financial assessment. Option C is incorrect as it overlooks the importance of financial criteria. Option D is incorrect as SSI considers both citizenship and financial need.

Question 76: Correct Answer: C) Comprehensive assessment of social determinants of health
Rationale: A comprehensive assessment of social

determinants of health is crucial as it identifies external factors affecting health outcomes related to gender. While A enhances understanding, it doesn't directly address individual needs. B may support decision-making but doesn't consider broader social influences. D focuses on medical aspects rather than psychosocial elements. Understanding social determinants allows case managers to tailor interventions effectively, addressing barriers such as economic status, education, and social support systems that impact gender health.

Question 77: Correct Answer: B) Fostering oscillation between loss-oriented and restoration-oriented activities
Rationale: The Dual Process Model emphasizes the importance of oscillating between confronting and avoiding grief (loss-oriented) and engaging in life changes (restoration-oriented). Option A focuses solely on emotional expression, neglecting restoration. Option C suggests avoidance, which can hinder processing grief. Option D implies ignoring grief by immersing in routines. Thus, B is correct as it balances both aspects, aligning with contemporary bereavement theories.

Question 78: Correct Answer: A) Early discharge planning
Rationale: The correct answer is A) Early discharge planning because it helps reduce hospital length of stay and prevents unnecessary readmissions, aligning with PPS incentives to minimize costs while ensuring quality care. While comprehensive medication review and coordination of follow-up are crucial for patient outcomes, they do not directly impact inpatient resource utilization like early discharge planning does. Utilization of outpatient services helps in managing long-term care but isn't prioritized within the inpatient PPS framework.

Question 79: Correct Answer: B) Allocate more time to patients with complex social determinants of health.
Rationale: Allocating more time to patients with complex social determinants of health (Option B) is crucial as these factors significantly impact health outcomes and resource utilization. While focusing solely on high acuity (Option A) or potential for quick discharge (Option C) may seem efficient, it overlooks the broader context affecting patient care. Balancing time equally (Option D) ignores individual patient needs. Addressing social determinants can lead to more sustainable and effective care management, aligning with contemporary research emphasizing holistic approaches in case management.

Question 80: Correct Answer: B) The complexity and acuity of client conditions
Rationale: The complexity and acuity of client conditions are paramount in determining caseload because they directly impact the time and resources required for effective management. While factors like length of stay, geographical distribution, and community resources are important, they do not capture the nuanced demands that complex cases impose. Understanding the intricate needs associated with high-acuity cases ensures that case managers can allocate sufficient attention and resources to each client, promoting better outcomes.

Question 81: Correct Answer: C) PPS creates financial risk if patient care exceeds DRG payment limits.
Rationale: The Prospective Payment System assigns a fixed payment based on DRGs, creating financial risk if care costs exceed these payments, encouraging efficiency and cost management. Option A is incorrect as PPS does not guarantee higher revenue; it controls costs through fixed payments. Option B is misleading because payments are predetermined, not aligned with actual incurred costs. Option D is incorrect since services are bundled under DRGs rather than billed separately,

emphasizing cost containment over itemized billing.

Question 82: Correct Answer: A) Patient-Centered Medical Home (PCMH) Recognition

Rationale: PCMH Recognition emphasizes patient-centered care by fostering partnerships between patients and their primary care providers. This approach aligns with NCQA's focus on improving care quality through enhanced patient engagement. Utilization Management Accreditation focuses on resource use, LTSS targets long-term care services, and Health Plan Accreditation evaluates health plans broadly. While each option supports quality improvement, PCMH directly targets patient-centered initiatives, making it the most relevant choice for enhancing patient-centered care according to NCQA standards.

Question 83: Correct Answer: D) Adopting bundled payment systems for specific conditions

Rationale: Bundled payment systems promote cost-effectiveness by providing a single payment for all services related to a treatment episode, encouraging coordinated and efficient care. Option A's fee-for-service model can lead to increased costs through service overuse. Option B's capitated payments may risk under-provision if not carefully managed. Option C encourages overutilization, increasing costs without necessarily improving outcomes. Bundled payments incentivize providers to deliver necessary and efficient care within a fixed budget.

Question 84: Correct Answer: C) Mindfulness-based stress reduction (MBSR) programs

Rationale: Mindfulness-based stress reduction (MBSR) programs are comprehensive as they integrate meditation, awareness training, and education to effectively reduce stress-related disorders. Yoga and meditation classes (A), time management workshops (B), and social support groups (D) each offer benefits but lack the holistic approach of MBSR that combines multiple elements tailored to stress reduction. MBSR's structured program addresses both cognitive and emotional components of stress, making it more effective than other singular approaches.

Question 85: Correct Answer: A) Implementing regular telehealth check-ins to monitor the patient's condition

Rationale: Regular telehealth check-ins align with PCMH principles by enhancing access and continuous care, crucial for managing chronic conditions. Option B lacks coordination, contrary to PCMH's integrated approach. Option C encourages fragmented care, not aligned with PCMH's proactive management. Option D focuses narrowly on medication, while PCMH emphasizes holistic care. Telehealth supports timely interventions and continuity, embodying PCMH's patient-centered ethos.

Question 86: Correct Answer: C) Administering benzodiazepines for withdrawal symptoms

Rationale: Administering benzodiazepines is critical for managing acute alcohol withdrawal symptoms such as cravings and anxiety, which can be life-threatening. While CBT (Option B) is effective long-term, it doesn't address immediate physical withdrawal. Exercise (Option A) aids recovery but isn't suitable for acute management. Long-term programs (Option D) are beneficial post-withdrawal stabilization. Therefore, Option C is prioritized to ensure John's safety during withdrawal.

Question 87: Correct Answer: B) Reflective listening

Rationale: Reflective listening is most effective as it involves understanding and validating the client's feelings, which can reduce resistance. Assertive confrontation (A) may escalate tension, direct persuasion (C) can be perceived as pressure, and information

overload (D) may overwhelm the client. Reflective listening fosters trust and openness, encouraging clients to express concerns without feeling judged or pressured, aligning with contemporary communication theories emphasizing empathy and active listening.

Question 88: Correct Answer: B) Engage Sarah in setting small, achievable health goals that align with her interests.

Rationale: Engaging Sarah in setting small, achievable goals (Option B) is most effective as it directly involves her in the change process, enhancing motivation and readiness. While educational materials (Option A), support groups (Option C), and nutritionist consultations (Option D) are beneficial, they do not actively involve Sarah in goal-setting, which is crucial for activation and sustained behavior change according to contemporary theories like the Transtheoretical Model of Change.

Question 89: Correct Answer: B) Integrate Mr. Lee's use of herbal remedies with his prescribed medications after consulting with his healthcare provider

Rationale: Option B acknowledges and respects Mr. Lee's cultural beliefs by integrating them into his care plan, promoting adherence and trust. Consulting with a healthcare provider ensures safety and addresses potential interactions, unlike option A which disregards his beliefs, option C which might dismiss beneficial practices without evaluation, and option D which lacks integration of his cultural practices into the care plan.

Question 90: Correct Answer: C) To enable individuals to receive care in their own homes or communities

Rationale: The primary objective of Medicaid HCBS waiver programs is to allow individuals, particularly those with disabilities or chronic conditions, to receive necessary services in their homes or communities rather than institutions. Option A and B focus on institutional and acute care, which are contrary to the community-based emphasis of HCBS waivers. Option D misrepresents the preventive and supportive nature of waiver programs, which aim to maintain independence outside of emergency contexts.

Question 91: Correct Answer: B) It offers emotional support by integrating spiritual beliefs into coping strategies.

Rationale: Pastoral counseling uniquely combines spiritual beliefs with emotional support, helping patients like Emily find meaning and hope amid suffering. Unlike option A, it doesn't provide medical advice; option C ignores spiritual integration; and option D may not be holistic or practical for all patients. The correct answer acknowledges the comprehensive approach of pastoral counseling that respects both psychological and spiritual dimensions.

Question 92: Correct Answer: A) Gender Role Socialization

Rationale: Gender Role Socialization refers to the process by which individuals learn and internalize societal expectations for behaviors and roles based on their assigned sex at birth. It involves cultural norms and social influences. Gender Fluidity (B) describes a flexible range of gender expressions. Gender Dysphoria (C) is the distress experienced due to a mismatch between one's gender identity and assigned sex. Gender Constancy (D) is the understanding that one's gender remains stable over time; it doesn't focus on societal expectations like socialization does.

Question 93: Correct Answer: C) Facilitating a detailed handover meeting between hospital and facility staff

Rationale: Facilitating a detailed handover meeting ensures that all necessary information regarding John's medical history, current treatment plan, and specific needs are communicated effectively between healthcare providers. While medication reconciliation (A), transportation arrangement (B), and providing contact information (D) are important steps, they do not directly address the comprehensive communication required for seamless continuity of care during transitions.

Question 94: Correct Answer: B) Outpatient physician visits.

Rationale: Medicare Part B covers outpatient physician visits, distinguishing it from Part A, which covers inpatient hospital stays (Option A), skilled nursing facility care (Option C), and hospice care (Option D). Part A focuses on inpatient services, while Part B primarily handles outpatient services and preventive care. This distinction is crucial in understanding how different parts of Medicare allocate coverage based on the setting and type of service provided to beneficiaries.

Question 95: Correct Answer: B) Facilitate a discussion on John's personal values and how they relate to his health goals.

Rationale: Facilitating a discussion on personal values helps align John's health goals with what matters most to him, enhancing motivation and adherence. This approach is grounded in motivational interviewing principles. Option A may overwhelm rather than motivate. Option C focuses on education but not emotional support. Option D provides social support but doesn't address individual values directly. The correct option integrates psychosocial support with goal-setting effectively.

Question 96: Correct Answer: D) Modified Mini Screen (MMS)

Rationale: The Modified Mini Screen (MMS) is designed to identify both mental health and substance use issues concurrently, making it suitable for co-occurring disorders. The CAGE Questionnaire (A), while useful for alcohol dependency, lacks mental health assessment. Beck Depression Inventory (B), focuses solely on depression symptoms. The Addiction Severity Index (C), though comprehensive for substance use, does not effectively screen for mental health conditions in tandem. MMS provides a balanced evaluation crucial for integrated treatment planning.

Question 97: Correct Answer: D) Diagnostic analytics identifying causes of readmissions

Rationale: Diagnostic analytics focuses on understanding the reasons behind events, making it ideal for identifying causes of John's repeated hospitalizations. Predictive analytics (A) forecasts future trends, while descriptive analytics (B) merely summarizes current data without providing insights into causality. Prescriptive analytics (C) offers solutions but requires understanding the underlying issues first. Thus, diagnostic analytics is crucial for uncovering the specific factors contributing to John's readmissions, enabling targeted interventions.

Question 98: Correct Answer: A) Increased independence by reducing reliance on family members for meals

Rationale: Meal delivery services significantly enhance independence for individuals with limited mobility by decreasing their reliance on family for daily nutrition. While option B suggests social interaction, it is minimal compared to the autonomy gained. Option C addresses financial aspects but not psychosocial benefits. Option D focuses on cultural exposure, which is less relevant than independence. The primary psychosocial advantage lies in empowering individuals to manage their own nutritional needs independently.

Question 99: Correct Answer: C) Integrate both medical urgency and socio-economic factors into his triage system.

Rationale: Integrating both medical urgency and socio-economic factors (Option C) allows John to address immediate health needs while considering broader influences on patient access and outcomes. A first-come, first-served policy (Option A) lacks nuance in resource allocation. Focusing solely on medical urgency (Option B) may overlook critical socio-economic barriers affecting health equity. Prioritizing long-term patients (Option D), though beneficial for continuity, can marginalize new patients with urgent needs. This balanced approach ensures comprehensive care delivery aligned with current best practices in case management.

Question 100: Correct Answer: B) Conditional Value at Risk (CVaR)

Rationale: CVaR is designed to assess the expected losses beyond the VaR threshold, making it suitable for understanding rare but severe financial risks in healthcare reimbursement. VaR (Option A) estimates potential loss within a confidence interval, but doesn't focus on extreme outcomes. Monte Carlo Simulation (Option C) is a technique for estimating probabilities, not specifically for extreme losses. Scenario Analysis (Option D) explores different future states but lacks focus on rare severe events like CVaR.

Question 101: Correct Answer: B) Difficulty in predicting costs due to variable patient needs and outcomes.

Rationale: Transitioning to a case rate model can be challenging because it requires accurate predictions of average costs across diverse patient needs, which can vary significantly. Option A is incorrect; while billing complexity might decrease, predicting costs remains challenging. Option C incorrectly suggests increased specificity in tracking costs, which is less feasible under bundled payments. Option D is misleading as case rates typically lack flexibility in adjusting payments based on individual outcomes without prior contractual agreements.

Question 102: Correct Answer: A) Encourage John to join a support group for emotional abuse survivors.

Rationale: Encouraging John to join a support group provides him with a community of individuals who have shared similar experiences, fostering understanding and validation, which are crucial for rebuilding trust and self-esteem. While journaling (B) and coping strategies (C) can be beneficial, they do not directly address the need for social support. Medication evaluation (D) may be necessary but does not specifically target emotional healing through shared experiences and peer support.

Question 103: Correct Answer: C) Benchmarking

Rationale: Benchmarking is the most effective method for identifying improvement areas by comparing performance metrics with established standards. While process mapping helps visualize workflows, it doesn't provide external comparisons. Root cause analysis identifies underlying issues but lacks comparative insight. SWOT analysis evaluates strengths and weaknesses internally without benchmarking against external standards. Benchmarking uniquely offers a structured approach to measure performance against industry standards, highlighting gaps and opportunities for enhancement.

Question 104: Correct Answer: B) Contemplation

Rationale: The Contemplation stage involves awareness of the need for change and consideration of making a change, often accompanied by information-seeking. This differs from Precontemplation, where clients are unaware or resistant to change. Preparation involves planning specific actions, while Action is the active implementation of change strategies. The subtlety lies in the client's mental readiness and willingness to engage with information without committing to immediate action.

Question 105: Correct Answer: B) Ensuring clients have access to evidence-based information about their conditions

Rationale: Option B is correct as it emphasizes providing clients with evidence-based information, enabling informed choices in self-care management. This aligns with contemporary research advocating for informed patient engagement. Option A lacks guidance, potentially overwhelming clients. Option C disregards the importance of evidence and professional advice, while Option D undermines client autonomy and empowerment, contradicting shared decision-making principles.

Question 106: Correct Answer: B) Employing reflective listening to validate feelings

Rationale: Reflective listening involves paraphrasing what the client says, validating their feelings, and showing understanding, which enhances rapport by making clients feel heard and valued. Using technical jargon (A) can alienate clients. Problem-solving focus (C), while important, might bypass emotional connections needed initially. A formal tone (D), though professional, can hinder warmth in communication. Reflective listening directly supports emotional engagement, crucial for building strong relationships.

Question 107: Correct Answer: A) Encourage John to write down his questions and concerns before each appointment.

Rationale: Encouraging John to write down his questions and concerns empowers him to actively participate in his healthcare, enhancing self-advocacy. Option B, providing pamphlets, offers information but doesn't directly enhance communication skills. Option C undermines self-advocacy by relying on others rather than empowering John himself. Option D, attending with an advocate, may support communication but doesn't build John's personal advocacy skills as effectively as preparing questions in advance.

Question 108: Correct Answer: B) Decreased medication errors

Rationale: Decreased medication errors lead to improved patient safety and potential cost savings from avoiding adverse events, making it a pivotal benefit in justifying the system's adoption. While increased documentation time (Option A) and software licensing costs (Option C) are factors to consider, they are outweighed by the critical nature of reducing errors. Improved staff morale (Option D), although beneficial, does not have as direct an impact on patient safety and financial outcomes as decreasing medication errors does.

Question 109: Correct Answer: B) Incorporating spiritual history taking as part of the initial assessment

Rationale: Incorporating spiritual history taking as part of the initial assessment allows case managers to understand a client's spiritual needs and integrate them into care plans. Option A is too narrow, focusing only on rituals. Option C lacks depth by relying solely on expressed beliefs without deeper exploration. Option D ignores spirituality, which is crucial in pastoral counseling. Spiritual history taking ensures a holistic approach, addressing both psychological and spiritual needs.

Question 110: Correct Answer: B) Highlight the atypical presentation of heart attack symptoms in women.

Rationale: Women often experience atypical heart attack symptoms such as nausea or fatigue rather than chest pain, making it crucial for Jamie to emphasize these differences (Option B). General dietary changes (Option A), smoking cessation (Option C), and exercise plans

(Option D) are important but do not specifically address the unique symptomatology of heart disease in women, which can lead to delayed diagnosis and treatment if not properly understood by the patient.

Question 111: Correct Answer: D) Developing personalized care plans incorporating patient preferences

Rationale: Personalized care plans (D) align with contemporary theories emphasizing patient-centered care, enhancing engagement and autonomy. Strict routines (A), while useful, may not accommodate individual needs or preferences. Peer support groups (B) provide social support but lack personalization. Reward systems (C) can motivate but may not sustain long-term behavior change. Personalized plans ensure that interventions resonate with patients' values and lifestyles, fostering better self-management.

Question 112: Correct Answer: B) Hospital Value-Based Purchasing (VBP) Program

Rationale: The Hospital Value-Based Purchasing (VBP) Program is designed to reward hospitals with financial incentives based on their performance across various quality measures. Unlike HRRP, which penalizes hospitals for excessive readmissions, VBP focuses on a broader set of quality metrics. MSSP is more related to accountable care organizations, and IQR emphasizes data reporting rather than direct financial incentives. Thus, VBP specifically aligns with CMS's goal of improving care quality through performance-based rewards.

Question 113: Correct Answer: B) Group Home

Rationale: A Group Home offers social support and supervision necessary for individuals like Sarah's client, promoting medication adherence and stability. A Psychiatric Hospital (A) is too restrictive for someone stable on medication. A Homeless Shelter (C) lacks the structured support needed, and an Independent Apartment (D) does not provide adequate supervision or community engagement. The balance of independence and support in a Group Home makes it the optimal choice.

Question 114: Correct Answer: B) The net monetary benefit after comparing costs and savings

Rationale: The most critical factor is the net monetary benefit after comparing costs and savings. This reflects true economic value (Option B), essential for deciding implementation. While alignment with policies (Option A), reduction in readmissions (Option C), and innovation (Option D) are valuable considerations, they do not directly measure financial viability, which is central to cost-benefit analysis.

Question 115: Correct Answer: B) Navigating complex eligibility criteria for clients

Rationale: A significant challenge for case managers is navigating the intricate eligibility criteria associated with Medicaid Waiver Programs, which can vary significantly by state and program type. Option A and D are more related to hospital management rather than waiver coordination. Option C incorrectly emphasizes surgical interventions, whereas waiver programs focus on comprehensive community-based care. Understanding these criteria is crucial for ensuring that clients receive appropriate services without unnecessary institutionalization.

Question 116: Correct Answer: B) The hospital will receive a fixed amount regardless of actual costs incurred during the patient's stay.

Rationale: Case rate reimbursement involves paying a predetermined, fixed amount for an entire episode of care, such as surgery, regardless of actual costs. Option

A is incorrect because it describes per diem payment; Option C refers to fee-for-service; and Option D suggests cost-based reimbursement. Each option reflects different payment methodologies, but only B accurately represents how case rates function by providing predictable financial outcomes for healthcare providers.

Question 117: Correct Answer: B) Contemplation
Rationale: Sarah is in the Contemplation stage as she recognizes her smoking habit and is considering quitting by researching options, but hasn't made a commitment yet. In the Precontemplation stage (Option A), individuals are not considering change. Preparation (Option C) involves planning to take action soon, while Action (Option D) involves actively modifying behavior.

Question 118: Correct Answer: B) Offers intensive rehabilitation services and 24-hour medical supervision.
Rationale: Skilled Nursing Facilities (SNFs) are distinct due to their provision of intensive rehabilitation services and continuous medical supervision, catering to patients needing significant post-acute care. Option A is incorrect as it describes long-term care facilities. Option C inaccurately represents hospice or palliative care centers, while option D aligns more with inpatient rehabilitation facilities that focus on short-term recovery rather than ongoing SNF services.

Question 119: Correct Answer: A) Longitudinal Study
Rationale: John is employing a Longitudinal Study, which involves repeated observations of the same variables over an extended period to assess long-term impacts. This method allows for tracking changes in quality of life over time among participants. In contrast, cross-sectional studies (Option B) provide a snapshot at one point in time, cohort studies (Option C) focus on following specific groups without necessarily repeated measures over time, and time-series analysis (Option D) examines patterns within data points but not necessarily on individual-level changes over years.

Question 120: Correct Answer: B) Routine dental check-ups for children
Rationale: Medicaid typically covers routine dental check-ups for children as part of the Early and Periodic Screening, Diagnostic, and Treatment (EPSDT) benefit. This makes option B correct. Cosmetic surgery (A), over-the-counter medications (C), and experimental treatments (D) are generally not covered unless deemed medically necessary or part of a specific state plan, making them incorrect in this context.

Question 121: Correct Answer: C) The external manifestation of gender through behavior, clothing, and other expressions.
Rationale: Gender expression refers to how individuals express their gender identity outwardly through choices such as clothing, behavior, and personal style. Unlike option A, which pertains to biological sex, or option B, which addresses internal gender identity, gender expression is about outward presentation. Option D focuses on legal aspects rather than personal expression. Thus, option C correctly captures the essence of gender expression as understood in contemporary research and theories.

Question 122: Correct Answer: C) Preferred Provider Organization (PPO) Plan
Rationale: A PPO Plan offers flexibility in choosing healthcare providers and covers out-of-network services at higher costs, similar to group plans Linda might have had. Marketplace plans vary widely in coverage and cost-sharing structures; HMOs restrict provider choice more than PPOs; catastrophic plans are designed for emergencies with high deductibles and limited routine

care coverage. Thus, a PPO provides comprehensive coverage aligning with Linda's previous employer-sponsored benefits.

Question 123: Correct Answer: C) Sarah must require assistance with activities of daily living (ADLs).
Rationale: The Aid and Attendance program provides additional financial support for veterans who need help with ADLs such as bathing or dressing. This requirement makes Option C correct. Option A is incorrect because there is no specific disability rating required; it focuses on the need for assistance. Option B is incorrect because while pension benefits are related, they are not mandatory for Aid and Attendance eligibility. Option D is misleading; wartime service may influence pension eligibility but not specifically Aid and Attendance criteria.

Question 124: Correct Answer: B) Contemplation
Rationale: In the Contemplation stage, individuals recognize the need for change and express a desire to change but have not yet committed to taking action. John's awareness and desire to quit smoking align with this stage. The Precontemplation stage (Option A) involves no intention to change; Preparation (Option C) involves planning and small steps towards change; Action (Option D) requires actual behavioral changes. John's situation fits best with contemplation as he acknowledges the problem without action.

Question 125: Correct Answer: B) Advocate for workplace sensitivity training on gender diversity.
Rationale: Advocating for workplace sensitivity training (Option B) addresses systemic issues by fostering an inclusive environment, aligning with best practices in supporting diverse gender expressions. Option A suggests altering personal expression for acceptance, which can be harmful. Option C implies hiding one's identity, contributing to internalized stigma. Option D may not address broader systemic issues and could limit opportunities without resolving discrimination at its source.

Question 126: Correct Answer: C) Pay-for-Performance
Rationale: Pay-for-Performance links reimbursement to the quality and efficiency of care, thereby incentivizing improved health outcomes in chronic care management. Fee-for-Service compensates based on volume rather than quality, potentially leading to overutilization without improving outcomes. Capitation involves a fixed payment per patient, which may not directly incentivize quality improvements. Bundled Payments cover a set of services for a specific condition but do not inherently link payment to performance metrics. Therefore, Pay-for-Performance directly aligns financial incentives with quality improvement goals in chronic care.

Question 127: Correct Answer: C) Improved patient outcomes through collaborative decision-making.
Rationale: The primary benefit of an interdisciplinary/interprofessional care team is improved patient outcomes, achieved through collaborative decision-making. This approach leverages diverse expertise to develop comprehensive care plans, addressing all aspects of a patient's condition. While options A, B, and D are potential advantages, they are secondary to the central goal of enhancing patient outcomes. Enhanced satisfaction (A), efficiency (B), and cost reduction (D) may occur but do not directly reflect the core objective of improved health results as collaboration does.

Question 128: Correct Answer: C) Accountable Care Organizations (ACOs)
Rationale: Accountable Care Organizations (ACOs) incentivize providers to deliver efficient, high-quality care

by allowing them to share in savings achieved through improved patient outcomes and reduced costs. Unlike Capitation, which provides a fixed payment per patient regardless of services rendered, ACOs focus on quality and efficiency. Pay-for-Performance rewards specific quality metrics but doesn't inherently include cost-sharing. Diagnosis-Related Groups offer fixed payments based on diagnosis but don't directly reward shared savings or quality improvements like ACOs do.

Question 129: Correct Answer: C) Recent changes in functional status

Rationale: Recent changes in functional status are critical for identifying high-acuity clients as they indicate immediate and significant shifts in health requiring intensive intervention. While age (A) can influence health needs, it doesn't directly reflect current acuity. Comorbid conditions (B), though relevant, don't necessarily indicate recent changes or increased immediate care needs. Family support availability (D), while important for discharge planning, does not directly measure clinical acuity or severity levels. Functional status changes provide direct insight into current care demands.

Question 130: Correct Answer: C) Help Tom access manufacturer-sponsored PAPs

Rationale: Manufacturer-sponsored Patient Assistance Programs (PAPs) are often the quickest way to secure medications for individuals like Tom who have lost insurance coverage. These programs provide medications at no cost or at a reduced price directly from pharmaceutical companies. While Medicaid and exchange plans offer coverage options, they may involve delays or costs that PAPs can mitigate immediately. The 340B program supports clinics but does not directly assist individuals without insurance as effectively as PAPs do.

Question 131: Correct Answer: C) Bundled payments covering post-operative care

Rationale: Bundled payments incentivize comprehensive care delivery by covering all related services in one payment, encouraging efficient use of telehealth. Fee-for-service (A) may lead to overutilization. Capitation (B) might not adequately cover specific post-operative needs. Pay-for-performance (D), while outcome-focused, doesn't directly address service bundling. The bundled payment model aligns with contemporary reimbursement strategies that support integrated care pathways via telehealth, ensuring cost control and quality outcomes.

Question 132: Correct Answer: B) To encourage detailed client responses

Rationale: Open-ended questions in Motivational Interviewing are designed to elicit more comprehensive and thoughtful responses from clients, facilitating deeper exploration of their thoughts and feelings. Unlike gathering specific information quickly (A), providing direct advice (C), or confronting behaviors (D), open-ended questions help clients articulate their motivations and ambivalence, fostering a collaborative environment for change. This approach aligns with Motivational Interviewing's goal of enhancing intrinsic motivation through client-centered dialogue.

Question 133: Correct Answer: D) Presence of comorbidities

Rationale: The presence of comorbidities significantly influences DRG assignment as it can change the complexity and resource utilization, leading to different DRG classifications. While the primary diagnosis and length of stay are important, they do not adjust the DRG as dynamically as comorbidities. Patient's age may affect treatment but isn't a primary factor in DRG assignment. Understanding these nuances ensures accurate

reimbursement and reflects the true cost of care.

Question 134: Correct Answer: C) Transportation availability

Rationale: Transportation availability is a critical determinant as it directly affects an individual's ability to physically access healthcare services. Without reliable transportation, even those with employment or education may struggle to attend appointments. While employment status and educational attainment can indirectly influence healthcare access through income and health literacy, respectively, they do not address the immediate logistical challenge of reaching healthcare facilities. Social support networks can provide assistance but are not a direct solution to transportation issues.

Question 135: Correct Answer: D) Eye Movement Desensitization and Reprocessing (EMDR)

Rationale: EMDR is specifically designed to address complex trauma by processing distressing memories and reducing their psychological impact. While CBT and TF-CBT are effective for various mental health issues, they may not fully address the depth of complex trauma. DBT is tailored for emotional regulation and interpersonal effectiveness but isn't primarily focused on trauma processing. EMDR's unique approach makes it particularly effective for those with a history of prolonged abuse.

Question 136: Correct Answer: B) J44.0 - COPD with acute lower respiratory infection

Rationale: Option B is correct because it captures both the acute bronchitis and the underlying chronic condition (COPD), which affects care complexity and reimbursement. Option A only codes for acute bronchitis, missing the chronic aspect. Option C captures an exacerbation of COPD without specifying an infection, which isn't as precise in this scenario. Option D is unrelated to the patient's conditions and does not accurately reflect the medical situation.

Question 137: Correct Answer: B) It helps identify variations due to special causes.

Rationale: A control chart's primary benefit is identifying variations due to special causes by distinguishing them from common cause variations within processes over time. Option A describes a static assessment not characteristic of control charts. Option C relates more to forecasting methods like regression analysis. Option D involves comparative studies rather than process variation monitoring. Therefore, option B is correct as it highlights the unique ability of control charts to pinpoint specific variations impacting quality outcomes.

Question 138: Correct Answer: B) Balancing clinical outcomes with resource allocation efficiency

Rationale: The primary objective in cost-benefit analysis is to balance clinical outcomes with resource allocation efficiency. While maximizing patient satisfaction (Option A) and ensuring equitable access (Option D) are important, they do not directly address the economic evaluation aspect. Achieving the highest quality regardless of cost (Option C) overlooks the necessity for efficient resource use, which is critical in cost-benefit analysis.

Question 139: Correct Answer: D) A recent increase in hospital readmissions

Rationale: An increase in hospital readmissions indicates a need for enhanced care to prevent further admissions, justifying expanded coverage under private insurance plans focused on reducing costs associated with frequent hospital stays. While improved outcomes and family support are beneficial, they do not directly influence coverage eligibility like readmission rates do. Proximity to hospitals is irrelevant to qualifying criteria for expanded benefits.

Question 140: Correct Answer: A) No-Fault Liability
Rationale: The principle of No-Fault Liability ensures that workers receive compensation for injuries sustained on the job regardless of who was at fault. This contrasts with Comparative Negligence, where fault is divided among parties, Assumption of Risk, which involves accepting known risks, and Contributory Negligence, where any fault by the injured party can bar recovery. No-Fault Liability simplifies the claims process by removing the need to establish negligence, focusing instead on providing timely support to injured workers.

Question 141: Correct Answer: B) Social support networks
Rationale: Social support networks play a pivotal role in mental health by providing emotional resources and coping mechanisms. While access to nutritious food (A), housing stability (C), and educational opportunities (D) contribute to overall health, they do not have as direct an impact on mental health disparities as social support networks. The presence of strong social ties can mitigate stress and improve mental resilience, making it a significant determinant in mental health outcomes across diverse populations.

Question 142: Correct Answer: B) Interest-Based Negotiation
Rationale: Interest-based negotiation emphasizes understanding underlying interests rather than positions, promoting sustainable partnerships with insurance companies. Hard bargaining and adversarial approaches may damage relationships by creating conflict. Zero-sum tactics imply one party's gain is another's loss, unsuitable for long-term partnerships. Interest-based negotiation allows case managers to explore creative solutions that satisfy both parties' interests, enhancing collaboration and trust in reimbursement negotiations.

Question 143: Correct Answer: A) Patient-centered care planning
Rationale: Patient-centered care planning is central to Joint Commission standards as it ensures that care is tailored to individual patient needs, thereby improving quality and outcomes. While financial resource allocation (B), staff credentialing (C), and technology integration (D) are important, they do not directly address the personalization of care that enhances patient outcomes. The emphasis on individualized care plans distinguishes option A from the others, which focus more on systemic or administrative aspects rather than direct patient impact.

Question 144: Correct Answer: C) Exploring John's beliefs and attitudes towards diabetes management
Rationale: Exploring John's beliefs and attitudes addresses underlying barriers to engagement by aligning interventions with his perspectives. Option A focuses on control rather than understanding. Option B informs but doesn't address personal barriers or motivation. Option D provides data without addressing behavioral change drivers. Understanding beliefs and attitudes allows tailored interventions that resonate personally, enhancing commitment and compliance through empathy and shared decision-making strategies grounded in psychosocial concepts.

Question 145: Correct Answer: C) Educate John on using a pill organizer and involve him in meal planning.
Rationale: Educating John on using a pill organizer and involving him in meal planning empowers him to take control of his health, promoting independence and adherence. While providing written schedules (Option A) offers guidance, it lacks interactive engagement. Arranging for a nurse (Option B) might reduce self-reliance. Weekly check-ins (Option D) are supportive but not as proactive in fostering self-management skills as Option C, which directly involves John in managing his care.

Question 146: Correct Answer: D) Risk Adjustment Model
Rationale: The Risk Adjustment Model effectively predicts financial risks by accounting for patient population variability, adjusting payments based on health status and demographic factors. Predictive Modeling (Option A) forecasts future trends but isn't specific to payment adjustments. Retrospective Cost Analysis (Option B) examines past costs without predicting future variability. The Prospective Payment System (Option C) sets fixed rates in advance, not adjusting for individual patient differences like the Risk Adjustment Model does.

Question 147: Correct Answer: C) TRICARE for Life
Rationale: TRICARE for Life is the plan designed specifically for retirees who are eligible for Medicare Part A and enrolled in Part B. It offers comprehensive coverage by acting as a secondary payer to Medicare, covering most out-of-pocket costs. While TRICARE Prime and Select are available to retirees, they do not coordinate with Medicare like TRICARE for Life does. TRICARE Reserve Select is not applicable as it targets reservists, not retirees.

Question 148: Correct Answer: A) Person-Centered Counseling
Rationale: Person-Centered Counseling emphasizes empathy and unconditional positive regard, fostering a supportive environment where John can explore his feelings and build self-confidence essential for rehabilitation. Psychoeducational Counseling (B) provides information but may not address emotional support needs directly. Gestalt Therapy (C), while focusing on present experiences, may not offer the empathetic support John requires. Narrative Therapy (D) helps reframe stories but might not focus on immediate emotional support as effectively as Person-Centered Counseling does.

Question 149: Correct Answer: B) Assist Lisa in creating a personalized meal plan based on her preferences and nutritional needs.
Rationale: Assisting Lisa in creating a personalized meal plan supports self-directed care by tailoring strategies to her unique needs and preferences, fostering ownership of her health management. Option A might overwhelm her without guidance, C could lead to conflicting advice without personalization, and D offers community support but lacks individualization. Personalized planning is crucial for effective self-care management in chronic conditions like diabetes, ensuring alignment with recognized theories of patient-centered care.

Question 150: Correct Answer: B) DRGs necessitate precise coding to ensure proper reimbursement rates
Rationale: Precise coding under DRG systems is crucial for accurate reimbursement, as errors can lead to financial losses or audits. Option A focuses more on clinical documentation than coding specificity. Option C, while important, does not directly impact coding practices related to DRG classification. Option D highlights record updates but misses the core aspect of precision in coding tied to reimbursement outcomes, making option B the most relevant and correct choice in this context.

CCM Exam Practice Questions [SET 3]

Question 1: John, a 72-year-old diabetic patient with mobility issues, needs a care plan that accommodates his inability to frequently visit healthcare facilities. As his case manager, which non-traditional site of care would best suit John's needs?
A) Remote patient monitoring via wearable devices
B) Adult day care center with medical supervision
C) Community health clinic visits twice a week
D) Assisted living facility with on-site medical staff

Question 2: Sarah, a case manager, is working with Mr. Thompson, a 68-year-old patient who struggles to afford his multiple prescriptions for chronic conditions. Which strategy should Sarah prioritize to ensure Mr. Thompson accesses necessary medications through Pharmacy Assistance Programs?
A) Encourage Mr. Thompson to apply for Medicare Part D coverage.
B) Assist Mr. Thompson in enrolling in a manufacturer-sponsored patient assistance program.
C) Recommend Mr. Thompson use a mail-order pharmacy service for discounts.
D) Suggest Mr. Thompson join a local medication discount club.

Question 3: In integrated case management services, what is the primary role of a case manager when working with an interdisciplinary team?
A) Solely providing administrative support to healthcare providers.
B) Ensuring effective communication and collaboration among team members for comprehensive care delivery.
C) Limiting their role to discharge planning and follow-up appointments.
D) Delegating all responsibilities to specialized healthcare professionals.

Question 4: Which payment methodology is designed to encourage cost-effective care by providing a fixed amount per patient, regardless of the number or nature of services provided?
A) Fee-for-service
B) Capitation
C) Bundled payments
D) Pay-for-performance

Question 5: As a case manager, you are reviewing the care plan for Maria, a 65-year-old patient with chronic heart failure. To improve the quality of care and patient outcomes, which quality indicator should be prioritized in her care management?
A) Reduction in hospital readmission rates
B) Increase in patient satisfaction scores
C) Improvement in medication adherence
D) Decrease in emergency department visits

Question 6: Which part of Medicare primarily covers inpatient hospital stays, skilled nursing facility care, hospice, and some home health care services?
A) Medicare Part A
B) Medicare Part B
C) Medicare Part C
D) Medicare Part D

Question 7: As a case manager, you are reviewing the financial risk models for a new bundled payment program at your hospital. The program aims to manage costs while maintaining quality care for patients undergoing hip replacement surgery. What is the most critical factor to consider when predicting financial risk in this scenario?

A) Historical cost data of similar surgeries
B) Patient demographics and comorbidities
C) Length of hospital stay
D) Readmission rates within 30 days

Question 8: Which organization primarily provides comprehensive resources and advocacy for uninsured individuals seeking healthcare services in the United States?
A) American Medical Association (AMA)
B) National Association of Free & Charitable Clinics (NAFC)
C) Centers for Disease Control and Prevention (CDC)
D) American Hospital Association (AHA)

Question 9: Which principle is crucial for case managers to consider when coordinating long-term care insurance benefits for clients?
A) Benefit Triggers
B) Premium Waivers
C) Elimination Periods
D) Inflation Protection

Question 10: Which of the following approaches is most effective in facilitating adaptive coping mechanisms in bereavement counseling for a client experiencing complicated grief?
A) Encouraging the client to avoid discussing the deceased to prevent emotional distress.
B) Promoting the expression of emotions and memories related to the deceased.
C) Suggesting the client focus on new relationships to replace the lost one.
D) Advising the client to maintain their usual routine without alterations.

Question 11: Which of the following neuropsychological assessments is most effective in evaluating executive function deficits in patients with frontal lobe damage?
A) Wisconsin Card Sorting Test (WCST)
B) Beck Depression Inventory (BDI)
C) Mini-Mental State Examination (MMSE)
D) Hamilton Anxiety Rating Scale (HAM-A)

Question 12: Maria is tasked with reducing hospital readmissions for elderly patients transitioning from hospital to home care. She must choose a model of care delivery that emphasizes continuity of care and effective communication between healthcare providers during this transition period. Which model should Maria select?
A) Chronic Care Model (CCM)
B) Transitional Care Model (TCM)
C) Patient-Centered Medical Home (PCMH)
D) Integrated Care Model (ICM)

Question 13: In an Accountable Care Organization (ACO), how are savings typically shared among providers?
A) Based solely on the volume of patients treated
B) Proportional to individual provider performance metrics
C) Equally distributed regardless of performance
D) Based on achieving specific quality and efficiency benchmarks

Question 14: In a rural community setting, which of the following strategies is most beneficial for a case manager to enhance access to healthcare services?
A) Establishing telehealth services
B) Partnering with local gyms
C) Organizing transportation services
D) Developing educational workshops

Question 15: Sarah, a 78-year-old woman with limited mobility, has been experiencing unexplained bruises on her arms and legs. As her case manager, you suspect potential elder abuse. What is the most appropriate first step in addressing this situation?
A) Confront the suspected abuser directly to gather more information.
B) Document the bruises and report the suspicion to Adult Protective Services (APS).
C) Discuss your concerns with Sarah in a private setting to understand her perspective.
D) Conduct a full physical examination to rule out medical causes for the bruising.

Question 16: Which of the following strategies is most effective for a case manager to establish trust with clients during the initial phase of relationship building?
A) Demonstrating professional expertise and authority
B) Actively listening and showing empathy
C) Providing detailed information about all available resources
D) Setting strict boundaries to maintain professionalism

Question 17: In the context of care delivery and reimbursement methods, which healthcare provider is primarily responsible for coordinating patient care across various settings to ensure continuity and cost-effectiveness?
A) Primary Care Physician
B) Registered Nurse
C) Case Manager
D) Social Worker

Question 18: John is a 45-year-old patient recently diagnosed with diabetes. He is overwhelmed by his diagnosis and unsure about managing his condition. As his case manager, what strategy should you prioritize to support John in making informed decisions about his self-care management?
A) Direct John to online forums where other patients share their experiences.
B) Provide John with a comprehensive list of dietary restrictions and exercise routines.
C) Collaborate with John to set realistic goals and develop an individualized care plan based on his preferences and lifestyle.
D) Advise John to strictly follow the standard medical guidelines for diabetes management.

Question 19: In terms of reimbursement methods, what is a significant consideration for case managers when coordinating care in group homes?
A) Ensuring eligibility for Medicaid waiver programs.
B) Guaranteeing private insurance coverage for all residents.
C) Prioritizing out-of-pocket payments to streamline services.
D) Focusing on reimbursement through Medicare Part A.

Question 20: In the context of accreditation standards, which element is essential for ensuring continuous quality improvement in case management practices?
A) Regular staff training programs
B) Comprehensive data analysis
C) Increased patient throughput
D) Standardized communication protocols

Question 21: Which care delivery model emphasizes the coordination of care by a primary care provider to improve health outcomes and reduce costs, often using a team-based approach?
A) Accountable Care Organizations (ACOs)
B) Patient-Centered Medical Home (PCMH)
C) Bundled Payments for Care Improvement (BPCI)
D) Fee-for-Service (FFS)

Question 22: In a multidisciplinary team meeting, John, a case manager, observes conflicts arising due to poor communication among team members. Which approach should John use to facilitate effective interpersonal communication and resolve conflicts based on contemporary research?
A) Encourage team members to express their emotions freely without constraints
B) Use reflective listening techniques to acknowledge each member's perspective
C) Focus on identifying the root cause of each conflict immediately
D) Implement strict guidelines for turn-taking during discussions

Question 23: As a case manager evaluating the introduction of a new telehealth program for managing chronic illnesses in rural areas, you need to perform a cost-benefit analysis. Which factor should be prioritized to ensure that the program's benefits outweigh its costs?
A) Initial setup costs of telehealth equipment
B) Reduction in hospital readmissions
C) Training costs for healthcare providers
D) Patient satisfaction scores

Question 24: Lisa, a case manager, is assisting Mr. Chen, who follows Confucian principles emphasizing family decision-making in healthcare matters. Mr. Chen's family wants to delay surgery until they consult with extended family members abroad. How should Lisa address this situation while respecting Mr. Chen's cultural values?
A) Advise the family that delaying surgery may not be in Mr. Chen's best interest due to medical urgency.
B) Respect the family's decision entirely without providing any medical input or urgency considerations.
C) Facilitate communication between the healthcare team and Mr. Chen's family to discuss potential risks of delay and explore feasible options together.
D) Insist on proceeding with the surgery as scheduled, prioritizing medical protocols over cultural considerations.

Question 25: Sarah, a case manager at a community health center, is tasked with implementing the Patient-Centered Medical Home (PCMH) model for a group of patients with chronic illnesses. Which of the following strategies best aligns with the core principles of PCMH to enhance care coordination and improve patient outcomes?
A) Implementing electronic health records (EHR) to track patient visits
B) Establishing a multidisciplinary team to manage patient care collaboratively
C) Scheduling monthly check-ups for all patients regardless of their condition
D) Encouraging patients to use telemedicine services for convenience

Question 26: In the context of health literacy, which factor is most critical for case managers to consider when developing a care plan for patients from diverse cultural backgrounds?
A) Patients' socioeconomic status
B) Language proficiency and communication preferences
C) Access to transportation for healthcare visits
D) Availability of family support systems

Question 27: Which of the following non-traditional sites of care is most effective in reducing hospital readmissions for chronic disease management through the use of telehealth technology?

A) Retail clinics
B) Urgent care centers
C) Home health care
D) Skilled nursing facilities

Question 28: Which of the following is a key advantage of employer-sponsored health coverage in terms of risk pooling?
A) It allows employees to choose any healthcare provider without restrictions.
B) It helps distribute healthcare costs across a larger group, reducing individual risk.
C) It guarantees lower premiums for all employees regardless of health status.
D) It provides tax-free benefits only for high-income employees.

Question 29: During a team meeting to discuss patient care plans, Case Manager Sarah notices that one team member consistently dominates the conversation, while others remain silent. Which group dynamic principle should Sarah apply to ensure balanced participation from all team members?
A) Norming
B) Storming
C) Facilitation
D) Adjourning

Question 30: During a routine utilization review meeting, the case manager, Tom, encounters a situation where a patient's length of stay is longer than expected due to unforeseen complications. What action should Tom take to align with utilization management principles?
A) Recommend immediate discharge to reduce costs
B) Extend the stay without further review if complications arise
C) Conduct a peer review to assess medical necessity for the extended stay
D) Focus on negotiating lower rates for extended services

Question 31: Which program offers comprehensive healthcare benefits specifically designed for veterans with service-connected disabilities, ensuring they receive the necessary medical care and support?
A) TRICARE
B) Veterans Health Administration (VHA)
C) CHAMPVA
D) Armed Forces Retirement Home

Question 32: Mr. Johnson, a 78-year-old patient with multiple chronic conditions, is being evaluated for long-term care options. As a case manager, you need to determine the most appropriate funding source for his long-term care needs. Considering his eligibility for Medicaid and Medicare, which option would best cover the costs of skilled nursing facility care?
A) Medicare Part A
B) Medicare Part B
C) Medicaid
D) Private Long-Term Care Insurance

Question 33: John, a case manager for an employer-based wellness program, needs to present a report on the long-term sustainability of the program to senior management. Which strategy should he prioritize to ensure continued support and funding?
A) Highlighting short-term employee engagement metrics
B) Demonstrating alignment with corporate goals
C) Focusing on anecdotal success stories from employees
D) Emphasizing cost savings from reduced absenteeism

Question 34: Jane, a case manager, is evaluating the potential benefits of implementing predictive modeling in her healthcare facility. She aims to reduce hospital readmissions by identifying high-risk patients. Which factor should Jane prioritize when selecting a predictive model for this purpose?
A) Model accuracy in predicting patient satisfaction scores
B) Model's ability to integrate with electronic health records (EHRs)
C) Model's sensitivity in identifying high-risk patients
D) Model's cost-effectiveness in terms of implementation

Question 35: Sarah, a case manager, is working with a patient who has been recently diagnosed with a chronic illness. She needs to ensure that the patient receives comprehensive care while minimizing costs. Which managed care concept should Sarah prioritize to achieve this goal?
A) Capitation
B) Utilization Review
C) Fee-for-Service
D) Point of Service Plan

Question 36: According to the Health Belief Model, which factor is most likely to motivate an individual to adopt a health-promoting behavior?
A) Perceived severity
B) Perceived susceptibility
C) Perceived barriers
D) Self-efficacy

Question 37: Sarah, a case manager, is working with a client named John who has been diagnosed with chronic depression. To effectively engage John in his treatment plan, Sarah decides to utilize motivational interviewing techniques. Which of the following strategies is most aligned with motivational interviewing to enhance client engagement?
A) Confronting John's resistance directly and firmly
B) Encouraging John to explore his own reasons for change
C) Providing John with detailed advice on what he should do
D) Highlighting the negative consequences of not adhering to the treatment

Question 38: Sarah, a case manager, is reviewing the medication list of Mr. Thompson, a 65-year-old patient with multiple chronic conditions. During the reconciliation process, she notices that Mr. Thompson has been prescribed both Lisinopril and Losartan. What should be Sarah's primary concern in this scenario?
A) Risk of hyperkalemia due to dual therapy
B) Increased risk of hypotension
C) Potential for renal impairment
D) Drug-drug interaction causing dizziness

Question 39: In the context of SSI eligibility, which factor primarily differentiates Supplemental Security Income from Social Security Disability Insurance (SSDI)?
A) SSI eligibility depends on work history, while SSDI does not.
B) SSI provides benefits regardless of age, whereas SSDI requires recipients to be over 50.
C) SSI is need-based without regard to work history; SSDI requires sufficient work credits.
D) Both SSI and SSDI require proof of citizenship but differ in residency requirements.

Question 40: In the context of chronic illness, which coping strategy is characterized by seeking social support to manage stress?
A) Problem-focused coping
B) Emotion-focused coping
C) Avoidance coping
D) Active coping

Question 41: When addressing physical neglect in an elderly client, what should be the primary focus of the case manager's intervention strategy?
A) Enhancing social support networks
B) Ensuring adequate nutritional intake
C) Facilitating access to healthcare services
D) Improving living conditions

Question 42: In the context of client support system dynamics, which model emphasizes the reciprocal relationship between a client's environment and their individual behavior, considering both as interdependent factors?
A) Biopsychosocial Model
B) Ecological Systems Theory
C) Social Learning Theory
D) Health Belief Model

Question 43: What is a primary function of Workers Compensation in the context of care delivery and reimbursement methods?
A) To provide punitive damages for workplace injuries
B) To ensure prompt medical treatment and wage replacement
C) To determine liability in workplace accidents
D) To cover all personal injury claims regardless of location

Question 44: In the context of pastoral counseling, which approach emphasizes the integration of spiritual and psychological care, considering both as essential for holistic healing?
A) Cognitive-Behavioral Therapy
B) Narrative Therapy
C) Biopsychosocial-Spiritual Model
D) Psychoanalytic Theory

Question 45: Sarah, a 45-year-old case manager, is assessing a client who has experienced a traumatic brain injury. The client exhibits difficulties in memory retention and executive functioning. Which psychological assessment tool is most appropriate for evaluating these cognitive deficits?
A) Beck Depression Inventory (BDI)
B) Wechsler Adult Intelligence Scale (WAIS)
C) Minnesota Multiphasic Personality Inventory (MMPI)
D) Wisconsin Card Sorting Test (WCST)

Question 46: In the context of psychosocial support systems, which factor is most crucial for effectively identifying and managing cases of elder neglect?
A) Regular home visits by healthcare professionals
B) Comprehensive family interviews
C) Utilization of standardized assessment tools
D) Community awareness programs

Question 47: As a case manager, you are working with Sarah, a patient who has been diagnosed with a chronic illness. She is struggling to adhere to her treatment plan due to lack of family support. Which strategy would be most effective in building a supportive relationship that encourages her adherence?
A) Provide Sarah with educational materials about her condition.
B) Arrange regular family meetings to discuss her treatment plan.
C) Encourage Sarah to join a support group for individuals with similar conditions.
D) Schedule frequent follow-up appointments to monitor her progress.

Question 48: In the context of employer-sponsored health coverage, what primary factor contributes to the tax advantages for both employers and employees?

A) The Affordable Care Act mandates
B) Pre-tax salary deductions for premiums
C) Employer contributions are considered taxable income
D) State-specific insurance regulations

Question 49: Sarah, a case manager, is evaluating John, a 30-year-old with a cognitive impairment who receives SSI benefits. John has recently started working part-time. How should Sarah advise him regarding the impact of his earnings on his SSI benefits?
A) All earnings will be deducted from SSI benefits
B) A portion of earnings will be excluded before affecting SSI benefits
C) Earnings do not affect SSI benefits if under $1,000 monthly
D) Earnings will only affect Medicaid eligibility

Question 50: Sarah, a case manager, is assisting a client who recently relocated and is seeking community support for emotional well-being. The client has expressed interest in joining a fraternal organization for social connections and moral support. Which of the following is the most appropriate initial step for Sarah to take in facilitating this process?
A) Research local fraternal organizations and provide contact information.
B) Encourage the client to attend a general community event to meet new people.
C) Refer the client to a religious counselor for spiritual guidance.
D) Suggest online forums for connecting with like-minded individuals.

Question 51: Sarah, a case manager, is working with a patient who has multiple chronic conditions and frequently visits the emergency department. To improve care coordination and reduce hospital admissions, Sarah decides to implement a model of care that emphasizes team-based, patient-centered care with a strong focus on primary care. Which model of care delivery should Sarah choose?
A) Patient-Centered Medical Home (PCMH)
B) Accountable Care Organization (ACO)
C) Transitional Care Model (TCM)
D) Chronic Care Model (CCM)

Question 52: Jane, a case manager, is working with an elderly patient, Mr. Thompson, who has been financially exploited by a family member. As part of her intervention strategy, which financial support system should Jane prioritize to prevent further abuse and ensure Mr. Thompson's financial security?
A) Establishing a joint bank account with another family member
B) Setting up a durable power of attorney for finances
C) Encouraging Mr. Thompson to manage his finances independently
D) Enrolling Mr. Thompson in a financial literacy program

Question 53: Sarah, a case manager, is working with a client who has recently been diagnosed with a chronic illness that significantly limits their daily activities. The client is seeking disability benefits. Which of the following is the most crucial factor Sarah should consider when assessing eligibility for these benefits under Social Security Disability Insurance (SSDI)?
A) The client's age and education level
B) The client's ability to perform any type of work
C) The client's medical diagnosis alone
D) The duration of the client's condition

Question 54: Which of the following is a primary focus of the Joint Commission's accreditation standards for

case management in healthcare settings?
A) Ensuring financial profitability of healthcare organizations
B) Enhancing patient safety and quality of care
C) Increasing patient throughput and reducing wait times
D) Expanding the range of services offered by healthcare facilities

Question 55: In the context of anxiety disorders, which cognitive symptom is most commonly associated with Generalized Anxiety Disorder (GAD)?
A) Obsessive thoughts
B) Intrusive memories
C) Excessive worry
D) Flashbacks

Question 56: In the context of crisis intervention, which strategy is best suited for helping a client regain control over their immediate environment to reduce stress and anxiety?
A) Narrative Therapy
B) Solution-Focused Brief Therapy
C) Environmental Manipulation
D) Psychoeducation

Question 57: How can fraternal/religious organizations enhance the psychosocial well-being of individuals within a community setting?
A) By offering financial assistance programs exclusively for their members
B) By providing opportunities for social interaction and emotional support
C) By facilitating access to healthcare services only for affiliated members
D) By organizing religious ceremonies as their primary focus

Question 58: In the context of reimbursement methods for alternative care sites, which factor most significantly influences reimbursement rates?
A) Geographic location of the facility
B) Type of services provided
C) Patient satisfaction scores
D) Volume of patients treated

Question 59: John is a 45-year-old patient recently diagnosed with chronic obstructive pulmonary disease (COPD). Despite understanding his treatment plan, he frequently forgets to use his inhaler. As his case manager, what intervention would most likely improve John's adherence to his inhaler regimen?
A) Setting up daily phone reminders for inhaler use
B) Involving John's family in monitoring his inhaler use
C) Scheduling weekly check-ins to discuss inhaler usage
D) Educating John on the long-term benefits of consistent inhaler use

Question 60: In the context of psychosocial support systems, which approach is most effective in addressing the emotional needs of a child experiencing neglect?
A) Punitive measures to enforce discipline
B) Cognitive-behavioral therapy to modify thought patterns
C) Ignoring negative behavior to avoid reinforcement
D) Medication to manage behavioral symptoms

Question 61: Which of the following is most effective in reducing relapse rates in individuals with opioid use disorder according to contemporary research?
A) Cognitive Behavioral Therapy (CBT)
B) Contingency Management
C) Medication-Assisted Treatment (MAT)
D) Motivational Interviewing

Question 62: In the context of psychosocial support

systems, which approach is considered most effective in enhancing health literacy among diverse patient populations?
A) Tailoring educational content to cultural preferences
B) Distributing standardized educational pamphlets
C) Relying on family members to interpret medical information
D) Utilizing online resources for self-education

Question 63: John, a 60-year-old patient recovering from cardiac surgery, expresses anxiety about managing his post-discharge care at home. What is the most effective approach for a case manager to facilitate John's self-care management?
A) Scheduling frequent follow-up appointments with his cardiologist.
B) Developing a personalized self-care plan with input from John's family members.
C) Providing John with comprehensive written instructions on post-operative care.
D) Arranging for home visits by a healthcare professional for the first month post-discharge.

Question 64: Emily, a 45-year-old single mother of two, is experiencing high levels of stress due to job insecurity and financial instability. As her case manager, you need to address the social determinants affecting her health. Which intervention is most likely to improve Emily's health outcomes?
A) Refer Emily to a financial advisor for budgeting assistance.
B) Enroll Emily in a stress management workshop.
C) Connect Emily with local employment resources and job training programs.
D) Provide Emily with information on healthy eating and exercise routines.

Question 65: Which strategy is most effective for case managers when coordinating care for clients with multiple chronic conditions?
A) Developing individualized care plans based on client preferences
B) Focusing on symptom management through pharmacological interventions
C) Establishing multidisciplinary team meetings for integrated care planning
D) Prioritizing cost-effective treatment options to reduce financial burden

Question 66: What is a key indicator that a client has moved from the Preparation stage to the Action stage in the Transtheoretical Model of Change?
A) Expressing awareness of potential benefits
B) Actively modifying behavior
C) Gathering resources and support
D) Weighing pros and cons

Question 67: Sarah, a case manager, is working with a healthcare team to implement a value-based care model for patients with chronic illnesses. The goal is to reduce hospital readmissions and improve patient outcomes. Which of the following strategies should Sarah prioritize to align with value-based care principles?
A) Implementing more frequent follow-up visits regardless of patient needs
B) Coordinating care across providers to ensure comprehensive management
C) Increasing the number of diagnostic tests to catch potential issues early
D) Focusing solely on reducing costs without considering patient outcomes

Question 68: In the context of cost containment, which

approach primarily aims to align financial incentives with quality improvements in healthcare delivery?
A) Bundled Payments
B) Health Maintenance Organization (HMO)
C) Accountable Care Organizations (ACOs)
D) Value-Based Purchasing

Question 69: Which of the following public benefit programs is primarily designed to provide healthcare coverage for low-income individuals and families, and is jointly funded by state and federal governments in the United States?
A) Medicare
B) Medicaid
C) CHIP (Children's Health Insurance Program)
D) SNAP (Supplemental Nutrition Assistance Program)

Question 70: Which of the following factors is most critical for a case manager to consider when selecting a meal delivery service for a client with dietary restrictions due to chronic kidney disease?
A) Cost-effectiveness of the meal plan
B) Customization options for low-sodium meals
C) Availability of organic ingredients
D) Delivery frequency and timing

Question 71: What is the primary benefit of integrating Pharmacy Assistance Programs into community health initiatives for case managers working with low-income populations?
A) Reducing medication errors through increased oversight
B) Enhancing medication adherence by alleviating financial barriers
C) Streamlining the prescription process for healthcare providers
D) Increasing pharmaceutical company profits through expanded program usage

Question 72: In health counseling, what is considered a critical component for building a successful therapeutic alliance?
A) Providing detailed educational materials
B) Demonstrating empathy and active listening
C) Establishing strict boundaries and authority
D) Offering solutions and advice early in sessions

Question 73: John, a case manager, is working with an elderly patient who requires home health care services after surgery. The patient's Medicare plan covers only part of these services. To optimize financial resources while ensuring continuity of care, what should John focus on?
A) Identify community-based volunteer programs
B) Arrange co-pay assistance through non-profit organizations
C) Assess eligibility for Medicare Advantage plans
D) Suggest borrowing from family members

Question 74: John, a 65-year-old male with a history of congestive heart failure (CHF), is being discharged from the hospital after an acute exacerbation. As his case manager, which of the following interventions is most critical to prevent readmission?
A) Schedule a follow-up appointment with his primary care physician within two weeks.
B) Arrange for home health services to monitor his weight and vital signs.
C) Educate him on recognizing early signs of CHF exacerbation and when to seek help.
D) Ensure he has a 30-day supply of all prescribed medications before discharge.

Question 75: In the context of bundled payments, what is the primary advantage of this reimbursement model over traditional fee-for-service models?
A) Increased administrative complexity
B) Enhanced provider accountability for patient outcomes
C) Greater flexibility in billing individual services
D) Higher financial risk for patients

Question 76: Which factor most significantly influences the success of a self-directed care program for individuals with chronic conditions?
A) Availability of financial resources
B) Access to comprehensive health education
C) Support from family and peers
D) Regular monitoring by healthcare providers

Question 77: Which principle is most crucial in pastoral counseling to ensure effective communication and support for clients dealing with psychosocial issues?
A) Active Listening
B) Directive Counseling
C) Solution-Focused Brief Therapy
D) Cognitive Restructuring

Question 78: During a home visit, Case Manager Emily notices that Mrs. Thompson, an elderly client, has unexplained bruises and appears fearful when her son is present. Emily suspects elder abuse. What should be her immediate course of action?
A) Confront the son about the suspected abuse.
B) Report the suspected abuse to Adult Protective Services (APS).
C) Document the findings and monitor the situation for further evidence.
D) Discuss her concerns with Mrs. Thompson in private.

Question 79: Which of the following best describes the eligibility criteria for TRICARE coverage for retired military personnel and their families?
A) Retired military personnel and their families are eligible for TRICARE Prime only if they reside within a 50-mile radius of a military treatment facility.
B) Retired military personnel and their families are automatically eligible for TRICARE Select, regardless of location.
C) Retired military personnel must enroll in Medicare Part B to maintain eligibility for TRICARE For Life.
D) Retired military personnel and their families are only eligible for TRICARE Standard if they have no other health insurance coverage.

Question 80: In managing elder care services, which intervention is most aligned with enhancing autonomy while ensuring safety in community-dwelling older adults?
A) Installing home monitoring systems
B) Encouraging participation in community exercise programs
C) Providing transportation services for medical appointments
D) Implementing medication management programs

Question 81: Sarah, a case manager, is assisting a patient who has recently been discharged from the hospital. The patient needs ongoing physical therapy, but their insurance plan has limited coverage for outpatient services. Which financial resource strategy should Sarah prioritize to ensure the patient receives necessary care without incurring excessive out-of-pocket expenses?
A) Negotiate a payment plan with the therapy provider
B) Apply for a medical grant from a local charity
C) Explore Medicaid eligibility for additional coverage
D) Recommend the patient use savings to cover costs

Question 82: Which of the following is a critical quality indicator for evaluating the effectiveness of case management interventions in a healthcare setting?
A) Patient satisfaction scores
B) Length of stay reduction
C) Readmission rates
D) Cost per patient

Question 83: Alex, a 35-year-old transgender male, is seeking assistance from a case manager to access appropriate healthcare services. As a case manager, what is the most critical factor to consider when coordinating Alex's care to ensure his gender identity is respected and supported throughout his healthcare journey?
A) Ensuring that all medical records reflect Alex's preferred name and gender identity
B) Focusing solely on the medical procedures related to gender transition
C) Prioritizing mental health support over physical health needs
D) Encouraging family involvement in all healthcare decisions

Question 84: Which concept in client support system dynamics suggests that a client's behavior is shaped by both internal personal factors and external environmental influences, requiring case managers to consider multiple levels of influence?
A) Transactional Model of Stress and Coping
B) Socio-Ecological Model
C) Cognitive Behavioral Therapy
D) Transtheoretical Model

Question 85: John, a 68-year-old patient with chronic heart failure, is being discharged from the hospital. As his case manager, you need to ensure that his home care benefits are maximized under his private insurance plan. Which of the following actions would most effectively utilize his home care benefits while ensuring continuity of care?
A) Arrange for weekly physical therapy sessions at home.
B) Schedule daily visits from a registered nurse for medication management.
C) Set up telehealth consultations with his cardiologist twice a week.
D) Coordinate with a home health aide for assistance with daily living activities.

Question 86: In the context of age-specific care, which approach is most effective in managing chronic conditions in older adults while considering their unique physiological changes?
A) Implementing a one-size-fits-all medication regimen
B) Prioritizing polypharmacy to address multiple conditions simultaneously
C) Utilizing a comprehensive geriatric assessment to tailor interventions
D) Focusing solely on acute symptom management

Question 87: In the context of home care benefits, which factor most significantly influences reimbursement decisions by private benefit programs?
A) The cost-effectiveness of home care versus hospitalization
B) The frequency of service utilization
C) The patient's previous hospitalizations
D) The geographic location of the patient

Question 88: Sarah, a case manager, has a client named Tom who is seeking ways to enhance his spiritual well-being after a major surgery. Sarah suggests exploring local religious organizations. Which of the following roles of these organizations would most effectively address Tom's spiritual needs?
A) Providing educational workshops on health management
B) Offering spiritual counseling and guidance
C) Organizing recreational activities for physical recovery
D) Facilitating peer support groups focused on chronic illness

Question 89: John, a 45-year-old man with multiple sclerosis, is experiencing significant stress due to his inability to perform daily activities independently. As a case manager, which psychosocial intervention would be most effective in enhancing John's coping mechanisms?
A) Cognitive-behavioral therapy (CBT)
B) Group therapy with peers
C) Family counseling sessions
D) Medication management

Question 90: During an initial interview with a new patient, Mr. Thompson, a case manager notices signs of anxiety. To build rapport and gather accurate information, which interviewing technique should the case manager prioritize?
A) Direct questioning to obtain specific answers
B) Reflective listening to show empathy and understanding
C) Confrontational approach to address inconsistencies
D) Closed-ended questions to maintain control

Question 91: John, a veteran, is seeking assistance to cover his healthcare expenses. He is eligible for both TRICARE and the Veterans Health Administration (VHA) benefits. As his case manager, how should you advise him to maximize his healthcare coverage?
A) Use TRICARE for all primary care services and VHA for specialty care.
B) Use VHA for all services as it covers everything TRICARE does.
C) Use TRICARE as primary insurance and VHA as secondary insurance.
D) Use VHA as primary insurance and TRICARE as secondary insurance.

Question 92: Mrs. Thompson, an 82-year-old woman with mild cognitive impairment, lives alone and is increasingly struggling with daily activities. Her daughter is concerned about her safety and well-being. As a case manager, which community resource would be most appropriate to recommend for addressing Mrs. Thompson's needs while promoting her independence?
A) Adult Day Care Services
B) In-Home Personal Care Services
C) Assisted Living Facility
D) Nursing Home Placement

Question 93: In the context of gender identity development, which concept refers to the internalization of societal norms and expectations about gender roles?
A) Gender Role Socialization
B) Gender Dysphoria
C) Gender Fluidity
D) Gender Constancy

Question 94: John, a case manager, needs to determine the most appropriate level of care for a patient recently discharged from surgery. What should John consider first according to utilization management guidelines?
A) The patient's insurance coverage limits
B) The patient's current health status and care needs
C) The hospital's available resources for continued care
D) The standard length of stay for similar surgeries

Question 95: In the context of financial risk models, which approach best aligns with reducing unnecessary hospital readmissions through improved case management practices?
A) Pay-for-Performance (P4P)
B) Diagnosis-Related Groups (DRGs)
C) Accountable Care Organizations (ACOs)
D) Retrospective Cost-Based Reimbursement

Question 96: When evaluating care delivery methods under managed care systems, which approach primarily focuses on preventive care and coordination among healthcare providers?
A) Fee-for-service model
B) Health Maintenance Organization (HMO)
C) Preferred Provider Organization (PPO)
D) Point of Service Plan (POS)

Question 97: In behavioral health, which cognitive distortion involves interpreting neutral events as negative?
A) Catastrophizing
B) Overgeneralization
C) Mental filtering
D) Personalization

Question 98: John, a 50-year-old patient with diabetes and anxiety, is experiencing difficulty managing his condition post-discharge. As his case manager, what is the most effective strategy to address both his physical and behavioral health challenges?
A) Enroll him in a diabetes management program with peer counseling sessions.
B) Set up weekly telehealth appointments with his endocrinologist only.
C) Provide educational materials about diabetes self-care without psychological support.
D) Encourage self-monitoring of blood glucose levels with no further interventions.

Question 99: Sarah, a case manager, is developing a wellness program for a corporate client. The client wants to reduce employee stress and improve mental health. Which of the following strategies should Sarah prioritize to effectively address these goals?
A) Implementing regular physical fitness challenges
B) Organizing monthly mindfulness and meditation workshops
C) Providing nutritional counseling sessions
D) Offering financial planning seminars

Question 100: Which of the following roles is most critical for a disease-based organization in providing psychosocial support to individuals with chronic illnesses?
A) Offering financial assistance for medical treatments
B) Facilitating peer support groups and community connections
C) Conducting clinical research on disease progression
D) Providing educational materials about disease management

Question 101: Emily, a case manager, is coordinating care for a patient with chronic heart failure who lives in a rural area. The patient has limited access to in-person healthcare services. Emily decides to implement virtual care strategies. Which of the following is the most effective approach for ensuring continuous monitoring and management of the patient's condition?
A) Schedule monthly telehealth visits with a cardiologist.
B) Use remote patient monitoring devices to track vital signs daily.
C) Encourage the patient to use online health forums for support.
D) Arrange weekly phone calls for symptom check-ins.

Question 102: What is the primary purpose of the CMS's Inpatient Quality Reporting (IQR) Program in the context of healthcare quality improvement?
A) To reduce hospital-acquired infections
B) To provide public reporting of hospital performance data
C) To financially penalize hospitals with high readmission rates
D) To incentivize electronic health record adoption

Question 103: As a case manager, you are coordinating the care for Mr. Johnson, a 68-year-old patient with multiple chronic conditions, including diabetes and heart failure. During an interdisciplinary team meeting, what is the most critical aspect to ensure effective collaboration among team members?
A) Establishing clear communication channels
B) Assigning tasks based on professional hierarchy
C) Focusing solely on cost-effective treatment plans
D) Prioritizing the patient's immediate medical needs

Question 104: Maria, a case manager, is helping Jordan, who identifies as gay and faces discrimination at work. Jordan is considering whether to report this discrimination. What should Maria emphasize when advising Jordan on this matter?
A) The importance of documenting incidents for legal purposes.
B) The potential negative impact on workplace relationships if reported.
C) The likelihood of resolution through informal discussions with colleagues.
D) The benefits of ignoring minor incidents to maintain job security.

Question 105: In the context of transitional care, which approach best ensures continuity of care for elderly patients transitioning from hospital to home?
A) Assigning a case manager to coordinate all services
B) Developing a detailed discharge summary for the primary care provider
C) Scheduling a follow-up appointment with a specialist before discharge
D) Utilizing electronic health records to share patient information

Question 106: In the context of financial abuse and neglect, which of the following actions is most indicative of financial exploitation of an elderly client by a caregiver?
A) The caregiver regularly uses the client's funds to purchase groceries for both the client and themselves.
B) The caregiver is added as a joint account holder on the client's bank account for convenience.
C) The caregiver makes large withdrawals from the client's account without clear justification.
D) The caregiver assists the client in paying bills and managing finances with full transparency.

Question 107: Sarah, a case manager, is tasked with coordinating care for a patient with chronic heart failure who lives in a rural area. The patient's condition requires frequent monitoring and adjustments to medication. Which non-traditional site of care would be most effective in managing this patient's condition while minimizing hospital visits?
A) Telehealth services
B) Urgent care centers
C) Home health visits
D) Community health clinics

Question 108: Which of the following criteria must be met for an individual to qualify for Supplemental Security Income (SSI) benefits under the Social Security Administration guidelines?
A) The individual must have a work history of at least 10 years.
B) The individual must be aged 65 or older, blind, or disabled with limited income and resources.
C) The individual must have a disability that is expected to last less than one year.
D) The individual must have dependents who are also receiving SSI benefits.

Question 109: In which model of care delivery do healthcare providers share responsibility for quality and cost of care, often involving risk-sharing arrangements with payers?
A) Patient-Centered Medical Home (PCMH)
B) Integrated Delivery System (IDS)
C) Accountable Care Organization (ACO)
D) Health Maintenance Organization (HMO)

Question 110: Which of the following strategies is most effective in reducing hospital readmissions during transitions of care for patients with chronic conditions?
A) Implementing a patient-centered discharge plan
B) Conducting medication reconciliation at discharge
C) Providing telephonic follow-up within 48 hours post-discharge
D) Ensuring comprehensive in-hospital education sessions

Question 111: In the context of viatical settlements, which factor most significantly affects the valuation of a life insurance policy?
A) The policyholder's current health status and life expectancy.
B) The original amount of premiums paid by the policyholder.
C) The number of beneficiaries listed on the policy.
D) The age at which the policy was originally purchased.

Question 112: A case manager, Sarah, is reviewing the hospital stay of a patient named John, who was admitted for a complex surgical procedure. To ensure that John's care aligns with utilization management principles, what should Sarah prioritize in her review?
A) Ensuring all diagnostic tests are completed regardless of necessity
B) Verifying that each service provided is supported by clinical guidelines
C) Approving extended hospital stays to ensure comprehensive care
D) Focusing solely on cost reduction strategies

Question 113: In the context of medication reconciliation, which step is most critical to ensure accuracy and prevent adverse drug events during patient transitions of care?
A) Reviewing the patient's electronic health record (EHR) for previous prescriptions
B) Conducting a thorough interview with the patient about their current medication regimen
C) Verifying medication lists with the patient's pharmacy records
D) Consulting with the patient's primary care physician for medication history

Question 114: Sarah, a case manager in a rehabilitation center, is tasked with creating a care plan for Maria, who has recently suffered a stroke. Which function should Sarah prioritize to maximize Maria's recovery and independence?
A) Develop an interdisciplinary team meeting schedule
B) Assess Maria's home environment for safety

modifications
C) Monitor Maria's progress through regular assessments
D) Facilitate family meetings to discuss Maria's care preferences

Question 115: In what way do fraternal/religious organizations enhance community resources for case managers working with diverse populations?
A) They provide specialized medical training programs
B) They organize cultural competence workshops
C) They facilitate interfaith dialogues and collaborative initiatives
D) They offer direct healthcare services

Question 116: John, a 68-year-old patient with chronic heart failure, is being discharged from the hospital. The case manager must decide on an alternative care site to ensure continuous monitoring and management of his condition. Which of the following options is most appropriate for John's needs?
A) Skilled Nursing Facility (SNF)
B) Home Health Care
C) Assisted Living Facility
D) Adult Day Care Center

Question 117: Which of the following strategies is most effective for a case manager to establish trust and rapport with a client during the initial stages of relationship building?
A) Providing detailed information about healthcare processes
B) Actively listening and showing empathy towards the client's concerns
C) Setting strict boundaries to maintain professional distance
D) Offering solutions to problems immediately

Question 118: Emily, a case manager at a large hospital, is reviewing a patient's discharge plan. The patient, Mr. Johnson, is covered under Medicare's Prospective Payment System (PPS). Emily needs to ensure that the hospital maximizes reimbursement while maintaining high-quality care. Which of the following should Emily focus on to achieve this goal?
A) Length of Stay (LOS)
B) Severity of Illness
C) Diagnosis-Related Group (DRG) assignment
D) Patient Satisfaction Scores

Question 119: In the context of pediatric care management, what is the primary benefit of incorporating family-centered care principles?
A) Enhancing medication adherence through direct instructions
B) Increasing healthcare costs due to extended consultations
C) Improving child health outcomes by involving families in decision-making
D) Reducing the need for interdisciplinary team meetings

Question 120: John, a 55-year-old male, presents with memory issues and difficulty in executive functioning. His case manager suspects mild cognitive impairment and needs to decide on the most appropriate psychological and neuropsychological assessment tool. Which assessment should be prioritized for John's condition?
A) Beck Depression Inventory (BDI)
B) Mini-Mental State Examination (MMSE)
C) Wechsler Adult Intelligence Scale (WAIS)
D) Wisconsin Card Sorting Test (WCST)

Question 121: In the context of accreditation standards, what is a critical component of evaluating case management effectiveness?
A) Patient satisfaction surveys

B) Cost reduction metrics
C) Evidence-based practice implementation
D) Length of hospital stay

Question 122: What is a primary consideration when determining the appropriateness of an assisted living facility for a client with mild cognitive impairment?
A) The availability of 24-hour skilled nursing care
B) The facility's ability to provide personalized care plans
C) The proximity to a major hospital
D) The presence of advanced technological monitoring systems

Question 123: You are working with Ms. Garcia, a 55-year-old patient recently discharged after surgery. To manage her recovery cost-effectively, which approach should you prioritize as her case manager?
A) Scheduling frequent follow-up appointments with her surgeon
B) Coordinating home health services to support her recovery
C) Advising Ms. Garcia to self-manage her wound care without professional input
D) Recommending immediate readmission if any complications arise

Question 124: In the context of gender health, which psychosocial factor is most likely to impact the mental health outcomes of transgender individuals during their transition process?
A) Access to hormone replacement therapy
B) Social support from family and friends
C) Availability of gender-affirming surgeries
D) Legal recognition of gender identity

Question 125: Maria has been receiving SSDI benefits due to a chronic illness. She is considering taking up a part-time job to supplement her income. As her case manager, what should you advise her regarding how this employment might affect her SSDI benefits?
A) Her SSDI benefits will be terminated immediately upon starting work
B) She can earn up to a certain amount without affecting her SSDI benefits
C) Any amount of earned income will reduce her SSDI benefits proportionally
D) She must first report her earnings before any determination can be made

Question 126: Sarah, a case manager, is working with John, a 60-year-old man who recently lost his spouse. John expresses feelings of intense sadness and isolation. Sarah wants to implement an evidence-based approach to help John process his grief. Which intervention should she prioritize based on contemporary bereavement counseling theories?
A) Encourage John to avoid talking about his loss to prevent emotional distress
B) Facilitate regular group therapy sessions with others who have experienced similar losses
C) Recommend medication to alleviate symptoms of depression associated with grief
D) Suggest journaling as a way for John to express and process his emotions

Question 127: What benefit program provides financial assistance for education and training to eligible veterans and their dependents, focusing on post-service educational advancement?
A) Post-9/11 GI Bill
B) Montgomery GI Bill
C) Vocational Rehabilitation and Employment (VR&E)
D) Survivors' and Dependents' Educational Assistance

(DEA)

Question 128: Which of the following non-traditional care sites is most effective for managing chronic conditions through integrated care coordination, while minimizing hospital readmissions?
A) Retail Clinics
B) Telehealth Services
C) Home Health Care
D) Urgent Care Centers

Question 129: In the context of long-term care, which reimbursement method is most effective in promoting cost-efficient care delivery while maintaining quality standards?
A) Fee-for-Service (FFS)
B) Capitation
C) Bundled Payments
D) Pay-for-Performance (P4P)

Question 130: In the context of group dynamics, which concept explains the phenomenon where individuals exert less effort when working in a group compared to when working alone?
A) Social Facilitation
B) Groupthink
C) Social Loafing
D) Deindividuation

Question 131: Sarah, a case manager, is working with an elderly client, Mr. Thompson, who has been recently diagnosed with dementia. His family is concerned about his financial management and potential financial abuse by a distant relative. What initial step should Sarah take to address these concerns effectively?
A) Recommend the family consult a lawyer to establish power of attorney
B) Advise Mr. Thompson to open a joint bank account with a trusted family member
C) Conduct a comprehensive assessment of Mr. Thompson's financial situation
D) Suggest the family monitor Mr. Thompson's financial transactions regularly

Question 132: As a case manager at a healthcare facility, you are tasked with improving patient outcomes by utilizing quality indicators. URAC accreditation emphasizes certain key areas for quality and outcomes evaluation. Which of the following would be most aligned with URAC's standards for measuring quality in case management?
A) Patient satisfaction surveys
B) Readmission rates within 30 days
C) Length of hospital stay
D) Number of patient complaints

Question 133: Which of the following best describes the role of a "gatekeeper" in group dynamics, particularly in the context of psychosocial support systems?
A) Ensures that all group members have an equal opportunity to participate
B) Dominates the conversation and controls group decisions
C) Provides expert opinions to guide the group's direction
D) Observes and evaluates group performance for improvements

Question 134: Sarah, a case manager, is evaluating the suitability of a residential treatment facility for her client, John, who has been struggling with severe substance use disorder. Which factor should Sarah prioritize when determining if a residential treatment facility is appropriate for John?
A) The distance of the facility from John's home

B) The accreditation status of the facility
C) The availability of individualized treatment plans
D) The number of recreational activities offered

Question 135: In the context of Prospective Payment Systems (PPS), which of the following is a primary advantage of implementing a Diagnosis-Related Group (DRG) system for hospitals?
A) Reduces administrative costs by eliminating the need for detailed billing processes
B) Encourages hospitals to discharge patients as soon as possible to maximize revenue
C) Provides a fixed payment rate based on the average cost of care for similar patient groups
D) Allows hospitals to negotiate individual payment rates with insurers

Question 136: As a case manager, you are evaluating the financial risk models applicable to a patient named John, who is transitioning from hospital care to a long-term rehabilitation facility. Considering contemporary reimbursement methods, which financial risk model would most effectively align with ensuring cost-effective care without compromising quality?
A) Capitation Model
B) Fee-for-Service Model
C) Bundled Payment Model
D) Pay-for-Performance Model

Question 137: Which factor is most likely to enhance the effectiveness of informed decision-making in case management by promoting client engagement in their care plan?
A) Providing comprehensive medical jargon
B) Encouraging passive listening
C) Facilitating shared decision-making
D) Imposing expert opinions

Question 138: In the context of community resources, what is the primary advantage of utilizing a case management approach for coordinating care among diverse service providers?
A) Reduces overall healthcare costs
B) Improves communication between providers
C) Ensures patient adherence to treatment plans
D) Facilitates timely access to resources

Question 139: Mrs. Thompson, a 78-year-old patient with multiple chronic conditions, is being discharged from the hospital. Her case manager is exploring options to provide in-home care services that are not covered by Medicare. Which waiver program should the case manager consider to provide these additional services?
A) Medicaid Home and Community-Based Services (HCBS) Waiver
B) Medicare Advantage Plan
C) Private Long-Term Care Insurance
D) Supplemental Security Income (SSI)

Question 140: Jamie, a non-binary individual seeking medical care, reports feeling uncomfortable with their current healthcare provider due to perceived bias. As a case manager, what is the best course of action to ensure Jamie receives appropriate care?
A) Recommend Jamie communicate directly with the provider about their concerns.
B) Assist Jamie in finding a new provider known for LGBTQ+ inclusivity.
C) Suggest Jamie bring an advocate during medical appointments for support.
D) Encourage Jamie to educate the current provider on non-binary identities.

Question 141: In assessing a patient's physical functioning and behavioral health, which standardized tool is most effective for evaluating both mobility limitations and psychological well-being in older adults?
A) Barthel Index
B) SF-36 Health Survey
C) Geriatric Depression Scale (GDS)
D) Mini-Mental State Examination (MMSE)

Question 142: Sarah, a 45-year-old woman recently diagnosed with type 2 diabetes, is struggling to adhere to her self-care regimen. As a case manager, you are tasked with developing an effective self-care management plan. Which strategy is most likely to enhance Sarah's adherence to her self-care regimen?
A) Providing Sarah with detailed educational materials about diabetes management.
B) Establishing a daily check-in routine via phone or email to monitor her progress.
C) Encouraging Sarah to join a peer support group for individuals with diabetes.
D) Setting up regular meetings with a nutritionist to review her dietary habits.

Question 143: In the context of Adjusted Clinical Groups, what is a key advantage of using this system for case management?
A) It reduces administrative costs by simplifying billing processes
B) It enhances predictive accuracy for future healthcare needs
C) It focuses solely on acute care episodes for analysis
D) It eliminates the need for electronic health records

Question 144: In developing a comprehensive case management plan for Ms. Smith, who requires both physical rehabilitation and mental health support, what is the most effective approach to ensure integrated service delivery?
A) Assign separate case managers for each service area
B) Develop a unified care plan incorporating both needs
C) Schedule sequential treatments for physical and mental health issues
D) Focus on immediate physical rehabilitation needs first

Question 145: When considering individually purchased health insurance, which factor most significantly influences premium costs for the policyholder?
A) Age of the policyholder
B) Geographic location
C) Type of coverage selected
D) Health status of the policyholder

Question 146: During an accreditation review, Case Manager John needs to demonstrate how his hospital ensures quality care through evidence-based practices. Which measure should he highlight to best meet accreditation standards?
A) Adopting new medical technologies as they become available.
B) Regularly updating clinical guidelines based on recent research findings.
C) Increasing the number of specialists available in the hospital.
D) Expanding patient access to telehealth services.

Question 147: Sarah, a 68-year-old woman with multiple chronic conditions, is transitioning from hospital to home care. As a case manager, which life span consideration is most crucial in ensuring her successful transition and adherence to her care plan?
A) Ensuring Sarah's understanding of her medication regimen.

B) Arranging for Sarah's follow-up appointments with specialists.
C) Assessing Sarah's social support network at home.
D) Providing Sarah with dietary guidelines suitable for her age.

Question 148: In the context of managing clients with disabilities, which approach is most effective in promoting client autonomy while ensuring comprehensive care coordination?
A) Client-centered care approach
B) Multidisciplinary team meetings
C) Standardized care pathways
D) Evidence-based practice guidelines

Question 149: In clients with dual diagnoses, what is a primary challenge that case managers face when coordinating care between mental health and addiction services?
A) Ensuring consistent medication adherence
B) Managing differing treatment philosophies
C) Facilitating family involvement in therapy
D) Scheduling regular follow-up appointments

Question 150: Which of the following methods is most effective in identifying high-risk patients within a population using health risk assessment tools?
A) Retrospective claims data analysis
B) Predictive analytics models
C) Patient self-reported surveys
D) Routine clinical assessments

ANSWER WITH DETAILED EXPLANATION SET [3]

Question 1: Correct Answer: A) Remote patient monitoring via wearable devices
Rationale: Remote patient monitoring allows continuous tracking of John's vital signs and glucose levels from home, providing timely alerts and interventions without frequent travel. While adult day care centers offer supervision, they require daily attendance. Community clinics necessitate travel and may not provide immediate feedback. Assisted living facilities offer on-site care but are more suitable for those needing residential support rather than independent living with remote oversight.

Question 2: Correct Answer: B) Assist Mr. Thompson in enrolling in a manufacturer-sponsored patient assistance program.
Rationale: Manufacturer-sponsored patient assistance programs are designed to provide free or low-cost medications to individuals who cannot afford them, particularly those without insurance or inadequate coverage, like Medicare Part D might not fully cover all costs (A). Mail-order pharmacies (C) and discount clubs (D) may offer savings but don't provide the comprehensive support needed for those with limited financial resources like manufacturer programs do.

Question 3: Correct Answer: B) Ensuring effective communication and collaboration among team members for comprehensive care delivery.
Rationale: The primary role of a case manager in integrated services is to facilitate communication and collaboration within an interdisciplinary team, ensuring that all aspects of a patient's care are addressed comprehensively. Option A limits the role to administrative tasks, which undermines the collaborative aspect. Option C restricts the scope to specific tasks rather than ongoing coordination. Option D incorrectly suggests that delegation replaces active involvement in managing patient care collaboratively.

Question 4: Correct Answer: B) Capitation
Rationale: Capitation involves paying a fixed amount per patient to a provider for a specified period, incentivizing cost-effective care by managing resources efficiently. Unlike fee-for-service, which pays per service rendered, capitation discourages unnecessary services. Bundled payments provide a single payment for all services related to a treatment episode, while pay-for-performance rewards quality and efficiency improvements. Capitation uniquely focuses on comprehensive care management across various services without additional compensation for increased service volume.

Question 5: Correct Answer: A) Reduction in hospital readmission rates
Rationale: Reducing hospital readmission rates is a critical quality indicator for chronic heart failure management, as it directly reflects the effectiveness of outpatient care and continuity of care. While increasing patient satisfaction (Option B), improving medication adherence (Option C), and decreasing emergency department visits (Option D) are important, they are often components that contribute to the broader goal of reducing readmissions. Focusing on this indicator aligns with contemporary research emphasizing the importance of continuity and comprehensive care plans to prevent unnecessary hospitalizations.

Question 6: Correct Answer: A) Medicare Part A
Rationale: Medicare Part A covers inpatient hospital stays, skilled nursing facility care, hospice, and some home health care services. It is often referred to as hospital insurance. Option B (Medicare Part B) covers outpatient care and preventive services. Option C (Medicare Part C), also known as Medicare Advantage, includes Parts A and B but is offered by private companies. Option D (Medicare Part D) covers prescription drugs. The key distinction is that Part A specifically addresses inpatient services.

Question 7: Correct Answer: B) Patient demographics and comorbidities
Rationale: Patient demographics and comorbidities are crucial in predicting financial risk because they directly influence the complexity and cost of care. While historical cost data (Option A) provides a baseline, it doesn't account for individual patient variability. Length of stay (Option C) is influenced by patient health, but it's a consequence rather than a predictor. Readmission rates (Option D) are important for quality metrics but are an outcome rather than a predictive factor. Thus, understanding patient demographics and comorbidities allows for more accurate risk stratification.

Question 8: Correct Answer: B) National Association of Free & Charitable Clinics (NAFC)
Rationale: The National Association of Free & Charitable Clinics (NAFC) focuses on supporting free and charitable clinics, offering resources and advocacy for uninsured individuals. While AMA advocates for physicians, CDC focuses on public health, and AHA represents hospitals' interests, NAFC directly aids clinics serving the uninsured. Its primary mission aligns with providing healthcare access to those without insurance, distinguishing it as the correct option among organizations listed.

Question 9: Correct Answer: A) Benefit Triggers
Rationale: Benefit Triggers are essential as they determine eligibility for receiving long-term care insurance benefits. Understanding these triggers ensures appropriate coordination of services. While Premium Waivers and Elimination Periods are important, they primarily affect payment timing rather than service coordination. Inflation Protection is vital for maintaining benefit value over time but does not directly impact immediate service eligibility like Benefit Triggers do.

Question 10: Correct Answer: B) Promoting the expression of emotions and memories related to the deceased.
Rationale: Option B is correct as contemporary research emphasizes that expressing emotions and memories helps clients process grief and fosters adaptive coping. Option A might suppress emotions, leading to unresolved grief. Option C can be premature, as replacing relationships without processing loss may hinder healing. Option D suggests maintaining routine but lacks addressing emotional needs, crucial for coping with complicated grief.

Question 11: Correct Answer: A) Wisconsin Card Sorting Test (WCST)
Rationale: The Wisconsin Card Sorting Test (WCST) is specifically designed to assess executive functions, such as problem-solving, flexibility, and abstract thinking, which are often affected by frontal lobe damage. The Beck Depression Inventory (BDI) and Hamilton Anxiety Rating Scale (HAM-A) focus on mood disorders, while the Mini-Mental State Examination (MMSE) is a general cognitive screening tool. WCST's specificity in targeting executive functions makes it the appropriate choice for evaluating deficits related to frontal lobe impairment.

Question 12: Correct Answer: B) Transitional Care Model (TCM)

Rationale: The TCM is specifically designed to manage transitions between different levels of care, focusing on reducing hospital readmissions by ensuring continuity and effective communication. CCM targets long-term management of chronic diseases, PCMH emphasizes comprehensive primary care but not specifically transitions, and ICM integrates services across sectors without focusing solely on transitions. TCM's emphasis on transition-specific strategies makes it the most suitable choice for Maria's objective.

Question 13: Correct Answer: D) Based on achieving specific quality and efficiency benchmarks

Rationale: Savings in an ACO are shared based on achieving specific quality and efficiency benchmarks. Option A incorrectly emphasizes volume over value, contradicting ACO principles. Option B suggests individual metrics alone determine sharing, ignoring collective goals. Option C inaccurately implies equal distribution without performance consideration. Only option D aligns with the ACO model, where shared savings depend on meeting predefined quality and efficiency standards, promoting both cost-effectiveness and high-quality care delivery.

Question 14: Correct Answer: A) Establishing telehealth services

Rationale: Telehealth services are crucial in rural areas where access to healthcare facilities may be limited due to distance and availability of specialists. This strategy allows patients to receive medical consultations remotely. Partnering with local gyms (B) and organizing transportation services (C) address physical activity and mobility but don't directly improve healthcare access. Educational workshops (D), while informative, do not solve the accessibility issue as effectively as telehealth does, making option A the most beneficial choice.

Question 15: Correct Answer: B) Document the bruises and report the suspicion to Adult Protective Services (APS).

Rationale: The correct answer is B. Reporting suspicions of abuse to APS is crucial for ensuring Sarah's safety and initiating an investigation. While discussing concerns with Sarah (Option C) is important, it should not delay reporting. Confronting the abuser (Option A) could escalate danger without proper authority involvement. A physical examination (Option D) is useful but secondary to immediate safety concerns. Documentation supports legal processes and protects Sarah's welfare.

Question 16: Correct Answer: B) Actively listening and showing empathy

Rationale: Actively listening and showing empathy are foundational to building trust, as they demonstrate genuine interest and understanding of the client's needs. While demonstrating expertise (A) is important, it may not immediately foster trust. Providing information (C) is useful but can overwhelm clients initially. Setting strict boundaries (D) is necessary but may create distance rather than connection at the start. Listening and empathy directly address the emotional needs, fostering a trusting relationship.

Question 17: Correct Answer: C) Case Manager

Rationale: The Case Manager is primarily responsible for coordinating patient care across different settings, ensuring continuity and cost-effectiveness. Unlike Primary Care Physicians who focus on medical diagnosis and treatment, or Registered Nurses who provide direct patient care, Case Managers integrate services and resources. Social Workers address psychosocial aspects but do not typically coordinate across all healthcare settings. Thus, the Case Manager's role is unique in its comprehensive approach to managing patient transitions and optimizing resource utilization.

Question 18: Correct Answer: C) Collaborate with John to set realistic goals and develop an individualized care plan based on his preferences and lifestyle.

Rationale: Option C is correct as it emphasizes collaboration between the case manager and John, fostering informed decision-making tailored to his needs and circumstances. This approach respects John's autonomy while providing support aligned with contemporary self-care management theories. Option A might not provide reliable information; Option B could overwhelm him without context; Option D does not consider John's unique situation or preferences, which are crucial for effective self-management.

Question 19: Correct Answer: A) Ensuring eligibility for Medicaid waiver programs.

Rationale: Medicaid waiver programs are crucial in funding group home services, making it vital for case managers to ensure residents meet eligibility criteria. Option B is incorrect as private insurance may not cover all aspects of group home care. Option C is misleading; relying on out-of-pocket payments can limit accessibility and affordability for residents. Option D is incorrect because Medicare Part A primarily covers hospital and inpatient services, not typically applicable to group homes.

Question 20: Correct Answer: B) Comprehensive data analysis

Rationale: Comprehensive data analysis is vital for continuous quality improvement as it allows for the identification of trends, inefficiencies, and areas needing enhancement. While regular staff training (A), increased patient throughput (C), and standardized communication protocols (D) contribute to overall efficiency and effectiveness, they do not provide the analytical insights necessary for targeted improvements. Option B stands out as it involves evaluating performance metrics to drive strategic enhancements in case management practices.

Question 21: Correct Answer: B) Patient-Centered Medical Home (PCMH)

Rationale: The Patient-Centered Medical Home (PCMH) model emphasizes coordinated, comprehensive care led by a primary care provider, focusing on improving health outcomes and reducing costs through team-based approaches. Unlike ACOs, which involve multiple providers sharing responsibility for patient populations, PCMH centers around individual patient care management. Bundled Payments focus on cost control for specific episodes of care rather than ongoing management. Fee-for-Service incentivizes volume over value, lacking the coordinated approach inherent in PCMH.

Question 22: Correct Answer: B) Use reflective listening techniques to acknowledge each member's perspective

Rationale: Reflective listening acknowledges individual perspectives, promoting understanding and resolution of conflicts. Encouraging free expression (A) can escalate tensions without structure. Focusing on root causes (C) may overlook emotional dynamics crucial for resolution. Strict turn-taking guidelines (D) might stifle spontaneous dialogue necessary for genuine communication. Reflective listening fosters empathy and collaboration by ensuring all voices are heard and understood in line with contemporary communication strategies.

Question 23: Correct Answer: B) Reduction in hospital readmissions

Rationale: The reduction in hospital readmissions is crucial as it directly impacts healthcare costs and patient outcomes, making it a primary benefit of telehealth programs. While initial setup and training costs (Options A and C) are important, they are one-time investments. Patient satisfaction (Option D), though significant, does not directly equate to financial savings or improved clinical outcomes like reduced readmissions do. Prioritizing reduced readmissions aligns with both cost reduction and enhanced patient care.

Question 24: Correct Answer: C) Facilitate communication between the healthcare team and Mr. Chen's family to discuss potential risks of delay and explore feasible options together.

Rationale: Option C is correct as it balances respect for cultural values with medical considerations by fostering open dialogue and collaborative decision-making. Option A may disregard cultural importance by focusing solely on medical urgency, potentially alienating the family. Option B lacks proactive engagement from the case manager, risking adverse outcomes due to lack of informed decision-making. Option D dismisses cultural values entirely, which could lead to non-compliance or dissatisfaction with care received.

Question 25: Correct Answer: B) Establishing a multidisciplinary team to manage patient care collaboratively

Rationale: The PCMH model emphasizes comprehensive, coordinated care delivered by a multidisciplinary team. Option B aligns with this by promoting collaborative management. While EHRs (Option A) support coordination, they don't inherently ensure collaborative care. Regular check-ups (Option C) may not address individual needs and can be inefficient. Telemedicine (Option D), while convenient, is just one tool among many in enhancing access and doesn't fully encompass the collaborative aspect crucial in PCMH.

Question 26: Correct Answer: B) Language proficiency and communication preferences

Rationale: Language proficiency and communication preferences are crucial as they directly impact a patient's ability to understand health information and instructions. While socioeconomic status (A), access to transportation (C), and family support (D) are important considerations, they do not directly influence the comprehension of health-related content as language does. Ensuring that communication is clear and culturally appropriate helps in developing an effective care plan tailored to the patient's needs, thereby enhancing health literacy.

Question 27: Correct Answer: C) Home health care

Rationale: Home health care effectively reduces hospital readmissions for chronic diseases by utilizing telehealth technology to monitor patients remotely and provide timely interventions. Unlike retail clinics and urgent care centers, which focus on acute conditions, home health care offers continuous monitoring and management. Skilled nursing facilities provide post-acute care but lack the home-based, patient-centered approach that telehealth in home health care offers. This integration allows for better adherence to treatment plans and early detection of complications.

Question 28: Correct Answer: B) It helps distribute healthcare costs across a larger group, reducing individual risk.

Rationale: Employer-sponsored health coverage effectively pools risks by distributing healthcare costs among a large group, thereby minimizing individual risk and stabilizing premiums. Option A is incorrect as network restrictions often apply. Option C is misleading since premiums may vary based on plan specifics. Option D incorrectly suggests tax benefits are exclusive to high-

income employees, whereas such benefits generally apply across income levels.

Question 29: Correct Answer: C) Facilitation

Rationale: Facilitation involves guiding group discussions to ensure equitable participation. Unlike norming or storming, which describe stages of group development, facilitation actively addresses imbalances in participation. Adjourning is related to group dissolution, not active engagement. By employing facilitation techniques, Sarah can encourage quieter members to contribute, fostering a more collaborative and inclusive environment.

Question 30: Correct Answer: C) Conduct a peer review to assess medical necessity for the extended stay

Rationale: Option C is correct because it involves evaluating the medical necessity of an extended stay through peer review, ensuring decisions are clinically justified. Option A risks patient safety by prioritizing cost over care needs. Option B lacks accountability without further assessment. Option D focuses on financial aspects rather than appropriate care delivery. The correct choice balances patient safety and resource use by relying on peer-reviewed assessments in line with contemporary utilization management practices.

Question 31: Correct Answer: B) Veterans Health Administration (VHA)

Rationale: The Veterans Health Administration (VHA) provides comprehensive healthcare benefits to veterans, particularly those with service-connected disabilities. Unlike TRICARE, which serves active-duty members and their families, or CHAMPVA, which covers dependents of disabled veterans, the VHA is specifically tailored to address the unique healthcare needs of veterans. The Armed Forces Retirement Home offers long-term care but not comprehensive healthcare services. Thus, VHA is uniquely positioned to cater to service-connected health issues among veterans.

Question 32: Correct Answer: C) Medicaid

Rationale: Medicaid is the primary payer for long-term care services in skilled nursing facilities for eligible individuals like Mr. Johnson. While Medicare Part A covers short-term stays post-hospitalization, it does not cover extended long-term care. Medicare Part B focuses on outpatient services and not long-term facility care. Private insurance can be costly and not accessible to all. Thus, Medicaid remains the most viable option due to its comprehensive coverage for long-term needs.

Question 33: Correct Answer: B) Demonstrating alignment with corporate goals

Rationale: Aligning the wellness program with corporate goals ensures strategic relevance and increases likelihood of continued support. While short-term engagement metrics (A) and cost savings from reduced absenteeism (D) are important, they may not guarantee long-term sustainability if not tied to broader organizational objectives. Anecdotal success stories (C), though compelling, lack quantitative evidence needed for strategic decisions. Thus, option B best supports sustained funding by linking wellness initiatives to overarching business priorities.

Question 34: Correct Answer: C) Model's sensitivity in identifying high-risk patients

Rationale: Jane should prioritize the model's sensitivity because it directly impacts the identification of high-risk patients, which is crucial for reducing readmissions. While integration with EHRs (Option B) and cost-effectiveness (Option D) are important, they do not directly affect the model's primary goal. Accuracy in predicting patient satisfaction scores (Option A) is unrelated to readmission risks. Sensitivity ensures that most high-risk patients are emotional support-seeking behavior.

Question 35: Correct Answer: B) Utilization Review

Rationale: Utilization review is crucial for ensuring that patients receive necessary and efficient care while controlling costs. It involves assessing the necessity and efficiency of healthcare services. Capitation (A) involves a fixed payment per patient, which doesn't directly address service appropriateness. Fee-for-service (C) can lead to unnecessary services and higher costs. Point of Service Plan (D) offers flexibility in choosing providers but doesn't inherently control cost or service necessity like utilization review does.

Question 36: Correct Answer: D) Self-efficacy

Rationale: Self-efficacy refers to an individual's belief in their capability to execute behaviors necessary for specific performance attainments. It directly influences motivation and behavior adoption more than perceived severity (A), susceptibility (B), or barriers (C), which are considerations that might influence decision-making but do not directly drive behavior. High self-efficacy enhances confidence in overcoming obstacles, thus promoting health behaviors. This makes it challenging as all factors are interrelated, but self-efficacy has a direct motivational impact according to contemporary research.

Question 37: Correct Answer: B) Encouraging John to explore his own reasons for change

Rationale: Motivational interviewing focuses on enhancing intrinsic motivation by helping clients explore their own reasons for change. Option B aligns with this principle, fostering self-motivation. Option A contradicts motivational interviewing's non-confrontational approach. Option C is directive rather than collaborative, while Option D may increase resistance by focusing on negatives rather than encouraging self-exploration.

Question 38: Correct Answer: A) Risk of hyperkalemia due to dual therapy

Rationale: The concurrent use of Lisinopril and Losartan, both affecting the renin-angiotensin-aldosterone system, increases the risk of hyperkalemia. While options B and C are potential concerns with these medications individually, the combination heightens the risk of elevated potassium levels more significantly. Option D is less relevant as dizziness is not a primary concern in this context. Hyperkalemia poses immediate risks requiring intervention.

Question 39: Correct Answer: C) SSI is need-based without regard to work history; SSDI requires sufficient work credits.

Rationale: The primary distinction between SSI and SSDI lies in their eligibility requirements; SSI is need-based, focusing on financial need without considering work history, making Option C correct. Option A incorrectly reverses the roles of work history in eligibility. Option B falsely attributes an age requirement to SSDI that does not exist. Option D misrepresents both programs by focusing on citizenship rather than the core difference in financial versus work credit requirements.

Question 40: Correct Answer: B) Emotion-focused coping

Rationale: Emotion-focused coping involves seeking social support to manage emotional responses to stressors, particularly relevant in chronic illness contexts. Problem-focused coping targets solving the issue causing stress, while avoidance coping involves evading the problem altogether. Active coping is a broader term encompassing both problem-solving and emotional regulation strategies. Emotion-focused coping specifically aligns with using social support to handle stress, distinguishing it from other strategies that do not prioritize

Question 41: Correct Answer: B) Ensuring adequate nutritional intake

Rationale: Ensuring adequate nutritional intake (Option B) is often critical in cases of physical neglect, as malnutrition can lead to severe health issues. While enhancing social support (Option A), facilitating healthcare access (Option C), and improving living conditions (Option D) are important, addressing nutrition directly impacts health outcomes. Malnutrition can exacerbate existing health problems, making it a priority in intervention strategies for neglected clients. This choice aligns with contemporary research emphasizing nutrition's role in elder care.

Question 42: Correct Answer: B) Ecological Systems Theory

Rationale: The Ecological Systems Theory, developed by Urie Bronfenbrenner, highlights the interaction between a person and their environment, emphasizing that they influence each other reciprocally. Unlike the Biopsychosocial Model (A), which integrates biological, psychological, and social factors but does not focus on reciprocal interaction, or Social Learning Theory (C), which centers on learning through observation, this theory considers broader environmental influences. The Health Belief Model (D) primarily addresses health behaviors based on individual perceptions rather than environmental interactions.

Question 43: Correct Answer: B) To ensure prompt medical treatment and wage replacement

Rationale: Workers Compensation aims to provide immediate medical care and replace lost wages for employees injured at work. Unlike punitive damages (Option A), it focuses on rehabilitation and economic stability rather than punishment. It does not determine liability (Option C), as it operates under a no-fault system. Furthermore, it specifically addresses workplace injuries (Option D), not all personal injury claims. This approach emphasizes swift recovery and financial security, crucial aspects of effective care delivery and reimbursement methods.

Question 44: Correct Answer: C) Biopsychosocial-Spiritual Model

Rationale: The Biopsychosocial-Spiritual Model integrates spiritual care with psychological and physical health, recognizing spirituality as a core component of holistic healing. Cognitive-Behavioral Therapy (A) and Psychoanalytic Theory (D) focus more on psychological aspects without explicit spiritual integration. Narrative Therapy (B) involves storytelling but does not inherently integrate spiritual care. The correct answer emphasizes a comprehensive approach that acknowledges the importance of spirituality in overall well-being, aligning with contemporary research on holistic health.

Question 45: Correct Answer: D) Wisconsin Card Sorting Test (WCST)

Rationale: The Wisconsin Card Sorting Test (WCST) is specifically designed to assess executive functions, such as problem-solving and cognitive flexibility, which are often affected by traumatic brain injuries. While the WAIS can evaluate general intelligence and cognitive ability, it does not focus on executive functioning as directly as the WCST. The BDI assesses depressive symptoms, and the MMPI evaluates personality structure and psychopathology, making them less suitable for this specific cognitive assessment.

Question 46: Correct Answer: C) Utilization of standardized assessment tools

Rationale: Utilizing standardized assessment tools is

crucial for effectively identifying and managing elder neglect as they provide objective criteria and consistency in evaluation. Regular home visits may help observe conditions but lack standardization. Comprehensive family interviews can provide insights but might be biased or incomplete. Community awareness programs increase general awareness but do not directly identify or manage specific cases. Standardized tools ensure a reliable and systematic approach, making them essential in this context.

Question 47: Correct Answer: C) Encourage Sarah to join a support group for individuals with similar conditions.
Rationale: Encouraging Sarah to join a support group is the most effective strategy as it provides emotional support from peers facing similar challenges, fostering a sense of community and understanding. While educational materials (A) and follow-up appointments (D) are important, they do not directly address the psychosocial aspect of relationship building. Family meetings (B) might help but may not be feasible if family support is lacking. Support groups specifically target relationship building through shared experiences and empathy.

Question 48: Correct Answer: B) Pre-tax salary deductions for premiums
Rationale: The primary tax advantage arises from pre-tax salary deductions for premiums, reducing taxable income for employees and payroll taxes for employers. Option A is incorrect as the ACA does not directly provide these tax advantages. Option C is misleading; employer contributions are generally not taxable income. Option D does not directly relate to federal tax advantages. Therefore, option B accurately identifies pre-tax deductions as the main factor contributing to tax benefits in employer-sponsored health coverage.

Question 49: Correct Answer: B) A portion of earnings will be excluded before affecting SSI benefits
Rationale: Under the SSI program's work incentives, a portion of an individual's earnings is excluded before calculating the reduction in benefits, encouraging work while maintaining some support. Option A is incorrect as not all earnings are deducted; exclusions apply. Option C is misleading since there's no fixed threshold like $1,000; exclusions are percentage-based. Option D confuses Medicaid with SSI rules; earnings impact both but through different mechanisms.

Question 50: Correct Answer: A) Research local fraternal organizations and provide contact information.
Rationale: Option A is correct because it directly addresses the client's interest in joining a fraternal organization by providing specific resources. Options B and D are more general approaches that do not specifically address the client's expressed interest in fraternal organizations. Option C, while potentially beneficial, shifts focus away from fraternal organizations to religious counseling, which may not align with the client's specific request.

Question 51: Correct Answer: A) Patient-Centered Medical Home (PCMH)
Rationale: The Patient-Centered Medical Home (PCMH) focuses on comprehensive, team-based care that is coordinated through primary care providers, making it ideal for managing patients with multiple chronic conditions. This model emphasizes accessibility, quality, and patient-centeredness. While ACOs also aim to improve coordination, they are more focused on population health management and financial accountability. The TCM is specific to transitions between care settings, and the CCM focuses on chronic disease

management without the primary care team emphasis seen in PCMH.

Question 52: Correct Answer: B) Setting up a durable power of attorney for finances
Rationale: A durable power of attorney for finances allows Mr. Thompson to designate a trusted individual to manage his financial affairs, protecting him from further exploitation. Option A could lead to more exploitation if the new family member is not trustworthy. Option C risks continued mismanagement due to vulnerability. Option D might not address immediate safety concerns. Thus, option B is the most effective preventive measure in this scenario.

Question 53: Correct Answer: B) The client's ability to perform any type of work
Rationale: While age and education (A), medical diagnosis (C), and duration of condition (D) are relevant, SSDI primarily assesses whether the client can engage in any substantial gainful activity (B). This focuses on functional capacity rather than just medical diagnosis or other factors. Thus, understanding the client's ability to perform any work is crucial for determining SSDI eligibility.

Question 54: Correct Answer: B) Enhancing patient safety and quality of care
Rationale: The Joint Commission's accreditation standards emphasize enhancing patient safety and quality of care, aligning with contemporary research on improving healthcare outcomes. While options A, C, and D are related to operational efficiency and service expansion, they do not directly address the core focus on patient safety and quality. The incorrect options are closely related to healthcare improvements but do not align with the primary goal of accreditation standards, which is ensuring high-quality patient care.

Question 55: Correct Answer: C) Excessive worry
Rationale: Excessive worry is a hallmark cognitive symptom of Generalized Anxiety Disorder (GAD). Unlike obsessive thoughts (A), which are characteristic of Obsessive-Compulsive Disorder (OCD), or intrusive memories and flashbacks (B and D), which are associated with Post-Traumatic Stress Disorder (PTSD), excessive worry pertains to persistent concerns about various aspects of life without specific triggers. This differentiation is crucial for accurate diagnosis and treatment planning within behavioral health contexts.

Question 56: Correct Answer: C) Environmental Manipulation
Rationale: Environmental Manipulation is the correct answer as it involves changing or controlling external factors to help clients manage stress. Narrative Therapy (A) focuses on storytelling, while Solution-Focused Brief Therapy (B) aims at finding solutions without altering the environment. Psychoeducation (D) provides information but does not directly alter environmental conditions. Environmental Manipulation specifically addresses modifying surroundings, distinguishing it from other strategies that focus more on internal or cognitive changes.

Question 57: Correct Answer: B) By providing opportunities for social interaction and emotional support
Rationale: Fraternal/religious organizations significantly contribute to psychosocial well-being by fostering environments that encourage social interaction and emotional support. Unlike options A and C, which emphasize exclusivity, option B highlights inclusivity, benefiting both members and non-members. Option D focuses on religious ceremonies, which may not directly address broader psychosocial needs. Therefore, option B

is most aligned with enhancing community well-being through inclusive support systems.

Question 58: Correct Answer: B) Type of services provided

Rationale: Reimbursement rates for alternative care sites are significantly influenced by the type of services provided, as different services carry different reimbursement levels based on complexity and resource utilization. While geographic location (A), patient satisfaction (C), and patient volume (D) can impact reimbursement indirectly, they do not have as direct an influence as the service type. Geographic factors may adjust rates slightly; satisfaction scores can affect incentives; and volume impacts overall revenue but not individual service reimbursement directly like option B does.

Question 59: Correct Answer: A) Setting up daily phone reminders for inhaler use

Rationale: Daily phone reminders serve as an immediate and consistent prompt for John, directly addressing forgetfulness and enhancing adherence. While involving family (Option B) can provide support, it may not be feasible or effective if they are unavailable. Weekly check-ins (Option C) offer periodic reinforcement but lack the immediacy needed for daily tasks. Education on benefits (Option D), though important, does not provide a tangible mechanism to combat forgetfulness like option A does.

Question 60: Correct Answer: B) Cognitive-behavioral therapy to modify thought patterns

Rationale: Cognitive-behavioral therapy (CBT) is recognized for effectively addressing the emotional needs of neglected children by modifying maladaptive thought patterns. Unlike punitive measures (A), which can exacerbate feelings of neglect, CBT (B) provides constructive coping strategies. Ignoring behavior (C) might worsen neglect issues, while medication (D), though sometimes necessary, does not address underlying cognitive-emotional processes as effectively as CBT.

Question 61: Correct Answer: C) Medication-Assisted Treatment (MAT)

Rationale: Medication-Assisted Treatment (MAT), which includes medications like methadone and buprenorphine, is recognized as the most effective method for reducing relapse rates in opioid use disorder. While CBT, Contingency Management, and Motivational Interviewing are beneficial psychosocial interventions, MAT directly addresses the physiological aspects of addiction by normalizing brain chemistry and blocking euphoric effects. The combination of medication with counseling and behavioral therapies enhances overall treatment efficacy, making MAT superior in managing opioid dependency compared to other standalone interventions.

Question 62: Correct Answer: A) Tailoring educational content to cultural preferences

Rationale: Tailoring educational content to cultural preferences is crucial because it respects and integrates the patient's cultural context, leading to improved understanding and retention of health information. Standardized pamphlets (B) lack personalization, while relying on family members (C) may introduce inaccuracies. Online resources (D), though useful, might not address specific cultural nuances. Culturally tailored content ensures relevance and engagement, promoting better health literacy outcomes among diverse populations.

Question 63: Correct Answer: B) Developing a personalized self-care plan with input from John's family

members.

Rationale: Involving family members in creating a personalized care plan (B) empowers John and ensures he has the necessary support system at home, addressing both practical and emotional needs. While follow-up appointments (A), written instructions (C), and professional home visits (D) are helpful, they might not fully engage John's immediate support network or tailor the care plan to his unique circumstances as effectively as involving family does.

Question 64: Correct Answer: C) Connect Emily with local employment resources and job training programs.

Rationale: Connecting Emily with employment resources addresses her job insecurity, a significant social determinant of health impacting her stress levels and financial instability. While A) offers budgeting help, it doesn't directly address job insecurity. B) targets stress but not its root cause. D) promotes general wellness but ignores the primary issue of employment stability, making C) the most comprehensive approach for improving her situation.

Question 65: Correct Answer: C) Establishing multidisciplinary team meetings for integrated care planning

Rationale: Multidisciplinary team meetings ensure comprehensive care by incorporating diverse expertise, crucial for managing complex cases with multiple conditions. While individualized plans (A), symptom management (B), and cost considerations (D) are essential, integrated planning through team collaboration addresses all aspects of a client's health holistically. This approach aligns with best practices in managing chronic illnesses, ensuring coordinated and efficient care delivery across different healthcare providers.

Question 66: Correct Answer: B) Actively modifying behavior

Rationale: The transition from Preparation to Action involves actively modifying behavior, which is distinct from merely gathering resources or expressing awareness (Preparation). Weighing pros and cons is typical of the Contemplation stage. Recognizing these transitions allows case managers to provide appropriate support and interventions tailored to each client's specific readiness level.

Question 67: Correct Answer: B) Coordinating care across providers to ensure comprehensive management

Rationale: Coordinating care across providers ensures comprehensive management, directly aligning with value-based care principles by improving outcomes and reducing unnecessary costs. Option A may lead to unnecessary visits, while C could increase costs without guaranteed outcome improvement. D focuses only on cost, neglecting quality, which contradicts value-based care's holistic approach.

Question 68: Correct Answer: D) Value-Based Purchasing

Rationale: Value-Based Purchasing aligns financial incentives with quality improvements by rewarding providers for delivering high-quality care. While Bundled Payments group services under a single payment, they do not directly link payments to quality improvements. HMOs focus on cost control through network restrictions rather than quality incentives. ACOs emphasize coordinated care but not explicitly aligning financial incentives with quality outcomes. Value-Based Purchasing uniquely integrates financial rewards with quality metrics, supporting contemporary principles of cost containment and improved healthcare delivery.

Question 69: Correct Answer: B) Medicaid

Rationale: Medicaid is a joint federal and state program that provides healthcare coverage to eligible low-income individuals and families. While Medicare also offers health coverage, it primarily serves those aged 65 and older or with certain disabilities. CHIP targets children in families with incomes too high for Medicaid but too low for private insurance. SNAP provides nutritional assistance, not healthcare. Therefore, Medicaid is the correct answer as it directly addresses healthcare for low-income populations.

Question 70: Correct Answer: B) Customization options for low-sodium meals

Rationale: Customization options for low-sodium meals are crucial for clients with chronic kidney disease, as sodium intake must be carefully managed. While cost-effectiveness (Option A) is important, it does not directly address dietary needs. Organic ingredients (Option C) might be beneficial but are not specific to kidney disease management. Delivery frequency and timing (Option D) are logistical concerns but secondary to dietary customization. Therefore, Option B is the most relevant choice.

Question 71: Correct Answer: B) Enhancing medication adherence by alleviating financial barriers

Rationale: Integrating Pharmacy Assistance Programs into community health initiatives primarily enhances medication adherence by removing financial obstacles, crucial for low-income populations. Option A is incorrect as oversight isn't directly related to PAPs. Option C focuses on provider convenience rather than patient benefit. Option D misinterprets the purpose of PAPs, which aim to assist patients, not profit companies. Therefore, option B correctly identifies the primary benefit concerning patient outcomes and adherence.

Question 72: Correct Answer: B) Demonstrating empathy and active listening

Rationale: Empathy and active listening are foundational for establishing trust and rapport in a therapeutic alliance. This approach fosters open communication and understanding. Option A can support education but lacks relational depth. Option C may create distance rather than connection. Option D might hinder exploration by prematurely focusing on solutions without understanding the client's perspective fully. Thus, B is crucial for creating a supportive environment conducive to effective counseling.

Question 73: Correct Answer: C) Assess eligibility for Medicare Advantage plans

Rationale: Assessing eligibility for Medicare Advantage plans (Option C) is optimal as these plans often offer extended benefits beyond standard Medicare, potentially covering more home health services. Community programs (Option A) and co-pay assistance (Option B) can supplement but not replace insurance benefits. Suggesting borrowing from family (Option D) may impose financial stress without providing sustainable solutions. Medicare Advantage offers structured support aligned with healthcare needs and financial constraints.

Question 74: Correct Answer: C) Educate him on recognizing early signs of CHF exacerbation and when to seek help.

Rationale: Educating John on recognizing early signs of CHF exacerbation is crucial as it empowers him to seek timely intervention, reducing the risk of readmission. While scheduling follow-ups (A), arranging home health services (B), and ensuring medication supply (D) are important, patient education directly addresses self-management and prevention, which are key in chronic illness management. This approach aligns with

contemporary research emphasizing patient empowerment in chronic disease management.

Question 75: Correct Answer: B) Enhanced provider accountability for patient outcomes

Rationale: Bundled payments enhance provider accountability by covering all services within an episode of care, promoting coordination and efficiency. Unlike traditional Fee-for-Service, which bills separately and may fragment care, bundled payments encourage comprehensive management. Although it increases provider risk rather than patients', it reduces administrative complexity by streamlining billing processes. Therefore, the primary advantage is improved accountability and care integration.

Question 76: Correct Answer: B) Access to comprehensive health education

Rationale: Access to comprehensive health education is crucial for enabling individuals to understand their condition and make informed decisions, a key component of successful self-directed care. While financial resources (A), family support (C), and regular monitoring (D) are beneficial, they do not directly equip individuals with the knowledge needed for effective self-management. Education empowers clients by enhancing their ability to navigate healthcare options and maintain their well-being independently, aligning with theories on patient empowerment and chronic disease management.

Question 77: Correct Answer: A) Active Listening

Rationale: Active listening is fundamental in pastoral counseling as it fosters understanding, empathy, and trust between the counselor and client. Directive Counseling (B) can be less effective in exploring personal beliefs. Solution-Focused Brief Therapy (C) focuses on solutions rather than underlying issues, while Cognitive Restructuring (D) targets thought patterns without emphasizing empathetic communication. Active listening allows counselors to connect deeply with clients' spiritual and emotional needs, making it essential for effective pastoral counseling.

Question 78: Correct Answer: B) Report the suspected abuse to Adult Protective Services (APS).

Rationale: Reporting to APS is crucial as it initiates an official investigation, ensuring Mrs. Thompson's safety. Confronting the son (A) may escalate the situation, while merely documenting (C) delays intervention. Discussing concerns privately (D) can help but does not replace mandatory reporting protocols aimed at immediate protection.

Question 79: Correct Answer: C) Retired military personnel must enroll in Medicare Part B to maintain eligibility for TRICARE For Life.

Rationale: Retired military personnel must enroll in Medicare Part B to remain eligible for TRICARE For Life, which acts as a secondary payer to Medicare. This requirement ensures comprehensive coverage. Option A is incorrect as TRICARE Prime is not restricted by proximity to a facility. Option B is misleading because automatic eligibility varies by plan type, while Option D incorrectly states a condition that doesn't apply to TRICARE Standard.

Question 80: Correct Answer: A) Installing home monitoring systems

Rationale: Installing home monitoring systems balances autonomy and safety by allowing older adults to live independently while ensuring their well-being through remote monitoring. While community exercise programs (B) promote physical health, they do not directly address safety. Transportation services (C) facilitate access to healthcare but do not enhance daily autonomy.

Medication management programs (D), although crucial for health, do not encompass the broader aspects of autonomy and safety provided by home monitoring systems (A).

Question 81: Correct Answer: C) Explore Medicaid eligibility for additional coverage

Rationale: Exploring Medicaid eligibility (Option C) is crucial as it may provide comprehensive coverage for outpatient services, minimizing out-of-pocket expenses. While negotiating a payment plan (Option A) and applying for grants (Option B) are helpful, they do not guarantee long-term coverage. Recommending the use of savings (Option D) should be a last resort due to financial strain. Medicaid offers broader and more sustainable support compared to other options.

Question 82: Correct Answer: C) Readmission rates

Rationale: Readmission rates are a critical quality indicator as they directly reflect the effectiveness of case management in ensuring continuity of care and preventing unnecessary hospitalizations. While patient satisfaction scores (A) and cost per patient (D) provide insights into service quality and financial efficiency, they do not specifically measure clinical outcomes. Length of stay reduction (B), although important, may not necessarily indicate successful intervention if patients are readmitted. Thus, readmission rates are a more direct measure of intervention success.

Question 83: Correct Answer: A) Ensuring that all medical records reflect Alex's preferred name and gender identity

Rationale: Ensuring that medical records accurately reflect Alex's preferred name and gender identity is crucial for respecting his gender identity and promoting a supportive healthcare environment. Option B, focusing solely on medical procedures, neglects the holistic approach needed. Option C undervalues the importance of integrating both mental and physical health. Option D may not always align with Alex's preferences or privacy rights. The correct choice emphasizes respect for identity across all interactions.

Question 84: Correct Answer: B) Socio-Ecological Model

Rationale: The Socio-Ecological Model asserts that behavior is influenced by multiple levels including personal, interpersonal, organizational, community, and policy levels. This comprehensive approach contrasts with the Transactional Model of Stress and Coping (A), which focuses on stress management processes; Cognitive Behavioral Therapy (C), which targets individual cognitive processes; and the Transtheoretical Model (D), which stages behavioral change without explicitly addressing multi-level influences. This model encourages case managers to consider diverse factors affecting client behavior.

Question 85: Correct Answer: B) Schedule daily visits from a registered nurse for medication management.

Rationale: Daily visits from a registered nurse for medication management are crucial in managing chronic heart failure at home, ensuring adherence to prescribed treatments and monitoring potential complications. While physical therapy (A) and telehealth (C) are beneficial, they do not directly address the immediate need for medication management. A home health aide (D) assists with daily activities but lacks the clinical expertise needed for managing complex medication regimens crucial in John's case.

Question 86: Correct Answer: C) Utilizing a comprehensive geriatric assessment to tailor interventions

Rationale: A comprehensive geriatric assessment (CGA) is crucial as it evaluates medical, psychosocial, and functional capabilities, allowing for personalized care plans that address the unique needs of older adults. Option A overlooks individual differences, B increases risks associated with polypharmacy, and D neglects chronic management. The CGA approach is supported by contemporary research emphasizing individualized care for optimal outcomes in older populations.

Question 87: Correct Answer: A) The cost-effectiveness of home care versus hospitalization

Rationale: Private benefit programs prioritize reimbursement decisions based on the cost-effectiveness of home care compared to hospitalization. This approach aligns with contemporary healthcare strategies focused on reducing costs while maintaining quality care. While service frequency (B), past hospitalizations (C), and geographic location (D) may impact reimbursement considerations, they do not carry as much weight as demonstrating overall cost savings through effective home care management. Understanding this prioritization aids case managers in navigating reimbursement processes effectively.

Question 88: Correct Answer: B) Offering spiritual counseling and guidance

Rationale: Religious organizations often offer spiritual counseling and guidance (Option B), which aligns directly with addressing spiritual well-being. Educational workshops on health management (Option A), recreational activities (Option C), and peer support groups (Option D) can contribute to overall well-being but do not specifically target spiritual needs. Spiritual counseling provides personalized support that helps individuals like Tom find meaning and comfort during challenging times, making it the most effective role in enhancing his spiritual well-being post-surgery.

Question 89: Correct Answer: A) Cognitive-behavioral therapy (CBT)

Rationale: CBT is effective in helping individuals reframe negative thought patterns and develop coping strategies. While group therapy (B) and family counseling (C) offer support, they may not directly address John's personal stressors. Medication management (D) focuses on physical symptoms rather than psychosocial aspects.

Question 90: Correct Answer: B) Reflective listening to show empathy and understanding

Rationale: Reflective listening is crucial for building rapport and understanding the patient's feelings, fostering trust, and encouraging open communication. Unlike direct questioning (A) or closed-ended questions (D), which may limit responses, reflective listening helps in exploring underlying issues. A confrontational approach (C) can increase anxiety, hindering effective communication. Thus, reflective listening aligns with contemporary theories on patient-centered care by promoting empathy and understanding.

Question 91: Correct Answer: C) Use TRICARE as primary insurance and VHA as secondary insurance.

Rationale: TRICARE serves as a comprehensive health program for military personnel, retirees, and their families, often providing more extensive coverage than VHA alone. By using TRICARE as primary and VHA as secondary, John can maximize his benefits and reduce out-of-pocket costs. Option A is incorrect because VHA can provide comprehensive care but might not cover everything that TRICARE does. Options B and D are incorrect because they do not utilize the full extent of coverage available through both programs.

Question 92: Correct Answer: B) In-Home Personal Care Services

Rationale: In-Home Personal Care Services provide assistance with daily activities while allowing Mrs. Thompson to remain in her home, thus promoting independence. Adult Day Care Services (Option A) offer socialization but do not address daily living needs comprehensively. An Assisted Living Facility (Option C) or Nursing Home Placement (Option D) might be considered too restrictive given her current level of impairment. The focus is on maintaining independence and safety in the least restrictive environment.

Question 93: Correct Answer: A) Gender Role Socialization

Rationale: Gender Role Socialization involves internalizing societal norms and expectations regarding gender roles, differentiating it from Gender Dysphoria, which pertains to distress due to incongruence between experienced and assigned gender. Gender Fluidity describes a flexible range of gender expressions, while Gender Constancy refers to understanding that one's gender remains consistent over time. The key distinction lies in socialization's focus on societal influence versus personal experience or cognitive understanding.

Question 94: Correct Answer: B) The patient's current health status and care needs

Rationale: Prioritizing the patient's current health status and care needs aligns with utilization management principles by ensuring that care decisions are patient-centered and clinically appropriate. Option A focuses on financial aspects rather than clinical needs. Option C considers resource availability but may not address specific patient requirements. Option D relies on generalized data that may not reflect individual patient circumstances. Evaluating health status ensures that decisions are tailored to the patient's unique situation, optimizing outcomes and resource use.

Question 95: Correct Answer: C) Accountable Care Organizations (ACOs)

Rationale: ACOs align well with reducing unnecessary readmissions by fostering coordinated care among providers, sharing savings from reduced costs. Pay-for-Performance incentivizes individual metrics, which may not directly address readmissions; DRGs focus on payment based on diagnosis rather than outcomes; Retrospective Cost-Based Reimbursement reimburses actual costs without promoting proactive management to prevent readmissions. Thus, ACOs provide a holistic approach to improving case management and reducing readmissions.

Question 96: Correct Answer: B) Health Maintenance Organization (HMO)

Rationale: HMOs emphasize preventive care and require members to use a network of providers, focusing on coordinated care. Option B is correct as it aligns with these principles. Option A lacks emphasis on prevention and coordination, being more transactional. Option C offers more flexibility and less coordination compared to HMOs. Option D combines elements of HMO and PPO but does not primarily focus on prevention like HMOs do. Therefore, B accurately represents the focus of HMOs within managed care systems.

Question 97: Correct Answer: C) Mental filtering

Rationale: Mental filtering involves focusing on negative aspects while ignoring positive ones, leading to a skewed perception of events. Catastrophizing (A) involves imagining the worst-case scenario. Overgeneralization (B) refers to making broad conclusions based on limited evidence. Personalization (D) is attributing personal responsibility for events outside one's control. Recognizing mental filtering aids case managers in

developing effective cognitive-behavioral interventions.

Question 98: Correct Answer: A) Enroll him in a diabetes management program with peer counseling sessions.

Rationale: Option A integrates physical health management through structured diabetes education and behavioral support via peer counseling, addressing both aspects of John's challenges effectively. Option B emphasizes medical oversight but lacks psychological support. Option C offers information without active engagement or emotional assistance. Option D promotes self-management without providing necessary guidance or addressing anxiety, which may lead to suboptimal outcomes.

Question 99: Correct Answer: B) Organizing monthly mindfulness and meditation workshops

Rationale: Mindfulness and meditation workshops directly target stress reduction and mental health improvement, making them the most effective strategy in this context. While physical fitness (Option A) and nutritional counseling (Option C) can indirectly benefit mental health, they primarily focus on physical wellness. Financial planning seminars (Option D), although beneficial for reducing financial stress, do not directly address mental health or stress reduction like mindfulness practices do.

Question 100: Correct Answer: B) Facilitating peer support groups and community connections

Rationale: Facilitating peer support groups and community connections is crucial as it directly addresses the psychosocial needs of individuals, offering emotional support and reducing feelings of isolation. While options A, C, and D are important functions, they do not specifically target the psychosocial aspect. Financial assistance (A) and educational materials (D) provide practical support, while clinical research (C) focuses on scientific advancement. Peer support uniquely fosters a sense of belonging and shared experience essential for psychosocial well-being.

Question 101: Correct Answer: B) Use remote patient monitoring devices to track vital signs daily.

Rationale: Remote patient monitoring (RPM) allows continuous tracking of vital signs, crucial for managing chronic heart failure effectively. Unlike monthly telehealth visits (Option A), RPM provides real-time data, enabling timely interventions. Online forums (Option C) offer support but lack clinical oversight, and weekly phone calls (Option D) do not provide objective data like RPM does. Thus, RPM is superior in ensuring comprehensive management and timely response to changes in the patient's condition.

Question 102: Correct Answer: B) To provide public reporting of hospital performance data

Rationale: The Inpatient Quality Reporting (IQR) Program aims to enhance transparency by publicly reporting hospital performance data, encouraging improvements in healthcare quality. While reducing infections and readmissions are important, they are not the primary focus of IQR; those are targeted by specific programs like HRRP. Option D pertains to EHR Incentive Programs. By emphasizing public reporting, IQR fosters accountability and drives hospitals to enhance care standards based on reported outcomes.

Question 103: Correct Answer: A) Establishing clear communication channels

Rationale: Establishing clear communication channels is essential for effective collaboration in an interdisciplinary team. It ensures that all team members are informed, aligned with the patient's goals, and can contribute their expertise effectively. Option B is incorrect as task assignment should be based on expertise rather than hierarchy. Option C overlooks comprehensive care by focusing only on cost-effectiveness. Option D is important but does not encompass the broader need for cohesive team communication.

Question 104: Correct Answer: A) The importance of documenting incidents for legal purposes.

Rationale: Documenting incidents is crucial for substantiating claims if legal action becomes necessary, ensuring Jordan's rights are protected. While Option B addresses potential repercussions, it does not empower Jordan legally or emotionally. Option C may not be effective if discrimination persists despite informal efforts. Option D undermines the seriousness of discrimination and may perpetuate harm. Thorough documentation supports accountability and can facilitate formal resolutions, making it the most strategic advice Maria can provide.

Question 105: Correct Answer: A) Assigning a case manager to coordinate all services

Rationale: Assigning a case manager ensures continuity by providing personalized oversight and coordination across various services, which is essential for complex elderly patient needs. B and D focus on information transfer but lack proactive management. C addresses specific care aspects but does not encompass overall service integration. Case managers facilitate comprehensive care plans tailored to individual patient requirements, bridging gaps between healthcare settings effectively.

Question 106: Correct Answer: C) The caregiver makes large withdrawals from the client's account without clear justification.

Rationale: Option C is correct because unexplained large withdrawals are a hallmark of financial exploitation, where funds are taken without consent or benefit to the client. Option A could be seen as sharing resources, while B might be for ease in managing finances, though it can also be risky. Option D indicates supportive behavior with transparency, which is not exploitative. Each incorrect option lacks the clear signs of unauthorized or unjustified financial activity present in Option C.

Question 107: Correct Answer: A) Telehealth services

Rationale: Telehealth services are optimal for managing chronic conditions like heart failure, especially in rural areas where access to healthcare facilities is limited. They allow for frequent monitoring and medication adjustments without requiring travel. While home health visits (C) offer personalized care, they may not provide the frequency or immediacy needed. Urgent care centers (B) and community health clinics (D) are not designed for ongoing management of chronic conditions and focus more on acute issues.

Question 108: Correct Answer: B) The individual must be aged 65 or older, blind, or disabled with limited income and resources.

Rationale: Option B is correct because SSI benefits are designed for individuals who are aged, blind, or disabled with limited income and resources. Option A is incorrect as work history is not required for SSI but for Social Security Disability Insurance (SSDI). Option C is incorrect because the disability must last at least one year or result in death. Option D is incorrect as having dependents on SSI does not qualify an individual for SSI benefits.

Question 109: Correct Answer: C) Accountable Care Organization (ACO)

Rationale: Accountable Care Organizations (ACOs) involve healthcare providers sharing responsibility for the quality and cost of care, often including risk-sharing with payers. While Integrated Delivery Systems (IDSs) also aim for coordinated care, they do not necessarily include shared financial risk. Patient-Centered Medical Homes focus on comprehensive primary care rather than financial models. Health Maintenance Organizations emphasize pre-paid health plans but are not structured around shared responsibility for cost and quality in the same way ACOs are.

Question 110: Correct Answer: C) Providing telephonic follow-up within 48 hours post-discharge

Rationale: Telephonic follow-up within 48 hours post-discharge is crucial as it allows for immediate identification and resolution of potential issues, thus reducing readmissions. While A and B are important, they do not offer the immediacy and continuous engagement that telephonic follow-ups provide. D, although beneficial, lacks the personalized attention that telephonic follow-ups can achieve. Research supports that early post-discharge contact is key to successful transitions.

Question 111: Correct Answer: A) The policyholder's current health status and life expectancy.

Rationale: The valuation of a viatical settlement primarily hinges on the policyholder's health status and expected lifespan, as shorter life expectancies increase settlement value. Option B is incorrect as premiums paid do not directly affect valuation; C is incorrect because beneficiaries do not impact valuation; D is incorrect as age at purchase does not directly influence current settlement value compared to health status and expectancy.

Question 112: Correct Answer: B) Verifying that each service provided is supported by clinical guidelines

Rationale: Option B is correct as utilization management emphasizes aligning services with evidence-based clinical guidelines to ensure appropriate and necessary care. Option A could lead to unnecessary testing, which contradicts efficient resource use. Option C may result in unnecessary hospital stays without clinical justification. Option D focuses only on cost, neglecting quality and necessity of care. The key difference lies in balancing quality care with cost-efficiency through adherence to clinical guidelines.

Question 113: Correct Answer: B) Conducting a thorough interview with the patient about their current medication regimen

Rationale: Conducting a thorough interview with the patient is crucial as it provides real-time, firsthand information about all medications, including over-the-counter drugs and supplements. While EHRs, pharmacy records, and consultations with physicians are valuable, they might not reflect recent changes or non-prescription medications. Interviews help uncover discrepancies that could lead to adverse drug events. This step is essential in capturing comprehensive and accurate medication information directly from the patient.

Question 114: Correct Answer: B) Assess Maria's home environment for safety modifications

Rationale: Assessing the home environment is vital to ensure it supports Maria's recovery and independence post-rehabilitation. Although developing team schedules (A), monitoring progress (C), and facilitating family meetings (D) are integral parts of case management, ensuring safety modifications directly impacts her ability to function independently at home, which is crucial after a stroke.

Question 115: Correct Answer: C) They facilitate interfaith dialogues and collaborative initiatives

Rationale: Fraternal/religious organizations enhance community resources by fostering interfaith dialogues and collaborative initiatives, promoting understanding among diverse groups. This differs from specialized medical training (A), which is not their primary role. Cultural competence workshops (B) might occur but are less common. Direct healthcare services (D) are typically outside their main activities. Their strength lies in building bridges across communities, enhancing cooperation, and supporting case managers in navigating diverse cultural landscapes effectively.

Question 116: Correct Answer: B) Home Health Care
Rationale: Home Health Care is the most appropriate option for John as it allows for continuous monitoring and management of his chronic heart failure in the comfort of his home. Skilled Nursing Facilities are more suitable for patients requiring intensive rehabilitation or nursing care, while Assisted Living Facilities cater to those needing minimal assistance with daily activities. Adult Day Care Centers provide social and health services during the day but lack continuous medical monitoring. Home Health Care ensures personalized care tailored to John's specific health needs.

Question 117: Correct Answer: B) Actively listening and showing empathy towards the client's concerns
Rationale: Actively listening and showing empathy are crucial for establishing trust, as they demonstrate genuine interest and understanding, fostering a strong client-manager relationship. Option A focuses on information sharing, which is important but secondary to building rapport. Option C may hinder connection by creating distance. Option D might rush problem-solving without fully understanding the client's needs, potentially undermining trust. Active listening and empathy align with contemporary research emphasizing their foundational role in relationship building.

Question 118: Correct Answer: C) Diagnosis-Related Group (DRG) assignment
Rationale: The correct answer is C) Diagnosis-Related Group (DRG) assignment because DRGs are the basis for payment under Medicare's PPS. They categorize hospitalization costs and determine how much Medicare pays for a patient's hospital stay. While LOS and severity of illness are important, they do not directly impact reimbursement under PPS as DRG does. Patient satisfaction scores affect quality metrics but not directly PPS reimbursement. Thus, focusing on accurate DRG assignment ensures appropriate payment reflecting the resources used.

Question 119: Correct Answer: C) Improving child health outcomes by involving families in decision-making
Rationale: Family-centered care involves families in the healthcare process, leading to improved child health outcomes through shared decision-making and tailored interventions. Option A focuses on adherence but lacks family involvement. Option B inaccurately suggests increased costs without considering long-term benefits. Option D reduces collaboration opportunities essential for comprehensive care. Family involvement ensures that care plans align with the child's needs and family dynamics, promoting better adherence and satisfaction.

Question 120: Correct Answer: B) Mini-Mental State Examination (MMSE)
Rationale: The MMSE is a widely used tool for screening cognitive impairment, making it suitable for assessing mild cognitive impairment in John's case. Option A, BDI, assesses depression rather than cognitive function. Option C, WAIS, measures intelligence and is not specific for mild cognitive impairment. Option D, WCST, evaluates executive function but does not provide a comprehensive assessment of overall cognitive status like the MMSE.

Question 121: Correct Answer: C) Evidence-based practice implementation
Rationale: Evaluating case management effectiveness critically involves implementing evidence-based practices, which ensures that care decisions are grounded in the best available research. While patient satisfaction (A), cost reduction (B), and length of stay (D) are important metrics, they do not directly assess the application of evidence-based methodologies. These incorrect options focus on outcomes or efficiency rather than the foundational process that evidence-based practice provides in achieving high-quality care.

Question 122: Correct Answer: B) The facility's ability to provide personalized care plans
Rationale: Personalized care plans are crucial in assisted living for clients with mild cognitive impairment, as they ensure tailored support that addresses specific needs. While 24-hour skilled nursing (Option A) is more relevant for nursing homes, proximity to hospitals (Option C) and advanced monitoring (Option D) are beneficial but not as critical as personalized care, which directly impacts daily quality of life and adaptation to the environment.

Question 123: Correct Answer: B) Coordinating home health services to support her recovery
Rationale: Coordinating home health services provides necessary medical support at a lower cost than hospital readmissions or frequent office visits, aligning with cost containment principles by reducing unnecessary healthcare utilization. Option A increases healthcare costs without substantial benefit unless clinically indicated; C risks inadequate care leading to complications; D promotes costly hospital readmissions rather than preventive measures at home. Home health services balance quality care and cost efficiency by ensuring proper monitoring and intervention when needed.

Question 124: Correct Answer: B) Social support from family and friends
Rationale: Social support from family and friends significantly influences mental health outcomes for transgender individuals during transition. While access to hormone therapy (A), gender-affirming surgeries (C), and legal recognition (D) are important, the immediate psychosocial environment, particularly social support, has a profound impact on mental well-being. Supportive relationships can buffer stress and promote resilience, whereas lack of support can lead to increased anxiety and depression. Thus, social support is a critical factor in improving mental health outcomes.

Question 125: Correct Answer: B) She can earn up to a certain amount without affecting her SSDI benefits
Rationale: Under the SSDI program's Trial Work Period, beneficiaries like Maria can earn up to a specific threshold without affecting their benefits. This allows individuals to test their ability to work without immediate loss of income support. Option D is incorrect as it implies mandatory reporting before earning; while reporting is necessary, it doesn't preclude earning up to the threshold. Options A and C incorrectly suggest immediate or proportional reduction in benefits, which does not align with SSDI's provisions for trial work periods.

Question 126: Correct Answer: B) Facilitate regular group therapy sessions with others who have experienced similar losses
Rationale: Facilitating group therapy (Option B) is supported by contemporary theories emphasizing social support in processing grief. It provides a space for shared experiences and validation, crucial for healing. Option A is incorrect as avoidance can hinder emotional

processing. Option C, while useful for some, doesn't directly address the need for social support. Option D is beneficial but less effective alone compared to the communal aspect of group therapy.

Question 127: Correct Answer: A) Post-9/11 GI Bill
Rationale: The Post-9/11 GI Bill offers financial assistance for education and training to eligible veterans and their dependents, focusing on post-service educational advancement. While the Montgomery GI Bill also provides educational benefits, it is less comprehensive than the Post-9/11 GI Bill. VR&E focuses on employment rather than education alone, and DEA specifically targets survivors and dependents. The Post-9/11 GI Bill is distinguished by its broad coverage of tuition, housing, and other educational costs for eligible veterans.

Question 128: Correct Answer: C) Home Health Care
Rationale: Home Health Care is most effective for managing chronic conditions by providing integrated care coordination, which reduces hospital readmissions. It offers personalized care plans and regular monitoring in the patient's home, promoting continuity of care. Retail clinics and urgent care centers focus on acute, episodic care rather than chronic management. Telehealth services offer remote monitoring but may lack the hands-on approach needed for complex chronic conditions. The correct choice reflects comprehensive, patient-centered management strategies.

Question 129: Correct Answer: C) Bundled Payments
Rationale: Bundled Payments incentivize providers to deliver cost-efficient care by offering a single payment for all services related to a treatment episode. Unlike Fee-for-Service, which can lead to unnecessary services, and Capitation, which might compromise care quality due to fixed payments, Bundled Payments balance cost control with quality outcomes. Pay-for-Performance focuses on rewarding quality but lacks the comprehensive cost-control mechanism of Bundled Payments.

Question 130: Correct Answer: C) Social Loafing
Rationale: Social Loafing describes reduced individual effort in groups due to perceived diffusion of responsibility. Social Facilitation (A) refers to improved performance in presence of others. Groupthink (B) involves conformity pressures leading to poor decisions, and Deindividuation (D) is loss of self-awareness in groups. Unlike these, Social Loafing specifically addresses diminished personal accountability within group settings, making it distinct as the correct choice for explaining decreased effort levels among group members.

Question 131: Correct Answer: C) Conduct a comprehensive assessment of Mr. Thompson's financial situation
Rationale: Conducting a comprehensive assessment allows Sarah to understand Mr. Thompson's current financial state and identify any signs of financial abuse or mismanagement. This step is crucial before taking further actions like legal consultations or monitoring transactions. While establishing power of attorney (A) and opening joint accounts (B) are important, they should follow an assessment. Regular monitoring (D) is also beneficial but not the initial step without understanding the full picture.

Question 132: Correct Answer: B) Readmission rates within 30 days
Rationale: URAC emphasizes using readmission rates as a critical quality indicator because it directly reflects the effectiveness of care transitions and ongoing patient management. While patient satisfaction surveys (A), length of hospital stay (C), and number of patient complaints (D) are important, they do not directly measure the continuity and efficacy of care like readmission rates do. Readmissions indicate potential gaps in care or discharge planning, making them a vital metric for evaluating case management quality.

Question 133: Correct Answer: A) Ensures that all group members have an equal opportunity to participate
Rationale: The "gatekeeper" role is crucial in maintaining balanced participation within a group, ensuring everyone has a voice. Unlike option B, which describes a dominator, or C, which refers to a contributor of expertise, or D, which is more aligned with an evaluator's role, the gatekeeper focuses on inclusivity. This role fosters effective communication and equitable interaction among members, supporting positive group dynamics by preventing monopolization of discussions.

Question 134: Correct Answer: C) The availability of individualized treatment plans
Rationale: Individualized treatment plans are crucial in addressing John's unique needs and ensuring effective recovery. While accreditation (B) ensures quality standards and is important, it doesn't guarantee personalized care. Distance (A) might affect family involvement but isn't as critical as tailored interventions. Recreational activities (D) support engagement but don't directly influence treatment efficacy. Prioritizing individualized care aligns with contemporary research emphasizing personalized approaches in residential settings.

Question 135: Correct Answer: C) Provides a fixed payment rate based on the average cost of care for similar patient groups
Rationale: The DRG system assigns a fixed payment rate for patient groups with similar clinical conditions, incentivizing efficient care delivery. Option A is incorrect as administrative costs can remain significant. Option B is misleading; while early discharge might occur, it's not the primary advantage. Option D is incorrect because DRGs standardize payments, not negotiate them.

Question 136: Correct Answer: C) Bundled Payment Model
Rationale: The Bundled Payment Model consolidates payments for multiple services during an episode of care, encouraging providers to coordinate and reduce unnecessary costs. Unlike the Fee-for-Service Model, which incentivizes volume over value, or the Capitation Model, which may risk under-service, bundled payments balance cost and quality. The Pay-for-Performance Model focuses on outcomes but doesn't directly manage episodic costs. Thus, for John's transition to rehabilitation, bundled payments ensure comprehensive care management.

Question 137: Correct Answer: C) Facilitating shared decision-making
Rationale: Facilitating shared decision-making enhances informed decision-making by actively involving clients in their care plans, promoting engagement and adherence. Providing comprehensive medical jargon can overwhelm clients, while encouraging passive listening limits their involvement. Imposing expert opinions may undermine clients' preferences and autonomy. Shared decision-making respects clients' values and preferences, leading to more personalized and effective care outcomes. This approach aligns with contemporary research emphasizing patient-centered care as a cornerstone of effective case management.

Question 138: Correct Answer: D) Facilitates timely access to resources
Rationale: The primary advantage of a case management

approach is facilitating timely access to necessary resources by coordinating among diverse service providers. This ensures that clients receive appropriate services without delay. While reducing costs (A), improving communication (B), and ensuring adherence (C) are benefits, they are secondary outcomes of effective coordination. Timely access directly impacts client well-being by addressing immediate needs through streamlined resource allocation and service delivery.

Question 139: Correct Answer: A) Medicaid Home and Community-Based Services (HCBS) Waiver
Rationale: The Medicaid HCBS Waiver allows states to provide services in a home or community setting for individuals who would otherwise require institutional care, addressing Mrs. Thompson's needs. Option B, Medicare Advantage Plan, typically does not cover extensive home-based services. Option C, Private Long-Term Care Insurance, requires prior purchase and may not be accessible. Option D, SSI, provides financial support but not specific healthcare services like the HCBS Waiver does.

Question 140: Correct Answer: B) Assist Jamie in finding a new provider known for LGBTQ+ inclusivity.
Rationale: Assisting Jamie in finding an inclusive provider ensures they receive respectful and knowledgeable care tailored to their identity. Option A risks continued discomfort without guaranteed change. Option C offers temporary support but doesn't address systemic bias. Option D places undue responsibility on Jamie rather than ensuring immediate access to competent care.

Question 141: Correct Answer: B) SF-36 Health Survey
Rationale: The SF-36 Health Survey is a comprehensive tool that assesses both physical and mental health domains, making it ideal for evaluating mobility limitations and psychological well-being. The Barthel Index focuses primarily on physical functioning related to daily activities. The Geriatric Depression Scale is specific to depression assessment, while the MMSE evaluates cognitive function. The SF-36's dual focus on physical and mental health makes it uniquely suited for holistic assessments in older adults.

Question 142: Correct Answer: C) Encouraging Sarah to join a peer support group for individuals with diabetes.
Rationale: Encouraging participation in peer support groups can significantly enhance adherence by providing emotional support and shared experiences, which are crucial in self-care management (C). While educational materials (A), daily check-ins (B), and nutritionist meetings (D) are beneficial, they may not address the psychosocial aspects as effectively as peer support groups do, which foster motivation and accountability through community interaction.

Question 143: Correct Answer: B) It enhances predictive accuracy for future healthcare needs
Rationale: The ACG system enhances predictive accuracy for future healthcare needs by analyzing comprehensive clinical data, allowing case managers to better allocate resources. While reducing costs (A) might be an indirect benefit, it is not the primary advantage. Focusing solely on acute care (C) would limit its scope, and eliminating EHRs (D) contradicts its reliance on detailed health information. The system's strength lies in its ability to forecast patient needs accurately through data analysis.

Question 144: Correct Answer: B) Develop a unified care plan incorporating both needs
Rationale:A unified care plan ensures that both physical and mental health needs are addressed concurrently, promoting integrated service delivery. Assigning separate case managers (A) could lead to fragmented care, while sequential treatments (C) may delay comprehensive recovery. Prioritizing one need over another (D) overlooks the interconnected nature of Ms. Smith's conditions. Research supports integrated planning as it facilitates holistic treatment and improved outcomes by considering all aspects of patient health simultaneously.

Question 145: Correct Answer: A) Age of the policyholder
Rationale: Age is a primary determinant in premium costs due to increased health risks associated with aging. While geographic location (B) and type of coverage (C) also affect premiums, they are secondary compared to age. Health status (D) can impact premiums but is often regulated to prevent discrimination, thus making age the most consistent factor across policies.

Question 146: Correct Answer: B) Regularly updating clinical guidelines based on recent research findings.
Rationale: Regularly updating clinical guidelines based on recent research ensures that care is evidence-based, aligning with accreditation standards focused on quality and outcomes evaluation. While adopting new technologies (A), increasing specialists (C), and expanding telehealth (D) are beneficial, they do not inherently guarantee evidence-based practice integration into daily operations as effectively as continuously updated clinical guidelines do, which directly reflect current best practices in patient care.

Question 147: Correct Answer: C) Assessing Sarah's social support network at home.
Rationale: Assessing Sarah's social support network is critical as it directly impacts her ability to adhere to the care plan and manage chronic conditions effectively. While understanding medication (A), scheduling follow-ups (B), and dietary guidelines (D) are important, they are secondary to the foundational support system that ensures these elements are actionable and sustainable. A strong support network can facilitate transportation, reminders, and emotional encouragement, which are essential for successful long-term management.

Question 148: Correct Answer: A) Client-centered care approach
Rationale: The client-centered care approach prioritizes the client's preferences and values, promoting autonomy by actively involving them in decision-making. This method ensures that care plans are tailored to individual needs, enhancing satisfaction and outcomes. While multidisciplinary team meetings (B) foster collaboration, they may not focus solely on client autonomy. Standardized care pathways (C) and evidence-based practice guidelines (D) provide structured frameworks but can limit personalized input, making A the superior choice for autonomy and individualized care.

Question 149: Correct Answer: B) Managing differing treatment philosophies
Rationale: Differing treatment philosophies between mental health and addiction services often pose significant challenges. Mental health services might focus on long-term therapy, while addiction services may prioritize immediate abstinence. This divergence can create barriers to cohesive care.

Question 150: Correct Answer: B) Predictive analytics models
Rationale: Predictive analytics models are most effective as they utilize large datasets and advanced algorithms to forecast future health risks, offering a proactive approach. Retrospective claims data (A) looks backward and may miss emerging risks. Patient self-reported surveys (C) can be subjective and less reliable. Routine clinical

assessments (D) provide current health status but lack predictive capability. Thus, predictive analytics models best integrate various data sources for comprehensive risk prediction.

CCM Exam Practice Questions [SET 4]

Question 1: Sarah, a case manager, is working with John, a 65-year-old patient with chronic heart failure. During their consultation, Sarah aims to implement shared decision-making to enhance John's self-care management. Which of the following actions best exemplifies shared decision-making in this context?
A) Sarah provides John with a detailed treatment plan and asks him to follow it strictly.
B) Sarah discusses various treatment options with John and helps him understand the potential outcomes of each.
C) Sarah encourages John to rely on her expertise and make decisions based on her recommendations.
D) Sarah gives John educational materials and schedules a follow-up visit for further discussion.

Question 2: Mark, a case manager, is tasked with selecting a residential treatment facility for Lisa, a patient with co-occurring mental health disorders and substance abuse issues. Which characteristic should Mark consider essential in choosing the right facility?
A) Facility's proximity to major hospitals
B) Integration of dual-diagnosis treatment programs
C) Availability of luxury amenities
D) High staff-to-patient ratio

Question 3: Which of the following psychosocial interventions is most effective in enhancing resilience among survivors of domestic abuse, according to contemporary research and theories?
A) Cognitive Behavioral Therapy (CBT)
B) Solution-Focused Brief Therapy (SFBT)
C) Motivational Interviewing (MI)
D) Narrative Therapy

Question 4: In bereavement counseling, which strategy is most aligned with Worden's tasks of mourning to help a client accept the reality of loss?
A) Encouraging denial until the client feels ready to face reality.
B) Facilitating rituals or activities that acknowledge the loss.
C) Advising immediate return to normalcy to distract from grief.
D) Promoting avoidance of places associated with the deceased.

Question 5: As a case manager, you are working with Mr. Thompson, a patient who is resistant to engaging in his care plan. To build a stronger relationship and encourage his participation, which approach should you prioritize?
A) Provide Mr. Thompson with detailed information about the benefits of the care plan.
B) Establish trust by actively listening to Mr. Thompson's concerns and validating his feelings.
C) Encourage Mr. Thompson to independently explore other care options available to him.
D) Focus on consistently reminding Mr. Thompson of the potential negative outcomes if he does not follow the care plan.

Question 6: Mrs. Garcia, a 72-year-old woman with chronic heart failure, is considering enrolling in a Medicare Advantage Plan instead of Original Medicare. She asks her case manager about potential differences in coverage. Which statement accurately describes a potential benefit of choosing a Medicare Advantage Plan?
A) Coverage of all prescription drugs without additional costs
B) Access to any healthcare provider nationwide without referrals
C) Additional benefits like vision and dental not typically covered by Original Medicare
D) Lower out-of-pocket costs guaranteed compared to Original Medicare

Question 7: Sarah, a 65-year-old patient with a history of depression and recent hip surgery, is being assessed for her discharge plan. As a case manager, you must consider both her physical functioning and behavioral health needs. Which of the following interventions is most appropriate to ensure comprehensive care for Sarah?
A) Arrange for home physical therapy and weekly psychiatric evaluations.
B) Schedule daily visits from a nurse to monitor medication adherence only.
C) Refer to a community support group for depression without physical therapy.
D) Coordinate with family members to manage her daily activities independently.

Question 8: Which coding methodology is primarily used for capturing the complexity of chronic conditions in case management, ensuring comprehensive care planning and reimbursement accuracy?
A) ICD-10-CM
B) CPT
C) DRG
D) SNOMED CT

Question 9: Sarah, a case manager, is handling a claim for a construction worker who was injured on the job. The worker's employer disputes the claim, arguing that the injury was due to a pre-existing condition. Which of the following actions should Sarah prioritize to ensure proper handling of this workers' compensation case?
A) Advise the worker to seek legal counsel immediately.
B) Gather comprehensive medical records and expert opinions.
C) Request an independent medical examination (IME).
D) Initiate mediation between the worker and employer.

Question 10: Sarah, a case manager, is assisting Tom, a veteran who recently separated from the military and now seeks mental health services. Tom is eligible for both VA benefits and TRICARE. Which of the following should Sarah advise Tom to prioritize using for accessing mental health services given his eligibility?
A) Use VA benefits exclusively
B) Use TRICARE exclusively
C) Use VA benefits as primary and TRICARE as secondary
D) Use TRICARE as primary and VA benefits as secondary

Question 11: In the context of case management, how does the transition from ICD-9 to ICD-10 impact the specificity and granularity of coding for healthcare services?
A) It reduces specificity by using fewer codes.
B) It increases specificity with more detailed codes.
C) It maintains the same level of specificity.
D) It simplifies coding by merging multiple conditions into single codes.

Question 12: Jane, a 65-year-old woman with chronic kidney disease, is learning to navigate her healthcare needs. As her case manager, you want to empower her to engage in self-advocacy effectively. Which of the following strategies would most effectively enhance Jane's self-advocacy skills?
A) Encourage Jane to research her condition independently.
B) Provide Jane with resources and coach her on asking informed questions during medical appointments.

C) Advise Jane to rely solely on healthcare professionals for decision-making.
D) Suggest Jane join a support group without further guidance.

Question 13: As a case manager, you are developing a care plan for John, a 45-year-old client with a spinal cord injury who is transitioning from hospital to home care. Which of the following strategies is most effective in ensuring continuity of care and reducing hospital readmissions?
A) Schedule weekly telehealth check-ins with John's primary care physician.
B) Arrange for daily home visits by a physical therapist.
C) Coordinate with a multidisciplinary team for comprehensive discharge planning.
D) Provide John with educational materials on managing his condition independently.

Question 14: Sarah is evaluating her options for individually purchased health insurance to ensure she has comprehensive maternity coverage. What aspect should Sarah prioritize when comparing plans?
A) The network of healthcare providers included in the plan
B) The deductible amount associated with maternity services
C) Whether maternity care is considered an essential health benefit
D) The co-payment required for prenatal visits

Question 15: In the scope of case management practice, which objective is crucial for integrating reimbursement methods with effective care delivery?
A) Enhancing patient autonomy by allowing unrestricted access to services.
B) Coordinating multidisciplinary teams to align treatment plans with reimbursement policies.
C) Prioritizing rapid discharge to optimize bed availability and reduce costs.
D) Implementing standardized treatment protocols to minimize variation in care delivery.

Question 16: How do fraternal/religious organizations primarily contribute to the psychosocial support of individuals in community settings?
A) By offering financial aid for medical expenses
B) By providing structured social networks and a sense of belonging
C) By delivering professional counseling services
D) By facilitating access to employment opportunities

Question 17: When managing polypharmacy in elderly patients, which strategy is most effective in reducing the risk of medication-related complications?
A) Prioritizing medications based on cost-effectiveness
B) Discontinuing medications that have not been prescribed by a specialist
C) Regularly reviewing all medications for necessity and potential interactions
D) Switching to generic medications to reduce financial burden

Question 18: Sarah, a 32-year-old woman with bipolar disorder and opioid addiction, is experiencing frequent mood swings and difficulty maintaining employment. As her case manager, which strategy should you prioritize to support her recovery?
A) Implement a harm reduction strategy focusing on opioid use only.
B) Encourage abstinence from opioids while stabilizing mood with mood stabilizers.
C) Utilize motivational interviewing to enhance readiness for change in both disorders.
D) Refer her to separate specialists for each disorder to ensure focused care.

Question 19: As a case manager, you are assisting Mrs. Patel in choosing an assisted living facility that aligns with her needs for personal independence while managing her chronic health conditions. Which feature of an assisted living facility is most essential in meeting Mrs. Patel's requirements?
A) On-site nursing staff available 24/7
B) Personalized meal planning services
C) Access to a fitness center with guided exercise programs
D) Regular transportation services for medical appointments

Question 20: In the context of case rate reimbursement, which factor is most crucial in determining the fixed payment amount for a specific case type?
A) Patient's length of stay
B) Average resource utilization for similar cases
C) Patient's demographic data
D) Hospital's location

Question 21: Mary, a 60-year-old patient diagnosed with chronic illness, is struggling with feelings of hopelessness and seeks meaning in her condition. As her case manager, how can pastoral counseling be most effectively integrated into her care?
A) Schedule regular sessions with a pastoral counselor to explore existential questions.
B) Recommend Mary attend group therapy sessions focusing on chronic illness management.
C) Advise Mary to join a meditation class to enhance mindfulness and stress relief.
D) Provide Mary with pamphlets on positive thinking techniques.

Question 22: When interpreting data for quality improvement in case management, which statistical method is most appropriate for identifying trends over time?
A) Cross-sectional analysis
B) Regression analysis
C) Chi-square test
D) Time series analysis

Question 23: As a case manager, you are overseeing the care of Mr. Johnson, a 65-year-old patient with multiple chronic conditions. To ensure a holistic approach in his care plan, which strategy should you prioritize to integrate services effectively?
A) Focus solely on coordinating medical appointments
B) Emphasize interdisciplinary team meetings involving all stakeholders
C) Concentrate on managing medication adherence
D) Prioritize financial counseling for medical expenses

Question 24: John, who suffered a severe spinal injury, is considering applying for long-term disability insurance benefits through his employer. As his case manager, you need to explain the key requirement he must meet to qualify for these benefits. Which of the following should you emphasize?
A) John's previous earnings history
B) John's inability to perform his specific job duties
C) John's inability to perform any occupation for which he is reasonably qualified
D) The cause of John's disability

Question 25: In the context of insurance principles, which concept allows an insurer to recover the amount paid on a claim from a third party responsible for causing the loss?
A) Contribution
B) Subrogation

C) Indemnity
D) Proximate Cause

Question 26: John, a 45-year-old freelance graphic designer, is considering purchasing an individual health insurance plan. He is concerned about coverage for pre-existing conditions. Which factor most likely influences the extent of coverage for his pre-existing conditions under individually purchased insurance?
A) The specific state regulations where John resides
B) The duration of John's previous insurance coverage
C) The type of plan John selects (e.g., HMO, PPO)
D) The premium amount John is willing to pay

Question 27: Sarah, a case manager, is working with a client recently diagnosed with multiple sclerosis (MS). She wants to connect her client to a disease-based organization that offers both educational resources and emotional support specifically for MS patients. Which of the following organizations should Sarah consider referring her client to?
A) American Diabetes Association
B) National Multiple Sclerosis Society
C) Alzheimer's Association
D) American Cancer Society

Question 28: John, a case manager, needs to evaluate the outcomes of a Medicaid-funded program aimed at reducing hospital readmissions. Which CMS tool should he use to effectively measure and report these outcomes?
A) Consumer Assessment of Healthcare Providers and Systems (CAHPS)
B) Outcome and Assessment Information Set (OASIS)
C) Medicare Advantage Star Ratings
D) Medicaid Adult Core Set

Question 29: During a case management meeting, you are tasked with verifying the procedural coding for Ms. Smith's recent outpatient surgery involving laparoscopic cholecystectomy. Which CPT code should be applied to accurately reflect this minimally invasive procedure?
A) 47562 - Laparoscopic cholecystectomy
B) 47600 - Open cholecystectomy
C) 49320 - Laparoscopy, surgical; abdomen, peritoneum, and omentum
D) 47563 - Laparoscopic cholecystectomy with cholangiography

Question 30: As a case manager, you are responsible for managing the care of Mr. Thompson, a 67-year-old patient with multiple chronic conditions. To ensure cost containment while maintaining quality care, which strategy would be most effective in coordinating his care?
A) Implementing a disease management program tailored to Mr. Thompson's conditions
B) Increasing the frequency of specialist visits to monitor his conditions
C) Encouraging Mr. Thompson to use emergency services for acute issues
D) Reducing the number of medications to minimize costs

Question 31: Sarah, a 65-year-old patient with limited mobility and dietary restrictions due to diabetes, is considering using a meal delivery service. As her case manager, what is the most crucial factor to consider when recommending a suitable service?
A) The variety of meal options available
B) The cost of the meal delivery service
C) The nutritional content tailored to her dietary needs
D) The delivery schedule flexibility

Question 32: Which healthcare provider is primarily responsible for coordinating a patient's comprehensive care plan, ensuring continuity of care across various practice settings?
A) Primary Care Physician
B) Nurse Practitioner
C) Case Manager
D) Social Worker

Question 33: Which of the following community resources is most effective for case managers when coordinating care for clients with chronic mental health conditions in urban settings?
A) Local food banks
B) Community mental health centers
C) Faith-based organizations
D) Recreational clubs

Question 34: Sarah is a case manager assisting Tom, an elderly patient with multiple chronic conditions. Tom has difficulty following his treatment plan due to low health literacy and cognitive decline. Which intervention should Sarah implement first to improve Tom's adherence to his treatment plan?
A) Simplify Tom's medication schedule using color-coded charts and pill organizers.
B) Refer Tom to a community support group for patients with similar conditions.
C) Schedule frequent check-in calls with Tom to remind him of his medications.
D) Provide Tom's family with detailed instructions for managing his care.

Question 35: Sarah, a case manager at a busy urban hospital, is tasked with evaluating the quality of care provided to diabetic patients over the past year. She has access to patient records, laboratory results, and follow-up visit data. Which of the following would be the most effective initial step in interpreting this data for quality improvement purposes?
A) Conduct a statistical analysis of lab results to identify trends.
B) Perform a root cause analysis on cases with poor outcomes.
C) Develop a dashboard summarizing key performance indicators.
D) Compare current data with national benchmarks for diabetes care.

Question 36: Sarah, a case manager, is working with an elderly client, Mr. Thompson, who lives alone and has recently been discharged from the hospital after hip surgery. He needs to attend regular physical therapy sessions but lacks personal transportation. Which community resource should Sarah prioritize to ensure Mr. Thompson's consistent attendance at his therapy appointments?
A) Volunteer driver programs
B) Public bus services
C) Taxi voucher systems
D) Non-emergency medical transportation (NEMT) services

Question 37: How do Diagnosis-Related Groups (DRGs) primarily influence hospital reimbursement under the prospective payment system?
A) By reimbursing hospitals based on the length of patient stay
B) By reimbursing hospitals based on the severity of patient illness
C) By reimbursing hospitals based on a predetermined fixed amount per case
D) By reimbursing hospitals based on actual costs incurred during treatment

Question 38: Which of the following principles of Motivational Interviewing focuses on recognizing and reinforcing the client's strengths and efforts towards change?
A) Expressing Empathy
B) Developing Discrepancy
C) Supporting Self-Efficacy
D) Rolling with Resistance

Question 39: Which of the following resources is most effective in providing comprehensive healthcare services to uninsured or underinsured individuals, particularly focusing on preventive care and chronic disease management?
A) Emergency Room Services
B) Community Health Centers
C) Retail Clinics
D) Urgent Care Centers

Question 40: When designing care plans for pediatric patients, which principle is essential to ensure age-appropriate interventions?
A) Applying adult-centric treatment protocols with minor adjustments
B) Integrating family-centered care principles throughout the treatment process
C) Emphasizing autonomy and decision-making similar to adult patients
D) Relying solely on standardized growth charts for developmental assessments

Question 41: In the context of managing financial abuse within psychosocial support systems, which of the following strategies is most effective for a case manager to implement when working with elderly clients who may be victims of financial exploitation?
A) Establishing a joint bank account with the client.
B) Collaborating with a multidisciplinary team to assess the client's financial situation.
C) Encouraging the client to make large cash withdrawals for safety.
D) Advising the client to change their will immediately.

Question 42: Which emotional response is most commonly observed in individuals who have experienced long-term emotional abuse, according to contemporary psychological theories?
A) Resilience and optimism
B) Anxiety and hyper-vigilance
C) Indifference and apathy
D) Increased self-esteem

Question 43: Emily, a case manager, is planning discharge options for Mrs. Lopez, who has stabilized after a severe bout of pneumonia but still requires respiratory therapy and close monitoring. Which alternative care site should Emily recommend to ensure continuity of care while minimizing hospital readmission risks?
A) Inpatient Rehabilitation Facility
B) Long-Term Acute Care Hospital
C) Skilled Nursing Facility
D) Home Health Care

Question 44: Which factor is crucial for a case manager to consider when selecting a pharmacy assistance program for a patient with chronic illness?
A) Geographic location of the pharmacy.
B) Duration of the program's benefits.
C) Formulary restrictions of the program.
D) Patient's previous usage of similar programs.

Question 45: John, a 60-year-old diabetic patient, lives alone and often misses medical appointments due to transportation issues and lack of motivation. What intervention should a case manager prioritize to improve his adherence to medical care?
A) Schedule weekly motivational interviewing sessions with John.
B) Set up a home visit program by healthcare professionals.
C) Connect John with a volunteer driver service for appointments.
D) Enroll John in a diabetes self-management education class.

Question 46: As a case manager, you are coordinating care for Sarah, a 65-year-old patient with chronic heart failure. She lives in a rural area with limited access to healthcare facilities. Which telehealth strategy would be most effective in managing her condition while considering cost-effectiveness and accessibility?
A) Regular in-person visits to the nearest urban hospital
B) Remote monitoring of vital signs and symptoms
C) Weekly phone consultations with her cardiologist
D) Monthly video conferencing with a multidisciplinary team

Question 47: Which program provides cash benefits to eligible disabled individuals with limited income and resources, ensuring they can meet basic needs for food, clothing, and shelter?
A) Social Security Disability Insurance (SSDI)
B) Supplemental Security Income (SSI)
C) Temporary Assistance for Needy Families (TANF)
D) Medicaid

Question 48: Which pastoral counseling intervention is most effective for enhancing coping mechanisms in patients experiencing chronic illness?
A) Encouraging participation in community worship services
B) Providing cognitive-behavioral therapy with a focus on religious texts
C) Facilitating group therapy sessions focused on shared faith experiences
D) Offering meditation techniques rooted in secular mindfulness practices

Question 49: In the context of Patient-centered Medical Home (PCMH), which principle primarily focuses on fostering a strong relationship between patients and their healthcare providers?
A) Enhanced access to care
B) Personal physician
C) Quality and safety improvement
D) Coordinated care

Question 50: John, a case manager, is assisting Maria, a single mother with two children, who recently lost her job. She is seeking public assistance to cover healthcare expenses. Which program should John prioritize to ensure Maria and her children receive comprehensive healthcare coverage?
A) Supplemental Nutrition Assistance Program (SNAP)
B) Temporary Assistance for Needy Families (TANF)
C) Medicaid
D) Children's Health Insurance Program (CHIP)

Question 51: Which of the following reimbursement models is designed to encourage collaboration among healthcare providers by offering a single payment for all services related to a treatment or condition over a specified period?
A) Fee-for-Service
B) Accountable Care Organizations (ACOs)
C) Bundled Payments
D) Capitation

Question 52: Maria, a case manager, is working with Ahmed, a client from a Middle Eastern background who is experiencing anxiety. Ahmed believes that his condition is due to spiritual imbalance and insists on traditional healing practices. How should Maria incorporate Ahmed's beliefs into his care plan while ensuring effective management of his anxiety?
A) Encourage Ahmed to solely rely on traditional healing practices and avoid conventional treatment.
B) Integrate traditional healing practices with evidence-based anxiety treatments as part of a holistic approach.
C) Suggest Ahmed prioritize conventional treatments over traditional practices to ensure efficacy.
D) Recommend Ahmed seek spiritual counseling exclusively for his anxiety management.

Question 53: Mr. Johnson, a 68-year-old retiree, is enrolled in Medicare Part A and Part B. He recently underwent a knee replacement surgery and is now being discharged from the hospital. As his case manager, you need to coordinate his post-acute care. Which of the following services will Medicare Part A cover for Mr. Johnson after his discharge?
A) Outpatient physical therapy sessions
B) Skilled nursing facility care for up to 20 days
C) Home health aide services for daily personal care
D) Durable medical equipment rental

Question 54: In an interview with Ms. Garcia, who has been non-compliant with her treatment plan, the case manager aims to explore underlying reasons for her behavior. Which technique is most effective for this purpose?
A) Offering advice based on professional experience
B) Motivational interviewing to explore ambivalence
C) Using authority to emphasize treatment importance
D) Focusing on past successes in treatment adherence

Question 55: Sarah, a case manager, is working with John, who recently lost his spouse. John exhibits signs of prolonged grief and struggles to resume daily activities. What is the most appropriate initial step for Sarah in providing bereavement counseling to John?
A) Encourage John to join a support group immediately.
B) Suggest John write a letter to his deceased spouse expressing unresolved feelings.
C) Assess John's readiness and willingness to engage in counseling sessions.
D) Refer John to a psychiatrist for medication evaluation.

Question 56: Emily is coordinating care for Mrs. Lee, a patient with cognitive impairment who needs weekly dialysis treatments. Mrs. Lee's family is concerned about her safety during travel due to her condition. What transportation option should Emily recommend to address both the safety and consistency of Mrs. Lee's travel?
A) Ride-sharing apps with GPS tracking
B) Family member accompaniment in private vehicles
C) Specialized transport services with trained staff
D) Public transit with senior discounts

Question 57: You are tasked with evaluating different financial risk models for an Accountable Care Organization (ACO). Which model would best minimize financial risks while ensuring high-quality care delivery?
A) Fee-for-service model
B) Capitation model
C) Shared savings model
D) Pay-for-performance model

Question 58: John, a 45-year-old male with a history of alcohol use disorder, has recently been diagnosed with major depressive disorder. As his case manager, what is the most appropriate initial step in managing his dual diagnosis to ensure effective treatment?
A) Prioritize treating the alcohol use disorder first to prevent further health deterioration.
B) Initiate simultaneous treatment for both disorders to address all symptoms concurrently.
C) Focus on treating the major depressive disorder first to stabilize mood and improve overall function.
D) Refer John to a specialized dual diagnosis program for integrated treatment.

Question 59: Sarah, a case manager, is working with a client who has experienced emotional abuse in a domestic setting. The client is hesitant to seek help due to fear of stigma and potential retaliation from the abuser. What is the most appropriate initial step for Sarah to take in supporting her client?
A) Encourage the client to immediately report the abuse to law enforcement.
B) Develop a safety plan tailored to the client's specific situation.
C) Refer the client to a mental health professional for counseling services.
D) Suggest joining a support group for individuals experiencing similar issues.

Question 60: Alex, a 17-year-old patient, is exploring their gender identity and expresses discomfort with the gender assigned at birth. As a case manager, which approach should you prioritize to support Alex's psychosocial needs effectively?
A) Encourage Alex to conform to societal gender norms.
B) Facilitate access to gender-affirming counseling services.
C) Recommend delaying exploration until adulthood.
D) Focus on addressing only immediate physical health concerns.

Question 61: Sarah, a case manager, is evaluating the most suitable alternative care facility for a patient with chronic heart failure who requires continuous monitoring but prefers a home-like environment. Which facility should she recommend to balance medical supervision and comfort?
A) Skilled Nursing Facility
B) Long-term Acute Care Hospital
C) Assisted Living Facility
D) Home Health Care

Question 62: Sarah, a 68-year-old patient with congestive heart failure, is being discharged from the hospital. As her case manager, you are responsible for ensuring a smooth transition to home care. Which of the following actions is most critical in preventing hospital readmissions for Sarah?
A) Scheduling a follow-up appointment with her primary care physician within two weeks
B) Providing Sarah with educational materials about her condition
C) Coordinating a home health nurse visit within 48 hours of discharge
D) Ensuring Sarah has access to her prescribed medications before discharge

Question 63: Which function of a case manager is pivotal in enhancing patient satisfaction and outcomes in a patient-centered medical home (PCMH) model?
A) Coordinating specialty referrals
B) Managing electronic health records
C) Implementing evidence-based guidelines
D) Advocating for patient-centered care

Question 64: In supportive care programs, which aspect is considered most critical when developing a patient-centered approach?
A) Standardized treatment protocols
B) Individualized care plans based on patient preferences
C) Focus solely on physical health outcomes
D) Uniform application of psychosocial interventions

Question 65: During a multidisciplinary team meeting for a patient with complex psychosocial needs, which healthcare provider is best suited to address issues related to housing instability and access to community resources?
A) Registered Nurse
B) Occupational Therapist
C) Social Worker
D) Physical Therapist

Question 66: John, a 32-year-old man, reports feeling extremely energetic and elated for several days at a time but also experiences periods of deep depression where he cannot function. As his case manager, what behavioral health concept should you consider as the primary diagnosis?
A) Cyclothymic Disorder
B) Major Depressive Disorder
C) Bipolar I Disorder
D) Persistent Depressive Disorder

Question 67: Sarah, a case manager, is working with a patient who has been recently diagnosed with a chronic illness. The patient expresses feelings of frustration and isolation. Which communication strategy should Sarah prioritize to effectively support the patient's emotional needs?
A) Use closed-ended questions to gather specific information about the patient's condition.
B) Employ reflective listening to validate the patient's emotions and encourage expression.
C) Provide detailed medical information to educate the patient about their condition.
D) Focus on setting future goals to motivate the patient toward recovery.

Question 68: Sarah, a case manager, is working with Emily, a patient who has been emotionally neglected by her family. Emily often expresses feelings of worthlessness and struggles to maintain relationships. What is the most effective initial intervention Sarah should consider to address Emily's emotional needs?
A) Encourage Emily to join a support group for individuals with similar experiences.
B) Refer Emily to a psychiatrist for medication evaluation.
C) Develop a safety plan with Emily in case of emotional distress.
D) Focus on building a therapeutic alliance to foster trust and open communication.

Question 69: In the Transtheoretical Model of Change, which stage is characterized by an individual intending to take action within the next six months but not having a specific plan yet?
A) Precontemplation
B) Contemplation
C) Preparation
D) Action

Question 70: As a case manager, you are working with John, a 45-year-old patient recovering from surgery who is experiencing anxiety and spiritual distress. John has expressed a desire for support in aligning his medical treatment with his spiritual beliefs. Which approach should you take to effectively incorporate pastoral counseling into his care plan?
A) Refer John to a hospital chaplain for spiritual guidance without further involvement.
B) Collaborate with John's religious leader to integrate spiritual practices into his recovery plan.
C) Encourage John to focus solely on medical treatments and avoid spiritual discussions.
D) Suggest John read self-help books on spirituality independently.

Question 71: Which of the following is a primary consideration for determining eligibility for home care benefits under private benefit programs?
A) The patient's age
B) The availability of family caregivers
C) The patient's medical necessity and plan of care
D) The proximity to healthcare facilities

Question 72: In managing a client who believes in traditional medicine, what approach should a case manager take to ensure effective communication and treatment adherence?
A) Dismiss traditional beliefs as unscientific and focus on evidence-based medicine.
B) Educate the client solely on the superiority of modern medicine.
C) Collaborate with traditional healers to complement medical treatment.
D) Insist on discontinuing all traditional practices for safety reasons.

Question 73: Mr. Garcia, a low-income elderly patient with disabilities, needs assistance with daily living activities but wishes to remain at home rather than move to a nursing facility. What waiver program could assist in funding his home-based care?
A) PACE (Program of All-Inclusive Care for the Elderly)
B) Medicaid State Plan Personal Care Services
C) Medicaid Home and Community-Based Services (HCBS) Waiver
D) Medicare Part D

Question 74: Sarah, a 45-year-old woman, presents with symptoms of persistent sadness, lack of interest in activities, and significant weight loss over the past two months. She reports feeling worthless and has difficulty concentrating. Based on behavioral health concepts, which diagnosis is most likely for Sarah?
A) Generalized Anxiety Disorder
B) Major Depressive Disorder
C) Bipolar Disorder
D) Persistent Depressive Disorder

Question 75: In the context of reimbursement methods for telehealth services, which factor most significantly influences the decision-making process for healthcare providers in alternative care sites?
A) The availability of high-speed internet connections
B) The integration with existing electronic health record systems
C) The parity laws governing telehealth reimbursements
D) The number of patients preferring telehealth over in-person visits

Question 76: Which of the following best describes the primary objective of a continuum of care in the context of health and human services?
A) To ensure all patients receive the same level of care regardless of their individual needs.
B) To provide a seamless transition between different levels and types of care tailored to patient needs.
C) To prioritize acute care settings over community-based services for cost efficiency.

D) To focus primarily on post-acute care services to reduce hospital readmissions.

Question 77: In the context of value-based care, which payment model incentivizes healthcare providers to deliver high-quality care while controlling costs by rewarding them for achieving specific health outcomes?
A) Fee-for-Service
B) Capitation
C) Pay-for-Performance
D) Bundled Payments

Question 78: In the context of care delivery and reimbursement methods, what is a primary role of case managers in coordinating patient care within an integrated care system?
A) To ensure patients receive only the services covered by their insurance.
B) To facilitate communication between multidisciplinary teams to optimize patient outcomes.
C) To solely focus on reducing hospital readmission rates.
D) To manage the financial aspects of patient care exclusively.

Question 79: John, a case manager, is designing an employer-based wellness program aimed at reducing employee stress. Which component is most likely to lead to measurable reductions in workplace stress?
A) Monthly team-building activities
B) Access to an on-site fitness center
C) Implementation of mindfulness training sessions
D) Offering healthy snacks in the break room

Question 80: Sarah, a 65-year-old patient with hypertension and diabetes, has been struggling to adhere to her prescribed medication regimen. As a case manager, which strategy would be most effective in improving Sarah's adherence to her care regimen?
A) Simplifying her medication schedule by coordinating doses with her daily routine
B) Increasing the frequency of follow-up appointments to monitor adherence
C) Educating Sarah on the potential complications of non-adherence
D) Providing Sarah with written instructions for each medication

Question 81: Sarah, a case manager, is developing a wellness program for a community with high rates of cardiovascular disease. She aims to incorporate psychosocial support to enhance the program's effectiveness. Which strategy should Sarah prioritize to effectively address both wellness and illness prevention in this context?
A) Implementing regular health screenings for early detection of cardiovascular issues.
B) Organizing community fitness events to encourage physical activity.
C) Establishing peer support groups for emotional and social support.
D) Providing educational workshops on healthy eating habits.

Question 82: During a care plan meeting, you are negotiating with a multidisciplinary team to secure additional home health services for Mrs. Garcia, an elderly patient with multiple chronic conditions. The team is concerned about budget constraints. Which negotiation strategy should you employ to ensure Mrs. Garcia receives adequate care?
A) Argue that denying services could lead to ethical concerns and liability issues.
B) Suggest reallocating existing resources to cover the

additional services needed.
C) Use interest-based negotiation to identify shared goals among team members.
D) Propose reducing other non-essential services to fund Mrs. Garcia's care.

Question 83: You are managing the case of Mrs. Garcia, who is struggling with adherence to her medication regimen due to personal beliefs. To effectively build rapport and address this challenge, what should be your primary focus?
A) Educate Mrs. Garcia on the scientific evidence supporting her medication regimen.
B) Collaborate with Mrs. Garcia by exploring her beliefs and finding common ground for mutual understanding.
C) Refer Mrs. Garcia to a specialist who can provide more detailed medical advice regarding her medication.
D) Emphasize the importance of following medical advice strictly as prescribed by her healthcare provider.

Question 84: Maria, a single mother of two, recently lost her employer-sponsored health insurance and is seeking affordable healthcare options for her family. As her case manager, what would be the most appropriate first step in ensuring Maria has access to necessary healthcare services?
A) Apply for COBRA continuation coverage
B) Enroll in the Children's Health Insurance Program (CHIP)
C) Seek assistance from local non-profit health organizations
D) Explore options in the Health Insurance Marketplace

Question 85: Which of the following strategies is most effective in enhancing client self-care management through health education, according to contemporary research in case management?
A) Providing clients with detailed written instructions
B) Utilizing motivational interviewing techniques
C) Offering regular group educational sessions
D) Distributing educational pamphlets

Question 86: In the context of Pharmacy Benefits Management, which strategy is primarily used to encourage the use of cost-effective medications by patients while maintaining therapeutic outcomes?
A) Step Therapy
B) Prior Authorization
C) Quantity Limits
D) Formulary Tiers

Question 87: Sarah, a 45-year-old employee at a mid-sized company, has just been laid off. She is concerned about losing her health insurance coverage and wants to know her options under COBRA. Which of the following statements accurately describes Sarah's eligibility for COBRA continuation coverage?
A) Sarah is eligible for COBRA coverage for up to 12 months.
B) Sarah can extend her COBRA coverage indefinitely if she pays the premiums.
C) Sarah is eligible for COBRA coverage for up to 18 months.
D) Sarah can only receive COBRA coverage if she finds new employment within 60 days.

Question 88: In the context of reimbursement methods for virtual care services, which model is most likely to incentivize providers to deliver comprehensive and continuous care?
A) Fee-for-service model
B) Value-based reimbursement model
C) Capitation payment model
D) Bundled payment model

Question 89: John, a case manager, is analyzing the outcomes of a new integrated care program aimed at reducing hospital readmissions for diabetic patients. To accurately measure the program's success, which key performance indicator should John prioritize?
A) Patient Satisfaction Scores
B) Average Length of Hospital Stay
C) Readmission Rates within 30 Days
D) Number of Emergency Room Visits

Question 90: John, a 60-year-old male with a history of alcohol use, presents with confusion, memory issues, and unsteady gait. As his case manager, which diagnosis should be considered based on these symptoms?
A) Alzheimer's Disease
B) Korsakoff Syndrome
C) Parkinson's Disease
D) Schizophrenia

Question 91: John, a 60-year-old patient recovering from a stroke, is hesitant about participating in rehabilitation exercises. As his case manager, how can you best assess John's readiness to engage in these exercises?
A) Ask John directly if he plans to start the exercises this week.
B) Explore John's beliefs and feelings about the benefits of rehabilitation exercises.
C) Provide John with statistics on recovery rates for those who participate in rehabilitation.
D) Schedule regular check-ins to remind John of his rehabilitation schedule.

Question 92: In utilization management, which principle is most critical when evaluating the necessity of a medical procedure?
A) Cost-effectiveness
B) Patient preference
C) Evidence-based practice
D) Provider convenience

Question 93: Sarah, a case manager, is working with an elderly client who has recently been diagnosed with early-stage Alzheimer's disease. The client lives alone and has no immediate family nearby. Which community resource should Sarah prioritize to ensure the client's safety and well-being?
A) Adult Day Care Services
B) Meals on Wheels
C) Home Health Aide Services
D) Alzheimer's Support Group

Question 94: In psychological assessment, which test is primarily used to measure a person's cognitive processing speed and attention?
A) Wechsler Adult Intelligence Scale (WAIS-IV)
B) Trail Making Test Part A
C) Rorschach Inkblot Test
D) Thematic Apperception Test (TAT)

Question 95: John is a case manager tasked with reducing readmissions for heart failure patients at his hospital. He needs to select a model of care that enhances communication between hospital staff and community resources while ensuring follow-up after discharge. Which model should John implement?
A) Chronic Care Model (CCM)
B) Integrated Care Model
C) Transitional Care Model (TCM)
D) Patient-Centered Medical Home (PCMH)

Question 96: Which of the following strategies is most effective in improving patient adherence to a care regimen in a value-based care model?
A) Providing detailed educational materials
B) Implementing shared decision-making processes
C) Increasing frequency of follow-up appointments
D) Utilizing financial incentives for adherence

Question 97: In the context of case management for chronic illness, which factor is most critical when assessing the interplay between physical functioning and behavioral health?
A) Medication adherence
B) Social support networks
C) Pain management strategies
D) Cognitive-behavioral therapy

Question 98: In the context of URAC's approach to quality indicators, what is considered a significant source for developing these measures?
A) Historical financial data
B) National clinical guidelines
C) Administrative policy documents
D) Marketing research reports

Question 99: A case manager named John is dealing with a conflict between a patient's family members regarding the treatment plan. The family is divided on whether to continue aggressive treatment or shift to palliative care. Which conflict resolution strategy should John employ to facilitate an agreement that respects the family's values and the patient's best interests?
A) Mediation
B) Arbitration
C) Avoidance
D) Forcing

Question 100: John, a case manager, is reviewing quarterly reports on patient readmission rates to assess the effectiveness of discharge planning protocols. Which method should he prioritize to ensure accurate interpretation and reporting of these rates?
A) Analyze readmission rates across all departments collectively.
B) Segregate data by specific patient demographics and conditions.
C) Focus on readmissions occurring within 7 days post-discharge.
D) Compare readmission rates solely against previous quarter's data.

Question 101: In evaluating a new case management program's effectiveness for diabetic patients, which quality indicator would best assess its impact on long-term health outcomes?
A) Number of educational sessions attended by patients
B) Reduction in HbA1c levels across the patient population
C) Increase in follow-up appointment attendance
D) Improvement in patient-reported lifestyle changes

Question 102: Maria, a 32-year-old woman with generalized anxiety disorder (GAD) and opioid dependence, struggles with social interactions due to her anxiety. As her case manager, which intervention would best support her recovery and improve her social functioning?
A) Cognitive Behavioral Therapy (CBT) focusing solely on anxiety management
B) Medication-assisted therapy (MAT) exclusively for opioid dependence
C) Dual-focused CBT integrating anxiety and substance use strategies
D) Group therapy concentrating on anxiety reduction only

Question 103: Which of the following is a primary

characteristic of a Health Maintenance Organization (HMO) within private benefit programs that distinguishes it from other managed care plans?
A) Flexibility in choosing any healthcare provider
B) Requirement for a primary care physician referral for specialist services
C) Fee-for-service payment model
D) High out-of-pocket costs for out-of-network services

Question 104: Which of the following crisis intervention strategies is primarily focused on restoring the individual's cognitive equilibrium by restructuring their thought processes during a crisis?
A) Cathartic Release
B) Cognitive Reframing
C) Emotional Ventilation
D) Behavioral Activation

Question 105: Which of the following strategies is most effective for enhancing client engagement in case management by addressing psychosocial barriers?
A) Implementing a standardized communication protocol
B) Establishing a trusting relationship through empathy and active listening
C) Providing educational materials tailored to the client's condition
D) Utilizing technology for regular follow-up communications

Question 106: Emily, a case manager, is reviewing a patient's pharmacy benefits to ensure cost-effective medication management. The patient has been prescribed a high-cost specialty drug. Which strategy should Emily prioritize to optimize the patient's pharmacy benefits while ensuring adherence?
A) Encourage the use of generic alternatives
B) Implement step therapy protocols
C) Facilitate enrollment in a patient assistance program
D) Recommend mail-order pharmacy services

Question 107: Jacob, a 16-year-old recovering from surgery, requires ongoing care at home. What age-specific intervention should the case manager prioritize to promote his recovery and independence?
A) Encourage his parents to manage all aspects of his care.
B) Involve him in creating his own recovery schedule with supervision.
C) Focus on providing educational materials about his condition to his parents.
D) Schedule routine visits from healthcare professionals without involving him.

Question 108: Sarah is a case manager working with a client, Mark, who has significant disabilities and recently received a large inheritance. Mark's family wants to ensure that this inheritance does not disqualify him from receiving Medicaid benefits. Which type of trust should Sarah recommend to protect Mark's eligibility for these benefits?
A) Revocable Trust
B) Irrevocable Trust
C) Special Needs Trust
D) Charitable Remainder Trust

Question 109: Sarah, a case manager, is working with John, a 65-year-old patient with multiple chronic conditions who is struggling to afford his medications. John has limited income and is not eligible for Medicaid. Which of the following pharmacy assistance programs would be most suitable for John to explore first?
A) State Pharmaceutical Assistance Program (SPAP)
B) Patient Assistance Programs (PAPs)
C) Medicare Part D Low-Income Subsidy (LIS)
D) 340B Drug Pricing Program

Question 110: Which of the following programs is specifically designed to provide healthcare access to uninsured children in families with incomes too high to qualify for Medicaid but too low to afford private coverage?
A) Medicare
B) Children's Health Insurance Program (CHIP)
C) Supplemental Nutrition Assistance Program (SNAP)
D) Temporary Assistance for Needy Families (TANF)

Question 111: In managed care, what is the primary purpose of utilizing gatekeepers such as primary care physicians?
A) To increase patient autonomy in choosing specialists
B) To facilitate direct access to specialty services
C) To coordinate patient care and manage resource utilization
D) To limit patients' access to necessary medical treatments

Question 112: Which of the following best describes the primary benefit of a viatical settlement for a terminally ill policyholder?
A) Provides immediate cash to cover medical expenses and improve quality of life.
B) Ensures continued health insurance coverage for dependents.
C) Guarantees full face value payout of the life insurance policy.
D) Eliminates the need to pay future premiums on the life insurance policy.

Question 113: Which of the following insurance principles is most critical when determining eligibility for disability benefits under a private disability insurance plan?
A) Principle of Utmost Good Faith
B) Principle of Indemnity
C) Principle of Subrogation
D) Principle of Proximate Cause

Question 114: When diagnosing a mental health disorder, which diagnostic tool is most commonly used to ensure standardized criteria are applied across different cases?
A) DSM-5 (Diagnostic and Statistical Manual of Mental Disorders, Fifth Edition)
B) ICD-10 (International Classification of Diseases, Tenth Revision)
C) MMPI (Minnesota Multiphasic Personality Inventory)
D) Rorschach Inkblot Test

Question 115: Maria, a case manager, is working with John, a patient who has been recently diagnosed with a chronic illness. Maria wants to empower John to take an active role in managing his health. Which approach should Maria prioritize to effectively empower John?
A) Provide John with comprehensive educational materials about his condition.
B) Encourage John to set personal health goals and create an action plan.
C) Schedule regular follow-ups to monitor John's adherence to treatment.
D) Connect John with peer support groups for shared experiences.

Question 116: In bereavement counseling, what is considered a key component when assisting clients in meaning reconstruction following a significant loss?
A) Encouraging clients to forget the deceased
B) Facilitating narrative development about the loss
C) Advising clients to avoid discussing their feelings
D) Promoting immediate replacement of lost relationships

Question 117: Alex, a 45-year-old transgender male, is experiencing increased stress due to lack of family support after his transition. As a case manager, what is the most appropriate initial step to address Alex's psychosocial needs related to gender health?
A) Encourage Alex to join a local transgender support group.
B) Refer Alex to a mental health professional specializing in gender issues.
C) Suggest Alex participate in family therapy sessions with his relatives.
D) Advise Alex to engage in stress-reduction techniques independently.

Question 118: Which of the following best describes the concept of gender expression as it relates to psychosocial support systems in healthcare settings?
A) Gender expression is solely determined by biological sex and should align with it.
B) Gender expression involves a person's external presentation of gender, which may not necessarily align with their biological sex.
C) Gender expression is defined by societal norms and must conform to them for effective psychosocial support.
D) Gender expression is irrelevant in healthcare settings and does not impact psychosocial support systems.

Question 119: Which of the following is a primary goal of Accountable Care Organizations (ACOs) in the context of care delivery and reimbursement methods?
A) Increasing patient volume to maximize revenue
B) Enhancing care coordination to improve patient outcomes
C) Reducing healthcare provider autonomy
D) Implementing strict cost-cutting measures

Question 120: Which conflict resolution strategy is most effective in maintaining long-term relationships while addressing both parties' needs in a healthcare setting?
A) Competing
B) Avoiding
C) Collaborating
D) Compromising

Question 121: Which of the following methodologies is most effective in identifying the root cause of a quality issue within a healthcare setting, focusing on systematic analysis and evidence-based solutions?
A) Lean Six Sigma
B) Root Cause Analysis (RCA)
C) Plan-Do-Study-Act (PDSA) Cycle
D) Failure Mode and Effects Analysis (FMEA)

Question 122: What is a key feature of Medicaid that distinguishes it from Medicare in terms of eligibility criteria?
A) Medicaid eligibility is based solely on age.
B) Medicaid eligibility is determined by income and family size.
C) Medicaid eligibility requires individuals to have a disability.
D) Medicaid eligibility is based on prior work history.

Question 123: In the context of outpatient care, which coding system is utilized to describe medical services and procedures to facilitate billing and ensure appropriate reimbursement?
A) HCPCS Level II
B) CPT
C) ICD-10-PCS
D) LOINC

Question 124: John, a 55-year-old factory worker, recently suffered a severe back injury that prevents him from continuing his job. He has been out of work for 5 months and is considering applying for Social Security Disability Insurance (SSDI). Which of the following criteria must John meet to qualify for SSDI benefits?
A) John must demonstrate that his condition will last at least 12 months or result in death.
B) John must prove that he cannot perform any work whatsoever.
C) John needs to show that he has no income from any source.
D) John must have been employed for at least 20 years before applying.

Question 125: Emily, a case manager, is developing a care plan for Mark, who has chronic obstructive pulmonary disease (COPD). Mark struggles with maintaining exercise routines due to fatigue and shortness of breath. Which self-care management intervention should Emily prioritize to enhance Mark's physical activity while considering his condition?
A) Recommend Mark join a high-intensity interval training program at the local gym.
B) Suggest Mark engage in daily brisk walking sessions for at least 30 minutes.
C) Encourage Mark to participate in pulmonary rehabilitation programs tailored for COPD patients.
D) Advise Mark to rest more frequently to conserve energy.

Question 126: John, a case manager, is evaluating the most appropriate living arrangement for a 45-year-old patient with moderate intellectual disability who requires some assistance with daily activities but desires a level of independence. Considering the patient's needs and preferences, which type of alternative care facility would be most suitable?
A) Skilled Nursing Facility
B) Assisted Living Facility
C) Group Home
D) Independent Living Community

Question 127: Sarah, a 65-year-old patient with chronic obstructive pulmonary disease (COPD), is being discharged from the hospital. Her case manager is exploring non-traditional sites of care to manage her condition effectively while minimizing hospital readmissions. Which option would be most appropriate for Sarah's ongoing care?
A) Telehealth monitoring with regular virtual consultations
B) Skilled nursing facility for ongoing rehabilitation
C) Home health care with periodic nurse visits
D) Outpatient pulmonary rehabilitation program

Question 128: In the context of indemnity insurance plans, which of the following best describes the primary financial responsibility of the insured individual?
A) Pay a fixed copayment for each healthcare service.
B) Cover a percentage of healthcare costs after meeting a deductible.
C) Pay for services upfront and seek reimbursement from the insurer.
D) Share costs equally with the insurer from the first dollar spent.

Question 129: Maria, a case manager, notices that her client, Lisa, has started attending weekly fitness classes after discussing her sedentary lifestyle during previous sessions. According to the Transtheoretical Model of Change, which stage is Lisa most likely in?
A) Maintenance
B) Action
C) Preparation
D) Termination

Question 130: Maria is a case manager assisting Emily,

whose father passed away unexpectedly. Emily has been experiencing prolonged grief and struggles with daily functioning. Which approach should Maria consider first to effectively support Emily's adjustment according to current bereavement counseling models?
A) Introduce Emily to mindfulness-based stress reduction techniques
B) Encourage Emily to focus on creating new routines without her father
C) Suggest that Emily engage in legacy-building activities honoring her father
D) Advise Emily to immerse herself in work or hobbies to distract from her grief

Question 131: Sarah, a case manager, is assisting a patient with newly diagnosed multiple sclerosis (MS). The patient expresses feelings of isolation and seeks support. Which disease-based organization should Sarah recommend to provide the patient with comprehensive support and resources specifically tailored to MS patients?
A) American Heart Association
B) National Multiple Sclerosis Society
C) Alzheimer's Association
D) Arthritis Foundation

Question 132: Which cost containment strategy focuses on improving patient outcomes while simultaneously reducing healthcare costs through coordinated care across multiple settings?
A) Capitation
B) Integrated Delivery System (IDS)
C) Fee-for-Service (FFS)
D) Pay-for-Performance (P4P)

Question 133: Which theory emphasizes the role of social interaction in the development of gender identity, suggesting that gender roles are learned through reinforcement and modeling?
A) Social Learning Theory
B) Biological Determinism Theory
C) Cognitive Developmental Theory
D) Gender Schema Theory

Question 134: John, a case manager, is assisting Maria, an elderly client who shows signs of neglect in her care facility. Maria often appears malnourished and unkempt but denies any issues when questioned. What should be John's primary focus in addressing this situation?
A) Report the neglect to adult protective services immediately.
B) Build rapport with Maria to encourage her disclosure of any issues.
C) Conduct an unannounced visit to assess Maria's living conditions further.
D) Discuss concerns with facility staff to gather more information.

Question 135: In the context of self-directed care, which of the following strategies most effectively enhances client autonomy and empowerment in managing their health care needs?
A) Providing clients with a list of pre-approved healthcare providers
B) Encouraging clients to set their own health goals and create action plans
C) Assigning case managers to make decisions on behalf of clients
D) Offering standardized care plans for all clients

Question 136: John, a case manager, has a client suffering from Parkinson's disease. He seeks to involve his client in a supportive care program that offers both community engagement and up-to-date research information about Parkinson's. Which organization should John contact?
A) Parkinson's Foundation
B) American Heart Association
C) Muscular Dystrophy Association
D) Lupus Foundation of America

Question 137: Jane, a 35-year-old case manager, is working with a client who identifies as bisexual. The client expresses feeling marginalized within both heterosexual and LGBTQ+ communities. Which of the following concepts best describes this experience?
A) Intersectionality
B) Minority Stress
C) Identity Confusion
D) Internalized Homophobia

Question 138: As a case manager, you are working with Mr. Johnson, who has multiple chronic conditions and frequently visits the emergency department. Your goal is to reduce his hospital admissions by coordinating a comprehensive care plan. Which reimbursement method would most effectively support this approach by promoting coordinated care and reducing unnecessary hospitalizations?
A) Fee-for-Service
B) Capitation
C) Bundled Payments
D) Pay-for-Performance

Question 139: Emily, a case manager in a large urban hospital, is tasked with coordinating care for Mr. Johnson, a 72-year-old patient with multiple chronic conditions. Her primary goal is to ensure seamless transitions between care settings. Which action best exemplifies her role in this context?
A) Scheduling regular follow-up appointments with Mr. Johnson's primary care physician
B) Developing a comprehensive discharge plan that includes home health services
C) Educating Mr. Johnson about his medication regimen
D) Facilitating communication between Mr. Johnson's family and healthcare providers

Question 140: Which of the following is a primary characteristic of the Patient-centered Medical Home (PCMH) model that distinguishes it from traditional care models?
A) Emphasis on acute care services
B) Focus on physician-led care
C) Comprehensive, coordinated care across all elements of the healthcare system
D) Prioritization of specialty care referrals

Question 141: John, a case manager, is tasked with reducing hospital readmissions for diabetic patients through virtual care interventions. Which strategy should he prioritize to achieve this goal effectively?
A) Implement an educational webinar series on diabetes management.
B) Establish a virtual support group for peer interactions.
C) Develop a personalized telemedicine follow-up schedule post-discharge.
D) Provide access to an online library of diabetes resources.

Question 142: Which of the following components is most critical in ensuring the success of an employer-based health and wellness program according to contemporary research?
A) Financial incentives for employees
B) Comprehensive health education sessions
C) Strong leadership support and commitment

D) Regular biometric screenings

Question 143: What is the maximum duration that COBRA coverage can be extended for a qualified beneficiary after an employee's termination, excluding cases of disability?
A) 12 months
B) 18 months
C) 24 months
D) 36 months

Question 144: Tom, a 60-year-old patient with diabetes, expresses frustration about managing his diet during motivational interviewing. Which approach should the case manager take to align with motivational interviewing principles?
A) Telling Tom the importance of strict dietary adherence.
B) Discussing Tom's past successes in managing his diet.
C) Creating a detailed meal plan for Tom to follow.
D) Explaining the health risks associated with poor diet control.

Question 145: What is a key difference between SSDI and Supplemental Security Income (SSI) that affects eligibility determination?
A) SSDI eligibility is based solely on financial need, while SSI requires a history of work.
B) SSDI requires a medical condition expected to last at least one year or result in death, while SSI does not require any medical condition.
C) SSDI is funded through payroll taxes and requires sufficient work history; SSI is funded by general tax revenues and does not require work history.
D) Both SSDI and SSI require recipients to be over age 65 to qualify.

Question 146: John, a diabetic patient recently discharged from the hospital, needs ongoing education and support to manage his condition effectively. As his case manager, which non-traditional site of care should you prioritize to ensure he receives comprehensive diabetes education and support?
A) Retail health clinics
B) Virtual diabetes management programs
C) Skilled nursing facilities
D) Emergency departments

Question 147: When assisting uninsured or underinsured clients in accessing medications, which program is specifically designed to help patients obtain prescription drugs at reduced costs through pharmaceutical manufacturers?
A) Medicaid
B) 340B Drug Pricing Program
C) Patient Assistance Programs
D) Medicare Part D

Question 148: In the context of reimbursement methods within the continuum of care, which approach most effectively supports integrated service delivery?
A) Fee-for-service payment models that reimburse each service separately.
B) Capitation payments that provide a fixed amount per patient regardless of services used.
C) Bundled payments that cover all services for an episode of care across providers.
D) Cost-plus reimbursement that adds a percentage profit to actual costs incurred.

Question 149: Which characteristic primarily differentiates indemnity insurance plans from managed care plans in terms of provider choice?
A) Restricted network of providers.
B) No requirement for primary care physician referrals.
C) Mandatory use of in-network specialists only.
D) Pre-authorization needed for all services.

Question 150: John, an elderly patient recovering from surgery, expresses feelings of isolation and desires involvement with a religious organization for community support. As his case manager, what should be your primary consideration when connecting him with such an organization?
A) Ensure the organization's beliefs align with John's personal values.
B) Select an organization based on proximity to John's residence.
C) Choose an organization known for its strong volunteer programs.
D) Recommend an organization that offers financial assistance programs.

ANSWER WITH DETAILED EXPLANATION SET [4]

Question 1: Correct Answer: B) Sarah discusses various treatment options with John and helps him understand the potential outcomes of each.
Rationale: Option B is correct as it embodies shared decision-making by involving John in understanding his treatment options and potential outcomes, empowering him in the decision process. Option A lacks patient involvement, while C discourages patient autonomy. Option D provides information but does not engage in an interactive decision-making process.

Question 2: Correct Answer: B) Integration of dual-diagnosis treatment programs
Rationale: Dual-diagnosis programs are vital for treating Lisa's co-occurring disorders effectively, ensuring comprehensive care. Proximity to hospitals (A) is beneficial for emergencies but not specific to dual needs. Luxury amenities (C), while enhancing comfort, do not impact clinical outcomes. A high staff-to-patient ratio (D) suggests better supervision but doesn't guarantee specialized dual-diagnosis expertise. Emphasizing integrated programs reflects evidence-based practices supporting concurrent management of mental health and substance use disorders.

Question 3: Correct Answer: A) Cognitive Behavioral Therapy (CBT)
Rationale: Cognitive Behavioral Therapy (CBT) is recognized for its efficacy in enhancing resilience among domestic abuse survivors by addressing negative thought patterns and promoting adaptive coping strategies. Solution-Focused Brief Therapy (SFBT) emphasizes solutions rather than problems, which may not fully address underlying trauma. Motivational Interviewing (MI) focuses on behavioral change, not necessarily resilience. Narrative Therapy helps reframe personal stories but lacks CBT's empirical support for resilience enhancement. Thus, CBT is the most comprehensive approach for fostering resilience in this context.

Question 4: Correct Answer: B) Facilitating rituals or activities that acknowledge the loss.
Rationale: Option B aligns with Worden's tasks by helping clients accept loss through acknowledgment rituals, essential for mourning progression. Option A delays acceptance, counterproductive in processing grief. Option C may provide temporary distraction but doesn't address acceptance of loss. Option D encourages avoidance, potentially reinforcing denial rather than fostering acceptance, contrary to Worden's framework for healthy mourning.

Question 5: Correct Answer: B) Establish trust by actively listening to Mr. Thompson's concerns and validating his feelings.
Rationale: Establishing trust through active listening and validation is crucial for relationship building, as it fosters an environment where patients feel heard and respected, encouraging engagement (contemporary research supports this). Option A, while informative, lacks relational depth; C may lead to disengagement; D could increase resistance due to its negative focus.

Question 6: Correct Answer: C) Additional benefits like vision and dental not typically covered by Original Medicare
Rationale: Medicare Advantage Plans often provide additional benefits such as vision and dental (C), which are not usually covered by Original Medicare, making this option correct. Prescription drug coverage (A) may require an additional premium or plan selection; access to any provider (B) can be restricted by network requirements; lower out-of-pocket costs (D) are not guaranteed as they depend on plan specifics. Understanding these nuances helps differentiate between the options available within Medicare plans.

Question 7: Correct Answer: A) Arrange for home physical therapy and weekly psychiatric evaluations.
Rationale: The correct option A ensures comprehensive care by addressing both physical rehabilitation through home physical therapy and mental health needs via psychiatric evaluations. Option B focuses solely on medication adherence, neglecting physical and mental health recovery. Option C provides emotional support but lacks physical rehabilitation. Option D relies on family support without professional intervention, potentially compromising recovery outcomes.

Question 8: Correct Answer: A) ICD-10-CM
Rationale: ICD-10-CM is designed to capture detailed information about chronic conditions, crucial for case management. It supports comprehensive care planning and accurate reimbursement by providing specific diagnostic codes. CPT focuses on procedures, DRG groups diagnoses for inpatient reimbursement, and SNOMED CT is a clinical terminology system rather than a coding methodology. ICD-10-CM's specificity in chronic condition coding makes it essential for effective case management.

Question 9: Correct Answer: B) Gather comprehensive medical records and expert opinions.
Rationale: Gathering comprehensive medical records and expert opinions is crucial as it provides objective evidence regarding the injury's cause and its relation to work activities, which can help in resolving disputes about pre-existing conditions. Option A might be premature without substantial evidence. Option C is useful but should follow initial evidence gathering. Option D could be considered later if disputes persist after evidence review. Thus, option B ensures a strong foundation for any further action.

Question 10: Correct Answer: C) Use VA benefits as primary and TRICARE as secondary
Rationale: Veterans are generally encouraged to use VA benefits first due to the specialized care available through the VA system, particularly for mental health services tailored to veterans' unique needs. Using VA benefits first allows access to these specialized programs while keeping TRICARE as secondary ensures broader coverage if needed. Options A and B limit service access by focusing on one program only, while D incorrectly prioritizes TRICARE over VA benefits.

Question 11: Correct Answer: B) It increases specificity with more detailed codes.
Rationale: The transition from ICD-9 to ICD-10 significantly increased the specificity and granularity of coding by expanding the number of codes available, allowing for more precise descriptions of diagnoses and procedures. This change supports improved accuracy in case management and reimbursement processes. Options A and D incorrectly suggest a reduction in detail, while C suggests no change in specificity, which is inaccurate as ICD-10 provides a much richer dataset compared to its predecessor.

Question 12: Correct Answer: B) Provide Jane with resources and coach her on asking informed questions during medical appointments.
Rationale: Option B is correct because it empowers Jane by providing tools and skills to actively participate in her care, aligning with self-advocacy principles. Option A is

incorrect as it lacks guidance, potentially overwhelming Jane. Option C undermines self-advocacy by discouraging personal involvement. Option D offers support but lacks the personalized coaching needed for effective advocacy.

Question 13: Correct Answer: C) Coordinate with a multidisciplinary team for comprehensive discharge planning.

Rationale: Coordinating with a multidisciplinary team ensures all aspects of John's care are addressed, promoting continuity and reducing readmissions. While A) offers regular monitoring, it lacks the comprehensive approach. B) focuses on physical therapy but misses other needs. D) empowers John but doesn't ensure professional oversight. The multidisciplinary approach integrates diverse expertise, essential for complex cases like spinal cord injuries.

Question 14: Correct Answer: C) Whether maternity care is considered an essential health benefit

Rationale: Under the Affordable Care Act, maternity care must be included as an essential health benefit in individual plans, making option C crucial. While provider networks (A), deductibles (B), and co-payments (D) are important financial considerations, they do not ensure comprehensive maternity coverage like essential benefits do. Therefore, C is correct as it guarantees inclusion by law, whereas A, B, and D focus on cost management without ensuring benefit inclusion.

Question 15: Correct Answer: B) Coordinating multidisciplinary teams to align treatment plans with reimbursement policies.

Rationale: Coordinating multidisciplinary teams ensures that treatment plans are consistent with reimbursement policies, promoting integrated care delivery. Option A focuses on autonomy without considering cost or policy alignment. Option C aims at rapid discharge, potentially compromising quality care for cost savings. Option D emphasizes standardization, which may reduce flexibility in aligning with specific reimbursement policies. The correct answer reflects the necessity of interdisciplinary collaboration for effective integration of care delivery and reimbursement strategies.

Question 16: Correct Answer: B) By providing structured social networks and a sense of belonging

Rationale: Fraternal/religious organizations primarily offer psychosocial support by creating structured social networks, fostering a sense of belonging, and promoting community integration. This contrasts with professional counseling (C), which is more clinical. Financial aid (A) and employment opportunities (D) are secondary benefits that may be offered but are not the core function related to psychosocial support. The focus is on community bonds and emotional support, which are crucial for mental health and well-being.

Question 17: Correct Answer: C) Regularly reviewing all medications for necessity and potential interactions

Rationale: Regularly reviewing all medications ensures that each drug is still necessary and checks for potential interactions, which is crucial in managing polypharmacy effectively. While cost-effectiveness, specialist prescriptions, and generic alternatives are important considerations, they do not directly address safety concerns like unnecessary or interacting medications. Frequent reviews help identify drugs that can be discontinued or adjusted to minimize risks associated with polypharmacy in elderly patients.

Question 18: Correct Answer: C) Utilize motivational interviewing to enhance readiness for change in both disorders.

Rationale: Motivational interviewing is an evidence-based practice that effectively enhances engagement and readiness for change in individuals with co-occurring disorders by exploring ambivalence and promoting self-efficacy. Option A focuses solely on opioid use without addressing mood stabilization, which is critical in bipolar disorder management. Option B may not be feasible without initial patient readiness or engagement strategies. Option D could lead to fragmented care, lacking the holistic integration necessary for effective management of co-occurring conditions.

Question 19: Correct Answer: A) On-site nursing staff available 24/7

Rationale: On-site nursing staff available 24/7 is essential for managing Mrs. Patel's chronic health conditions, providing immediate medical attention when needed. While personalized meal planning (Option B), fitness programs (Option C), and transportation services (Option D) contribute to her independence and well-being, they do not offer the same level of direct healthcare management as continuous nursing availability. This ensures that any health issues are promptly addressed, crucial for residents with chronic conditions seeking both independence and medical support.

Question 20: Correct Answer: B) Average resource utilization for similar cases

Rationale: The case rate is primarily determined by the average resource utilization for similar cases, as it reflects the expected costs associated with treating a particular condition. While the patient's length of stay (A), demographic data (C), and hospital's location (D) may influence costs, they do not directly determine the fixed payment amount like resource utilization does. Resource utilization provides a standardized measure to establish consistent reimbursement rates across similar cases.

Question 21: Correct Answer: A) Schedule regular sessions with a pastoral counselor to explore existential questions.

Rationale: Option A is correct as it directly addresses Mary's need for existential exploration through structured pastoral counseling sessions, offering personalized support in finding meaning. Option B focuses on group dynamics rather than individual spiritual needs; C offers general stress relief but not specific existential guidance; D lacks the depth required for addressing profound questions of meaning and hope. Pastoral counseling provides tailored interventions aligned with recognized theories of holistic care.

Question 22: Correct Answer: D) Time series analysis

Rationale: Time series analysis is the most appropriate method for identifying trends over time because it evaluates data points collected at successive points in time. Unlike cross-sectional analysis, which examines data at a single point, and regression analysis, which predicts relationships between variables, time series specifically focuses on temporal patterns. The chi-square test is used for categorical data comparison rather than trend identification. Thus, option D is correct as it directly addresses temporal trend evaluation.

Question 23: Correct Answer: B) Emphasize interdisciplinary team meetings involving all stakeholders

Rationale: Interdisciplinary team meetings are essential for integrating diverse healthcare services, ensuring that all aspects of Mr. Johnson's needs are addressed collaboratively. While coordinating appointments (A) and managing medication (C) are important, they don't encompass the full scope of holistic care. Financial counseling (D) is a component but not the primary strategy for integration. The interdisciplinary approach aligns with contemporary research advocating for comprehensive care through collaboration among various healthcare professionals.

Question 24: Correct Answer: C) John's inability to perform any occupation for which he is reasonably qualified

Rationale: Long-term disability insurance often requires proving inability to work in any occupation for which one is qualified (C), rather than just one's specific job (B). Previous earnings history (A) and cause of disability (D) are less critical in this context. Emphasizing the broader occupational criteria helps clarify eligibility requirements and aligns with typical policy definitions.

Question 25: Correct Answer: B) Subrogation

Rationale: Subrogation permits insurers to pursue recovery from third parties responsible for an insured loss, aligning with legal and financial recovery processes. Contribution (A) involves multiple insurers sharing a claim payment. Indemnity (C) focuses on compensating without profit. Proximate cause (D) identifies the primary cause of loss in claims assessment. Therefore, subrogation specifically addresses recouping losses from liable third parties.

Question 26: Correct Answer: A) The specific state regulations where John resides

Rationale: State regulations significantly impact the coverage of pre-existing conditions in individually purchased insurance plans. While previous insurance duration (B), plan type (C), and premium amount (D) may influence overall coverage, state laws primarily dictate pre-existing condition policies. This makes option A the correct choice as it directly addresses regulatory factors influencing policy terms, whereas B, C, and D relate more to general coverage features rather than specific legal mandates.

Question 27: Correct Answer: B) National Multiple Sclerosis Society

Rationale: The National Multiple Sclerosis Society is dedicated to supporting individuals with MS through educational resources and emotional support. While the other organizations focus on specific diseases like diabetes, Alzheimer's, and cancer, they do not provide specialized support for MS. This makes Option B the correct choice as it directly addresses the needs of Sarah's client with MS, unlike the other options which cater to different conditions.

Question 28: Correct Answer: D) Medicaid Adult Core Set

Rationale: The Medicaid Adult Core Set provides standardized measures specifically designed for evaluating Medicaid programs, making it ideal for John's task. CAHPS focuses on patient experience rather than specific outcomes. OASIS is used primarily in home health settings, while Medicare Advantage Star Ratings pertain to Medicare plans, not Medicaid programs. Thus, the Medicaid Adult Core Set is the best tool for measuring outcomes in John's context.

Question 29: Correct Answer: A) 47562 - Laparoscopic cholecystectomy

Rationale: The correct code, 47562, represents a standard laparoscopic cholecystectomy without additional procedures like cholangiography. Option B (47600) is incorrect as it refers to an open cholecystectomy rather than laparoscopic. Option C (49320) is too general and doesn't specify the gallbladder removal. Option D (47563), though close, includes cholangiography which wasn't performed in Ms. Smith's case. Accurate selection ensures proper reimbursement and reflects the surgical method used.

Question 30: Correct Answer: A) Implementing a disease management program tailored to Mr. Thompson's conditions

Rationale: Implementing a disease management program is effective in coordinating care and controlling costs by providing structured support and education, leading to better self-management and reduced hospitalizations. Option B increases costs without necessarily improving outcomes, C leads to higher expenses and potential overuse of emergency services, and D may compromise treatment effectiveness if not clinically justified. Disease management aligns with contemporary principles of cost containment by focusing on preventive care and efficient resource utilization.

Question 31: Correct Answer: C) The nutritional content tailored to her dietary needs

Rationale: While variety (A), cost (B), and delivery flexibility (D) are important, ensuring meals meet Sarah's specific dietary needs is paramount for managing her diabetes. Nutritional content directly impacts her health outcomes, making it the most critical factor. Variety may not ensure diabetic-friendly meals, cost savings are irrelevant if health deteriorates, and flexible schedules don't guarantee nutritional adequacy.

Question 32: Correct Answer: C) Case Manager

Rationale: The Case Manager is pivotal in coordinating a patient's comprehensive care plan across diverse settings, ensuring continuity and addressing all aspects of the patient's needs. While Primary Care Physicians (A) and Nurse Practitioners (B) provide direct medical care, they do not focus on the coordination aspect as intensively as Case Managers. Social Workers (D) assist with psychosocial support but are not primarily responsible for overall care coordination. This distinction highlights the unique role of Case Managers in integrating various services and providers.

Question 33: Correct Answer: B) Community mental health centers

Rationale: Community mental health centers are specifically designed to provide comprehensive services for individuals with chronic mental health conditions, offering therapy, medication management, and support groups. Local food banks (A), while helpful for addressing nutritional needs, do not specialize in mental health. Faith-based organizations (C) may offer support but lack specialized mental health services. Recreational clubs (D) focus on social interaction rather than targeted mental health care. Thus, option B is the most effective resource in this context.

Question 34: Correct Answer: A) Simplify Tom's medication schedule using color-coded charts and pill organizers.

Rationale: Simplifying the medication schedule using visual aids like color-coded charts directly addresses Tom's low health literacy by making complex information more accessible and easier to follow independently.

Question 35: Correct Answer: D) Compare current data with national benchmarks for diabetes care.

Rationale: Comparing current data with national benchmarks helps identify gaps and areas needing improvement by providing context and standards for quality evaluation. Option A is useful but lacks context without benchmarks. Option B focuses on specific cases rather than overall trends. Option C aids in visualization but doesn't inherently provide comparative insights like benchmarks do.

Question 36: Correct Answer: D) Non-emergency medical transportation (NEMT) services

Rationale: Non-emergency medical transportation

(NEMT) services are specifically designed to assist individuals like Mr. Thompson who require regular medical appointments but lack personal transportation. Unlike public bus services or volunteer programs, NEMT ensures timely and reliable transport tailored for medical needs. While taxi vouchers provide flexibility, they may not be as cost-effective or reliable for frequent trips. Volunteer programs can be inconsistent due to availability issues, making NEMT the most dependable option for consistent attendance.

Question 37: Correct Answer: C) By reimbursing hospitals based on a predetermined fixed amount per case

Rationale: DRGs primarily influence hospital reimbursement by assigning a fixed payment for each case, regardless of actual costs or length of stay, promoting cost efficiency. Option A is incorrect as it does not reflect the fixed nature of DRG payments. Option B is partially true but does not capture the essence of fixed payments. Option D is incorrect as DRGs do not account for actual costs incurred. This system encourages hospitals to manage resources efficiently within the predetermined budget.

Question 38: Correct Answer: C) Supporting Self-Efficacy

Rationale: Supporting self-efficacy involves bolstering the client's belief in their ability to change, which is crucial in Motivational Interviewing. While expressing empathy (A) builds rapport, developing discrepancy (B) highlights differences between current behavior and goals, and rolling with resistance (D) involves adapting to client pushback, they do not directly focus on reinforcing client strengths. Supporting self-efficacy empowers clients by affirming their capacity for change, making it distinct from the other principles.

Question 39: Correct Answer: B) Community Health Centers

Rationale: Community Health Centers offer comprehensive services, including preventive care and chronic disease management, which are crucial for uninsured or underinsured individuals. They provide a sliding fee scale based on income, making them accessible. Emergency Room Services (A) and Urgent Care Centers (D) focus on acute issues rather than ongoing care. Retail Clinics (C) provide limited services and lack comprehensive care coordination. Community Health Centers integrate medical, dental, and mental health services, making them the most effective option.

Question 40: Correct Answer: B) Integrating family-centered care principles throughout the treatment process

Rationale: Family-centered care is vital in pediatrics as it involves families in decision-making, recognizing their role in a child's development and well-being. Option A fails to account for developmental differences, C is inappropriate given children's cognitive levels, and D provides limited insight into complex needs. Research supports family engagement as crucial for effective pediatric care planning, enhancing outcomes through collaborative approaches.

Question 41: Correct Answer: B) Collaborating with a multidisciplinary team to assess the client's financial situation.

Rationale: Option B is correct as it involves comprehensive assessment and intervention by leveraging diverse expertise, crucial for addressing complex financial abuse cases effectively. A multidisciplinary team can provide a holistic view and create a tailored plan to protect the client's assets. Option

A may increase risk, option C could exacerbate vulnerability, and option D might not address immediate exploitation concerns and could be inappropriate without proper legal advice.

Question 42: Correct Answer: B) Anxiety and hyper-vigilance

Rationale: Contemporary research highlights that long-term emotional abuse often results in anxiety and hyper-vigilance due to the constant anticipation of negative outcomes. Unlike resilience (A), which suggests positive adaptation, or indifference (C), which implies a lack of emotional response, anxiety (B) is a direct consequence of sustained emotional stress. Increased self-esteem (D) contradicts the typical effects of emotional abuse, as victims usually experience diminished self-worth.

Question 43: Correct Answer: C) Skilled Nursing Facility

Rationale: A Skilled Nursing Facility provides necessary respiratory therapy and continuous monitoring post-pneumonia stabilization. Inpatient Rehabilitation Facilities focus on intense physical rehabilitation rather than ongoing medical care; Long-Term Acute Care Hospitals cater to patients needing extended hospital-level care; Home Health Care offers limited monitoring and might increase readmission risk due to insufficient support. Therefore, an SNF balances medical oversight with therapeutic needs effectively for Mrs. Lopez's condition.

Question 44: Correct Answer: C) Formulary restrictions of the program.

Rationale: Formulary restrictions are critical because they dictate which medications are covered under the program, impacting treatment plans for chronic illnesses. Geographic location (Option A), duration (Option B), and previous usage (Option D) may influence convenience and continuity but do not directly affect medication availability. Understanding formulary limitations ensures that patients receive necessary medications without interruptions, aligning with their clinical needs.

Question 45: Correct Answer: C) Connect John with a volunteer driver service for appointments.

Rationale: Connecting John with transportation services directly addresses the practical barrier preventing him from attending appointments, thus improving adherence. Option A targets motivation but doesn't resolve logistical issues. Option B provides care at home but doesn't encourage John's active participation in his health management outside the home setting. Option D enhances knowledge but may not impact attendance if transportation remains unresolved, making option C the most comprehensive choice for immediate adherence improvement.

Question 46: Correct Answer: B) Remote monitoring of vital signs and symptoms

Rationale: Remote monitoring is the most effective strategy as it allows continuous tracking of Sarah's health status without requiring frequent travel, thus being cost-effective and accessible. In-person visits (A) are less feasible due to distance. Phone consultations (C) lack visual assessment capabilities, and monthly video conferences (D) might not provide timely interventions. Remote monitoring aligns with contemporary telehealth practices by enabling proactive management through data-driven insights.

Question 47: Correct Answer: B) Supplemental Security Income (SSI)

Rationale: SSI offers cash benefits to disabled individuals with limited income/resources for basic needs. SSDI (A), while also aiding disabled persons, is based on work history rather than financial need. TANF (C) provides temporary financial aid to families but isn't specifically for disabled individuals. Medicaid (D), though a public benefit program for low-income individuals, focuses on healthcare rather than cash assistance. SSI's specific focus on providing cash benefits based on financial need sets it apart as the correct answer.

Question 48: Correct Answer: C) Facilitating group therapy sessions focused on shared faith experiences

Rationale: Facilitating group therapy sessions focused on shared faith experiences effectively enhances coping by fostering community support and shared understanding among participants. Option A may not directly address individual coping mechanisms. Option B combines cognitive-behavioral therapy with religion but may not suit all patients. Option D, while beneficial for stress reduction, lacks the communal and faith-based elements crucial for those seeking pastoral support. Group therapy leverages both social and spiritual dimensions for better coping strategies.

Question 49: Correct Answer: B) Personal physician

Rationale: The principle of having a "Personal physician" ensures that each patient has an ongoing relationship with a personal clinician who provides first contact and continuous, comprehensive care. This fosters trust and improves health outcomes. Enhanced access to care (Option A), while important, focuses on availability rather than relationships. Quality and safety improvement (Option C) emphasize system-level enhancements. Coordinated care (Option D) involves various providers working together but doesn't necessarily focus on the personal bond between patient and provider, making Option B the correct choice.

Question 50: Correct Answer: C) Medicaid

Rationale: Medicaid is the primary public benefit program providing comprehensive healthcare coverage for low-income individuals and families, including adults and children. While SNAP provides food assistance and TANF offers temporary financial aid, they do not cover healthcare. CHIP specifically targets children's health insurance but may not cover the mother. Therefore, Medicaid is the most appropriate choice to address Maria's entire family's healthcare needs.

Question 51: Correct Answer: C) Bundled Payments

Rationale: Bundled Payments encourage provider collaboration by offering one comprehensive payment for all services related to a treatment episode. This contrasts with Fee-for-Service, which pays separately for each service, potentially discouraging coordination. ACOs focus on overall population health management rather than specific episodes. Capitation provides a fixed per-patient fee without linking it to specific treatments or conditions. Therefore, Bundled Payments best align with promoting collaborative care in value-based frameworks.

Question 52: Correct Answer: B) Integrate traditional healing practices with evidence-based anxiety treatments as part of a holistic approach.

Rationale: Option B is correct because it respects Ahmed's cultural beliefs while ensuring he receives effective care through an integrated approach. Option A disregards evidence-based treatments, potentially compromising care quality. Option C undermines Ahmed's cultural values, which could lead to non-compliance. Option D neglects the benefits of evidence-based interventions for anxiety. A holistic approach enhances adherence and outcomes by acknowledging and incorporating diverse cultural perspectives in healthcare.

Question 53: Correct Answer: B) Skilled nursing facility care for up to 20 days

Rationale: Medicare Part A covers skilled nursing facility (SNF) care for up to 20 days following a qualifying hospital stay, making option B correct. Outpatient physical therapy (A) is covered under Part B, while home health aide services (C) are limited and not typically daily under Part A. Durable medical equipment (D) is also covered under Part B, not Part A. The key distinction lies in understanding which specific post-acute services are covered by each part of Medicare.

Question 54: Correct Answer: B) Motivational interviewing to explore ambivalence

Rationale: Motivational interviewing is designed to explore and resolve ambivalence, encouraging patients like Ms. Garcia to articulate their reasons for non-compliance. This technique contrasts with offering advice (A), which may not address underlying issues, or using authority (C), which could be perceived as coercive. Focusing on past successes (D) might not uncover current barriers. Motivational interviewing aligns with contemporary research emphasizing patient autonomy and collaboration in healthcare decisions.

Question 55: Correct Answer: C) Assess John's readiness and willingness to engage in counseling sessions.

Rationale: The initial step in bereavement counseling is assessing the individual's readiness and willingness to participate in the process, as this determines the effectiveness of subsequent interventions. Option A may be beneficial later but not as an initial step. Option B can be therapeutic but requires prior assessment of John's emotional state. Option D might be necessary if symptoms are severe, but assessing readiness is crucial first.

Question 56: Correct Answer: C) Specialized transport services with trained staff

Rationale: Specialized transport services with trained staff are ideal for patients like Mrs. Lee who have cognitive impairments and require safe and consistent travel for medical treatments. These services offer trained personnel who can handle specific health-related needs during transit, ensuring safety and reliability that ride-sharing apps or public transit cannot guarantee. While family accompaniment offers safety, it may not always be feasible due to scheduling conflicts, making specialized services the best choice for balancing safety and consistency in transport.

Question 57: Correct Answer: C) Shared savings model

Rationale: The shared savings model minimizes financial risks by incentivizing providers to reduce unnecessary spending while maintaining quality standards. Unlike fee-for-service (Option A), which may encourage overutilization, or capitation (Option B), which might lead to underutilization, shared savings aligns provider incentives with cost efficiency and quality outcomes. Pay-for-performance (Option D) focuses on quality but doesn't inherently manage costs effectively. Hence, shared savings strikes the best balance between cost control and quality assurance in an ACO setting.

Question 58: Correct Answer: D) Refer John to a specialized dual diagnosis program for integrated treatment.

Rationale: Integrated treatment in a specialized dual diagnosis program is crucial as it addresses both disorders simultaneously, improving outcomes by considering their interrelated nature. Option A overlooks the necessity of treating both conditions together, while B may overwhelm the patient without coordinated care. Option C neglects the importance of addressing substance use alongside mental health issues. Integrated programs provide comprehensive care, ensuring both disorders are treated effectively.

Question 59: Correct Answer: B) Develop a safety plan tailored to the client's specific situation.
Rationale: Developing a safety plan is crucial as it addresses immediate risks and empowers the client with actionable steps, considering their fears of stigma and retaliation. Option A may escalate danger without preparation. Option C is beneficial but secondary to ensuring immediate safety. Option D provides long-term support but doesn't address urgent needs. Safety planning aligns with contemporary practice by prioritizing immediate protection while respecting client autonomy and readiness.

Question 60: Correct Answer: B) Facilitate access to gender-affirming counseling services.
Rationale: Facilitating access to gender-affirming counseling services is crucial as it provides a supportive environment for exploring gender identity, consistent with contemporary research and best practices in psychosocial support. Option A is incorrect as it disregards individual identity exploration. Option C delays necessary support, potentially harming psychological well-being. Option D overlooks the importance of addressing mental health and identity issues, which are integral to holistic care.

Question 61: Correct Answer: A) Skilled Nursing Facility
Rationale: A Skilled Nursing Facility offers continuous medical supervision and monitoring, making it ideal for patients with chronic conditions like heart failure. It provides a balance between medical care and a more comfortable, home-like setting. In contrast, Long-term Acute Care Hospitals focus on intensive care for critically ill patients, Assisted Living Facilities offer minimal medical oversight, and Home Health Care lacks the comprehensive monitoring available in skilled facilities.

Question 62: Correct Answer: C) Coordinating a home health nurse visit within 48 hours of discharge
Rationale: Coordinating a home health nurse visit within 48 hours of discharge is crucial as it allows for immediate assessment and intervention, reducing the risk of complications that could lead to readmission. While scheduling follow-ups (A), providing educational materials (B), and ensuring medication access (D) are important, early post-discharge nursing support directly addresses potential issues promptly, which is vital in transitional care.

Question 63: Correct Answer: D) Advocating for patient-centered care
Rationale: Advocating for patient-centered care is fundamental in the PCMH model as it ensures that care decisions respect patients' preferences, needs, and values. While coordinating referrals (A), managing records (B), and implementing guidelines (C) are important tasks, they do not directly influence the alignment of healthcare delivery with patient expectations. Advocacy ensures that all aspects of care are centered around the patient's individual experience, thereby enhancing satisfaction and outcomes.

Question 64: Correct Answer: B) Individualized care plans based on patient preferences
Rationale: The most critical aspect in developing a patient-centered approach within supportive care programs is creating individualized care plans tailored to patient preferences (Option B). This ensures that care aligns with personal values and needs, enhancing engagement and satisfaction. Standardized protocols (Option A) lack personalization. Focusing only on physical health (Option C) ignores holistic needs. Uniform psychosocial interventions (Option D) fail to address

unique patient circumstances, underscoring the importance of individualized strategies in effective supportive care.

Question 65: Correct Answer: C) Social Worker
Rationale: Social workers are trained to address psychosocial issues such as housing instability and access to community resources. They have expertise in navigating community support systems and advocating for patients' needs. While registered nurses (A), occupational therapists (B), and physical therapists (D) play crucial roles in patient care, their primary focus is not on social determinants of health or resource coordination, making social workers the most appropriate choice for these concerns.

Question 66: Correct Answer: C) Bipolar I Disorder
Rationale: Bipolar I Disorder involves episodes of mania (extreme energy and elation) followed by depressive episodes, matching John's symptoms. Cyclothymic Disorder involves milder mood swings over a longer period without full manic or depressive episodes. Major Depressive Disorder lacks manic phases entirely. Persistent Depressive Disorder involves chronic depression without the manic episodes John experiences. Therefore, Bipolar I Disorder best accounts for John's alternating mood states.

Question 67: Correct Answer: B) Employ reflective listening to validate the patient's emotions and encourage expression.
Rationale: Reflective listening involves understanding and validating emotions, which helps build trust and rapport, essential in addressing emotional needs. Option A, closed-ended questions, limit emotional expression. Option C focuses on information rather than emotional support, while option D may overlook current emotional distress by focusing on future goals. Reflective listening aligns with contemporary research emphasizing empathy in interpersonal communication for effective psychosocial support.

Question 68: Correct Answer: D) Focus on building a therapeutic alliance to foster trust and open communication.
Rationale: Building a therapeutic alliance (Option D) is crucial as it establishes trust, allowing Emily to express her emotions safely, which is foundational before other interventions. Option A, while beneficial, may not be effective initially without trust. Option B focuses on medication without addressing immediate emotional needs. Option C is more relevant for imminent physical threats rather than ongoing emotional neglect. Hence, fostering trust through a therapeutic relationship is the most appropriate initial step.

Question 69: Correct Answer: B) Contemplation
Rationale: In the Contemplation stage, individuals are aware of the benefits of change and intend to take action within six months, but they lack a specific plan. This distinguishes it from Preparation (C), where individuals have a plan and intend to act soon. Precontemplation (A) involves no intention to change, while Action (D) involves active modification of behavior.

Question 70: Correct Answer: B) Collaborate with John's religious leader to integrate spiritual practices into his recovery plan.
Rationale: Option B is correct as it emphasizes collaboration between healthcare providers and spiritual leaders, ensuring holistic care that respects John's beliefs. Option A lacks ongoing integration, while C dismisses the importance of spirituality in healing. Option D provides passive support without professional guidance. Integrating spiritual practices can improve

emotional well-being and adherence to medical advice, aligning with contemporary research on holistic care.

Question 71: Correct Answer: C) The patient's medical necessity and plan of care

Rationale: Eligibility for home care benefits primarily hinges on the patient's medical necessity and an established plan of care. This ensures that services are tailored to meet specific health needs, aligning with private benefit program criteria. While age (A), family caregiver availability (B), and proximity to facilities (D) can influence care decisions, they are secondary to establishing medical necessity and a structured plan. Understanding these distinctions is crucial for case managers in optimizing benefit utilization.

Question 72: Correct Answer: C) Collaborate with traditional healers to complement medical treatment.

Rationale: Collaboration respects the client's cultural practices while ensuring safety and efficacy in treatment plans. Option A may create resistance by dismissing valued beliefs. Option B could be perceived as culturally insensitive, reducing trust. Option D might lead to non-compliance due to perceived disrespect for cultural traditions. Effective case management involves culturally competent care that values clients' perspectives and incorporates them into comprehensive care strategies.

Question 73: Correct Answer: C) Medicaid Home and Community-Based Services (HCBS) Waiver

Rationale: The HCBS Waiver provides funding for home-based care for eligible individuals like Mr. Garcia who prefer staying at home over institutionalization. Option A, PACE, offers comprehensive care but may require enrollment in specific programs. Option B provides personal care services but under different eligibility criteria than waivers. Option D focuses on prescription drug coverage under Medicare and does not address home-based care needs directly like the HCBS Waiver does.

Question 74: Correct Answer: B) Major Depressive Disorder

Rationale: The symptoms Sarah exhibits align with Major Depressive Disorder (MDD), characterized by persistent sadness, lack of interest in activities, significant weight changes, and feelings of worthlessness. Generalized Anxiety Disorder (A) involves excessive worry rather than persistent sadness. Bipolar Disorder (C) includes mood swings between depression and mania, which are not present here. Persistent Depressive Disorder (D), or dysthymia, involves chronic depression symptoms but typically less severe than MDD. Therefore, MDD is the most accurate diagnosis based on her symptoms.

Question 75: Correct Answer: C) The parity laws governing telehealth reimbursements

Rationale: Parity laws are crucial as they determine if telehealth services are reimbursed at the same rate as in-person services, directly influencing provider decisions. Option A is a technical requirement but not a decision-making factor. Option B affects implementation ease but not reimbursement decisions. Option D reflects patient preference rather than reimbursement influence, making C the most significant factor in this context.

Question 76: Correct Answer: B) To provide a seamless transition between different levels and types of care tailored to patient needs.

Rationale: The continuum of care aims to offer a seamless transition across various healthcare settings, ensuring that care is tailored to individual patient needs. Option A is incorrect as it suggests uniformity rather than personalization. Option C incorrectly prioritizes acute over community-based care, which contradicts the holistic

approach. Option D narrows focus only to post-acute services, missing the broader scope. The correct answer emphasizes comprehensive, coordinated care across all stages, reflecting contemporary healthcare models.

Question 77: Correct Answer: C) Pay-for-Performance

Rationale: Pay-for-Performance (P4P) models incentivize healthcare providers by linking compensation to the quality of care delivered and specific health outcomes achieved. Unlike Fee-for-Service, which rewards volume over quality, P4P focuses on efficiency and effectiveness. Capitation provides a fixed amount per patient regardless of services rendered, lacking direct outcome incentives. Bundled Payments offer a single payment for an episode of care but do not directly tie compensation to quality metrics. Thus, P4P is most aligned with value-based principles.

Question 78: Correct Answer: B) To facilitate communication between multidisciplinary teams to optimize patient outcomes.

Rationale: The primary role of case managers is to facilitate communication between multidisciplinary teams, ensuring coordinated and efficient patient care, which optimizes outcomes. Option A is incorrect as case managers focus on comprehensive care, not just insurance coverage. Option C, while important, is a subset of their broader role. Option D misrepresents their function; financial management is part of a larger coordination effort rather than an exclusive focus.

Question 79: Correct Answer: C) Implementation of mindfulness training sessions

Rationale: Mindfulness training directly targets stress reduction by teaching employees techniques to manage stress effectively. Team-building activities (A) and fitness centers (B) may improve morale and physical health but are less focused on stress management. Healthy snacks (D), while beneficial for overall health, do not specifically address stress. Mindfulness provides practical skills for immediate stress relief, making it the most effective option for this goal.

Question 80: Correct Answer: A) Simplifying her medication schedule by coordinating doses with her daily routine

Rationale: Simplifying Sarah's medication schedule by aligning it with her daily activities can significantly enhance adherence, as it reduces complexity and integrates seamlessly into her lifestyle. Option B, while helpful, may not directly address the root cause of non-adherence. Option C might increase awareness but does not provide practical solutions. Option D offers clarity but lacks the personalized approach that option A provides, making it less effective in promoting sustained adherence.

Question 81: Correct Answer: C) Establishing peer support groups for emotional and social support.

Rationale: Establishing peer support groups (Option C) effectively addresses both wellness and illness prevention by offering emotional and social support, crucial for sustainable lifestyle changes. While health screenings (Option A) aid in early detection, they don't provide ongoing psychosocial support. Community fitness events (Option B) promote physical activity but lack the emotional component. Educational workshops (Option D) offer knowledge but not the peer interaction vital for comprehensive wellness strategies.

Question 82: Correct Answer: C) Use interest-based negotiation to identify shared goals among team members.

Rationale: Interest-based negotiation (Option C) focuses on finding common interests and goals, which is crucial in multidisciplinary settings where collaboration is key. This approach encourages creative problem-solving and can lead to mutually beneficial solutions without compromising ethical standards or resource allocation unnecessarily, unlike Options A and D, which may create conflict or reduce necessary services elsewhere. Reallocating resources (Option B), while practical, might not fully address all team members' concerns or priorities comprehensively compared to interest-based methods.

Question 83: Correct Answer: B) Collaborate with Mrs. Garcia by exploring her beliefs and finding common ground for mutual understanding.
Rationale: Collaboration involves understanding patient perspectives and finding shared values, which strengthens relationships and improves adherence (supported by psychosocial theories). Option A might not address personal beliefs; C could alienate her from primary support; D may seem authoritative rather than collaborative, potentially damaging rapport.

Question 84: Correct Answer: D) Explore options in the Health Insurance Marketplace
Rationale: The Health Insurance Marketplace offers various plans tailored to income levels and family needs, providing an immediate solution for Maria's situation. COBRA (A), though useful, can be costly without employer contribution. CHIP (B) is beneficial but only covers children, not Maria herself. Local non-profit organizations (C) may provide support but lack comprehensive coverage options like those found in the Marketplace. Thus, exploring the Marketplace ensures Maria finds suitable and potentially subsidized plans for her entire family.

Question 85: Correct Answer: B) Utilizing motivational interviewing techniques
Rationale: Motivational interviewing is recognized as a highly effective strategy for enhancing client self-care management. It involves engaging clients in a collaborative conversation to strengthen their motivation and commitment to change. While providing written instructions (A) and distributing pamphlets (D) offer valuable information, they lack the personalized engagement needed for behavior change. Group sessions (C) can be beneficial but may not address individual needs as effectively as motivational interviewing, which tailors the approach to each client's readiness and willingness to change.

Question 86: Correct Answer: D) Formulary Tiers
Rationale: Formulary tiers categorize drugs based on cost-sharing levels, encouraging patients to choose more cost-effective medications. While step therapy (A) and prior authorization (B) manage drug use, they focus on clinical appropriateness rather than cost-effectiveness. Quantity limits (C) restrict usage but do not directly promote cost-effective choices. Formulary tiers (D), however, directly influence patient choice through financial incentives, aligning with both cost management and therapeutic outcomes.

Question 87: Correct Answer: C) Sarah is eligible for COBRA coverage for up to 18 months.
Rationale: Under the Consolidated Omnibus Budget Reconciliation Act (COBRA), individuals who lose their job-based health insurance due to job loss are generally eligible to continue their group health benefits for up to 18 months, provided they pay the full premium. Option A is incorrect as it understates the duration. Option B is incorrect because COBRA does not allow indefinite extension; extensions beyond 18 months are limited and specific. Option D incorrectly ties eligibility to new employment, which is not a requirement under COBRA.

Question 88: Correct Answer: B) Value-based reimbursement model
Rationale: The value-based reimbursement model incentivizes comprehensive and continuous care by linking payments to patient outcomes rather than service volume. A) fee-for-service encourages quantity over quality, C) capitation provides fixed payments regardless of outcomes, potentially limiting comprehensive care, and D) bundled payments focus on specific episodes of care rather than ongoing management. Therefore, B ensures that providers are motivated to maintain high-quality, continuous virtual care delivery.

Question 89: Correct Answer: C) Readmission Rates within 30 Days
Rationale: Readmission rates within 30 days are a direct indicator of the program's effectiveness in preventing unnecessary hospitalizations, making it essential for evaluating success. While patient satisfaction scores (Option A), average length of stay (Option B), and emergency room visits (Option D) provide useful insights, they do not directly measure readmissions—a critical outcome for integrated care programs targeting reduced hospitalizations in diabetic patients.

Question 90: Correct Answer: B) Korsakoff Syndrome
Rationale: Korsakoff syndrome is characterized by confusion, memory issues, and unsteady gait due to thiamine deficiency often associated with alcohol use. Alzheimer's disease (A) primarily affects memory but not typically gait at onset. Parkinson's disease (C) involves motor symptoms like tremors but not primarily confusion or memory issues initially. Schizophrenia (D) is characterized by psychotic symptoms rather than the described cognitive impairments linked to alcohol-related thiamine deficiency in Korsakoff syndrome.

Question 91: Correct Answer: B) Explore John's beliefs and feelings about the benefits of rehabilitation exercises.
Rationale: Exploring John's beliefs and feelings (Option B) helps assess his readiness by understanding his internal motivations and barriers, aligning with motivational interviewing techniques. Direct questioning (Option A), providing statistics (Option C), or reminders (Option D) may not uncover underlying attitudes influencing his readiness to change. Understanding these beliefs is crucial for tailoring interventions that enhance engagement according to psychosocial theories on behavior change.

Question 92: Correct Answer: C) Evidence-based practice
Rationale: Evidence-based practice is crucial in evaluating medical necessity, ensuring decisions are grounded in scientific research and clinical guidelines. A), while important, does not prioritize clinical appropriateness. B), patient preference, though significant, may not always align with clinical evidence. D), provider convenience, should not dictate medical necessity decisions. The emphasis on evidence-based practice aligns with modern utilization management principles focusing on quality and efficacy in healthcare delivery.

Question 93: Correct Answer: C) Home Health Aide Services
Rationale: Home Health Aide Services provide essential in-home care, ensuring safety and assistance with daily activities, crucial for clients with cognitive impairments like Alzheimer's. While Adult Day Care Services (A) offer socialization and some supervision, they do not provide continuous home monitoring. Meals on Wheels (B) address nutritional needs but not safety or daily care. Alzheimer's Support Group (D) offers emotional support

but does not address immediate safety concerns or daily living assistance.

Question 94: Correct Answer: B) Trail Making Test Part A

Rationale: The Trail Making Test Part A is designed to evaluate cognitive processing speed and attention by requiring individuals to connect numbered dots in sequence as quickly as possible. In contrast, the Wechsler Adult Intelligence Scale (WAIS-IV) assesses overall intelligence across multiple domains, while the Rorschach Inkblot Test and Thematic Apperception Test (TAT) are projective tests used to explore personality dynamics. Therefore, Trail Making Test Part A is specifically tailored for assessing processing speed and attention.

Question 95: Correct Answer: C) Transitional Care Model (TCM)

Rationale: The Transitional Care Model (TCM) is specifically designed to ensure continuity of care as patients move from hospital to home or other settings. It focuses on preventing readmissions by enhancing communication and coordinating follow-up care. While the CCM addresses long-term management of chronic diseases, it lacks the acute transition focus of TCM. The Integrated Care Model aims at broader integration across services but does not specifically target transitions. PCMH emphasizes ongoing primary care rather than acute transition processes.

Question 96: Correct Answer: B) Implementing shared decision-making processes

Rationale: Shared decision-making is pivotal in value-based care as it fosters patient engagement and ownership of their care plan, thus enhancing adherence. While educational materials (A) and frequent follow-ups (C) are beneficial, they lack the personalized approach that shared decision-making offers. Financial incentives (D), although effective in some contexts, may not lead to sustainable adherence compared to empowering patients through collaborative planning.

Question 97: Correct Answer: B) Social support networks

Rationale: Social support networks are crucial as they influence both physical recovery and mental well-being. Medication adherence impacts treatment efficacy but not directly behavioral aspects. Pain management is essential for physical comfort but doesn't address behavioral health comprehensively. Cognitive-behavioral therapy targets mental health specifically without integrating physical functioning considerations. Social support provides emotional and practical aid, fostering better outcomes in managing chronic illnesses through enhanced resilience and coping mechanisms.

Question 98: Correct Answer: B) National clinical guidelines

Rationale: National clinical guidelines serve as a significant source for developing quality indicators under URAC's framework. These guidelines provide evidence-based recommendations that ensure consistency and effectiveness in patient care practices. Unlike historical financial data (A), administrative policy documents (C), or marketing research reports (D), national clinical guidelines offer scientifically validated benchmarks essential for measuring healthcare quality and outcomes. They guide case managers in implementing best practices aligned with URAC's commitment to high-quality care delivery.

Question 99: Correct Answer: A) Mediation

Rationale: Mediation involves guiding discussions to help conflicting parties reach their own agreement, respecting individual values and interests. It contrasts with arbitration, where decisions are imposed by an external party, potentially disregarding personal values. Avoidance neglects the issue entirely, failing to address critical concerns. Forcing imposes one viewpoint over another, risking further discord. Mediation supports constructive dialogue and consensus-building, aligning with John's goal of respecting family dynamics and patient-centered care.

Question 100: Correct Answer: B) Segregate data by specific patient demographics and conditions.

Rationale: Segregating data by demographics and conditions provides detailed insights into patterns affecting specific groups, essential for targeted interventions. Option A may overlook subgroup variations. Option C narrows focus too much, missing broader trends. Option D lacks depth as it doesn't consider other influencing factors beyond temporal comparison.

Question 101: Correct Answer: B) Reduction in HbA1c levels across the patient population

Rationale: The reduction in HbA1c levels is a direct measure of blood glucose control and a key quality indicator for assessing long-term health outcomes in diabetic patients. It provides objective data on how well diabetes is being managed over time. While educational sessions (Option A), follow-up appointments (Option C), and lifestyle changes (Option D) are essential components of diabetes management, they serve as intermediate steps towards achieving better glycemic control, making HbA1c reduction the most relevant outcome measure.

Question 102: Correct Answer: C) Dual-focused CBT integrating anxiety and substance use strategies

Rationale: Dual-focused CBT is effective for co-occurring disorders like GAD and opioid dependence because it simultaneously targets both issues, fostering improved social functioning. Solely focusing on anxiety or opioid dependence through separate therapies may overlook their interconnected effects. MAT alone does not address the psychological aspects of anxiety. Group therapy limited to anxiety reduction fails to consider substance use impacts. Integrating approaches ensures comprehensive management of both conditions.

Question 103: Correct Answer: B) Requirement for a primary care physician referral for specialist services

Rationale: The defining feature of an HMO is the requirement for members to obtain referrals from their primary care physicians to see specialists, ensuring coordinated care. Option A is incorrect as HMOs restrict provider choice. Option C is incorrect because HMOs use capitation, not fee-for-service. Option D is misleading as HMOs typically have lower out-of-pocket costs but restrict out-of-network services.

Question 104: Correct Answer: B) Cognitive Reframing

Rationale: Cognitive Reframing is the correct answer as it directly involves altering an individual's thought patterns to restore cognitive balance. Cathartic Release (A) and Emotional Ventilation (C) focus on emotional expression rather than cognitive restructuring. Behavioral Activation (D) targets behavioral changes, not thought processes. The emphasis of Cognitive Reframing on changing perceptions and interpretations makes it distinct from the other options that focus on emotional or behavioral aspects.

Question 105: Correct Answer: B) Establishing a trusting relationship through empathy and active listening

Rationale: Establishing a trusting relationship through empathy and active listening is crucial for addressing psychosocial barriers, as it fosters trust and understanding, encouraging clients to participate actively. Option A, while important, lacks the personalized approach necessary for addressing individual psychosocial needs. Option C provides valuable information but doesn't directly engage the client on an emotional level. Option D enhances communication but might not address underlying psychosocial issues as effectively as building trust through empathy and listening.

Question 106: Correct Answer: C) Facilitate enrollment in a patient assistance program

Rationale: Facilitating enrollment in a patient assistance program can significantly reduce out-of-pocket costs for high-cost specialty drugs, ensuring affordability and adherence. While generic alternatives (A) and step therapy (B) are cost-saving strategies, they may not apply if no equivalents exist. Mail-order services (D) offer convenience but may not impact cost as effectively as assistance programs. Patient assistance programs are specifically designed to help with expensive medications, making them the most effective strategy in this scenario.

Question 107: Correct Answer: B) Involve him in creating his own recovery schedule with supervision.

Rationale: Involving Jacob in creating his own recovery schedule fosters autonomy and responsibility, key developmental tasks for adolescents. Option A undermines independence; Option C neglects Jacob's involvement; Option D misses opportunities for empowerment and engagement. Adolescents benefit from participatory approaches that respect their growing independence while ensuring necessary guidance, making B the optimal choice to support both recovery and personal development.

Question 108: Correct Answer: C) Special Needs Trust

Rationale: A Special Needs Trust is specifically designed to allow individuals with disabilities to receive inheritances or other funds without losing eligibility for government benefits like Medicaid. Unlike revocable or irrevocable trusts, which may affect eligibility, a Special Needs Trust ensures funds are used for the beneficiary's supplemental needs without impacting benefit qualification. A Charitable Remainder Trust is unrelated as it focuses on charitable giving. This distinction makes the Special Needs Trust the correct choice.

Question 109: Correct Answer: B) Patient Assistance Programs (PAPs)

Rationale: Patient Assistance Programs (PAPs) are designed to help individuals like John who have limited income but do not qualify for Medicaid. They provide free or low-cost medications directly from pharmaceutical companies. SPAPs and LIS are also valuable resources, but they often require state-specific eligibility or enrollment in Medicare Part D, which may not apply to John's situation. The 340B program benefits hospitals and clinics rather than individual patients directly.

Question 110: Correct Answer: B) Children's Health Insurance Program (CHIP)

Rationale: The Children's Health Insurance Program (CHIP) is tailored to offer health coverage to uninsured children whose families have incomes above Medicaid eligibility but still cannot afford private insurance. Unlike Medicare, which serves older adults, and SNAP or TANF, which focus on nutritional and financial aid respectively, CHIP directly addresses healthcare access for children. Its design bridges the gap between Medicaid and private insurance, making it the appropriate choice in this context.

Question 111: Correct Answer: C) To coordinate patient care and manage resource utilization

Rationale: Gatekeepers like primary care physicians coordinate care and manage resources by directing patients to appropriate services, ensuring efficiency and cost-effectiveness. Increasing patient autonomy (A) or facilitating direct access to specialists (B) contradicts the gatekeeper role's intent. Limiting access to necessary treatments (D) is not the primary goal; instead, gatekeepers aim to optimize treatment pathways. Therefore, coordination and resource management are central objectives in managed care through gatekeeping.

Question 112: Correct Answer: A) Provides immediate cash to cover medical expenses and improve quality of life.

Rationale: A viatical settlement allows terminally ill individuals to receive immediate cash by selling their life insurance policy, which can be used for medical expenses and enhancing their quality of life. Option B is incorrect as it does not ensure health coverage for dependents; C is incorrect because it does not guarantee full face value; D is incorrect because while it eliminates future premiums, this is not the primary benefit compared to receiving immediate funds.

Question 113: Correct Answer: A) Principle of Utmost Good Faith

Rationale: The principle of utmost good faith is crucial in disability insurance as it requires full disclosure of all relevant information by the insured. This principle ensures that both parties, the insurer and the insured, have access to all necessary details to assess risk accurately. While the principle of indemnity focuses on restoring the insured's financial position, subrogation involves transferring rights to claim damages, and proximate cause relates to identifying the primary cause of loss, none directly address eligibility determination like utmost good faith.

Question 114: Correct Answer: A) DSM-5 (Diagnostic and Statistical Manual of Mental Disorders, Fifth Edition)

Rationale: DSM-5 is the most commonly used tool for diagnosing mental health disorders as it provides standardized criteria based on contemporary research. ICD-10 (B), while also used for diagnosis, is broader and less detailed in psychiatric contexts compared to DSM-5. MMPI (C) is a psychological assessment tool but not specifically for diagnostic criteria. The Rorschach Inkblot Test (D), a projective test, lacks standardization for diagnosis compared to DSM-5's structured guidelines.

Question 115: Correct Answer: B) Encourage John to set personal health goals and create an action plan.

Rationale: Encouraging John to set personal health goals and create an action plan (Option B) directly involves him in the decision-making process, fostering empowerment by promoting autonomy and self-efficacy. While providing educational materials (Option A) is informative, it lacks the interactive component necessary for empowerment. Regular follow-ups (Option C) ensure adherence but do not necessarily enhance empowerment. Peer support groups (Option D) offer shared experiences but may not specifically focus on individual empowerment like goal-setting does.

Question 116: Correct Answer: B) Facilitating narrative development about the loss

Rationale: Meaning reconstruction involves creating narratives that help integrate the loss into one's life story. Option A contradicts this by suggesting forgetting. Option C discourages emotional processing, vital for healing. Option D overlooks personal growth through understanding loss. Therefore, B is correct as it aids in constructing meaning and adapting to life changes post-loss, supported by contemporary research on bereavement counseling.

Question 117: Correct Answer: B) Refer Alex to a mental health professional specializing in gender issues.

Rationale: Referring Alex to a mental health professional specializing in gender issues is crucial as it provides specialized support and addresses complex emotional and psychological needs specific to transgender individuals. Option A may help but lacks immediate professional guidance. Option C assumes family willingness, which may not be present. Option D might not adequately address underlying issues without professional intervention.

Question 118: Correct Answer: B) Gender expression involves a person's external presentation of gender, which may not necessarily align with their biological sex.

Rationale: Option B correctly identifies that gender expression refers to how individuals present their gender externally, which can differ from their biological sex. This understanding is crucial for effective psychosocial support in healthcare. Option A incorrectly limits gender expression to biological sex, ignoring the diverse ways people express themselves. Option C incorrectly implies conformity to societal norms, while D dismisses the importance of recognizing diverse gender expressions in healthcare settings.

Question 119: Correct Answer: B) Enhancing care coordination to improve patient outcomes

Rationale: The primary goal of ACOs is to enhance care coordination, thereby improving patient outcomes. Unlike option A, which focuses on revenue, ACOs prioritize quality over quantity. Option C misrepresents the collaborative nature of ACOs, which aim to integrate rather than diminish provider roles. Option D incorrectly implies that cost-cutting is the sole focus; instead, ACOs balance cost with quality improvements. Thus, option B accurately reflects the core mission of ACOs.

Question 120: Correct Answer: C) Collaborating

Rationale: Collaborating is the most effective strategy for maintaining long-term relationships as it seeks a win-win outcome by integrating the needs and concerns of both parties. Unlike competing, which focuses on winning, collaborating emphasizes mutual satisfaction. Avoiding neglects conflict resolution, potentially harming relationships. Compromising finds a middle ground but may not fully satisfy either party, unlike collaborating, which aims for comprehensive solutions.

Question 121: Correct Answer: B) Root Cause Analysis (RCA)

Rationale: Root Cause Analysis (RCA) is specifically designed to identify the underlying causes of a problem, ensuring that solutions address the root issue rather than symptoms. While Lean Six Sigma focuses on process improvement and waste reduction, PDSA is iterative for testing changes, and FMEA identifies potential failures before they occur. RCA's strength lies in its structured approach to uncovering fundamental issues through data collection and analysis, making it ideal for addressing quality issues at their source.

Question 122: Correct Answer: B) Medicaid eligibility is determined by income and family size.

Rationale: Medicaid eligibility is primarily based on income and family size, making it distinct from Medicare, which considers age or disability. Option A is incorrect as age alone doesn't determine Medicaid eligibility. Option C is misleading because while some disabled individuals qualify, it isn't the sole criterion. Option D incorrectly links Medicaid to work history, which pertains more to Medicare's qualification for Social Security benefits.

Therefore, B accurately reflects the fundamental income-based criterion of Medicaid.

Question 123: Correct Answer: B) CPT

Rationale: CPT (Current Procedural Terminology) is used to describe medical services and procedures in outpatient settings, facilitating billing and ensuring appropriate reimbursement. HCPCS Level II codes are for supplies/services not included in CPT. ICD-10-PCS is used for inpatient procedure coding, while LOINC is a standard for lab results. CPT's role in detailing outpatient procedures makes it critical for accurate billing and reimbursement processes.

Question 124: Correct Answer: A) John must demonstrate that his condition will last at least 12 months or result in death.

Rationale: To qualify for SSDI, an applicant's disability must be expected to last at least 12 months or result in death. This distinguishes it from short-term disabilities (Option B), which may not meet this criterion. Option C is incorrect as SSDI does not require zero income but rather limited substantial gainful activity. Option D is misleading; eligibility depends on work credits, not necessarily the length of employment.

Question 125: Correct Answer: C) Encourage Mark to participate in pulmonary rehabilitation programs tailored for COPD patients.

Rationale: Pulmonary rehabilitation programs are specifically designed for COPD patients, focusing on improving exercise capacity and reducing symptoms like fatigue and breathlessness. High-intensity training (Option A) may be too strenuous for Mark's condition. Brisk walking (Option B), although beneficial, might not be tailored enough for his needs. Advising more rest (Option D) does not actively address physical activity improvement like Option C does by offering structured support aligned with his condition.

Question 126: Correct Answer: C) Group Home

Rationale: A Group Home is ideal for individuals like the patient who need some assistance while maintaining independence. Unlike Skilled Nursing Facilities (A), which are for those needing extensive medical care, or Assisted Living Facilities (B), which cater to those needing significant personal care, Group Homes provide the right balance of support and independence. Independent Living Communities (D) offer minimal assistance, unsuitable for this patient's needs.

Question 127: Correct Answer: A) Telehealth monitoring with regular virtual consultations

Rationale: Telehealth monitoring provides continuous oversight and timely interventions, reducing the risk of readmissions for COPD patients like Sarah. Unlike a skilled nursing facility or home health care, telehealth offers real-time data and access to healthcare providers without requiring physical presence. Outpatient rehabilitation focuses on physical therapy but lacks the comprehensive monitoring provided by telehealth, making it less suitable for preventing acute exacerbations in chronic conditions.

Question 128: Correct Answer: C) Pay for services upfront and seek reimbursement from the insurer.

Rationale: Indemnity insurance plans require individuals to pay for healthcare services upfront and then seek reimbursement, aligning with traditional fee-for-service models. Option A is incorrect as it describes managed care plans. Option B relates to coinsurance, common in other plan types but not specific to indemnity plans' core function. Option D inaccurately suggests equal cost-sharing without initial payment, diverging from indemnity principles where initial financial responsibility lies with the insured.

Question 129: Correct Answer: B) Action
Rationale: The Action stage involves active modification of behavior, as seen with Lisa attending fitness classes. This distinguishes it from Preparation (Option C), where planning occurs without full commitment. Maintenance (Option A) follows sustained behavior change over time, while Termination (Option D) indicates complete confidence in maintaining the change without relapse risk. Lisa's consistent class attendance reflects active behavior modification typical of the Action stage.

Question 130: Correct Answer: C) Suggest that Emily engage in legacy-building activities honoring her father
Rationale: Legacy-building activities (Option C) are integral in contemporary bereavement counseling as they help individuals find meaning and maintain a bond with the deceased, aiding adjustment. Option A can reduce stress but may not address deeper emotional connections. Option B might help eventually but lacks immediate emotional processing elements. Option D focuses on distraction rather than confronting and integrating the loss into life narratives.

Question 131: Correct Answer: B) National Multiple Sclerosis Society
Rationale: The National Multiple Sclerosis Society is dedicated to providing support and resources specifically for individuals with MS. It offers educational materials, community programs, and advocacy tailored to MS patients' needs. While the American Heart Association, Alzheimer's Association, and Arthritis Foundation offer valuable resources, they focus on different conditions (heart disease, Alzheimer's disease, and arthritis respectively). Therefore, the National Multiple Sclerosis Society is the most relevant choice for MS-specific support.

Question 132: Correct Answer: B) Integrated Delivery System (IDS)
Rationale: Integrated Delivery Systems (IDS) aim to reduce costs and improve outcomes by coordinating care across various healthcare settings. Unlike Capitation, which involves a fixed payment per patient, IDS emphasizes integrated care delivery. Fee-for-Service (FFS) incentivizes volume over value, potentially increasing costs. Pay-for-Performance (P4P) focuses on quality metrics but does not inherently integrate care across settings. IDS uniquely combines coordination and outcome improvement, aligning with contemporary research on cost-effective care delivery.

Question 133: Correct Answer: A) Social Learning Theory
Rationale: Social Learning Theory posits that gender identity is shaped through social interaction, reinforcement, and modeling, making it distinct from Biological Determinism, which focuses on innate biological factors. Cognitive Developmental Theory emphasizes individual cognitive processes in understanding gender, while Gender Schema Theory highlights mental frameworks guiding perceptions of gender. The key difference is Social Learning's emphasis on external social influences over internal cognitive structures or biological determinants.

Question 134: Correct Answer: B) Build rapport with Maria to encourage her disclosure of any issues.
Rationale: Building rapport fosters trust, encouraging Maria to share her experiences openly, which is vital for understanding her situation accurately. Immediate reporting (Option A) may be premature without confirming neglect through Maria's perspective. An unannounced visit (Option C) could breach privacy or trust without consent. Discussing concerns with staff (Option D) might not reveal underlying issues if staff are complicit or unaware. Establishing trust aligns with best practices in elder care by emphasizing client-centered communication and advocacy.

Question 135: Correct Answer: B) Encouraging clients to set their own health goals and create action plans
Rationale: Option B empowers clients by allowing them to take control of their health decisions, fostering autonomy. This aligns with contemporary research emphasizing client-centered care. Option A limits choice, while C undermines autonomy by shifting decision-making to case managers. Option D fails to tailor care to individual needs, reducing personalization. Encouraging goal-setting and action planning is key to self-directed care, promoting engagement and responsibility.

Question 136: Correct Answer: A) Parkinson's Foundation
Rationale: The Parkinson's Foundation provides community engagement opportunities and disseminates current research information specifically tailored for individuals with Parkinson's disease. The other organizations focus on distinct medical conditions such as heart disease, muscular dystrophy, and lupus, which do not align with John's client's needs. Therefore, Option A is the valid choice as it directly supports individuals dealing with Parkinson's disease through relevant programs and information.

Question 137: Correct Answer: B) Minority Stress
Rationale: Minority stress refers to the unique stressors faced by individuals belonging to stigmatized minority groups, including bisexual individuals who may feel marginalized by both heterosexual and LGBTQ+ communities. While intersectionality (A) addresses overlapping social identities and related systems of oppression, it doesn't specifically focus on stress. Identity confusion (C) pertains to uncertainty about one's sexual orientation, not external marginalization. Internalized homophobia (D) involves negative feelings towards one's own sexual orientation rather than external community dynamics.

Question 138: Correct Answer: C) Bundled Payments
Rationale: Bundled payments incentivize providers to deliver efficient, coordinated care by offering a single payment for all services related to a treatment or condition over a specified period. This method encourages reducing unnecessary hospitalizations, aligning with the goal of managing Mr. Johnson's chronic conditions more effectively. Fee-for-service often leads to higher utilization without coordination incentives. Capitation provides a fixed amount per patient but may not adequately address specific care needs. Pay-for-performance focuses on quality metrics but does not directly address comprehensive care coordination.

Question 139: Correct Answer: B) Developing a comprehensive discharge plan that includes home health services
Rationale: The correct answer is B, as developing a comprehensive discharge plan ensures continuity of care across settings, which is crucial for patients with complex needs like Mr. Johnson. Option A focuses on follow-up appointments, which are important but do not encompass the broader coordination role. Option C is more about patient education than transition coordination. Option D involves communication but lacks the strategic planning needed for effective transitions.

Question 140: Correct Answer: C) Comprehensive, coordinated care across all elements of the healthcare system

Rationale: The PCMH model emphasizes comprehensive, coordinated care across all healthcare system elements, including specialty and community services. This approach ensures holistic patient management, contrasting with options A and D, which focus on specific aspects like acute or specialty care. Option B is incorrect as PCMH promotes team-based rather than solely physician-led care. The model's strength lies in its integration and coordination, aiming for improved outcomes and patient satisfaction through continuous and accessible healthcare.

Question 141: Correct Answer: C) Develop a personalized telemedicine follow-up schedule post-discharge.

Rationale: Personalized telemedicine follow-ups ensure tailored care and immediate problem-solving post-discharge, directly reducing readmissions by addressing individual needs promptly. While educational webinars (Option A) enhance knowledge, they lack personalization. Virtual support groups (Option B) foster community but don't address specific medical issues directly. An online library (Option D), although informative, doesn't offer real-time interaction or feedback like personalized follow-ups do, making Option C the most effective strategy.

Question 142: Correct Answer: C) Strong leadership support and commitment

Rationale: Strong leadership support and commitment are vital as they foster a culture of health, ensuring resources and policies align with wellness goals. Unlike financial incentives (A), which may offer short-term motivation, leadership involvement sustains long-term engagement. Comprehensive health education (B) is essential but less impactful without leadership backing. Regular biometric screenings (D) are beneficial for tracking health metrics but do not drive program success without strategic support from leadership.

Question 143: Correct Answer: B) 18 months

Rationale: The standard maximum duration for COBRA coverage after employment termination is 18 months. Option A (12 months) underestimates this period, while option C (24 months) exceeds it without disability extension. Option D (36 months) applies only in specific circumstances like divorce or death affecting dependents. Thus, B is correct as it aligns with the typical continuation period specified by COBRA regulations, reflecting the balance between immediate post-employment needs and long-term benefit planning.

Question 144: Correct Answer: B) Discussing Tom's past successes in managing his diet.

Rationale: Motivational interviewing emphasizes building confidence through past successes, making Option B correct as it encourages self-efficacy and positive reinforcement. Option A is prescriptive, Option C is overly directive, and Option D focuses on fear-based tactics rather than empowering change through motivation and self-reflection.

Question 145: Correct Answer: C) SSDI is funded through payroll taxes and requires sufficient work history; SSI is funded by general tax revenues and does not require work history.

Rationale: SSDI eligibility depends on a sufficient work history funded by payroll taxes, whereas SSI focuses on financial need without requiring prior employment. Option A incorrectly reverses these requirements. Option B misrepresents SSI's medical condition requirement—both programs require disability verification. Option D inaccurately suggests age-based qualification; both programs serve younger disabled individuals as well.

Question 146: Correct Answer: B) Virtual diabetes management programs

Rationale: Virtual diabetes management programs provide comprehensive education and support tailored to individual needs, making them ideal for ongoing diabetes management post-discharge. Retail health clinics (A), while convenient, typically focus on minor acute issues rather than chronic disease management. Skilled nursing facilities (C) are more appropriate for patients needing intensive rehabilitation or medical care. Emergency departments (D) are unsuitable for routine education and support as they address urgent health issues rather than ongoing management needs.

Question 147: Correct Answer: C) Patient Assistance Programs

Rationale: Patient Assistance Programs (PAPs) are specifically designed by pharmaceutical manufacturers to provide medications at reduced costs to those who qualify based on financial need. Medicaid (A) and Medicare Part D (D) are government programs with broader eligibility criteria but not specific to manufacturer discounts. The 340B Drug Pricing Program (B) is intended for healthcare facilities serving vulnerable populations, not directly for individual patients. PAPs directly address the needs of uninsured or underinsured individuals seeking affordable medication access.

Question 148: Correct Answer: C) Bundled payments that cover all services for an episode of care across providers.

Rationale: Bundled payments incentivize integrated service delivery by covering all services in an episode, encouraging coordination among providers. Option A's fee-for-service can lead to fragmented care due to separate reimbursements per service. Option B's capitation might not adequately support integration as it focuses on cost control over coordination. Option D's cost-plus model may promote inefficiency by reimbursing based on incurred costs plus profit, lacking incentive for integrated delivery. Bundled payments align with contemporary strategies for cohesive and efficient healthcare provision.

Question 149: Correct Answer: B) No requirement for primary care physician referrals.

Rationale: Indemnity insurance allows freedom to choose any healthcare provider without needing referrals, unlike managed care plans that often require such protocols. Option A incorrectly suggests network restrictions typical of HMOs or PPOs. Option C inaccurately implies network limitations not present in indemnity plans. Option D misrepresents indemnity plans by suggesting extensive pre-authorization processes, which are more characteristic of managed care structures aiming to control costs and service utilization.

Question 150: Correct Answer: A) Ensure the organization's beliefs align with John's personal values.

Rationale: Option A is correct because aligning organizational beliefs with John's values ensures meaningful engagement and emotional support, crucial for recovery. Options B and C focus on logistical convenience and activity availability but may not provide the emotional connection John seeks. Option D addresses financial needs rather than social or emotional support, which is John's primary concern in this context.

CCM Exam Practice Questions [SET 5]

Question 1: Sarah, a case manager, is assisting a client who recently lost their job and is struggling to afford healthcare coverage. The client qualifies for several public benefit programs. Which program should Sarah prioritize enrolling the client in to ensure they receive immediate healthcare coverage?
A) Supplemental Nutrition Assistance Program (SNAP)
B) Medicaid
C) Temporary Assistance for Needy Families (TANF)
D) Social Security Disability Insurance (SSDI)

Question 2: In managing clients with chronic heart failure, which of the following interventions is most effective in reducing hospital readmissions?
A) Implementing a daily exercise regimen tailored to the client's capabilities
B) Conducting regular telehealth consultations to monitor symptoms
C) Prescribing a low-sodium diet plan and monitoring adherence
D) Providing comprehensive medication management education

Question 3: You are tasked with evaluating the effectiveness of a new electronic health record (EHR) system designed to enhance quality and performance in patient care management. During your assessment, which key performance indicator (KPI) would best reflect improved quality and outcomes resulting from this implementation?
A) Reduction in medication errors
B) Increase in patient volume handled per day
C) Decrease in staff overtime hours
D) Improved staff satisfaction scores

Question 4: Which of the following is a core principle of Motivational Interviewing that emphasizes understanding the client's perspective without judgment?
A) Express Empathy
B) Develop Discrepancy
C) Roll with Resistance
D) Support Self-Efficacy

Question 5: Maria, a case manager, is working with a 45-year-old patient named John who has recently been diagnosed with diabetes. John is struggling to accept his condition and is hesitant about joining a support group. Maria wants to encourage him to participate in a support group by highlighting its benefits. Which of the following is the most compelling reason Maria should provide?
A) Support groups offer medical advice from professionals.
B) Support groups provide emotional support and shared experiences from peers.
C) Support groups guarantee improved medical outcomes.
D) Support groups reduce the need for medication.

Question 6: When assessing for Generalized Anxiety Disorder (GAD), which symptom is most critical to differentiate it from other anxiety disorders?
A) Panic attacks occurring unexpectedly
B) Excessive worry occurring more days than not for at least six months
C) Specific phobias related to certain objects or situations
D) Recurrent intrusive thoughts leading to compulsive behaviors

Question 7: In the context of health care analytics, which method is most effective for predicting patient readmissions by analyzing large datasets and identifying complex patterns?
A) Logistic Regression
B) Decision Trees
C) Support Vector Machines (SVM)
D) Neural Networks

Question 8: Which of the following is the most effective strategy for a case manager to employ when integrating support groups into a client's care plan to enhance psychosocial outcomes?
A) Encourage clients to attend any available support group in their area.
B) Match clients with support groups that align with their specific conditions and needs.
C) Recommend online forums as a substitute for in-person support groups.
D) Suggest participation in multiple support groups simultaneously for broader perspectives.

Question 9: John, a case manager, is working with a patient, Mary, who has been recently diagnosed with diabetes. During their sessions, John notices that Mary struggles to understand her medication regimen and dietary changes. Which strategy should John prioritize to enhance Mary's health literacy and ensure effective management of her condition?
A) Provide Mary with printed educational materials that include detailed medical terminology.
B) Use teach-back methods to confirm Mary's understanding of the information provided.
C) Encourage Mary to attend group education sessions without any follow-up on her comprehension.
D) Recommend online resources for Mary to explore independently at her own pace.

Question 10: Jamie, a 35-year-old case manager, is working with a transgender client who is experiencing distress due to societal expectations about gender expression. What should Jamie prioritize in their approach to support the client's gender expression?
A) Encourage the client to conform to societal norms for safety.
B) Validate the client's feelings and support their authentic gender expression.
C) Focus on helping the client pass as their identified gender.
D) Advise the client to avoid discussing their gender identity in public.

Question 11: Which community resource is most effective in providing comprehensive psychosocial support to elderly individuals living independently, focusing on enhancing their social engagement and mental well-being?
A) Home Health Care Services
B) Adult Day Care Centers
C) Assisted Living Facilities
D) Skilled Nursing Facilities

Question 12: John, a 72-year-old retiree, recently underwent a hip replacement surgery and is currently in a skilled nursing facility for rehabilitation. He is concerned about the coverage of his stay under Medicare. As his case manager, what should you inform him regarding Medicare's coverage for skilled nursing facility care?
A) Medicare Part A covers up to 20 days in a skilled nursing facility with no coinsurance.
B) Medicare Part B covers up to 100 days in a skilled nursing facility with full cost coverage.
C) Medicare Part A covers up to 100 days in a skilled

nursing facility with a coinsurance fee after 20 days.
D) Medicare Part C covers all costs for an unlimited number of days in a skilled nursing facility.

Question 13: In a multidisciplinary team within a hospital setting, which professional typically leads the discharge planning process to ensure appropriate post-hospitalization care?
A) Hospitalist
B) Registered Nurse
C) Physical Therapist
D) Discharge Planner

Question 14: Which of the following reimbursement methodologies best aligns with the goal of incentivizing quality care while controlling costs in a healthcare setting?
A) Fee-for-Service
B) Capitation
C) Value-Based Purchasing
D) Per Diem Payment

Question 15: Emily, a case manager, is supporting Maria, who lost her child six months ago and is experiencing intense sadness and avoidance behaviors. Which approach should Emily prioritize to help Maria process her grief effectively?
A) Encourage Maria to focus on creating new memories with friends and family.
B) Facilitate expressive arts therapy sessions for Maria to explore her emotions creatively.
C) Advise Maria to avoid places that trigger memories of her child until she feels better.
D) Suggest cognitive-behavioral therapy techniques to reframe negative thoughts.

Question 16: John, a case manager, is tasked with creating a holistic care plan for Maria, an elderly patient with complex medical and social needs. To ensure comprehensive service delivery, which strategy should John employ to address both medical and non-medical factors impacting Maria's health?
A) Focus solely on Maria's medical treatment adherence.
B) Coordinate with community resources for social support services.
C) Prioritize frequent medical check-ups and monitoring.
D) Develop an individualized exercise regimen.

Question 17: When considering community resources for patient transportation, what is the primary benefit of integrating telehealth options into a case management plan?
A) Reduces healthcare costs significantly
B) Eliminates the need for any physical travel
C) Increases patient engagement and adherence
D) Provides immediate access to specialist consultations

Question 18: Mr. Garcia, a 76-year-old man with limited mobility due to arthritis, lives with his wife who also has health issues. They are struggling to manage household tasks and are isolated from their community support network due to transportation challenges. What community resource should the case manager prioritize to enhance their quality of life?
A) Meals on Wheels Program
B) Senior Center Activities
C) Volunteer Transportation Services
D) Home Health Aide

Question 19: Which of the following is the most critical factor for a case manager to consider when assessing the risk of elder abuse in a community-dwelling older adult?

A) The older adult's financial status
B) The presence of cognitive impairment
C) The availability of social support
D) The older adult's living environment

Question 20: Mr. Johnson, a 55-year-old patient with a history of diabetes, is being discharged from the hospital after surgery. As his case manager, you need to ensure he receives Supplemental Security Income (SSI) benefits to support his post-operative care. Which of the following criteria must Mr. Johnson primarily meet to qualify for SSI?
A) Age over 65
B) Limited income and resources
C) U.S. citizenship
D) Disability status

Question 21: In the context of collaborative case management, which of the following strategies is most effective in ensuring comprehensive care coordination for patients with complex needs?
A) Establishing a single point of contact for all healthcare providers
B) Utilizing a multidisciplinary team approach
C) Implementing standardized care pathways
D) Focusing on cost-effective treatment options

Question 22: In the context of health coaching, which of the following strategies is most effective in facilitating behavior change according to the Transtheoretical Model (TTM)?
A) Providing immediate rewards for positive behavior changes
B) Tailoring interventions to match the individual's stage of change
C) Focusing on reducing barriers to change through environmental restructuring
D) Emphasizing the importance of goal-setting and self-monitoring

Question 23: Which of the following is a primary benefit of employer-based health and wellness programs in the context of care delivery and reimbursement methods?
A) Reduced absenteeism rates
B) Increased employee satisfaction
C) Lower healthcare costs for employees
D) Enhanced employee productivity

Question 24: Sarah, a case manager, is coordinating care for Mr. Johnson, who has limited mobility and lives in a rural area. She is considering virtual care options to ensure he receives regular monitoring and consultations. Which of the following strategies would be most effective in implementing virtual care for Mr. Johnson while addressing potential barriers?
A) Use video conferencing for all consultations without considering internet connectivity issues.
B) Implement remote patient monitoring devices and provide technical support to address connectivity issues.
C) Schedule periodic in-person visits to supplement virtual care without integrating technology.
D) Rely solely on telephone calls for consultations due to his rural location.

Question 25: John, a 68-year-old patient with chronic heart failure, is being discharged from the hospital. As his case manager, your goal is to ensure a smooth transition of care to prevent readmission. Which strategy is most effective in achieving this goal?
A) Schedule a follow-up appointment with his primary care physician within 30 days.
B) Arrange for home health services to visit John once a week.

C) Develop a comprehensive discharge plan including medication reconciliation and patient education.
D) Provide John with contact information for emergency services.

Question 26: How might a case manager best address the health needs of a client from a culture that views illness as a result of spiritual imbalance?
A) Encourage adherence to prescribed medical treatments only.
B) Integrate spiritual healing practices with medical treatments.
C) Focus solely on biomedical explanations of the illness.
D) Avoid discussing spiritual beliefs to maintain clinical objectivity.

Question 27: John, a case manager, is tasked with managing a complex case involving multiple chronic conditions requiring numerous medications. To optimize pharmacy benefits and improve outcomes, which approach should John consider first?
A) Conducting a comprehensive medication review
B) Implementing prior authorization for all medications
C) Encouraging the use of over-the-counter alternatives
D) Switching to formulary-preferred brand medications

Question 28: During a case management meeting, Sarah, a case manager, notices that her client, Mr. Thompson, is hesitant to share personal information. To improve interpersonal communication and encourage openness, which strategy should Sarah prioritize based on active listening principles?
A) Paraphrasing Mr. Thompson's statements to show understanding
B) Offering immediate solutions to Mr. Thompson's problems
C) Sharing her own experiences to build rapport
D) Asking closed-ended questions for clarity

Question 29: How does the Adjusted Clinical Group (ACG) system primarily classify patients to predict healthcare resource utilization?
A) By using demographic data such as age and gender
B) By evaluating clinical diagnoses and treatment patterns
C) By assessing socioeconomic status and geographic location
D) By analyzing patient-reported outcomes and satisfaction scores

Question 30: Sarah, a 75-year-old with diabetes and mobility issues, requires a setting that provides comprehensive support without hospitalization. The case manager needs to select an alternative care site that offers medical supervision and daily living assistance. Which site should be chosen?
A) Independent Living Community
B) Inpatient Rehabilitation Facility
C) Long-term Acute Care Hospital
D) Assisted Living Facility

Question 31: Sarah, a case manager, is reviewing a patient's request for an MRI scan. The patient's insurance plan requires prior authorization for imaging services. Which step should Sarah prioritize to ensure compliance with utilization management principles?
A) Submit the request without documentation to expedite approval
B) Verify the medical necessity and gather supporting documentation
C) Schedule the MRI before obtaining authorization to avoid delays
D) Assume approval based on previous similar cases

Question 32: In the context of case management, which transportation strategy is most effective for ensuring continuity of care for patients with limited mobility in urban areas?
A) Public transportation passes
B) Non-emergency medical transportation services
C) Ride-sharing services
D) Volunteer driver programs

Question 33: What is a primary advantage of using alternative care sites in the management of patient care during a public health crisis?
A) Reduced need for specialized medical equipment
B) Decreased burden on traditional healthcare facilities
C) Lower cost of care compared to hospital settings
D) Increased patient satisfaction due to personalized care

Question 34: Sarah, a case manager, is evaluating the effectiveness of a Health Home model for a patient with multiple chronic conditions. Which key feature should Sarah prioritize to ensure comprehensive care coordination under this model?
A) Emphasizing acute care interventions
B) Enhancing patient self-management education
C) Focusing on specialty care referrals
D) Increasing the frequency of home visits

Question 35: Sarah is managing the case of Mrs. Lopez, who has been neglected financially by her caregiver son, resulting in unpaid bills and potential eviction. What immediate financial intervention should Sarah consider to stabilize Mrs. Lopez's situation?
A) Applying for emergency rental assistance programs
B) Counseling the son on better financial management
C) Advising Mrs. Lopez to take legal action against her son
D) Suggesting Mrs. Lopez apply for a high-interest loan

Question 36: John, a veteran living alone with mild cognitive impairment, wants to maintain independence through meal delivery services. What should be prioritized in selecting an appropriate service for him?
A) Availability of senior discounts
B) Meals that require minimal preparation
C) Access to customer support for order adjustments
D) Delivery frequency that matches his routine

Question 37: Lisa is a case manager assisting Tom, who is resistant to lifestyle changes necessary for managing his chronic condition. During their conversation, Tom mentions feeling overwhelmed by the required changes. What Motivational Interviewing technique should Lisa use to support Tom in this situation?
A) Confront Tom about his resistance to change.
B) Highlight the discrepancies between Tom's current behavior and his goals.
C) Provide reassurance that change is easy once started.
D) Offer detailed solutions for overcoming barriers.

Question 38: Sarah, a 45-year-old single mother living in an urban area, frequently misses her medical appointments due to transportation issues. As her case manager, which social determinant of health should you prioritize to improve her healthcare access?
A) Economic Stability
B) Education Access and Quality
C) Neighborhood and Built Environment
D) Social and Community Context

Question 39: In the context of bundled payment models, which aspect is primarily intended to incentivize healthcare providers to improve care coordination and efficiency?
A) Fee-for-service reimbursement
B) Capitation payments

C) Shared savings programs
D) Episode-based payments

Question 40: In the context of individually purchased insurance, what is a primary advantage of selecting a high-deductible health plan (HDHP)?
A) Lower monthly premium payments
B) Broader network access
C) More comprehensive coverage options
D) Reduced out-of-pocket maximums

Question 41: In the context of Medicaid's reimbursement methods, which model involves a predetermined payment per patient regardless of the actual services provided?
A) Fee-for-Service
B) Capitation
C) Bundled Payments
D) Pay-for-Performance

Question 42: As part of a new initiative, Case Manager John must design a reimbursement model for a healthcare organization that aligns with value-based care principles. Which model should John advocate for to promote quality improvement and cost efficiency?
A) Fee-for-service model that incentivizes volume of services provided.
B) Capitation model providing fixed payments per patient regardless of services used.
C) Pay-for-performance model rewarding providers for meeting quality benchmarks.
D) Bundled payments covering all services for a specific condition over a period.

Question 43: Which of the following approaches is most effective in addressing the psychosocial needs of a patient experiencing domestic abuse, according to contemporary research?
A) Encouraging the patient to immediately leave the abusive environment
B) Facilitating access to a multidisciplinary support team
C) Providing individual therapy sessions focused on empowerment
D) Offering legal advice and resources

Question 44: John, a case manager, is working with an elderly client who recently lost his driver's license due to vision impairment. The client needs regular transportation for medical appointments and grocery shopping. Which transportation option should John recommend as the most sustainable solution?
A) Ride-sharing services
B) Paratransit services
C) Senior center shuttle service
D) Personal care assistant's vehicle

Question 45: Which principle is fundamental to implementing effective self-directed care in a case management setting?
A) Standardizing treatment protocols for all clients
B) Facilitating access to diverse resources and support networks
C) Prioritizing cost-effectiveness over client preferences
D) Limiting client participation in decision-making processes

Question 46: In the context of reimbursement methods for residential treatment facilities, which factor most significantly influences funding eligibility?
A) Patient's age and gender
B) Patient's diagnosis and treatment plan
C) Duration of stay at the facility
D) Facility's location in relation to urban centers

Question 47: As part of discharge planning, case manager Emily needs to ensure that her client, Mrs. Garcia, who has limited financial resources, can afford necessary medications post-hospitalization. Which strategy should Emily prioritize to secure Mrs. Garcia's access to her medications?
A) Refer Mrs. Garcia to a pharmaceutical assistance program
B) Advise Mrs. Garcia to apply for Medicaid immediately
C) Arrange for home delivery services from local pharmacies
D) Encourage Mrs. Garcia to use over-the-counter alternatives

Question 48: Which of the following strategies is most effective in promoting long-term adherence to wellness and illness prevention programs among individuals with chronic conditions?
A) Regular distribution of educational materials
B) Implementation of motivational interviewing techniques
C) Periodic health screenings
D) Incentivizing participation through financial rewards

Question 49: In the context of program evaluation methods, which approach emphasizes continuous feedback and improvement during the implementation phase of a case management program?
A) Impact Evaluation
B) Developmental Evaluation
C) Outcome Evaluation
D) Cost-Benefit Analysis

Question 50: During a team meeting, a case manager named Sarah notices increasing tension between two team members over differing opinions on a patient's discharge plan. As a conflict resolution strategy, which approach should Sarah prioritize to effectively manage and resolve the conflict while maintaining a collaborative environment?
A) Avoidance
B) Compromise
C) Collaboration
D) Accommodation

Question 51: What is the primary purpose of the Medicare Savings Programs (MSPs)?
A) To cover all prescription drug costs for low-income individuals
B) To provide additional benefits for those with chronic conditions
C) To assist low-income individuals in paying for Medicare premiums and out-of-pocket expenses
D) To offer supplemental insurance coverage for long-term care

Question 52: Which interview technique is most effective for ensuring that a case manager accurately understands the client's perspective during a psychosocial assessment?
A) Open-ended questions
B) Closed-ended questions
C) Leading questions
D) Reflective listening

Question 53: Sarah, a 35-year-old woman, presents with frequent unexplained bruises and a high level of anxiety. As a case manager, which physical sign should you prioritize to assess potential abuse or neglect?
A) Unexplained weight loss
B) Recurrent headaches
C) Multiple fractures at different healing stages
D) Insomnia

Question 54: John, a 55-year-old patient with terminal

cancer, is considering a viatical settlement to help cover his medical expenses. As his case manager, you need to advise him on the potential financial implications. Which of the following considerations is most critical when evaluating the benefits of a viatical settlement for John?
A) The potential impact on John's eligibility for Medicaid benefits.
B) The amount offered by the viatical settlement company compared to John's life insurance policy face value.
C) The tax implications of receiving funds from a viatical settlement.
D) The reputation and reliability of the viatical settlement provider.

Question 55: In what way do fraternal/religious organizations typically contribute to community resource development?
A) By establishing exclusive educational scholarships for members' children
B) By advocating for local policy changes that benefit the wider community
C) By offering vocational training solely to religious affiliates
D) By focusing resources primarily on internal organizational growth

Question 56: In the context of population health management, which approach is most aligned with contemporary research for reducing healthcare disparities?
A) Increasing hospital funding in urban areas
B) Enhancing community-based participatory research initiatives
C) Implementing universal screening programs for chronic diseases
D) Expanding telehealth services in rural regions

Question 57: Sarah, a case manager, is evaluating the quality of care provided to her patients under Medicare. She wants to use quality indicators that are recognized by the Centers for Medicare and Medicaid Services (CMS) to ensure compliance with national standards. Which of the following sources should she prioritize for obtaining these quality indicators?
A) National Committee for Quality Assurance (NCQA)
B) Healthcare Effectiveness Data and Information Set (HEDIS)
C) Hospital Compare Database
D) Joint Commission Accreditation Standards

Question 58: In utilization management, what is a critical factor in determining whether a healthcare service should be approved for reimbursement?
A) The length of stay in the hospital
B) The potential for positive patient outcomes
C) The patient's insurance plan details
D) The historical cost of similar procedures

Question 59: Mrs. Smith, a 65-year-old woman with Alzheimer's disease, requires continuous supervision and assistance with daily activities. Her family is exploring long-term care options that offer both medical support and personal care services. Which type of facility would best meet her needs?
A) Assisted Living Facility
B) Skilled Nursing Facility
C) Adult Day Care Center
D) Home Health Care

Question 60: Emily, a case manager, is tasked with reducing hospital readmissions for her patient, Robert, who has recently been discharged after heart surgery. Which process tool should Emily implement to effectively manage Robert's post-discharge care and

ensure adherence to his treatment plan?
A) Utilization Review
B) Transitional Care Planning
C) Disease Management Program
D) Patient-Centered Medical Home

Question 61: Maria, a case manager, is assisting Sam, an adult client who identifies as non-binary and wishes to express this through their appearance at work. What is the best strategy Maria should employ to help Sam navigate potential workplace challenges related to their gender expression?
A) Advise Sam to adhere strictly to the company's dress code regardless of personal discomfort.
B) Collaborate with HR to create inclusive policies that accommodate diverse gender expressions.
C) Suggest Sam gradually introduce subtle changes in appearance over time.
D) Encourage Sam to seek employment elsewhere if the current environment feels restrictive.

Question 62: John, a case manager at a community clinic, is tasked with designing an illness prevention program for elderly patients with chronic illnesses. Which component should be emphasized to ensure the program's success in enhancing patient outcomes?
A) Regular physical activity sessions tailored to individual capabilities
B) Bi-weekly group educational seminars on chronic disease management
C) Monthly social gatherings to encourage peer support
D) Access to online health information resources

Question 63: Sarah, a 32-year-old patient with a history of major depressive disorder, presents with symptoms of alcohol use disorder. As her case manager, which approach should be prioritized to effectively address her dual diagnosis?
A) Focus on treating the depressive disorder first to stabilize mood.
B) Address the alcohol use disorder first to prevent further substance-related harm.
C) Implement an integrated treatment plan addressing both disorders simultaneously.
D) Refer Sarah to separate specialists for each disorder for focused treatment.

Question 64: John, a case manager, is assisting a single mother of two who lost her job due to the COVID-19 pandemic. She is struggling to pay rent and afford basic necessities. Which community resource should John connect her with first to stabilize her situation?
A) Employment Assistance Programs
B) Temporary Shelter Programs
C) Food Banks
D) Rental Assistance Programs

Question 65: In the context of psychosocial support systems for diverse gender expressions, which approach is most effective in promoting inclusivity?
A) Implementing strict policies that enforce traditional gender norms.
B) Encouraging open dialogues about individual experiences and identities.
C) Mandating uniformity in dress codes to avoid attention to differences.
D) Prioritizing medical interventions for those expressing non-conforming genders.

Question 66: Which of the following statements accurately reflects a key characteristic of indemnity insurance plans compared to other types of health insurance?

A) Indemnity plans require patients to choose from a specific network of providers.
B) Indemnity plans offer greater flexibility in choosing healthcare providers without referrals.
C) Indemnity plans typically have lower out-of-pocket costs than managed care plans.
D) Indemnity plans mandate prior authorization for specialist visits.

Question 67: Maria, a 75-year-old woman recovering from hip surgery, is eligible for home care benefits through her private insurance. As her case manager, which strategy would best optimize her recovery while adhering to her benefit limitations?
A) Initiate a comprehensive rehabilitation program at an outpatient facility.
B) Implement a structured exercise regimen supervised by a visiting therapist at home.
C) Enroll her in an intensive inpatient rehabilitation program.
D) Provide her with educational materials on self-directed exercises.

Question 68: Sarah, a case manager, is evaluating a patient's eligibility for a private benefit program that offers coverage for home health services. The patient, Mr. Thompson, has a chronic condition requiring frequent in-home care. Which factor is most critical for Sarah to consider when determining Mr. Thompson's eligibility for this private benefit program?
A) The specific diagnosis of Mr. Thompson's chronic condition
B) The frequency of Mr. Thompson's required in-home care
C) The network status of the home health provider with the private benefit program
D) The total cost of Mr. Thompson's in-home care services

Question 69: Which program evaluation method is most effective for identifying causal relationships between program activities and outcomes in a healthcare setting?
A) Process Evaluation
B) Formative Evaluation
C) Summative Evaluation
D) Experimental Evaluation

Question 70: In the context of bundled payments, what is a critical factor for determining reimbursement rates for healthcare providers?
A) Historical billing amounts of individual providers.
B) Average costs of similar episodes in the region.
C) The highest charge submitted by any provider in the bundle.
D) The total number of patients treated by each provider annually.

Question 71: Which of the following best describes a key principle of value-based care in the context of reimbursement and payment methodologies for case managers?
A) Fee-for-service reimbursement
B) Capitation payment models
C) Bundled payments
D) Pay-for-performance incentives

Question 72: In Tuckman's stages of group development, which stage is characterized by the emergence of conflicts and competition as group members assert their individual personalities?
A) Forming
B) Storming
C) Norming
D) Performing

Question 73: In the context of relationship building, which communication technique is considered most effective for a case manager when dealing with a resistant client?
A) Utilizing open-ended questions to explore concerns
B) Providing immediate reassurance about outcomes
C) Emphasizing authority and expertise in decision-making
D) Sharing personal experiences to relate to the client

Question 74: Which of the following emotional responses is most commonly associated with individuals experiencing chronic abuse and neglect, according to contemporary psychological research?
A) Resilience
B) Emotional numbness
C) Hyperactivity
D) Optimism

Question 75: During a meeting with Emily, a 45-year-old patient recently diagnosed with diabetes, the case manager seeks to employ shared decision-making strategies. What approach should the case manager take to effectively involve Emily in managing her condition?
A) The case manager decides on the best medication for Emily based on clinical guidelines and informs her of this choice.
B) The case manager presents Emily with several lifestyle changes and allows her to choose which ones she prefers to implement.
C) The case manager explains the risks and benefits of different management strategies and collaborates with Emily to choose a plan that aligns with her values and preferences.
D) The case manager insists that Emily attend all recommended educational sessions before making any decisions.

Question 76: Which strategy is most effective in enhancing health literacy among patients with low literacy levels, according to contemporary research?
A) Providing comprehensive written materials with medical terminology
B) Utilizing teach-back methods to confirm understanding
C) Offering digital resources for self-paced learning
D) Conducting group educational sessions

Question 77: When conducting a behavioral health assessment as part of case management, which approach best integrates both psychological evaluation and social determinants of health?
A) Cognitive Behavioral Therapy (CBT) Assessment
B) Biopsychosocial Model Assessment
C) Psychoanalytic Assessment
D) Medical Model Assessment

Question 78: In conducting an interview with a client, which tool is most beneficial for identifying underlying psychosocial issues that may not be immediately apparent?
A) Structured interview guide
B) Genogram
C) Checklist of symptoms
D) Standardized questionnaire

Question 79: In the context of Prospective Payment Systems, which factor primarily influences the payment amount under Medicare's Skilled Nursing Facility (SNF) PPS?
A) Geographic location of the facility.
B) Resource Utilization Groups (RUGs).
C) Total number of nursing hours per patient day.
D) Patient's age and gender demographics.

Question 80: Sarah, a case manager, is working with Tom, who has been struggling with lifestyle changes recommended for managing his diabetes. What is the most effective counseling approach Sarah should use to enhance Tom's adherence to these changes?
A) Use directive counseling to provide clear instructions on lifestyle changes.
B) Implement motivational interviewing to explore Tom's ambivalence towards change.
C) Focus solely on educating Tom about the complications of unmanaged diabetes.
D) Regularly remind Tom of the consequences of non-adherence.

Question 81: Sarah, a case manager, is reviewing the indemnity insurance policy of a patient who requires surgery. The policy states that reimbursement is based on "usual, customary, and reasonable" (UCR) charges. Which of the following best describes how Sarah should interpret the UCR charges in this context?
A) UCR charges are determined by the patient's previous medical expenses.
B) UCR charges are based on the average fees charged by providers in the same geographic area.
C) UCR charges refer to the highest possible reimbursement rate for any procedure.
D) UCR charges are set by federal government standards.

Question 82: Sarah, a case manager, is assessing a patient who has been experiencing persistent sadness, loss of interest in activities, and changes in appetite. She needs to determine the appropriate DSM-5 diagnosis for this patient. Which of the following DSM-5 disorders should Sarah consider based on these symptoms?
A) Major Depressive Disorder
B) Persistent Depressive Disorder
C) Bipolar I Disorder
D) Cyclothymic Disorder

Question 83: John, a case manager, is conducting an initial assessment interview with a new client who seems anxious about discussing their personal history. Which technique should John use to help the client feel more at ease and willing to share sensitive information?
A) Silence
B) Clarification
C) Summarization
D) Empathy

Question 84: Sarah, a case manager, is analyzing data from a recent health risk assessment survey conducted among diabetic patients at her facility. She aims to identify the primary indicator for predicting hospital readmissions within 30 days. Which indicator should she focus on?
A) Glycated Hemoglobin (HbA1c) Levels
B) Frequency of Hypoglycemic Episodes
C) Patient Adherence to Medication
D) Number of Comorbidities

Question 85: Mark is a case manager helping his client, Lisa, navigate the complexities of maintaining her SSI benefits while she begins part-time work. Which strategy should Mark emphasize to ensure Lisa remains eligible for SSI?
A) Reporting all changes in Lisa's medical condition promptly
B) Encouraging Lisa to save any extra earnings in a savings account
C) Advising Lisa to track and report her earnings accurately each month
D) Suggesting that Lisa reduce her work hours below 10 per week

Question 86: Sarah, a case manager, is working with a patient who has multiple chronic conditions and requires coordinated care across various specialties. To ensure optimal healthcare delivery and reimbursement, which system should Sarah prioritize to enhance integrated care and cost-effectiveness?
A) Fee-for-Service Model
B) Accountable Care Organization (ACO)
C) Health Maintenance Organization (HMO)
D) Preferred Provider Organization (PPO)

Question 87: Sarah, a 68-year-old patient with chronic heart failure, is considering whether to undergo a new experimental treatment. As her case manager, you need to facilitate informed decision-making. Which of the following actions best supports Sarah in making an informed decision?
A) Provide Sarah with detailed medical journals about the experimental treatment.
B) Discuss the potential benefits and risks of the treatment in layman's terms.
C) Encourage Sarah to decide based on her emotional response to the treatment.
D) Advise Sarah to follow the most popular choice among other patients.

Question 88: Emily, a case manager, is tasked with evaluating the effectiveness of a new discharge planning program aimed at reducing hospital readmissions. She decides to use a method that involves comparing outcomes of patients who participated in the program with those who did not. Which evaluation method is Emily using?
A) Randomized Controlled Trial (RCT)
B) Quasi-Experimental Design
C) Cross-Sectional Study
D) Case-Control Study

Question 89: John, a 75-year-old man with chronic heart failure, frequently visits the emergency department due to exacerbations. As his case manager, which intervention is most likely to reduce his hospital readmissions while improving his overall quality of life?
A) Implementing a Disease Management Program
B) Enrolling in a Transitional Care Program
C) Increasing Frequency of Routine Check-ups
D) Referring to Specialist Consultations

Question 90: John, a 55-year-old man recently diagnosed with multiple sclerosis, is considering joining a supportive care program. As his case manager, you aim to recommend an intervention that best supports his psychological adjustment to the diagnosis. Which option should you prioritize?
A) Regular occupational therapy sessions
B) Access to an online peer support network
C) Bi-monthly family meetings with a counselor
D) Personalized exercise regimen

Question 91: Emily, a case manager, is evaluating the home care benefits for her patient, Mr. Johnson, who requires daily assistance with medication management and physical therapy. Which factor is most critical in determining the extent of home care benefits covered by Mr. Johnson's private insurance plan?
A) The patient's medical diagnosis
B) The frequency of required home visits
C) The cost-effectiveness of home care versus hospitalization
D) The availability of certified home health agencies

Question 92: Sarah, a case manager, is working with a

multidisciplinary team to develop a comprehensive care plan for a patient with multiple chronic conditions. The team aims to ensure seamless communication and coordination among all healthcare providers involved. Which approach should Sarah prioritize to achieve optimal integrated case management?
A) Encourage regular individual updates from each provider.
B) Implement a centralized electronic health record system.
C) Schedule bi-weekly face-to-face meetings with the entire team.
D) Focus on patient self-management education.

Question 93: John, a 65-year-old man living alone with mild cognitive impairment, is considering using a meal delivery service. As his case manager, which aspect should you prioritize when recommending a service?
A) Meals requiring minimal preparation
B) Meals with organic ingredients
C) Meals with diverse cultural flavors
D) Meals with high protein content

Question 94: Which strategy is most effective for a case manager when encountering conflicting religious practices that may affect a client's treatment plan?
A) Dismiss conflicting practices to maintain focus on evidence-based medical treatment.
B) Collaborate with religious leaders or cultural liaisons to find acceptable compromises.
C) Insist on adherence to medical recommendations regardless of religious concerns.
D) Document the conflict and proceed without addressing it further.

Question 95: As a case manager for an Accountable Care Organization (ACO), you are tasked with improving the care coordination for Mr. Smith, a 68-year-old patient with multiple chronic conditions. Which strategy should you prioritize to enhance care coordination and reduce hospital readmissions?
A) Implementing a patient-centered medical home model
B) Increasing the frequency of specialist referrals
C) Enhancing electronic health record (EHR) interoperability
D) Scheduling monthly in-person check-ups

Question 96: In the context of healthcare delivery systems, which model emphasizes the integration of care across various settings to enhance patient outcomes and reduce costs?
A) Fee-for-Service Model
B) Patient-Centered Medical Home (PCMH) Model
C) Capitation Model
D) Direct Primary Care Model

Question 97: Which public benefit program primarily aims to provide healthcare coverage for low-income individuals and families, and is jointly funded by state and federal governments?
A) Medicare
B) Medicaid
C) Children's Health Insurance Program (CHIP)
D) Supplemental Security Income (SSI)

Question 98: Alex, a case manager, is working with a transgender client who is experiencing significant stress related to their gender identity and social interactions. Which of the following interventions is most appropriate for Alex to prioritize in supporting this client's mental health?
A) Refer the client to a psychiatrist for medication management.
B) Encourage participation in a gender support group.
C) Focus on cognitive-behavioral therapy to address anxiety symptoms.

D) Initiate family therapy sessions to improve familial relationships.

Question 99: In the context of shared decision making (SDM) for case managers, which of the following is most critical to ensure effective client self-care management?
A) Providing clients with a detailed care plan without their input
B) Encouraging clients to express their values and preferences
C) Making decisions on behalf of the client based on clinical guidelines
D) Focusing solely on the medical aspects of care

Question 100: John, a case manager, is working with a patient who has multiple chronic conditions and frequently visits the emergency department due to unmanaged symptoms. To improve health outcomes and reduce hospital visits, which intervention should John prioritize?
A) Implementing a telehealth monitoring system.
B) Scheduling regular in-person follow-up appointments.
C) Coordinating care with a multidisciplinary team.
D) Educating the patient on lifestyle modifications.

Question 101: In the context of the Patient-centered Medical Home (PCMH), which element is crucial for enhancing patient engagement and self-management?
A) Regular emergency room visits
B) Access to electronic health records (EHRs)
C) Increased prescription medication use
D) Frequent specialist consultations

Question 102: Which of the following strategies is most effective for a case manager to ensure patients benefit from Pharmacy Assistance Programs (PAPs) when considering their psychosocial needs?
A) Identifying and applying for all available PAPs regardless of patient eligibility
B) Collaborating with social workers to assess patient eligibility and tailor PAP applications
C) Relying solely on pharmaceutical companies' websites for PAP information
D) Encouraging patients to independently research and apply for PAPs

Question 103: John, a newly appointed case manager, is reviewing the eligibility criteria for Medicaid with a client who recently lost their job. The client is worried about maintaining health coverage. Which factor primarily determines eligibility for Medicaid?
A) Employment status
B) Age of the individual
C) Income level and household size
D) Previous insurance coverage

Question 104: When assessing the effectiveness of a case management program, which approach provides the most comprehensive evaluation of both quality and outcomes?
A) Patient satisfaction surveys
B) Cost-benefit analysis
C) Integrated data analytics
D) Peer review

Question 105: Sarah, a case manager, is working with a client, Mr. Thompson, who has recently been diagnosed with Type 2 diabetes. To enhance Mr. Thompson's self-care management, Sarah decides to focus on health education. Which strategy is most effective in empowering Mr. Thompson to manage his condition?
A) Providing Mr. Thompson with pamphlets about diabetes management

B) Encouraging Mr. Thompson to attend group educational sessions
C) Collaborating with Mr. Thompson to set realistic and achievable health goals
D) Recommending online resources for diabetes education

Question 106: Which of the following strategies is most effective in promoting long-term self-care management for clients with chronic illnesses?
A) Regularly scheduled follow-up appointments
B) Providing educational materials about the illness
C) Collaborative goal-setting between client and healthcare provider
D) Frequent reminders about medication adherence

Question 107: Sarah, a case manager, is evaluating the best reimbursement model for a new integrated care program aimed at reducing hospital readmissions. Which payment methodology would most effectively incentivize providers to focus on quality and outcomes rather than volume?
A) Fee-for-Service
B) Capitation
C) Pay-for-Performance
D) Diagnosis-Related Groups (DRGs)

Question 108: Maria is a 60-year-old diabetic patient who feels overwhelmed by her treatment regimen. As her case manager, what strategy should you employ to foster her self-advocacy?
A) Teach Maria how to negotiate her treatment plan with her healthcare provider.
B) Suggest Maria attends group therapy sessions for emotional support.
C) Provide Maria with detailed instructions on managing her diabetes at home.
D) Encourage Maria to follow her doctor's orders without question.

Question 109: In the context of client activation, which factor is most likely to enhance a client's readiness to change by increasing their confidence in successfully making a change?
A) External motivation
B) Self-efficacy
C) Social support
D) Goal-setting

Question 110: During an interview with a patient named Sarah, a case manager notices that Sarah frequently avoids eye contact and gives short, minimal responses. Which interview technique should the case manager prioritize to encourage more open communication from Sarah?
A) Direct questioning
B) Reflective listening
C) Confrontation
D) Closed-ended questions

Question 111: In the context of psychosocial support for abuse survivors, which approach is most aligned with empowering clients by enhancing their sense of agency and autonomy?
A) Solution-Focused Therapy
B) Narrative Therapy
C) Psychodynamic Therapy
D) Cognitive Behavioral Therapy

Question 112: Sarah, a 45-year-old woman, has been experiencing persistent feelings of sadness, loss of interest in activities she once enjoyed, and changes in appetite and sleep patterns for over two months. As her case manager, which behavioral health concept is most
likely affecting Sarah's condition?
A) Generalized Anxiety Disorder
B) Major Depressive Disorder
C) Bipolar Disorder
D) Adjustment Disorder

Question 113: Which of the following scenarios would qualify an individual for an extended COBRA coverage period beyond the standard duration?
A) The individual experiences a reduction in working hours.
B) The individual becomes disabled within the first 60 days of COBRA coverage.
C) The individual gains new employment with health benefits.
D) The individual relocates to another state.

Question 114: John, a 55-year-old male with chronic obstructive pulmonary disease (COPD), is part of a managed care plan. Which reimbursement method is most likely to incentivize providers to offer cost-effective and quality care for his chronic condition?
A) Fee-for-Service
B) Capitation
C) Bundled Payments
D) Pay-for-Performance

Question 115: Sarah, a case manager, is tasked with developing a community health intervention program to reduce the incidence of diabetes in a high-risk population. Which of the following strategies should she prioritize to effectively address the social determinants of health impacting this population?
A) Implementing a community-wide educational campaign on healthy eating
B) Establishing partnerships with local food banks to increase access to fresh produce
C) Organizing regular health screenings for early detection of diabetes
D) Providing free gym memberships to promote physical activity

Question 116: What is a significant challenge faced by individuals when purchasing health insurance independently compared to obtaining it through an employer?
A) Limited availability of preventive care services.
B) Higher administrative costs and complexity in plan selection.
C) Reduced access to specialty care providers.
D) Decreased portability of health coverage across states.

Question 117: In the context of health education for promoting psychosocial support systems, which approach is considered most effective for empowering clients to manage their health conditions independently?
A) Encouraging participation in online health forums
B) Establishing peer support groups
C) Conducting one-on-one counseling sessions
D) Providing access to telehealth services

Question 118: Maria is experiencing a crisis after being diagnosed with a chronic illness, which has led to feelings of helplessness and depression. As her case manager, what initial intervention strategy should be employed to best assist Maria in coping with her new diagnosis?
A) Provide Maria with educational resources about her illness to empower her decision-making.
B) Encourage Maria to join a support group for individuals with similar health conditions.
C) Collaborate with Maria to identify and leverage her personal strengths in managing the illness.

D) Refer Maria to individual therapy sessions for professional psychological support.

Question 119: Sarah, a case manager, is working with a client named John who has recently lost his job and is experiencing significant stress and anxiety. As part of crisis intervention, which initial strategy should Sarah prioritize to effectively assist John in managing his current situation?
A) Encourage John to explore new career opportunities immediately.
B) Develop a long-term plan for John's financial stability.
C) Focus on building a strong support system around John.
D) Help John identify immediate coping mechanisms to manage stress.

Question 120: Which of the following is a primary goal of utilization management within the context of care delivery and reimbursement methods?
A) To maximize patient satisfaction by increasing service volume
B) To ensure the provision of medically necessary services at the lowest cost
C) To enhance healthcare provider revenue through increased procedures
D) To minimize administrative costs by reducing documentation requirements

Question 121: Which psychological theory is most relevant in understanding the impact of childhood abuse on adult attachment styles?
A) Cognitive Behavioral Theory
B) Attachment Theory
C) Social Learning Theory
D) Psychoanalytic Theory

Question 122: In the context of accreditation standards, what is a critical component of evaluating case management effectiveness?
A) Patient satisfaction surveys
B) Cost reduction metrics
C) Evidence-based practice implementation
D) Length of hospital stay

Question 123: Alex, a case manager, is working with Jamie, a 16-year-old client exploring their gender expression. Jamie feels most comfortable wearing clothing traditionally associated with a different gender than the one assigned at birth. Which approach should Alex prioritize to support Jamie's gender expression effectively?
A) Encourage Jamie to conform to societal norms for easier social acceptance.
B) Facilitate open discussions with Jamie about their feelings and preferences.
C) Suggest Jamie consults a fashion expert for clothing advice.
D) Advise Jamie to wait until adulthood to make any changes in gender expression.

Question 124: In the context of client engagement, which approach is most effective for enhancing a client's motivation to participate actively in their care plan?
A) Providing detailed educational materials about their condition
B) Establishing a collaborative goal-setting process
C) Implementing regular progress monitoring sessions
D) Offering incentives for adherence to the care plan

Question 125: In the context of employer-sponsored health coverage, what is the primary purpose of a Health Savings Account (HSA)?

A) To provide immediate access to emergency medical funds.
B) To cover out-of-pocket expenses with pre-tax dollars.
C) To offer additional retirement savings options.
D) To replace traditional insurance plans entirely.

Question 126: Emily, a case manager, is helping a patient named Mark understand his indemnity health insurance benefits. Mark wants to know how his insurer will handle payments if he chooses to see a specialist outside of his usual network. Which feature of indemnity insurance should Emily explain to clarify this process?
A) Fee-for-Service Reimbursement
B) In-Network Discounts
C) Prior Authorization
D) Global Payment System

Question 127: When assessing a client's support system dynamics, which factor is most crucial in determining the resilience of a client's social network?
A) The size of the social network.
B) The frequency of interactions within the network.
C) The quality and strength of relationships within the network.
D) The diversity of roles within the network.

Question 128: Which of the following criteria is essential for a case manager to consider when determining a client's eligibility for Social Security Disability Insurance (SSDI) benefits?
A) The client's age at the time of application
B) The client's total household income
C) The client's work history and contributions to Social Security
D) The client's educational background

Question 129: Emily, a case manager, is coordinating care for a patient recently diagnosed with diabetes. The patient has limited financial resources and is concerned about the cost of medication. Which strategy should Emily prioritize to ensure the patient receives necessary medication without financial strain?
A) Encourage the patient to apply for Medicaid.
B) Suggest switching to a less expensive over-the-counter alternative.
C) Explore pharmaceutical assistance programs.
D) Recommend reducing medication dosage to save costs.

Question 130: In the context of health risk assessment, which factor is most crucial for ensuring the accuracy and reliability of predictive models used in healthcare analytics?
A) Volume of data collected
B) Quality and relevance of data
C) Speed of data processing
D) Diversity of patient demographics

Question 131: During a session with Maria, a 45-year-old patient struggling with medication adherence, the case manager uses motivational interviewing to explore her ambivalence. Which of the following strategies best exemplifies the use of reflective listening in this context?
A) Asking Maria why she is not taking her medication regularly.
B) Summarizing Maria's reasons for and against taking her medication.
C) Providing information about the consequences of non-adherence.
D) Suggesting a specific schedule for medication intake.

Question 132: Which of the following community resources is most effective in providing comprehensive

psychosocial support to elderly individuals experiencing social isolation?
A) Senior Centers
B) Home Health Aides
C) Adult Day Care Services
D) Meals on Wheels

Question 133: Which communication theory emphasizes the importance of understanding the context and relationship between communicators to effectively interpret messages in interpersonal communication?
A) Social Penetration Theory
B) Uncertainty Reduction Theory
C) Coordinated Management of Meaning (CMM)
D) Communication Accommodation Theory

Question 134: In the context of substance use disorder treatment, which approach primarily focuses on altering the individual's thoughts and beliefs about substance use to effect behavior change?
A) Contingency management
B) Cognitive restructuring
C) Harm reduction
D) Twelve-step facilitation

Question 135: Which model of care delivery emphasizes the integration of healthcare services across different levels and sites of care, aiming to improve patient outcomes through coordinated efforts among various healthcare providers?
A) Patient-Centered Medical Home (PCMH)
B) Accountable Care Organization (ACO)
C) Primary Nursing Model
D) Functional Nursing Model

Question 136: Sarah, a case manager, is working with Tom, a 45-year-old patient recently diagnosed with a chronic illness. To enhance Tom's engagement in his care plan, Sarah focuses on understanding his personal goals and preferences. Which strategy is most effective for Sarah to improve Tom's client engagement?
A) Providing Tom with detailed educational materials about his illness
B) Encouraging Tom to attend support group meetings regularly
C) Collaborating with Tom to set personalized health goals
D) Scheduling frequent follow-up appointments for Tom

Question 137: Sarah, a 72-year-old widow, has recently been discharged from the hospital after a hip replacement surgery. She lives alone and expresses concerns about her ability to manage daily tasks during her recovery. As a case manager, which community resource would be most appropriate to ensure Sarah receives comprehensive support at home?
A) Home Health Care Services
B) Meals on Wheels
C) Adult Day Care
D) Senior Center Activities

Question 138: Which of the following criteria must be met for an individual to qualify for Social Security Disability Insurance (SSDI) benefits under the "work credits" requirement?
A) The individual must have earned at least 40 work credits, with 20 earned in the last 10 years ending with the year of disability.
B) The individual must have earned at least 20 work credits, all within the last 5 years.
C) The individual must have a minimum of 30 work credits, regardless of when they were earned.
D) The individual must have worked continuously for at least 10 years before becoming disabled.

Question 139: Sarah, a case manager, is reviewing a patient's medical records to ensure proper reimbursement. The patient underwent a complex surgical procedure that involved multiple stages and required extended postoperative care. Which coding methodology should Sarah use to accurately capture the complexity and resources utilized during this procedure?
A) ICD-10-CM
B) CPT
C) DRG
D) HCPCS

Question 140: Which interview technique is most effective in building rapport with a patient who is hesitant to share personal information during a case management assessment?
A) Closed-ended questioning
B) Reflective listening
C) Direct confrontation
D) Structured interviewing

Question 141: Which assessment tool is most appropriate for identifying memory deficits in patients with potential neurocognitive disorders?
A) Stroop Color and Word Test
B) Rey-Osterrieth Complex Figure Test
C) Mini-Mental State Examination (MMSE)
D) Trail Making Test

Question 142: In the management of co-occurring disorders, which integrated treatment approach is considered most effective according to contemporary research?
A) Sequential Treatment
B) Parallel Treatment
C) Integrated Dual Disorder Treatment (IDDT)
D) Separate Specialist Care

Question 143: John, a case manager, is evaluating the effectiveness of telehealth interventions for his patients with chronic conditions. He wants to measure outcomes related to patient engagement and satisfaction. Which metric should John prioritize to assess these outcomes effectively?
A) Number of virtual visits completed
B) Patient-reported experience measures (PREMs)
C) Reduction in hospital readmissions
D) Clinical health improvement scores

Question 144: Which of the following criteria is essential for diagnosing Major Depressive Disorder according to the DSM-5?
A) Presence of manic episodes
B) Depressed mood or loss of interest/pleasure for at least two weeks
C) Persistent delusions or hallucinations
D) Significant weight gain without dieting

Question 145: In the context of psychosocial support systems, which concept is crucial for developing resilience in individuals participating in wellness and illness prevention programs?
A) Social isolation
B) Emotional intelligence
C) Autonomy
D) Peer support

Question 146: Which of the following best describes a potential advantage of using case rate reimbursement models in healthcare?
A) Encourages extended patient stays

B) Promotes standardization in care delivery
C) Increases administrative complexity
D) Reduces focus on patient outcomes

Question 147: In the context of chronic disease management, which factor is most likely to predict long-term adherence to a prescribed medication regimen?
A) Patient's belief in the necessity of medication
B) Complexity of the medication regimen
C) Frequency of healthcare provider visits
D) Availability of social support

Question 148: In the context of Behavioral Change Theories, which process is most associated with helping individuals move from the preparation stage to the action stage in Prochaska's model?
A) Consciousness Raising
B) Self-Reevaluation
C) Counterconditioning
D) Self-Liberation

Question 149: As a case manager, you are working with John, a 45-year-old male diagnosed with both major depressive disorder and alcohol use disorder. He has been struggling to maintain sobriety and adhere to his antidepressant regimen. Which of the following approaches is most effective in addressing John's co-occurring disorders?
A) Focus on treating the alcohol use disorder first before addressing the depressive symptoms.
B) Integrate treatment for both disorders simultaneously using a coordinated care approach.
C) Prioritize the treatment of depressive symptoms to improve overall outcomes.
D) Use medication-assisted treatment (MAT) exclusively for alcohol use disorder.

Question 150: In the context of psychosocial support systems, which approach best aligns with contemporary theories of client empowerment?
A) Implementing standardized care plans for all clients to ensure consistency.
B) Facilitating peer support groups that encourage shared experiences and mutual aid.
C) Assigning case managers to monitor client progress closely and provide feedback.
D) Utilizing motivational interviewing techniques to explore and resolve ambivalence.

ANSWER WITH DETAILED EXPLANATION SET [5]

Question 1: Correct Answer: B) Medicaid
Rationale: Medicaid provides immediate healthcare coverage for low-income individuals, which is crucial for clients who have lost their jobs and need medical care. SNAP focuses on food assistance, TANF offers financial support but not direct healthcare, and SSDI requires a disability determination process. Therefore, Medicaid is prioritized due to its direct and immediate healthcare benefits.

Question 2: Correct Answer: B) Conducting regular telehealth consultations to monitor symptoms
Rationale: Regular telehealth consultations allow for timely monitoring and intervention, which can prevent exacerbations leading to hospital readmissions. While exercise (A), diet (C), and medication education (D) are important, they are more preventive in nature. Telehealth provides immediate feedback and adjustment possibilities, making it a proactive approach in chronic disease management. This option leverages technology for continuous care, aligning with contemporary practices in chronic illness management.

Question 3: Correct Answer: A) Reduction in medication errors
Rationale:A reduction in medication errors directly indicates improved quality and safety due to better EHR functionalities like alerts and cross-referencing. Increased patient volume (B) might reflect efficiency but not necessarily quality. Decreased overtime (C) relates more to staffing efficiency than care quality. Improved staff satisfaction (D), while beneficial, doesn't directly measure patient outcomes or care quality enhancements.

Question 4: Correct Answer: A) Express Empathy
Rationale: Expressing empathy involves understanding and reflecting the client's feelings and perspectives, which is central to Motivational Interviewing. It fosters a trusting relationship, making clients feel heard and respected. While developing discrepancy, rolling with resistance, and supporting self-efficacy are also essential principles, they focus on other aspects like resolving ambivalence and enhancing confidence. The key difference lies in empathy's role as the foundation for building rapport and facilitating open communication, crucial for effective motivational interviewing.

Question 5: Correct Answer: B) Support groups provide emotional support and shared experiences from peers.
Rationale: Option B is correct because support groups are primarily designed to offer emotional support and shared experiences, which can help individuals like John feel less isolated and more understood. Option A is incorrect as support groups are not primarily for medical advice; professionals may guide, but peer interaction is key. Option C is misleading; while they can improve outcomes indirectly, it's not guaranteed. Option D is incorrect as reducing medication needs isn't a direct function of support groups.

Question 6: Correct Answer: B) Excessive worry occurring more days than not for at least six months
Rationale: Generalized Anxiety Disorder (GAD) is characterized by excessive worry occurring more days than not for at least six months, as per DSM-5 criteria. Option A pertains to Panic Disorder, while Option C relates to Specific Phobia. Option D describes Obsessive-Compulsive Disorder (OCD). The chronic nature and pervasive worry are central to GAD, distinguishing it from other anxiety disorders with more episodic or specific triggers.

Question 7: Correct Answer: D) Neural Networks

Rationale: Neural Networks are highly effective in predicting patient readmissions due to their ability to process large datasets and identify complex, non-linear patterns. Unlike Logistic Regression and Decision Trees, which may oversimplify relationships, Neural Networks can model intricate interactions between variables. While Support Vector Machines also handle non-linear relationships, they are less efficient with very large datasets compared to Neural Networks, which excel in scalability and adaptability in health care analytics.

Question 8: Correct Answer: B) Match clients with support groups that align with their specific conditions and needs.
Rationale: Matching clients with condition-specific support groups is crucial because it ensures relevance and relatability, which enhances emotional and psychosocial benefits. Option A is less effective as generic groups may not address specific needs. Option C, while convenient, lacks the personal interaction of in-person groups. Option D can be overwhelming and dilute focus, reducing effectiveness. Hence, option B optimally supports personalized care plans by fostering meaningful connections and targeted support.

Question 9: Correct Answer: B) Use teach-back methods to confirm Mary's understanding of the information provided.
Rationale: The teach-back method is an evidence-based strategy that ensures patient comprehension by having them repeat the information in their own words. This approach allows the case manager to assess and address any misunderstandings immediately. While printed materials (A) and online resources (D) can be useful, they may not cater to Mary's individual learning needs or guarantee comprehension. Group sessions (C), without personalized follow-up, might not address specific misunderstandings or questions Mary may have.

Question 10: Correct Answer: B) Validate the client's feelings and support their authentic gender expression.
Rationale: Validating the client's feelings and supporting their authentic gender expression (Option B) aligns with contemporary research on promoting mental health and well-being for transgender individuals. It acknowledges the importance of self-identification and personal authenticity. Option A, encouraging conformity, may lead to further distress by denying personal identity. Option C focuses on passing, which might not align with the client's desires or experiences. Option D suggests avoidance, which can suppress identity rather than affirm it.

Question 11: Correct Answer: B) Adult Day Care Centers
Rationale: Adult Day Care Centers are specifically designed to provide social and recreational activities, promoting mental well-being for elderly individuals who live independently. They offer a structured environment that encourages social interaction, reducing feelings of isolation. While Home Health Care Services (A) focus on medical care at home, Assisted Living Facilities (C) and Skilled Nursing Facilities (D) cater to those needing more intensive care or residing in these facilities. Therefore, Adult Day Care Centers are best suited for enhancing social engagement among independent seniors.

Question 12: Correct Answer: C) Medicare Part A covers up to 100 days in a skilled nursing facility with a coinsurance fee after 20 days.
Rationale: Medicare Part A provides coverage for up to 100 days in a skilled nursing facility following at least a three-day inpatient hospital stay, with full cost covered for

the first 20 days and coinsurance required from day 21 to day 100. Option A is incorrect as it omits the coinsurance requirement after 20 days. Option B incorrectly attributes this coverage to Part B, which primarily covers outpatient services. Option D inaccurately suggests unlimited coverage by Part C, which varies by plan specifics.

Question 13: Correct Answer: D) Discharge Planner
Rationale: The Discharge Planner is specialized in leading the discharge planning process, ensuring patients receive appropriate post-hospitalization care. While Hospitalists (A) manage inpatient medical treatment, they do not focus on discharge logistics. Registered Nurses (B) provide essential care but do not typically lead discharge planning. Physical Therapists (C) contribute to rehabilitation but are not involved in overall discharge coordination. The Discharge Planner's role is crucial in organizing follow-up care and liaising with external providers to facilitate smooth transitions from hospital to home or other facilities.

Question 14: Correct Answer: C) Value-Based Purchasing
Rationale: Value-Based Purchasing (VBP) incentivizes providers to deliver high-quality care by linking payment to performance metrics. Unlike Fee-for-Service, which pays per service and may lead to overutilization, VBP focuses on outcomes. Capitation offers a fixed amount per patient but may not prioritize quality. Per Diem Payment provides a daily rate, potentially encouraging longer stays without quality focus. Thus, VBP effectively balances cost control with quality improvement.

Question 15: Correct Answer: B) Facilitate expressive arts therapy sessions for Maria to explore her emotions creatively.
Rationale: Expressive arts therapy allows individuals like Maria to process complex emotions non-verbally, which can be particularly effective in grief work. Option A can be helpful but might suppress rather than address feelings. Option C might reinforce avoidance behavior, hindering healing. Option D focuses on cognitive restructuring but doesn't directly engage with emotional processing like expressive arts therapy does at this stage of grief recovery.

Question 16: Correct Answer: B) Coordinate with community resources for social support services.
Rationale: Coordinating with community resources addresses both medical and non-medical factors by providing holistic support, including social determinants of health. Option A neglects non-medical needs critical for holistic care. Option C focuses on medical aspects without integrating social factors. Option D can benefit physical health but lacks the comprehensive approach needed to address broader socio-environmental factors impacting Maria's well-being like option B does.

Question 17: Correct Answer: C) Increases patient engagement and adherence
Rationale: Integrating telehealth into case management enhances patient engagement and adherence by providing convenient access to care without physical travel. While reducing costs (A) and eliminating travel (B) are benefits, they are secondary to the primary goal of improving adherence. Immediate specialist access (D), although advantageous, does not directly address ongoing engagement. Telehealth ensures consistent monitoring and interaction, thus fostering better health outcomes through increased patient participation in their care plan.

Question 18: Correct Answer: C) Volunteer Transportation Services
Rationale: Volunteer Transportation Services address Mr.

Garcia's isolation by enabling access to community resources and social activities, enhancing quality of life. Meals on Wheels (Option A) provides nutritional support but does not address social isolation directly. Senior Center Activities (Option B), while beneficial for socialization, require transportation access first. A Home Health Aide (Option D) assists with personal care but doesn't solve the transportation issue critical for community engagement and reducing isolation.

Question 19: Correct Answer: B) The presence of cognitive impairment
Rationale: Cognitive impairment is a significant risk factor for elder abuse, as it may increase vulnerability and dependency on caregivers. While financial status, social support, and living environment are important considerations, cognitive impairment directly affects the ability to recognize and report abuse. Financial status can influence vulnerability but is not as direct a factor as cognitive impairment. Social support can mitigate risk but does not directly indicate abuse potential. Living environment impacts safety but is secondary to cognitive issues.

Question 20: Correct Answer: B) Limited income and resources
Rationale: To qualify for SSI, the primary criterion is having limited income and resources. While age, citizenship, and disability are important factors, they alone do not determine eligibility without financial need. Option A is incorrect because age alone does not guarantee SSI; financial status is crucial. Option C is incorrect as citizenship is required but not sufficient without financial need. Option D is incorrect because disability must be coupled with financial criteria.

Question 21: Correct Answer: B) Utilizing a multidisciplinary team approach
Rationale: Utilizing a multidisciplinary team approach ensures comprehensive care by integrating diverse expertise to address complex patient needs. While establishing a single point of contact (Option A) can streamline communication, it lacks the breadth of perspectives provided by a team. Standardized care pathways (Option C) offer consistency but may not account for individual complexities. Focusing solely on cost-effectiveness (Option D) might overlook quality and holistic care aspects. The multidisciplinary approach fosters collaboration and personalized care, aligning with contemporary research on effective case management.

Question 22: Correct Answer: B) Tailoring interventions to match the individual's stage of change
Rationale: The Transtheoretical Model (TTM) emphasizes that behavior change is a process involving several stages. Tailoring interventions to match an individual's stage of change ensures that the strategies are relevant and effective. Option A focuses on rewards, which can be useful but may not address underlying readiness. Option C addresses environmental factors, which might not align with internal readiness. Option D is important but more general, whereas B specifically aligns with TTM principles.

Question 23: Correct Answer: A) Reduced absenteeism rates
Rationale: Employer-based health and wellness programs primarily aim to reduce absenteeism by promoting healthier lifestyles, leading to fewer sick days. While increased employee satisfaction (B), lower healthcare costs for employees (C), and enhanced productivity (D) are potential outcomes, they are secondary benefits. The direct link between wellness programs and reduced absenteeism is well-documented

in contemporary research, highlighting its immediate impact on attendance, which directly influences care delivery efficiency and cost-effectiveness.

Question 24: Correct Answer: B) Implement remote patient monitoring devices and provide technical support to address connectivity issues.

Rationale: The correct answer is B because it combines the use of technology with support to overcome connectivity barriers, crucial for rural areas. Option A fails to consider connectivity issues, C does not leverage virtual care effectively, and D limits the scope of care by relying only on phone calls, lacking comprehensive monitoring.

Question 25: Correct Answer: C) Develop a comprehensive discharge plan including medication reconciliation and patient education.

Rationale: A comprehensive discharge plan addresses multiple aspects of care, reducing readmissions by ensuring continuity and understanding of treatment. Option A, while important, lacks immediacy and comprehensiveness. Option B provides support but may not be frequent enough for John's condition. Option D offers emergency contact information but doesn't actively prevent issues. The correct answer integrates medication reconciliation and education, aligning with best practices in transitional care for chronic conditions.

Question 26: Correct Answer: B) Integrate spiritual healing practices with medical treatments.

Rationale: Integrating spiritual healing practices acknowledges the client's cultural beliefs, enhancing trust and compliance. Option A disregards cultural context, potentially alienating the client. Option C ignores the client's worldview, which may hinder acceptance of care. Option D neglects an essential aspect of holistic care. Recognizing and incorporating clients' beliefs can improve health outcomes by aligning treatment plans with their values and expectations.

Question 27: Correct Answer: A) Conducting a comprehensive medication review

Rationale: Conducting a comprehensive medication review allows identification of potential duplications, interactions, and opportunities for optimization, leading to better outcomes and cost savings. Prior authorization (B) can be burdensome without addressing underlying issues. Over-the-counter alternatives (C) may not provide equivalent efficacy for chronic conditions. Switching to formulary-preferred brands (D), while potentially cost-effective, doesn't address overall medication management comprehensively like option A does. The review ensures holistic assessment and alignment with best practices in pharmacy benefits management.

Question 28: Correct Answer: A) Paraphrasing Mr. Thompson's statements to show understanding

Rationale: Paraphrasing demonstrates active listening by reflecting the client's words, fostering trust and encouraging openness. While offering solutions (B) may seem helpful, it can hinder communication if done prematurely. Sharing personal experiences (C) might shift focus away from the client. Closed-ended questions (D) limit responses and do not promote detailed sharing. Paraphrasing aligns with active listening principles by validating the client's feelings and thoughts.

Question 29: Correct Answer: B) By evaluating clinical diagnoses and treatment patterns

Rationale: The ACG system primarily classifies patients based on clinical diagnoses and treatment patterns to predict healthcare resource utilization. This approach allows for a nuanced understanding of patient needs, unlike demographic data (A), which lacks specificity in predicting resource use. Socioeconomic factors (C) and patient-reported outcomes (D) provide context but do not directly drive classification in the ACG model. The focus on clinical data ensures accurate predictions of healthcare needs.

Question 30: Correct Answer: D) Assisted Living Facility

Rationale: An Assisted Living Facility is ideal for Sarah as it offers both medical supervision and assistance with daily activities, addressing her diabetes management and mobility issues. Independent Living Communities do not provide medical care or significant personal assistance. Inpatient Rehabilitation Facilities focus on intensive therapy post-hospitalization, unsuitable for Sarah's ongoing needs. Long-term Acute Care Hospitals are designed for patients requiring extended medical care beyond acute hospital stays, not fitting Sarah's requirement for daily living support combined with medical oversight.

Question 31: Correct Answer: B) Verify the medical necessity and gather supporting documentation

Rationale: Verifying medical necessity and gathering supporting documentation is crucial in utilization management to justify the need for services and obtain prior authorization. Option A overlooks necessary documentation, risking denial. Option C violates protocol by scheduling without approval, leading to potential financial liability. Option D assumes approval without verification, which can result in denial due to policy changes or case-specific factors. Proper documentation ensures compliance with guidelines and supports informed decision-making.

Question 32: Correct Answer: B) Non-emergency medical transportation services

Rationale: Non-emergency medical transportation (NEMT) services are designed specifically for patients requiring assistance to access healthcare facilities, ensuring continuity of care. While public transportation passes (A) offer affordability, they may not address accessibility needs. Ride-sharing services (C) provide flexibility but lack specialized support for medical needs. Volunteer driver programs (D), though helpful, may not consistently meet demand or have trained personnel.

Question 33: Correct Answer: B) Decreased burden on traditional healthcare facilities

Rationale: Alternative care sites help alleviate the pressure on hospitals by accommodating overflow patients, thus ensuring that traditional facilities can focus on critical cases. Option A is incorrect because alternative sites may still require specialized equipment. Option C is misleading as costs can vary based on setup and resources. Option D is incorrect because satisfaction levels depend on various factors and are not inherently higher in alternative sites.

Question 34: Correct Answer: B) Enhancing patient self-management education

Rationale: The Health Home model emphasizes patient-centered care, prioritizing self-management education to empower patients in managing their chronic conditions. While acute care interventions (A), specialty care referrals (C), and frequent home visits (D) are important, they do not directly enhance the patient's ability to manage their health independently. Option B is correct as it aligns with the core goal of Health Homes to improve health outcomes through active patient participation and education.

Question 35: Correct Answer: A) Applying for emergency rental assistance programs

Rationale: Emergency rental assistance can provide immediate relief and prevent eviction, addressing the urgent need for housing stability. Option B may not resolve the immediate crisis and relies on the son's cooperation. Option C could be lengthy and stressful without addressing current needs. Option D increases financial burden through high interest rates, worsening Mrs. Lopez's situation. Therefore, option A offers the most direct and practical solution in this urgent context.

Question 36: Correct Answer: B) Meals that require minimal preparation

Rationale: For John's cognitive impairment, minimizing meal preparation complexity (B) ensures he can safely manage his nutrition independently. While discounts (A), customer support (C), and frequency alignment (D) are beneficial, they do not address the immediate need for ease of use.

Question 37: Correct Answer: B) Highlight the discrepancies between Tom's current behavior and his goals.

Rationale: Highlighting discrepancies helps Tom recognize inconsistencies between his actions and personal goals, fostering motivation for change—central to Motivational Interviewing. Option A can increase defensiveness; Option C oversimplifies change processes; Option D may overwhelm without addressing readiness or autonomy. Each incorrect option overlooks the importance of self-motivated realization that option B effectively targets through reflective discussion and goal alignment within Motivational Interviewing principles.

Question 38: Correct Answer: C) Neighborhood and Built Environment

Rationale: The correct answer is C) Neighborhood and Built Environment because transportation issues are directly related to the infrastructure and accessibility within Sarah's community. Although economic stability (A) can influence access to resources, it does not directly address transportation. Education access (B) pertains to learning opportunities rather than physical mobility. Social context (D) involves support networks but not logistical barriers like transportation. Addressing neighborhood factors will help improve Sarah's ability to attend medical appointments.

Question 39: Correct Answer: D) Episode-based payments

Rationale: Episode-based payments, a core component of bundled payment models, are designed to encourage providers to enhance care coordination and efficiency by offering a single payment for all services related to a treatment or condition over a specific period. Unlike fee-for-service (A), which reimburses per service, or capitation (B), which provides a fixed amount per patient, episode-based payments focus on outcomes within an episode. Shared savings programs (C) incentivize cost reduction but do not inherently link payments to specific episodes of care.

Question 40: Correct Answer: A) Lower monthly premium payments

Rationale: High-deductible health plans (HDHPs) typically offer lower monthly premiums, making them attractive to individuals who prefer lower upfront costs. Although HDHPs may not provide broader network access (B), more comprehensive coverage options (C), or reduced out-of-pocket maximums (D), they are financially appealing for those who anticipate low healthcare utilization and wish to save on monthly expenses.

Question 41: Correct Answer: B) Capitation

Rationale: Capitation involves a fixed payment per patient to providers, irrespective of the services rendered, encouraging cost-effective care management. Fee-for-Service reimburses based on individual services, making

it distinct from Capitation. Bundled Payments cover a set of services for a particular treatment episode, differing from per-patient payments. Pay-for-Performance incentivizes quality improvements but doesn't involve fixed payments per patient. Capitation stands out by its focus on managing overall care within a set budget.

Question 42: Correct Answer: C) Pay-for-performance model rewarding providers for meeting quality benchmarks.

Rationale: The pay-for-performance model (Option C) aligns well with value-based care by directly linking financial incentives to quality improvements, encouraging providers to enhance service delivery and patient outcomes efficiently. The fee-for-service model (Option A), in contrast, promotes volume over value, potentially leading to unnecessary procedures. Capitation (Option B), while cost-effective, may risk under-provision of necessary care due to fixed payments. Bundled payments (Option D) focus on specific conditions rather than overall quality improvement across all services provided.

Question 43: Correct Answer: B) Facilitating access to a multidisciplinary support team

Rationale: Facilitating access to a multidisciplinary support team is most effective as it provides comprehensive care addressing various aspects of abuse, including medical, psychological, and social needs. While individual therapy (Option C) and legal advice (Option D) are important, they are components of broader support. Encouraging immediate departure (Option A) may not be feasible or safe for all patients. A multidisciplinary approach ensures holistic care tailored to each individual's situation, aligning with current best practices in managing domestic abuse cases.

Question 44: Correct Answer: B) Paratransit services

Rationale: Paratransit services are designed specifically for individuals with disabilities or impairments, offering door-to-door service that aligns with the client's specific needs. Ride-sharing services (Option A), while flexible, may not cater to specific accessibility needs or offer consistent scheduling. Senior center shuttles (Option C) could be limited by schedule and scope of service. Using a personal care assistant's vehicle (Option D) might lack sustainability due to potential availability issues or additional costs.

Question 45: Correct Answer: B) Facilitating access to diverse resources and support networks

Rationale: Option B is fundamental as it supports self-directed care by providing clients with various resources, enhancing informed decision-making. This approach aligns with theories advocating for personalized support systems. Option A contradicts individualization, while C disregards client-centered values. Option D restricts empowerment by minimizing client involvement. Access to diverse resources enables tailored interventions, respecting client preferences and promoting autonomy in managing their care effectively.

Question 46: Correct Answer: B) Patient's diagnosis and treatment plan

Rationale: Funding eligibility for residential treatment facilities is primarily influenced by the patient's diagnosis and treatment plan, as these determine medical necessity and appropriateness of care. While age and gender (A), duration of stay (C), and location (D) might be considered in some contexts, they do not directly impact reimbursement eligibility as much as having a clear, medically justified diagnosis and an evidence-based treatment plan. This ensures that funding is allocated based on clinical need rather than demographic or logistical factors.

Question 47: Correct Answer: A) Refer Mrs. Garcia to a pharmaceutical assistance program

Rationale: Referring Mrs. Garcia to a pharmaceutical assistance program can provide immediate relief by reducing medication costs through available subsidies or discounts tailored for low-income individuals. While applying for Medicaid (B) might help long-term, it may not offer immediate support due to processing timeframes. Home delivery services (C) improve convenience but do not address cost issues directly, and over-the-counter alternatives (D) may not be clinically appropriate or sufficient for her needs.

Question 48: Correct Answer: B) Implementation of motivational interviewing techniques

Rationale: Motivational interviewing is a counseling approach that enhances intrinsic motivation, making it highly effective for long-term adherence to wellness programs. Unlike regular educational materials (A), which may not engage individuals deeply, or periodic health screenings (C), which focus more on monitoring than behavior change, motivational interviewing encourages self-reflection and commitment. Financial incentives (D) can be effective short-term but may not sustain long-term behavioral change as they do not address underlying motivations.

Question 49: Correct Answer: B) Developmental Evaluation

Rationale: Developmental Evaluation emphasizes continuous feedback and improvement during implementation by adapting to complex environments and evolving needs. Unlike Impact Evaluation, which assesses long-term effects, or Outcome Evaluation, which measures end results, Developmental Evaluation is iterative and flexible. Cost-Benefit Analysis focuses on financial implications rather than process enhancement. This approach supports real-time decision-making and adaptation in dynamic settings, making it ideal for ongoing program development.

Question 50: Correct Answer: C) Collaboration

Rationale: Collaboration is the most effective strategy in this scenario as it seeks a win-win solution by addressing the concerns of both parties, fostering teamwork and innovation. Unlike avoidance, which ignores the conflict, or accommodation, which may lead to resentment by prioritizing one side's needs, collaboration encourages open dialogue and mutual respect. Compromise might offer a quick solution but doesn't fully satisfy either party's concerns, making collaboration the superior choice for long-term resolution.

Question 51: Correct Answer: C) To assist low-income individuals in paying for Medicare premiums and out-of-pocket expenses

Rationale: The primary purpose of Medicare Savings Programs (MSPs) is to help low-income individuals pay for Medicare premiums, deductibles, coinsurance, and copayments. Option A is incorrect as it focuses solely on prescription drug costs. Option B incorrectly suggests benefits for chronic conditions rather than financial assistance. Option D relates to long-term care coverage but does not align with MSPs' objectives. MSPs are crucial for making healthcare more affordable for eligible beneficiaries by reducing their financial burden.

Question 52: Correct Answer: D) Reflective listening

Rationale: Reflective listening is the most effective technique as it involves actively listening and reflecting back what the client has said, ensuring accurate understanding. While open-ended questions (Option A) allow clients to express themselves freely, they do not ensure understanding. Closed-ended questions (Option B) limit responses, and leading questions (Option C) may bias responses. Reflective listening confirms comprehension and builds rapport by validating the client's feelings and thoughts.

Question 53: Correct Answer: C) Multiple fractures at different healing stages

Rationale: Multiple fractures at different healing stages are a strong indicator of physical abuse, as they suggest repeated trauma over time. While unexplained weight loss (A), recurrent headaches (B), and insomnia (D) can be associated with stress or neglect, they are not as definitive for abuse as the presence of multiple fractures. This option directly points to physical harm, aligning with contemporary research that prioritizes physical signs in abuse assessments.

Question 54: Correct Answer: A) The potential impact on John's eligibility for Medicaid benefits.

Rationale: Option A is correct because receiving a lump sum from a viatical settlement could affect John's asset threshold for Medicaid eligibility, potentially disqualifying him from benefits. While Options B and C are important financial considerations, they don't directly impact his Medicaid status. Option D, though relevant for ensuring a trustworthy transaction, doesn't address immediate financial aid concerns like Medicaid eligibility. Understanding these distinctions ensures comprehensive advice aligned with John's healthcare needs and financial planning.

Question 55: Correct Answer: B) By advocating for local policy changes that benefit the wider community

Rationale: Fraternal/religious organizations play a crucial role in community resource development by advocating for policies that benefit the entire community. Option B reflects this broader impact, unlike options A and C, which focus on exclusivity. Option D's emphasis on internal growth does not align with community-wide benefits. Thus, option B best represents how these organizations can influence positive change beyond their immediate membership.

Question 56: Correct Answer: B) Enhancing community-based participatory research initiatives

Rationale: Community-based participatory research (CBPR) involves communities in identifying needs and developing interventions, effectively addressing social determinants of health and reducing disparities. Option A may improve infrastructure but doesn't directly tackle disparities. Option C targets disease detection rather than underlying causes. Option D increases access but may not address specific community needs. CBPR empowers communities, ensuring interventions are culturally relevant and sustainable, thereby aligning with contemporary research for disparity reduction.

Question 57: Correct Answer: C) Hospital Compare Database

Rationale: The Hospital Compare Database is a CMS initiative providing quality indicators for hospitals, helping case managers like Sarah assess care quality under Medicare. While NCQA and HEDIS offer valuable metrics, they are not CMS-specific. The Joint Commission focuses on accreditation rather than CMS quality measures. Therefore, the Hospital Compare Database is the most appropriate source for CMS-compliant quality indicators.

Question 58: Correct Answer: B) The potential for positive patient outcomes

Rationale: The potential for positive patient outcomes is crucial in utilization management to justify the medical necessity and effectiveness of a service, making it eligible for reimbursement. Option A focuses on length of stay, which doesn't directly assess necessity or outcomes. Option C emphasizes insurance details, which are logistical rather than clinical considerations. Option D considers historical costs, which don't directly relate to current patient-specific outcomes or needs.

Question 59: Correct Answer: B) Skilled Nursing Facility
Rationale: A Skilled Nursing Facility provides comprehensive medical support alongside personal care services necessary for patients like Mrs. Smith who have complex health needs such as Alzheimer's disease. Assisted living facilities generally offer less intensive medical support, focusing more on personal assistance. Adult day care centers provide temporary relief but not continuous supervision or medical care. Home health care offers limited in-home medical services but may lack the full-time supervision required for advanced Alzheimer's patients.

Question 60: Correct Answer: B) Transitional Care Planning
Rationale: Transitional Care Planning focuses on ensuring continuity of care during transitions between different healthcare settings, crucial for reducing hospital readmissions post-discharge. Unlike Utilization Review, which evaluates service use efficiency; Disease Management Programs that target chronic disease education; or Patient-Centered Medical Homes emphasizing comprehensive primary care access; Transitional Care Planning directly addresses post-discharge needs by coordinating follow-up appointments and medication management, making it ideal for managing Robert's post-surgery recovery and adherence to his treatment plan.

Question 61: Correct Answer: B) Collaborate with HR to create inclusive policies that accommodate diverse gender expressions.
Rationale: Collaborating with HR (Option B) promotes systemic change by fostering an inclusive environment that respects all employees' gender expressions, aligning with best practices in diversity management. Option A ignores personal comfort and perpetuates exclusionary norms. Option C may be insufficient without structural support, while Option D bypasses addressing workplace issues directly, potentially limiting opportunities for broader cultural change within the organization.

Question 62: Correct Answer: A) Regular physical activity sessions tailored to individual capabilities
Rationale: Tailored physical activity is crucial for managing chronic illnesses in the elderly, as it improves overall health outcomes by enhancing mobility and reducing comorbidities. Educational seminars (Option B), while informative, may not have immediate impacts on physical health. Social gatherings (Option C) foster support but don't directly influence disease management. Online resources (Option D) provide information but lack personalized engagement critical for elderly patients' adherence and improvement.

Question 63: Correct Answer: C) Implement an integrated treatment plan addressing both disorders simultaneously.
Rationale: Integrated treatment is crucial for dual diagnoses as it addresses both conditions concurrently, leading to better outcomes. Option A and B suggest sequential treatment, which may neglect the interrelated nature of dual diagnoses. Option D risks fragmented care without coordination. Contemporary research supports integrated approaches as they consider the complex interactions between mental health and substance use disorders, providing comprehensive support and improving recovery rates.

Question 64: Correct Answer: D) Rental Assistance Programs
Rationale: Rental Assistance Programs are critical in preventing homelessness by providing financial aid for housing stability. While Employment Assistance Programs (A) help with job placement, they do not offer immediate relief for housing needs. Temporary Shelter Programs (B) provide temporary housing but do not address long-term housing security. Food Banks (C) alleviate food insecurity but do not assist with rent payments or housing stability, which is the primary concern in this scenario.

Question 65: Correct Answer: B) Encouraging open dialogues about individual experiences and identities.
Rationale: Encouraging open dialogues fosters an inclusive environment by allowing individuals to share their unique experiences and identities without fear of judgment. Option A's enforcement of traditional norms can marginalize non-conforming expressions. Option C's uniformity suppresses individuality, while D's focus on medical interventions overlooks the importance of social acceptance and understanding. Thus, option B effectively supports inclusivity by valuing diverse gender expressions through communication and understanding within psychosocial frameworks.

Question 66: Correct Answer: B) Indemnity plans offer greater flexibility in choosing healthcare providers without referrals.
Rationale: Indemnity insurance plans are characterized by their flexibility, allowing patients to choose any healthcare provider without needing referrals, unlike managed care models like HMOs or PPOs (Option A). This flexibility often results in higher out-of-pocket costs (contrary to Option C). While some indemnity plans may require prior authorization for certain services (Option D), this is not a defining feature as it is with managed care plans where such controls are more prevalent.

Question 67: Correct Answer: B) Implement a structured exercise regimen supervised by a visiting therapist at home.
Rationale: A structured exercise regimen supervised by a visiting therapist maximizes Maria's recovery potential within her benefit limitations by providing personalized care and reducing the need for more costly inpatient services (C). Outpatient programs (A) might be less convenient and challenging post-surgery, and educational materials (D), though useful, lack professional guidance essential during recovery. This approach balances effective rehabilitation with cost-efficiency under private insurance constraints.

Question 68: Correct Answer: C) The network status of the home health provider with the private benefit program
Rationale: The network status of the provider is crucial as many private benefit programs only cover services from in-network providers to control costs and ensure quality standards. While diagnosis and frequency are important, they do not directly affect eligibility like network status does. Total cost may influence coverage limits but not initial eligibility.

Question 69: Correct Answer: D) Experimental Evaluation
Rationale: Experimental Evaluation is the most effective method for identifying causal relationships because it involves the use of control groups and randomization to establish cause-and-effect links. Unlike Process Evaluation, which focuses on how a program operates, or Formative Evaluation, which aims at improving program design, Experimental Evaluation provides robust

evidence of impact. Summative Evaluation assesses overall effectiveness but lacks the rigorous control needed to determine causality like Experimental Evaluation does.

Question 70: Correct Answer: B) Average costs of similar episodes in the region.
Rationale: Reimbursement rates under bundled payments are typically based on regional averages for similar episodes to ensure fairness and cost-effectiveness, promoting standardization across providers. Option A focuses on past billing, which can perpetuate inefficiencies. Option C could lead to inflated costs and is not representative of typical practices. Option D relates to volume rather than cost-effectiveness or quality, missing the core objective of bundled payments which is efficient resource utilization based on regional norms.

Question 71: Correct Answer: C) Bundled payments
Rationale: Bundled payments align with value-based care by encouraging cost efficiency and quality improvement across a patient's entire care episode. Unlike fee-for-service (A), which incentivizes volume, bundled payments focus on outcomes. Capitation (B) involves fixed per-member payments but lacks episode-specific incentives. Pay-for-performance (D) rewards specific metrics rather than comprehensive care episodes. Thus, bundled payments represent a holistic approach to enhancing value through coordinated care and shared accountability, aligning well with contemporary value-based care principles.

Question 72: Correct Answer: B) Storming
Rationale: The storming stage involves conflict and competition as individuals assert themselves, which distinguishes it from forming (initial orientation), norming (developing cohesion), and performing (achieving goals). During storming, differing opinions may lead to disputes but are essential for growth. Recognizing this phase is crucial for case managers to facilitate resolution strategies and promote constructive dialogue, helping groups progress towards harmony and productivity in subsequent stages.

Question 73: Correct Answer: A) Utilizing open-ended questions to explore concerns
Rationale: Open-ended questions encourage dialogue, allowing clients to express their thoughts freely, which can reduce resistance by making them feel heard and valued. This technique aligns with research highlighting its effectiveness in engaging clients. Option B might seem supportive but could dismiss underlying issues. Option C can create barriers by imposing authority rather than collaboration. Option D risks shifting focus from the client's needs to the manager's experiences. Open-ended questioning fosters a collaborative environment essential for overcoming resistance.

Question 74: Correct Answer: B) Emotional numbness
Rationale: Emotional numbness is a defense mechanism often developed by individuals subjected to chronic abuse and neglect as a means to cope with overwhelming stress. This response helps in minimizing emotional pain. In contrast, resilience (A) and optimism (D) are positive adaptive responses that typically require supportive environments. Hyperactivity (C), while a possible reaction, is more commonly linked to acute stress or attention disorders rather than long-term abuse. Therefore, emotional numbness is the most appropriate response in this context.

Question 75: Correct Answer: C) The case manager explains the risks and benefits of different management strategies and collaborates with Emily to choose a plan that aligns with her values and preferences.
Rationale: Option C is correct as it involves Emily in understanding management strategies while respecting her values, aligning with shared decision-making principles. Option A excludes patient input; B allows choice but lacks comprehensive discussion; D mandates education without immediate collaboration, reducing immediate engagement in decision-making.

Question 76: Correct Answer: B) Utilizing teach-back methods to confirm understanding
Rationale: Teach-back methods are effective as they ensure patients understand the information by having them repeat it in their own words. This approach directly engages patients, allowing healthcare providers to assess comprehension and clarify misunderstandings. While providing written materials (A) and digital resources (C) can be helpful, they may not be accessible or easily understood by all patients. Group sessions (D) might not address individual comprehension issues effectively. Teach-back is interactive and personalized, making it superior in improving health literacy.

Question 77: Correct Answer: B) Biopsychosocial Model Assessment
Rationale: The Biopsychosocial Model Assessment considers biological, psychological, and social factors, providing a comprehensive view of the patient's health. CBT focuses solely on cognitive processes, while Psychoanalytic Assessment emphasizes unconscious processes without addressing social factors. The Medical Model primarily targets biological aspects. The Biopsychosocial approach integrates multiple dimensions crucial for understanding the interplay between mental health and social determinants, offering a balanced assessment framework in case management.

Question 78: Correct Answer: B) Genogram
Rationale: A genogram is most beneficial for identifying underlying psychosocial issues as it visually maps family relationships and patterns that may influence the client's situation. A structured interview guide (Option A) provides consistency but lacks depth in uncovering hidden issues. A checklist of symptoms (Option C) focuses on specific problems rather than relationships. A standardized questionnaire (Option D) offers general insights but may miss nuanced familial dynamics. The genogram uniquely reveals intergenerational patterns impacting psychosocial health.

Question 79: Correct Answer: B) Resource Utilization Groups (RUGs).
Rationale: Under Medicare's SNF PPS, payments are primarily influenced by Resource Utilization Groups (RUGs), which categorize patients based on expected resource needs. This system ensures that payments reflect care complexity rather than geographic location (Option A), staffing levels (Option C), or demographic factors like age and gender (Option D). RUGs allow for precise alignment with patient care requirements, enhancing efficiency and resource allocation in skilled nursing facilities, consistent with current reimbursement strategies.

Question 80: Correct Answer: B) Implement motivational interviewing to explore Tom's ambivalence towards change.
Rationale: Motivational interviewing is effective in resolving ambivalence and enhancing intrinsic motivation for change by exploring personal reasons for lifestyle adjustments. Option A may not address underlying resistance. Option C emphasizes education without addressing motivation or readiness for change. Option D might induce fear rather than motivate positive behavior

change. The correct option prioritizes understanding and addressing Tom's internal conflicts regarding lifestyle modifications, promoting sustainable adherence.

Question 81: Correct Answer: B) UCR charges are based on the average fees charged by providers in the same geographic area.

Rationale: The UCR charges reflect average fees for services within a specific region, ensuring fair reimbursement without overpayment. Option A is incorrect as it does not consider regional averages. Option C is misleading because UCR does not guarantee maximum reimbursement but rather typical rates. Option D incorrectly attributes UCR determination to federal standards, whereas it is regionally and market-driven.

Question 82: Correct Answer: A) Major Depressive Disorder

Rationale: Major Depressive Disorder (MDD) is characterized by persistent sadness, loss of interest, and changes in appetite. Persistent Depressive Disorder (PDD), while similar, involves longer-term symptoms that are less severe. Bipolar I Disorder includes manic episodes, which are not present here. Cyclothymic Disorder involves fluctuating mood disturbances over a long period but does not match the acute presentation of symptoms seen in MDD. Therefore, MDD is the most accurate diagnosis given Sarah's patient's symptoms.

Question 83: Correct Answer: D) Empathy

Rationale: Demonstrating empathy helps build rapport and trust, making clients feel understood and supported. It encourages them to open up about sensitive topics. Silence (A), while sometimes useful, may heighten anxiety in this context; clarification (B) is for ensuring understanding but not necessarily comfort; summarization (C) aids in reinforcing information but doesn't inherently ease anxiety. Empathy directly addresses emotional needs, promoting a safe environment for sharing.

Question 84: Correct Answer: C) Patient Adherence to Medication

Rationale: Patient adherence to medication is the primary indicator for predicting hospital readmissions within 30 days because non-adherence can lead to poor glycemic control and subsequent complications requiring hospitalization. While HbA1c levels and hypoglycemic episodes are important, they often reflect past control rather than current adherence. The number of comorbidities contributes to overall risk but doesn't directly predict adherence-related issues leading to readmission. Adherence ensures effective management of diabetes and reduces hospitalization rates.

Question 85: Correct Answer: C) Advising Lisa to track and report her earnings accurately each month

Rationale: Accurate monthly reporting of earnings (Option C) ensures that SSA can adjust benefits according to Lisa's income changes, maintaining her eligibility. While reporting medical condition changes (Option A) is important, it doesn't directly address earnings impact on SSI. Saving extra earnings (Option B), without considering resource limits, may inadvertently jeopardize eligibility. Reducing work hours (Option D) unnecessarily limits potential income without guaranteeing continued eligibility; accurate reporting suffices to manage benefit adjustments effectively.

Question 86: Correct Answer: B) Accountable Care Organization (ACO)

Rationale: An ACO focuses on coordinated care, aiming to improve quality while reducing costs by aligning incentives across providers. Unlike the Fee-for-Service model that can lead to fragmented care, ACOs emphasize accountability for patient outcomes. HMOs offer managed care but may restrict provider choice more than ACOs. PPOs provide flexibility but lack the integrated approach of ACOs. Therefore, ACOs are best suited for managing complex cases like Sarah's patient, ensuring comprehensive and cost-effective care.

Question 87: Correct Answer: B) Discuss the potential benefits and risks of the treatment in layman's terms.

Rationale: Option B is correct as it involves translating complex medical information into understandable language, empowering Sarah to make an informed decision. Option A might overwhelm her with technical jargon, while C does not adequately inform her. Option D relies on others' choices rather than personalized information. Informing through clear communication aligns with contemporary theories emphasizing patient-centered care and shared decision-making.

Question 88: Correct Answer: B) Quasi-Experimental Design

Rationale: Emily is using a Quasi-Experimental Design, which compares outcomes between groups without random assignment, making it suitable for evaluating real-world interventions like discharge planning programs. Unlike RCTs (Option A), which require randomization, quasi-experimental designs are more practical in healthcare settings where randomization may be unethical or impractical. Cross-sectional studies (Option C) and case-control studies (Option D) do not involve intervention comparisons over time, focusing instead on observational data at a single point or retrospective analysis.

Question 89: Correct Answer: B) Enrolling in a Transitional Care Program

Rationale: Transitional Care Programs focus on ensuring smooth transitions from hospital to home, reducing readmissions by addressing gaps in care post-discharge. While Disease Management Programs target specific conditions and routine check-ups increase monitoring frequency, neither addresses the critical transition phase. Specialist consultations offer expertise but lack comprehensive transitional support. Thus, enrolling John in a Transitional Care Program provides coordinated follow-up and education crucial for managing heart failure effectively at home.

Question 90: Correct Answer: B) Access to an online peer support network

Rationale: Access to an online peer support network (B) provides continuous emotional and psychological support from individuals facing similar challenges, fostering adjustment and acceptance. While occupational therapy (A), family meetings (C), and exercise regimens (D) offer benefits in managing physical symptoms or family dynamics, they lack the direct peer interaction that significantly aids psychological adaptation by sharing experiences and coping mechanisms unique to those with similar conditions.

Question 91: Correct Answer: C) The cost-effectiveness of home care versus hospitalization

Rationale: The cost-effectiveness of home care versus hospitalization is crucial as insurers prioritize treatments that reduce overall healthcare expenses. While the patient's medical diagnosis and frequency of visits are important, they do not directly influence coverage decisions. Certified agency availability affects service provision but not benefit extent. Cost-effectiveness aligns with contemporary research emphasizing economic factors in private insurance decisions.

Question 92: Correct Answer: B) Implement a centralized electronic health record system.

Rationale: Implementing a centralized electronic health record system ensures real-time access to patient information for all providers, facilitating seamless communication and coordination. Option A, while useful, may lead to fragmented communication. Option C is beneficial but may not be feasible or timely enough for urgent updates. Option D enhances patient involvement but does not directly improve provider communication like option B does.

Question 93: Correct Answer: A) Meals requiring minimal preparation

Rationale: For John, who has mild cognitive impairment, it's essential that meals require minimal preparation to reduce confusion and ensure safety. While organic ingredients (B), cultural diversity (C), and high protein content (D) can be beneficial, they do not address the immediate need for simplicity in meal preparation.

Question 94: Correct Answer: B) Collaborate with religious leaders or cultural liaisons to find acceptable compromises.

Rationale: Collaborating with religious leaders or cultural liaisons helps bridge gaps between medical recommendations and religious practices, ensuring respectful and effective care. Option A disregards patient-centered care principles; C risks non-compliance by ignoring patient values; D neglects resolution efforts, potentially worsening conflicts. B is correct as it fosters understanding and cooperation, aligning with principles of culturally competent practice by integrating multiple perspectives into decision-making processes.

Question 95: Correct Answer: C) Enhancing electronic health record (EHR) interoperability

Rationale: Enhancing EHR interoperability allows seamless sharing of patient information across providers, crucial for coordinated care in ACOs. While the patient-centered medical home model (A) promotes primary care, it doesn't directly address information flow. Increasing specialist referrals (B) might lead to fragmented care without proper coordination. Monthly check-ups (D) alone don't ensure real-time data sharing essential for reducing readmissions.

Question 96: Correct Answer: B) Patient-Centered Medical Home (PCMH) Model

Rationale: The Patient-Centered Medical Home (PCMH) model focuses on coordinated care across multiple settings, ensuring comprehensive management and improved outcomes. Unlike the Fee-for-Service Model, which incentivizes volume over quality, PCMH emphasizes holistic and integrated care. The Capitation Model primarily deals with payment structures rather than care integration. Direct Primary Care is more about simplified payment methods without necessarily integrating care across settings. Thus, PCMH is uniquely designed for enhanced patient outcomes through integrated care.

Question 97: Correct Answer: B) Medicaid

Rationale: Medicaid is specifically designed to offer healthcare coverage to low-income individuals and families, funded by both state and federal governments. While Medicare (A) covers older adults and certain younger people with disabilities, CHIP (C) targets children's health insurance needs but isn't as comprehensive in scope as Medicaid. SSI (D), on the other hand, provides financial assistance rather than direct healthcare benefits. The joint funding structure of Medicaid distinguishes it from these other programs, making it the correct choice.

Question 98: Correct Answer: B) Encourage participation in a gender support group.

Rationale: Encouraging participation in a gender support group is crucial as it provides peer support and validation, which are vital for mental health in transgender individuals. While medication (Option A) and cognitive-behavioral therapy (Option C) can help manage symptoms, they do not directly address the unique social challenges faced by transgender individuals. Family therapy (Option D) might improve family dynamics but may not immediately address the client's need for social acceptance and understanding from peers who share similar experiences.

Question 99: Correct Answer: B) Encouraging clients to express their values and preferences

Rationale: Encouraging clients to express their values and preferences is essential in shared decision making, as it ensures that care plans are tailored to individual needs and promotes self-care management. Option A undermines SDM by excluding client input. Option C contradicts SDM principles by removing client autonomy. Option D neglects psychosocial factors crucial for comprehensive care. Therefore, option B aligns with contemporary research emphasizing client-centered care.

Question 100: Correct Answer: C) Coordinating care with a multidisciplinary team.

Rationale: Coordinating care with a multidisciplinary team ensures comprehensive management of multiple chronic conditions by integrating expertise from various healthcare professionals, thus improving outcomes and reducing emergency visits. Telehealth (Option A) offers monitoring but lacks holistic management; regular appointments (Option B) are beneficial but not as integrative; lifestyle education (Option D) supports self-management but doesn't directly address complex care coordination needs.

Question 101: Correct Answer: B) Access to electronic health records (EHRs)

Rationale: Access to EHRs is crucial for enhancing patient engagement and self-management in the PCMH model. It empowers patients by providing access to their health information, facilitating informed decision-making. Option A is incorrect as regular ER visits are not conducive to proactive management. Option C incorrectly emphasizes medication use without addressing engagement. Option D focuses on specialist consultations, which do not inherently enhance self-management. EHRs support transparency and active participation in one's own healthcare journey.

Question 102: Correct Answer: B) Collaborating with social workers to assess patient eligibility and tailor PAP applications

Rationale: Collaborating with social workers ensures a comprehensive assessment of the patient's psychosocial needs, enabling tailored applications that increase the likelihood of receiving assistance. Option A might overwhelm patients with inapplicable programs, while C could miss personalized insights. Option D places undue burden on patients, potentially leading to missed opportunities. Hence, option B is optimal as it combines professional expertise and personalized support.

Question 103: Correct Answer: C) Income level and household size

Rationale: Eligibility for Medicaid is primarily determined by income level and household size, aligning with federal poverty guidelines, making option C correct. Employment status (A), age (B), and previous insurance coverage (D) may influence eligibility but are not primary determinants in the way that income level and household size are considered under Medicaid regulations.

Question 104: Correct Answer: C) Integrated data

analytics
Rationale: Integrated data analytics offers a comprehensive evaluation by synthesizing various data sources to assess both qualitative and quantitative aspects of a case management program. Patient satisfaction surveys (A), while valuable for feedback, lack depth in outcome assessment. Cost-benefit analysis (B) primarily focuses on financial metrics rather than holistic evaluation. Peer review (D), although insightful for professional standards, does not encompass all facets of program effectiveness. Integrated data analytics thus ensures a thorough evaluation by combining diverse data points.

Question 105: Correct Answer: C) Collaborating with Mr. Thompson to set realistic and achievable health goals
Rationale: Collaborative goal-setting empowers patients by actively involving them in their care plan, increasing motivation and adherence. While pamphlets (A), group sessions (B), and online resources (D) provide valuable information, they may not address individual needs or foster personal accountability as effectively as personalized goal-setting does. This approach aligns with contemporary research emphasizing patient-centered care and self-efficacy theory.

Question 106: Correct Answer: C) Collaborative goal-setting between client and healthcare provider
Rationale: Collaborative goal-setting empowers clients by involving them in their care, increasing motivation and adherence to self-care practices. While regular appointments (A) and educational materials (B) provide support, they lack the personalized engagement that collaborative goal-setting offers. Frequent reminders (D), although helpful, may not foster the same level of personal responsibility and intrinsic motivation as setting goals together does. This approach aligns with contemporary theories emphasizing patient-centered care and shared decision-making.

Question 107: Correct Answer: C) Pay-for-Performance
Rationale: Pay-for-Performance (P4P) directly ties financial incentives to the quality and efficiency of care provided, encouraging providers to focus on outcomes. While Capitation (B) offers a fixed amount per patient, it may not specifically reward quality improvements. Fee-for-Service (A) incentivizes volume over quality, and DRGs (D) focus on cost containment for specific diagnoses rather than overall outcomes. P4P aligns financial rewards with improved patient care metrics, making it the most effective model for Sarah's goal.

Question 108: Correct Answer: A) Teach Maria how to negotiate her treatment plan with her healthcare provider.
Rationale: Teaching Maria negotiation skills empowers her to actively engage in decision-making about her care, fostering self-advocacy. Option B provides emotional support but doesn't specifically enhance advocacy skills. Option C offers practical management advice but lacks focus on communication and negotiation skills critical for self-advocacy. Option D discourages active participation in care decisions, which is contrary to promoting self-advocacy principles where patient involvement and empowerment are key aspects.

Question 109: Correct Answer: B) Self-efficacy
Rationale: Self-efficacy refers to a client's belief in their ability to succeed in specific situations or accomplish a task, directly influencing their readiness to change. While social support and goal-setting are important, they primarily serve as external aids rather than intrinsic motivators.

Question 110: Correct Answer: B) Reflective listening
Rationale: Reflective listening is crucial here as it involves actively listening and then reflecting back what the patient says, showing empathy and understanding. This can help Sarah feel more comfortable and willing to share. Direct questioning (A) might feel intrusive, confrontation (C) could increase resistance, and closed-ended questions (D) limit expression. Reflective listening fosters trust and openness, facilitating deeper communication.

Question 111: Correct Answer: A) Solution-Focused Therapy
Rationale: Solution-Focused Therapy emphasizes client strengths and future solutions rather than past problems, empowering clients by enhancing agency and autonomy. Unlike Psychodynamic Therapy, which delves into past experiences and unconscious processes, or Cognitive Behavioral Therapy that targets cognitive distortions, Solution-Focused Therapy centers on empowering clients through goal-setting. Narrative Therapy reshapes personal stories but doesn't primarily focus on agency like Solution-Focused Therapy. Understanding these differences aids case managers in selecting appropriate therapeutic approaches.

Question 112: Correct Answer: B) Major Depressive Disorder
Rationale: Major Depressive Disorder is characterized by persistent feelings of sadness, loss of interest, and changes in appetite and sleep, which align with Sarah's symptoms. Generalized Anxiety Disorder primarily involves excessive worry rather than pervasive sadness. Bipolar Disorder includes episodes of mania or hypomania, not described here. Adjustment Disorder relates to stress reactions within three months of a specific event, which is not indicated in Sarah's scenario. Thus, Major Depressive Disorder best explains her symptoms.

Question 113: Correct Answer: B) The individual becomes disabled within the first 60 days of COBRA coverage.
Rationale: If an individual becomes disabled within the first 60 days of COBRA coverage, they may qualify for an extension of up to 29 months. Option A is incorrect as a reduction in hours triggers initial eligibility but not an extension. Option C is incorrect as gaining new employment typically ends COBRA eligibility. Option D does not affect COBRA duration since relocation doesn't impact eligibility or duration under federal guidelines.

Question 114: Correct Answer: B) Capitation
Rationale: Capitation provides a fixed amount per patient, encouraging cost-effective management of chronic conditions like COPD by incentivizing providers to focus on preventive care and efficient resource use. Fee-for-Service can lead to unnecessary services; Bundled Payments are typically procedure-focused rather than chronic care; Pay-for-Performance rewards quality but doesn't inherently control costs. Therefore, Capitation aligns incentives with cost-effective, quality care for John's condition.

Question 115: Correct Answer: B) Establishing partnerships with local food banks to increase access to fresh produce
Rationale: Option B addresses social determinants by improving access to nutritious food, directly impacting dietary habits—a key factor in diabetes prevention. While options A and C focus on education and detection, they do not directly alter environmental factors. Option D promotes activity but doesn't address nutritional barriers. Partnerships with food banks provide sustainable dietary improvements crucial for long-term health outcomes.

Question 116: Correct Answer: B) Higher administrative

costs and complexity in plan selection.

Rationale: Individuals face higher administrative burdens and complexities when selecting independently purchased health insurance due to the vast array of options and lack of employer guidance, unlike employer-sponsored plans that streamline choices. Option A is incorrect as preventive care services are often included in independent plans due to ACA requirements. Option C is misleading since access depends on the chosen plan's network rather than purchase method. Option D is incorrect because independently purchased plans often offer greater portability across states than employer-based ones, which can be tied to job location.

Question 117: Correct Answer: B) Establishing peer support groups

Rationale: Establishing peer support groups empowers clients by fostering a sense of community and shared experience, which is crucial for psychosocial support and independent management of health conditions. Online forums (A) offer information but lack personal interaction. One-on-one counseling (C) provides personalized guidance but may not build the community aspect. Telehealth services (D) increase access to care but do not inherently provide peer interaction. Peer support groups uniquely combine emotional support with shared learning experiences, enhancing self-management skills.

Question 118: Correct Answer: C) Collaborate with Maria to identify and leverage her personal strengths in managing the illness.

Rationale: Identifying and leveraging personal strengths (Option C) empowers Maria, fostering resilience and self-efficacy crucial in crisis situations. Educational resources (Option A) are informative but may overwhelm initially. Support groups (Option B) offer peer connection but might not immediately address personal coping mechanisms. Therapy (Option D) provides long-term support but doesn't focus on immediate empowerment like leveraging strengths does, aligning best with contemporary crisis intervention theories emphasizing self-efficacy and empowerment in initial responses.

Question 119: Correct Answer: D) Help John identify immediate coping mechanisms to manage stress.

Rationale: In crisis intervention, the priority is to stabilize the individual by addressing immediate needs and reducing distress. Option D focuses on helping John manage his current stress through coping mechanisms, which aligns with the initial phase of crisis intervention. Option A and B are more future-oriented and not suitable for immediate crisis stabilization. Option C, while important, does not directly address John's immediate emotional state as effectively as identifying coping strategies.

Question 120: Correct Answer: B) To ensure the provision of medically necessary services at the lowest cost

Rationale: Utilization management aims to balance cost efficiency with quality care by ensuring that services provided are medically necessary and cost-effective. Option B correctly reflects this goal. Option A focuses on patient satisfaction through volume, which may not align with necessity or cost-effectiveness. Option C emphasizes provider revenue rather than patient-centered care. Option D highlights reducing documentation, which can compromise oversight and quality assurance.

Question 121: Correct Answer: B) Attachment Theory

Rationale: Attachment Theory, developed by John Bowlby and Mary Ainsworth, is pivotal in understanding how early experiences with caregivers shape adult attachment styles. It explains the lasting impact of childhood abuse on emotional bonds and relationships. Cognitive Behavioral Theory focuses more on thought patterns, Social Learning Theory emphasizes learned behaviors through observation, and Psychoanalytic Theory delves into unconscious motives, making them less directly related to attachment dynamics.

Question 122: Correct Answer: C) Evidence-based practice implementation

Rationale: Evaluating case management effectiveness critically involves implementing evidence-based practices, which ensures that care decisions are grounded in the best available research. While patient satisfaction (A), cost reduction (B), and length of stay (D) are important metrics, they do not directly assess the application of evidence-based methodologies. These incorrect options focus on outcomes or efficiency rather than the foundational process that evidence-based practice provides in achieving high-quality care.

Question 123: Correct Answer: B) Facilitate open discussions with Jamie about their feelings and preferences.

Rationale: Facilitating open discussions (Option B) supports Jamie's self-exploration and aligns with contemporary theories on gender identity, which emphasize understanding and respecting individual experiences. Option A contradicts these theories by prioritizing conformity over personal authenticity. Option C is superficial and does not address deeper emotional needs. Option D delays support unnecessarily, ignoring the importance of timely affirmation in adolescence.

Question 124: Correct Answer: B) Establishing a collaborative goal-setting process

Rationale: Establishing a collaborative goal-setting process empowers clients by involving them in decision-making, fostering ownership and intrinsic motivation. While providing educational materials (A) and regular monitoring (C) are supportive, they may not directly enhance motivation. Incentives (D), though potentially motivating, can lead to extrinsic rather than intrinsic motivation. Collaborative goal-setting aligns with contemporary research emphasizing shared decision-making as crucial for client engagement.

Question 125: Correct Answer: B) To cover out-of-pocket expenses with pre-tax dollars.

Rationale:HSAs are designed to help individuals save pre-tax dollars specifically for covering qualified medical expenses, thus reducing taxable income. Option A misrepresents HSAs as emergency funds, which are not their primary function. Option C conflates HSAs with retirement accounts, which are distinct financial tools. Option D inaccurately suggests that HSAs replace traditional insurance plans; instead, they complement high-deductible plans by offering tax advantages for medical expenses.

Question 126: Correct Answer: A) Fee-for-Service Reimbursement

Rationale: Indemnity insurance often operates on a fee-for-service basis, meaning the insurer reimburses a portion of each service after Mark pays upfront. This system allows flexibility in choosing providers but can lead to higher out-of-pocket costs compared to in-network discounts or global payment systems found in other plans. Prior authorization is not typically required in indemnity plans as it is in managed care settings. Therefore, understanding fee-for-service reimbursement helps Mark anticipate how payments are processed when choosing out-of-network specialists.

Question 127: Correct Answer: C) The quality and

strength of relationships within the network.

Rationale: Quality and strength of relationships (option C) are key determinants of a resilient social network as they provide emotional support and trust. Option A focuses on quantity rather than depth; option B may not reflect meaningful connections; option D's diversity is beneficial but secondary to relationship quality. Recognizing this allows case managers to foster supportive environments that enhance client resilience through strong interpersonal bonds.

Question 128: Correct Answer: C) The client's work history and contributions to Social Security

Rationale:SSDI eligibility primarily depends on the client's work history and contributions to Social Security, as it is an insurance program funded through payroll taxes. While age (A), income (B), and education (D) might influence other aspects of care, they are not primary factors in determining SSDI eligibility. This distinction is crucial for case managers to ensure appropriate guidance and support for clients seeking SSDI benefits.

Question 129: Correct Answer: C) Explore pharmaceutical assistance programs.

Rationale: Exploring pharmaceutical assistance programs is the best strategy as these programs often provide medications at reduced or no cost for eligible patients, addressing both financial and health needs effectively. Encouraging Medicaid application (Option A) may not be immediate or guaranteed, while over-the-counter alternatives (Option B) may not be appropriate for managing diabetes. Reducing dosage (Option D) compromises treatment efficacy and safety.

Question 130: Correct Answer: B) Quality and relevance of data

Rationale: The quality and relevance of data are crucial for the accuracy and reliability of predictive models, as they ensure that the insights drawn are based on accurate information reflecting true risk factors. While volume (A), speed (C), and diversity (D) contribute to model performance, without high-quality, relevant data, predictions can be inaccurate or misleading. Quality ensures precision, while relevance ensures applicability to real-world scenarios, making B the pivotal factor for effective health risk assessment.

Question 131: Correct Answer: B) Summarizing Maria's reasons for and against taking her medication.

Rationale: Reflective listening involves summarizing and clarifying what the patient has expressed, helping them explore their ambivalence. Option B directly aligns with this technique by capturing both sides of Maria's internal conflict. Option A is more confrontational, Option C is informative but not reflective, and Option D is directive rather than exploratory.

Question 132: Correct Answer: C) Adult Day Care Services

Rationale: Adult Day Care Services offer structured programs that include social activities, health services, and therapeutic activities, effectively addressing the psychosocial needs of isolated elderly individuals. Unlike Senior Centers (A), which primarily provide recreational activities without health services, and Home Health Aides (B), who focus on medical and personal care rather than social engagement, Adult Day Care Services (C) offer a comprehensive approach. Meals on Wheels (D) addresses nutritional needs but lacks the social interaction component critical for reducing isolation.

Question 133: Correct Answer: C) Coordinated Management of Meaning (CMM)

Rationale: The Coordinated Management of Meaning (CMM) theory highlights the significance of context and relationships in interpreting messages. Unlike Social Penetration Theory, which focuses on self-disclosure, or Uncertainty Reduction Theory, which deals with reducing ambiguity, CMM is centered on how individuals co-create meaning through interaction. Communication Accommodation Theory focuses on adapting communication styles rather than understanding context. Therefore, CMM is the most suitable choice for emphasizing contextual understanding in interpersonal communication.

Question 134: Correct Answer: B) Cognitive restructuring

Rationale: Cognitive restructuring is a technique within cognitive-behavioral therapy that aims to change maladaptive thought patterns related to substance use, thereby influencing behavior change. Contingency management (A) uses rewards to reinforce abstinence but doesn't address cognitive processes directly. Harm reduction (C) focuses on minimizing negative consequences rather than changing beliefs. Twelve-step facilitation (D), while supportive, centers more on spiritual principles than cognitive changes. Cognitive restructuring targets the root cognitive distortions driving substance use behaviors.

Question 135: Correct Answer: B) Accountable Care Organization (ACO)

Rationale: The ACO model focuses on integrating healthcare services across multiple providers to enhance patient outcomes through coordination. Unlike PCMH, which centers on primary care, ACOs involve a broader network of providers. The Primary Nursing Model emphasizes individualized care by a single nurse, while the Functional Nursing Model divides tasks among team members. ACOs are distinct in their emphasis on collaborative accountability and shared savings incentives, making them unique in promoting comprehensive care integration.

Question 136: Correct Answer: C) Collaborating with Tom to set personalized health goals

Rationale: Collaborating with Tom to set personalized health goals empowers him and aligns the care plan with his values, enhancing engagement. Option A provides information but may not address personal motivation. Option B offers support but may not directly involve him in decision-making. Option D ensures monitoring but lacks personalization. Personalized goal-setting is crucial as it fosters ownership and adherence by integrating personal relevance into the care process.

Question 137: Correct Answer: A) Home Health Care Services

Rationale: Home Health Care Services provide medical and rehabilitation support directly at home, essential for post-surgical recovery like Sarah's. Meals on Wheels (B) addresses nutritional needs but lacks medical support. Adult Day Care (C) offers social engagement but not in-home care. Senior Center Activities (D) focus on socialization rather than recovery support. Thus, A is the most comprehensive option for ensuring Sarah's well-being during recovery.

Question 138: Correct Answer: A) The individual must have earned at least 40 work credits, with 20 earned in the last 10 years ending with the year of disability.

Rationale: To qualify for SSDI, individuals typically need to earn 40 work credits, with at least 20 of these earned in the last decade before becoming disabled. Option B is incorrect as it reduces both total and recent credit requirements. Option C is misleading because it ignores recency, a critical factor. Option D inaccurately emphasizes continuous work rather than credit accumulation and timing.

Question 139: Correct Answer: C) DRG
Rationale: DRG (Diagnosis-Related Group) is used for hospital reimbursement and considers the complexity and resources used during a patient's stay. While ICD-10-CM provides diagnostic codes and CPT codes are used for outpatient procedures, they do not capture resource utilization like DRGs. HCPCS is mainly for billing Medicare services and supplies, not hospital stays. Therefore, DRG is the most appropriate choice to reflect the complexity of inpatient care in this scenario.

Question 140: Correct Answer: B) Reflective listening
Rationale: Reflective listening is crucial for building rapport as it involves understanding and validating the patient's feelings, encouraging them to open up. Unlike closed-ended questions (Option A), which limit responses, or direct confrontation (Option C), which can be intimidating, reflective listening fosters a supportive environment. Structured interviewing (Option D) may organize data but lacks the empathetic engagement essential for rapport. Reflective listening aligns with contemporary psychosocial theories emphasizing empathy and active engagement in patient interactions.

Question 141: Correct Answer: C) Mini-Mental State Examination (MMSE)
Rationale: The Mini-Mental State Examination (MMSE) is widely used to screen for cognitive impairment and assess memory deficits associated with neurocognitive disorders. Although the Stroop Test evaluates attention and inhibition, the Rey-Osterrieth Complex Figure Test assesses visuospatial abilities, and the Trail Making Test measures processing speed and mental flexibility. The MMSE's specific focus on memory makes it the most appropriate tool for identifying memory deficits.

Question 142: Correct Answer: C) Integrated Dual Disorder Treatment (IDDT)
Rationale: Integrated Dual Disorder Treatment (IDDT) is recognized as the most effective approach because it simultaneously addresses both mental health and substance use disorders within a single treatment plan. Unlike sequential (A) and parallel treatments (B), which treat disorders separately, IDDT ensures coordinated care, reducing fragmentation. Separate specialist care (D) often leads to communication gaps and inconsistent strategies. IDDT's holistic approach improves outcomes by considering the interplay between disorders, aligning with evidence-based practices.

Question 143: Correct Answer: B) Patient-reported experience measures (PREMs)
Rationale: PREMs are specifically designed to capture patients' experiences and satisfaction with healthcare services, including telehealth. While the number of virtual visits (A), reduction in hospital readmissions (C), and clinical health improvement scores (D) provide valuable data on utilization and clinical outcomes, they do not directly assess patient engagement or satisfaction like PREMs do. Therefore, option B is the most relevant metric for John's objective.

Question 144: Correct Answer: B) Depressed mood or loss of interest/pleasure for at least two weeks
Rationale: The DSM-5 requires a depressed mood or a loss of interest/pleasure in activities for at least two weeks as a core criterion for diagnosing Major Depressive Disorder. Option A (manic episodes) indicates Bipolar Disorder, not depression. Option C (delusions or hallucinations) is more indicative of psychotic disorders. Option D (significant weight gain without dieting) is a symptom but not a core diagnostic criterion. The focus on duration and core symptoms distinguishes Major Depressive Disorder.

Question 145: Correct Answer: D) Peer support
Rationale: Peer support fosters a sense of belonging and shared experience, crucial for building resilience in wellness programs. Unlike social isolation (A), which negatively impacts mental health, peer support provides encouragement and understanding. Emotional intelligence (B) aids personal insight but lacks the community aspect critical for resilience. Autonomy (C) emphasizes independence but may overlook the benefits of collective strength found in peer networks. Thus, peer support effectively combines emotional connection with practical assistance, enhancing program outcomes.

Question 146: Correct Answer: B) Promotes standardization in care delivery
Rationale: Case rate reimbursement models promote standardization in care delivery by providing a fixed payment for specific conditions, encouraging providers to adhere to established protocols to manage costs effectively. Option A is incorrect because it discourages extended stays; C is incorrect as it simplifies billing processes; D is incorrect as it maintains focus on outcomes by aligning incentives with efficient care delivery. Standardization ensures consistency and quality while managing financial resources effectively.

Question 147: Correct Answer: A) Patient's belief in the necessity of medication
Rationale: A patient's belief in the necessity of their medication strongly predicts long-term adherence as it aligns with health behavior theories emphasizing perceived benefits. Although regimen complexity (B), provider visits (C), and social support (D) are relevant, they do not directly address intrinsic motivation like belief does. Understanding this internal factor helps case managers tailor interventions more effectively, ensuring sustained compliance with treatment plans.

Question 148: Correct Answer: D) Self-Liberation
Rationale: Self-liberation emphasizes belief in one's ability to change and commitment to act, bridging preparation and action stages. Consciousness raising increases awareness but doesn't necessarily propel action. Self-reevaluation aids in contemplation by reassessing self-image. Counterconditioning replaces negative behaviors but is more relevant during maintenance. Understanding these processes aids case managers in facilitating client transitions effectively.

Question 149: Correct Answer: B) Integrate treatment for both disorders simultaneously using a coordinated care approach.
Rationale: The integrated treatment approach is widely recognized as the most effective method for managing co-occurring disorders, as it addresses both conditions concurrently, improving overall outcomes. Option A is incorrect because treating one disorder at a time can neglect crucial aspects of the other condition. Option C fails to consider the impact of untreated alcohol use on depression management. Option D limits intervention to MAT without addressing psychological aspects of depression, thus being less comprehensive.

Question 150: Correct Answer: D) Utilizing motivational interviewing techniques to explore and resolve ambivalence.
Rationale: Motivational interviewing (MI) aligns with empowerment by enhancing intrinsic motivation through collaborative dialogue, respecting client autonomy, and addressing ambivalence—core aspects of empowerment theories. Option A standardizes care without personalization, limiting empowerment potential. Option B

supports peer interaction but may lack individualized focus on empowerment goals. Option C emphasizes monitoring over collaboration, reducing client agency compared to MI's personalized approach that fosters self-directed change through respectful engagement.